Transition Methods
for Youth with Disabilities

Transition Methods for Youth with Disabilities

DAVID W. TEST
University of North Carolina at Charlotte

NELLIE P. ASPEL
Cleveland County Schools

JANE M. EVERSON
The Hickory Metro Higher Education Center
Appalachian State University

PEARSON
Merrill
Prentice Hall

Upper Saddle River, New Jersey
Columbus, OH

Library of Congress Cataloging-in-Publication Data

Test, David Wesley
  Transition methods for youth with disabilities / David W. Test, Nellie P. Aspel, Jane M. Everson.
    p. cm.
  Includes bibliographical references and index.
  ISBN 0-13-113064-1
    1. Youth with disabilities—Vocational education—United States. 2. Youth with
  disabilities—Services for—United States. 3. School-to-work transition—United States. I.
  Aspel, Nellie P. II. Everson, Jane M. III. Title.

LC4019.7.T47 2006
371.9'0473—dc22

2005043305

Vice President and Executive Publisher: Jeffery W. Johnston
Acquisitions Editor: Allyson P. Sharp
Editorial Assistant: Kathleen S. Burk
Production Editor: Sheryl Glicker Langner
Production Coordination: Ann Mohan, WordCrafters Editorial Services, Inc.
Design Coordinator: Diane C. Lorenzo
Photo Coordinator: Valerie Schultz
Cover Designer: Thomas Borah
Cover image: Superstock
Production Manager: Laura Messerly
Director of Marketing: Ann Castel Davis
Marketing Manager: Autumn Purdy
Marketing Coordinator: Brian Mounts

This book was set in Palatino by Pine Tree Composition, Inc. It was printed and bound by R. R. Donnelley & Sons Company. The cover was printed by R. R. Donnelley & Sons Company.

Photo Credits: Anne Vega/Merrill, pp. 2, 32; Barbara Schwartz/Merrill, p. 60; Scott Cunningham/Merrill, pp. 92, 140, 170; Todd Yarrington/Merrill, p. 218; Anthony Magnacca/Merrill, pp. 252, 368; Laimute E. Druskis/PH College, p. 302; Michael Littlejohn/PH College, p. 334.

Pearson Education Ltd.
Pearson Education Singapore Pte. Ltd.
Pearson Education Canada, Ltd.
Pearson Education—Japan

Pearson Education Australia Pty. Limited
Pearson Education North Asia Ltd.
Pearson Educación de Mexico, S.A. de C.V.
Pearson Education Malaysia Pte. Ltd.

10 9 8 7 6 5 4
ISBN: 0-13-113064-1

To Our Families

EDUCATOR LEARNING CENTER: AN INVALUABLE ONLINE RESOURCE

Merrill Education and the Association for Supervision and Curriculum Development (ASCD) invite you to take advantage of a new online resource, one that provides access to the top research and proven strategies associated with ASCD and Merrill—the Educator Learning Center. At **www.educator learningcenter.com**, you will find resources that will enhance your students' understanding of course topics and of current educational issues, in addition to being invaluable for further research.

How the Educator Learning Center Will Help Your Students Become Better Teachers

With the combined resources of Merrill Education and ASCD, you and your students will find a wealth of tools and materials to better prepare them for the classroom.

Research

♦ More than 600 articles from the ASCD journal *Educational Leadership* discuss everyday issues faced by practicing teachers.

♦ A direct link on the site to Research Navigator™ gives students access to many of the leading education journals, as well as extensive content detailing the research process.

♦ Excerpts from Merrill Education texts give your students insights on important topics of instructional methods, diverse populations, assessment, classroom management, technology, and refining classroom practice.

Classroom Practice

♦ Hundreds of lesson plans and teaching strategies are categorized by content area and age range.

♦ Case studies and classroom video footage provide virtual field experience for student reflection.

♦ Computer simulations and other electronic tools keep your students abreast of today's classrooms and current technologies.

Look into the Value of Educator Learning Center Yourself

A four-month subscription to Educator Learning Center is $25 but is **FREE** when packaged with any Merrill Education text. In order for your students to have access to this site, you must use this special value-pack ISBN number **WHEN** placing your textbook order with the bookstore: 0-13-169982-2. Your students will then receive a copy of the text packaged with a free ASCD pincode. To preview the value of this website to you and your students, please go to **www.educatorlearningcenter.com** and click on "Demo."

Preface

From the moment we are born, life is a series of transitions: from diapers to underpants, day care to preschool, preschool to elementary school, elementary school to middle school, and middle school to high school. While these and many other transitions occur throughout an individual's life, one of the most significant is graduating from high school and entering adult life. High school graduation traditionally signifies a time filled with challenges and changes. It is a time anxiously awaited by students and parents, filled with hopes and dreams of leaving high school and moving into the adult world of employment and/or postsecondary education. Halpern (1992) defined this transition as "a period of *floundering* that occurs for at least the first several years after leaving school as adolescents attempt to assume a *variety* of adult roles in their communities" (p. 203). Unfortunately for students with disabilities, the "floundering" period often lasts for years and, in some cases, for a lifetime.

Fortunately, the field of special education has responded to this challenge by developing strategies and programs designed to help students make a successful transition from high school to adulthood. Based on this work, *Transition Methods for Youth with Disabilities* is guided by four major themes:

1. The goal of education should be to prepare all students for high-quality adult lives.
2. Transition services must be student centered, and teachers need to be skilled in promoting transition and self-determination skills.
3. There is a set of evidence-based best practices for providing transition services as outlined in Kohler's (1996) taxonomy of transition programming.
4. While teachers need to understand the historical foundations and legal requirements for providing transition services, they also need practical information about how to provide high-quality transition services to their students.

A significant feature of this textbook is that it can be used in both introductory and methods courses. It includes the basics of transition (the introductory level material), as well as material on how to provide the different types of transition services introduced. We have designed the text to be used across disability areas by including examples and case studies that include students with mild, moderate, and severe disabilities. In addition, the text includes specific chapters on each of the major adult outcomes required by the Individuals with Disabilities Education Improvement Act (i.e., employment, postsecondary education, community living opportunities, and community participation). Finally, it is currently the only transition text that includes a chapter on program evaluation.

SPECIAL FEATURES

To bridge the gap between research and practice, this text has a number of special features designed to provide readers with practical, hands-on information.

Families Features

Research has demonstrated that parents and other family members want and need to become involved in planning and delivering transition services for their daughters and sons. As such, families should be encouraged to participate in the full range of transition activities, from assessment and planning to implementation and evaluation. To provide this encouragement, educators must learn to communicate effectively with families and create a supportive environment. At the same time, educators must be taught not to impose their own values and cultural biases on families; they must learn strategies for understanding and working with families with diverse cultural and linguistic backgrounds. Each chapter includes a special boxed feature that provides information directly related to involving families in the transition process.

Personal Perspectives

A key characteristic of a high-quality transition program is collaboration among many different people, businesses, and agencies to promote students' pursuit of successful postschool outcomes. Educators can learn to foster collaborative service delivery by use of interagency agreements that clearly articulate roles, responsibilities, communication strategies, student individualized education program meetings, and other cooperative actions that enhance curriculum and program development and service delivery. To this end, each chapter begins with a "Personal Perspective" from the viewpoint of one of the many people who may be involved in the transition process.

Case Studies

Since the text provides both introductory and methods material, it can be difficult for readers to see how all the information fits together for individual students. To help bring the material to life, case studies are provided in each chapter. Each case study is designed to provide specific examples of the information and concepts presented in the chapter.

Methods Focus

Because this text was designed for use in both introductory and methods courses, each chapter is organized around three questions: What is it? Why is it important? and How do you do it? Each chapter has a number of tables that provide information on implementing various transition strategies. In addition, some chapters include information on strategies for addressing common transition challenges.

Program Evaluation

Chapter 11, "Transition Program Evaluation," is unique among texts on transition. The chapter provides readers with the rationale for collecting program evaluation data and the types of data that can be gathered, as well as strategies for collecting data. All information gathered to evaluate a school system's transition practices must both link directly to continuous program improvement and ensure that students are achieving their dreams.

ACKNOWLEDGMENTS

We would like to acknowledge the contributions of the following people to the creation and development of this text:

Nancy L. Cooke, Dave's colleague, wife, and best friend, for her patience and ideas as this journey unwound.

Michael S. Aspel, Nellie's husband and best friend, for his continued love, support, and ability to make a great cup of coffee. And to her son Houston, for the hugs of encouragement and for helping her remember the important things in life.

Jane's colleagues and friends, especially in Louisiana, New York, North Carolina, South Carolina, and Virginia, who as teachers, counselors, parents, and advocates made the stories and examples in this book possible and kept the light focused on transition outcomes for the past 20 years.

Gail G. Bettis, for being the kind of teacher who inspires others with her energy, creativity, and total belief in the impact that effective transition services can have on the life of a young adult.

All the young people with disabilities who have inspired us through their courage in overcoming barriers and challenges on their way to becoming adults.

The administrators in Cleveland County Schools and the former Shelby City Schools who supported an environment in which TASSEL (Teaching All Students Skills for Employment and Life) could thrive and grow.

The staff of North Shelby School, for showing Nellie what it means to really put students first and to never give up.

Bill Heward, Dave's mentor and the reason that it took him so long to write a textbook. He was right. It really is a lot of work!

Bob Pittillo, Nellie's mentor, who made her believe that she could make a difference.

All the students who have taken our classes in transition. We hope that you have learned as much from us as we have learned from you.

Moira Konrad, who kept Dave organized and helped with all the little details.

Freda Lee, for her passion for transition and for using that passion to advocate for students across the state of North Carolina even in the face of what others would have viewed as overwhelming barriers. There has never been a better state-level transition coordinator.

Finally, to our reviewers for all their hard work and suggestions. Our textbook is definitely better because of you: Kathleen Chinn, New Mexico State University; Margaret Hutchins, Illinois State University; Larry Kortering, Appalachia State University; Cindy Marble, Arizona State University, East; Caron Mellblom-Nishioka, California State University, Dominguez Hills; Sara Pankaskie, Florida Atlantic University; Denise Smith, Indiana University, South Bend; Colleen Thoma, Virginia Commonwealth University; Jane M. Williams, University of Nevada, Las Vegas; Carolyn H. Wilson, Virginia State University; and Peggy Wittwer, Southern Utah University.

David W. Test
Nellie Aspel
Jane M. Everson

REFERENCE

Halpern, A. (1992). Transition: Old wine in new bottles. *Exceptional Children, 58,* 202–211.

Discover the Merrill Education Resources for Special Education Website

Technology is a constantly growing and changing aspect of our field that is creating a need for new content and resources. To address this emerging need, Merrill Education has developed an online learning environment for students, teachers, and professors alike to complement our products—the *Merrill Education Resources for Special Education* Website. This content-rich website provides additional resources specific to this book's topic and will help you—professors, classroom teachers, and students—augment your teaching, learning, and professional development.

Our goal is to build on and enhance what our products already offer. For this reason, the content for our user-friendly website is organized by topic and provides teachers, professors, and students with a variety of meaningful resources all in one location. With this website, we bring together the best of what Merrill has to offer: text resources, video clips, web links, tutorials, and a wide variety of information on topics of interest to general and special educators alike. Rich content, applications, and competencies further enhance the learning process.

The *Merrill Education Resources for Special Education* Website includes:

RESOURCES FOR THE PROFESSOR—

- ◆ The **Syllabus Manager**™, an online syllabus creation and management tool, enables instructors to create and revise their syllabus with an easy, step-by-step process. Students can access your syllabus and any changes you make during the course of your class from any computer with Internet access. To access this tailored syllabus, students will just need the URL of the website and the password assigned to the syllabus. By clicking on the date, the student can see a list of activities, assignments, and readings due for that particular class.

♦ In addition to the **Syllabus Manager**™ and its benefits listed above, professors also have access to all of the wonderful resources that students have access to on the site.

RESOURCES FOR THE STUDENT—

♦ Video clips specific to each topic, with questions to help you evaluate the content and make crucial theory-to-practice connections.

♦ Thought-provoking critical analysis questions that students can answer and turn in for evaluation or that can serve as basis for class discussions and lectures.

♦ Access to a wide variety of resources related to classroom strategies and methods, including lesson planning and classroom management.

♦ Information on all the most current relevant topics related to special and general education, including CEC and Praxis standards, IEPs, portfolios, and professional development.

♦ Extensive web resources and overviews on each topic addressed on the website.

♦ A message board with discussion starters where students can respond to class discussion topics, post questions and responses, or ask questions about assignments.

♦ A search feature to help access specific information quickly.

To take advantage of these and other resources, please visit the *Merrill Education Resources for Special Education* Website at

http://www.prenhall.com/test

About the Authors

David W. Test earned his Ph.D. from The Ohio State University. He is Professor of Special Education at the University of North Carolina at Charlotte and teaches courses in single-subject research, transition, secondary methods, and classroom management. Trained as a behavior analyst, his research interests lie in applying these strategies to teach students self-determination and self-advocacy skills, as well as daily living and social skills.

Dr. Test's previous experience includes the administration and supervision of more than $4 million in both federally and state funded personnel preparation and research and demonstration grants. He currently serves as Co-Director (with Dr. Wendy Wood) of the Self-Determination Technical Assistance Centers project and Co-Director (with Dr. Diane Browder) of UNC Charlotte's Special Education Leadership Preparation Program. His vita includes more than 65 articles and book chapters, the majority focusing on self-determination, transition, community-based training, and supported employment. He is honored to be the current recipient of the First Citizen's Scholar Medal, UNC Charlotte's highest award for scholarship.

Nellie Aspel earned her Ed.D. from the University of North Carolina at Chapel Hill. She has worked as a special education teacher and administrator in both private and public settings for the last 24 years. Her experience is with students with mild to moderate cognitive disabilities and emotional or behavioral disabilities. She is presently a principal in Cleveland County Schools and oversees TASSEL (Teaching All Students Skills for Employment and Life), an award-winning transition program that is implemented at the area high schools within her school system.

Dr. Aspel is an adjunct professor at UNC Charlotte, teaching courses in the special education program. She is also the author of the North Carolina Department of Public Instruction's Transition Manual. She facilitated the development of the Life Skills Science and Occupational Preparation courses for the North Carolina Occupational Course of Study. She received an Outstanding Service award from the North Carolina Department of Public Instruction in 1997 and was the North Carolina Southwest Region Principal of the Year in 1998. In July of 2000, she was honored with a Distinguished Service award from the North Carolina Department of Public Instruction.

Jane M. Everson is a graduate of the University of Virginia and earned her Ph.D. in Urban Services from Virginia Commonwealth University. She is the Director of the Hickory Metropolitan Higher Education Center (HMHEC) and a member of the Appalachian State University (ASU) faculty. Before accepting her current position with the HMHEC, she held a joint position as an Associate Professor with Louisiana State University Health Sciences Center in New Orleans and the University of South Carolina School of Medicine in Columbia. Before that she was the Director of the National Technical Assistance Center with the Helen Keller National Center in New York. She is also on the editorial board of the *Journal of Vocational Rehabilitation.*

Dr. Everson has more than 20 years of experience in higher education, community development, and workforce development specializing in the needs of individuals with disabilities. She has authored more than 100 books, chapters, and articles and has directed more than $5 million in federal grants.

Brief Contents

Contents

NOTE: Every effort has been made to provide accurate and current Internet information in this book. However, the Internet and information posted on it are constantly changing, and it is inevitable that some of the Internet addresses listed in this textbook will change.

Transition Methods
for Youth with Disabilities

Introduction to Transition

Chapter 1

Introduction

The goal of this chapter is to introduce educators to the field of transition from school to adulthood. The chapter begins by describing the historical trends and legislative mandates that have set the stage for current transition practices. By becoming familiar with what is required legislatively in the fields of education, special education, vocational education, and vocational rehabilitation, educators are better prepared to advocate for interagency collaboration.

The chapter concludes with an example of how a common challenge is being addressed and a case study demonstrating the impact of providing a full array of transition services on student postschool outcomes.

Key Terms

transition
work/study programs
career education movement
bridges model
Vocational Rehabilitation Act of 1973 and Amendments
Americans with Disabilities Act
Carl D. Perkins Vocational Acts
Individuals with Disabilities Education Act
transition perspective

A Personal Perspective on the Impact of Transition Services

Gail Bettis

Transition Teacher, Cleveland County Schools

Let me tell you about Davia. Davia's participation in developing her transition postsecondary goals began at the age of 14 when she completed a student mapping form and dream sheet. It continued when Davia and her mother attended an adult services provider meeting with all other sophomores and parents that addressed existing community services. Throughout Davia's high school career, we gradually taught her to prepare agendas for her team meetings and complete school-level team information forms that addressed her postsecondary goals in education, employment, recreation, and related issues such as transportation.

As a result, in one of Davia's early planning meetings she stated that she wanted to become employed in a retail setting, preferably a grocery store. She also stated that she had an interest in becoming a stocker/bagger if she had the opportunity. Her postsecondary plan was to attend special trade classes in the area of construction or automotive repair, depending on the availability of courses and her work schedule. Davia also stated that after graduation she wanted to continue to live at home with her parents. Finally, she mentioned that she didn't have a driver's license but was planning to apply for one prior to her senior year. She discussed transportation as a major issue and that she needed to locate a job in close proximity to her mother's work.

For the next few years, with the help of Davia's family, I, the transition coordinator, vocational rehabilitation counselors, career/technical education teachers, mental health agency representatives, and social security agency personnel, to name a few, worked on helping Davia achieve her goals. So, by the time Davia graduated she was working full time, attending a local community college, actively involved in sports, and considering getting a YMCA membership. She plans to continue to live at home with her parents until she becomes financially able to live independently.

Davia's story demonstrates the impact that high-quality transition services can have on a student's success in life. When it comes to providing transition services, it really does "take a community to raise a child." Without the assistance of all interagency team members and the resources that were developed and implemented, Davia would not be where she is today. Davia and her mother also credit her achievements to challenging transition planning activities and teachers who believed in her, motivated her to work, practiced excellent character traits, and presented her with the mission statement that they would never give up on her success.

The impact of transition services changed Davia's life, but more important, it taught her the lesson that if you work hard enough you will achieve success, but you must believe to achieve.

From the moment we are born, life is a series of transitions—from diapers to underpants; from bicycles to cars; from daycare to preschool, preschool to elementary school, elementary school to middle school, and middle school to high school. While these and many other transitions occur throughout a person's life, one of the most significant points of **transition** is graduating from high school and entering into adult life. High school graduation traditionally signifies a time filled with many challenges and changes. It is a time anxiously awaited by students and parents, filled with hopes and dreams of successfully leaving high school and moving into the adult world of employment and/or postsecondary education. Halpern (1992) defined this transition as "a period of *floundering* that occurs for at least the first several years after leaving school as adolescents attempt to assume a *variety* of adult roles in their communities" (p. 203). Unfortunately for students with disabilities, the "floundering period" often lasts for years, and in some cases a lifetime. The purpose of this text is to provide the reader with methods for providing students with skills that will enable them to make a successful transition to adulthood.

BACKGROUND

The following sections describe some of the problems faced by students with disabilities as they make the transition from school to adulthood.

Postschool Outcomes for Students with Disabilities Continue to Be Disturbing

In 2001–2002 there were approximately 2 million students with disabilities ages 14 to 21 receiving special education services. In 1998–1999, 57.4% of students ages 14 and older graduated with a standard diploma, and 28.9% dropped out of school (U.S. Department of Education, 2001). While these numbers show slight improvement over the past 5 years, they are still disturbing when considered along with data from the National Longitudinal Transition Study (NLTS; Blackorby & Wagner, 1996). Table 1.1 summarizes the NLTS data, which indicate low levels of employment, wages, involvement in postsecondary education, and independent living for students with disabilities in general, and a clear difference between students who graduated and students who dropped out.

As seen in Table 1.1, for students with disabilities, graduating from high school does not necessarily mean a successful entry into adulthood. For example, consider the quality of life of individuals who, within 5 years of leaving high school, have just better than a 50-50 chance of being employed, a less than 40% chance of earning over $6.00 per hour or living independently, and a less than 30% chance of entering postsecondary education.

Students with Disabilities Continue to Have Low Rates of School Completion

The low rate of school completion among youths in special education programs remains a persistent problem. On a national level, the Office of Special Education Programs (OSEP) suggests that, in general, youths with disabilities fail to

Table 1.1
Summary of National Longitudinal Transition Study Data

Category	≤ 2 Years Out (%)	3–5 Years Out (%)
Total Employed	45.7	56.8
High school graduates	53.3	64.8
Drop-outs	42.2	47.1
Total Earning ≥ $6.00/hr	9.0	39.8
High school graduates	6.8	41.7
Drop-outs	11.2	37.9
Total Entering Postsecondary Education	14.0	26.7
High school graduates	18.9	40.8
Drop-outs	6.3	11.1
Total Living Independently	11.2	37.4
High school graduates	9.9	40.8
Drop-outs	15.2	35.0

Note. Based on figures from Blackorby & Wagner (1996).

complete school at a rate twice that of their general education peers ("Special Education Dropout Rate," 1997). Specifically, (a) OSEP's *Twenty-Third Annual Report to Congress on the Implementation of the Individuals with Disabilities Education Act* (U.S. Department of Education, 2001) provided data indicating that 173,523 students exited with a diploma and 33,427 with a certificate, while (b) the National Council on Disability (2000) indicated that 150,000 students dropped out or were not known to continue school. Together, these two sets of data suggest a graduation rate for students with disabilities somewhere between 46% and 67%, falling well short of the 85% national average among all youths in 1995 (McMillan, Kaufman, & Klein, 1997). While this number includes the 7% of former students who earn the general education development (GED) diploma (Murnane, Willett, & Boudett, 1997), indications are that youths who drop out of a special education program seldom earn a GED (Westberry, 1994). Sadly, these school completion rates for students with disabilities have remained largely unchanged in recent years.

   The low rate of school completion causes some significant problems. For example, research indicates that students who fail to graduate from general education programs endure higher rates of unemployment or underemployment, a trend that continues to worsen (Bound & Johnson, 1995). School dropouts also experience higher rates of unexpected parenthood (Coley, 1995) and drug use (Swaim, Beauvis, Chavez, & Oetting, 1997), and they account for more than half of heads of households on welfare and prisoners (Coley, 1995). While research on what happens to youths with disabilities who fail to complete school is limited (Sitlington & Frank, 1993), it is unlikely that they enjoy adulthood outcomes as good as those reported for general education peers (Collett-Klingenberg, 1998; Kortering & Braziel, 1999).

Completion of High School Does Not Guarantee Being Prepared for Adulthood

Educational reform in the last decade has focused on both graduation rates and whether students who graduate are meeting specific standards set by states and districts. High school graduation is a key indicator of academic success for both individuals and education agencies. Unfortunately, completion of high school does not always guarantee preparation for the demands of adult living. For example, many young adults with learning disabilities leave the workforce because they are ill prepared to complete job-related activities and they face limited options for future job success (Adelman & Vogel, 1993). Similar findings are evident for individuals in other disability categories. Youths with emotional or behavioral disorders also struggle with finding and holding a job because they have difficulty following directions, staying on task in relation to specific job-related responsibilities (Schelly, Sample, & Kothe, 1995), and applying academic skills to job-related situations (Love & Malian, 1997). Graduates also report having difficulty with (a) completing job applications, because of the reading and writing required; (b) reading materials required for their jobs; and (c) using math skills in developing and maintaining a budget (Gottesman, 1994).

Thus, while high school completion is important to future success, it is even more critical that students obtain not just a diploma, but the skills critical to adult living. For example, Hasazi, Furney, and DeStefano (1999) noted that many students with disabilities are achieving academic success at the expense of careful transition planning. On the other hand, focusing on life skills often limits student access to interacting with their general education peers (Kohler, 1998). Finding the proper balance between academic and functional/vocational courses of study for students can be very difficult.

Taken together, the dismal postschool outcomes, drop-out rates, and apparent lack of academic and work-related skills could be disheartening for special educators. But we are an optimistic group. So instead, we have viewed theses outcomes as a challenge and set about to make things better. As you will discover, the journey has been uneven and filled with failed attempts, but we are always moving forward.

Transition: Old Wine in a New Bottle

In what could be considered one of the most important articles published in the field of transition, Halpern (1992) described three transition movements: (a) the cooperative work/study movement of the 1960s; (b) the career education movement of the 1970s; and (c) the transition movement of the 1980s and 1990s.

Cooperative Work/Study Programs (1960s).   Work/study programs emerged as a cooperative venture between public schools and local offices of state rehabilitation agencies to create an integrated program that included academic, social, and vocational curricula (Halpern, 1973). **Work/study programs** were primarily developed to help prepare students with mild disabilities to live in their home communities. The centerpiece of these programs was a formal cooperative agreement between a local school system and the vocational rehabilitation agency. The formal agreement typically involved assigning a classroom teacher as a work coordinator to spend a portion of the day helping students get work placements as a part of their high school program. In addition, the teacher/work coordinator helped refer students for vocational rehabilitation services.

Unfortunately, work/study programs were discontinued during the 1970s as a result of two problems. First, because of the way teachers/work coordinators' salaries were funded, a portion of the time had to be supervised by a representative of the rehabilitation agency. This extra supervision did not sit well with many high school principals. Second, the 1973 Rehabilitation Act Amendments (described in detail later in this chapter), stipulated that a rehabilitation agency could not pay for services that were the legitimate responsibility of another agency (for example, an educational agency such as a school system). This was not a problem until 1975, when Public Law (P.L.) 94–142, the Education for All Handicapped Children Act, resulted in work-experience programs being considered an "appropriate" educational service. As a result, rehabilitation agencies could no longer pay for part of the salary for a teacher/work coordinator and work/study programs fell out of favor. However, the needs of the students they served did not go away.

Career Education (1970s). The **career education movement** started in 1970 when Sidney Marland, Commissioner of Education, declared career education to be the top priority of the United States Office of Education (Halpern, 1992). The federal focus on career education was expanded in 1974 with the addition of the Office of Career Education to the U.S. Office of Education, and again in 1977 with the passage of P.L. 95–207, The Career Education Implementation Incentive Act. Until P.L. 95–207, the career education movement was viewed as primarily a general education movement. However, P.L. 95–207 specifically mentioned students with disabilities as a potential audience for receiving career education services.

At about the same time, in 1976, the Council for Exceptional Children approved the formation of Division of Career Development. This formal endorsement of the concept of career development (Brolin, 1983; Cegelka, 1979; Hoyt, 1982) helped preserve the career education philosophy for students with disabilities when, in 1982, Congress repealed the funding for P.L. 95–207. The career education movement had expanded the limited focus of preparing only high school

DID YOU KNOW?

Career education started out as a general education movement.

students with mild disabilities for the workplace to one of preparing all students across elementary, middle, and high school years.

Transition (1980s–1990s).   Given the foundations of work/study and career education programs, it is not surprising that the field of transition would rapidly expand during the 1980s and 1990s. This period started with Will's (1984) position paper on transition, Halpern's (1985) description of the three foundations of transition, and the special education outcome data from 1985 to 1990 and culminated in 1990 with P.L. 101–476, often called the "transition law."

In 1984, Madeline Will, the director of the Office of Special Education and Rehabilitative Services (OSERS), published a position paper on transition for her office that became known as the **"bridges" model** (see Figure 1.1). The OSERS transition model showed three bridges from high school to employment. The first bridge, called "No Special Services," referred to generic services that are available to anyone living in a community. For example, a trade school or a community college is one service people can use to facilitate their transition into employment. The second bridge, called "Time-Limited Services," referred to time-limited, special services for which a person with a disability must qualify. Vocational rehabilitation services are an example of time-limited services. The third bridge, called "Ongoing Services," referred to services available across an individual's life span. While Will recognized that this service was not widely available, since "supported employment" was still in its infancy, this model changed the focus to community employment and away from sheltered employment.

Shortly after the OSERS bridges model was introduced, the field responded by expanding the model to include additional pillars, including residential environments and social and interpersonal networks (Halpern, 1985). Figure 1.2

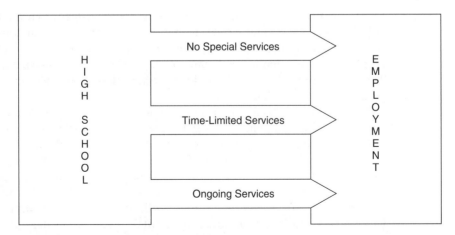

Figure 1.1
Major Components of the Transition Process

Note. From *OSERS Programming for the Transition of Youth with Disabilities: Bridges from School to Working Life* by M. Will, 1984, Washington, DC: U.S. Department of Education.

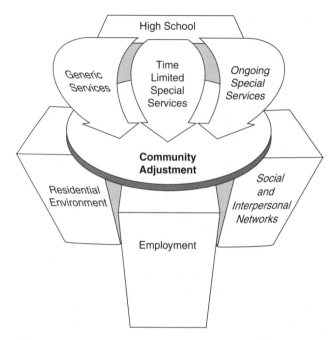

Figure 1.2
Revised Transition Model

Note. From *Transition: A look at the foundations* by Andrew S. Halpern, *Exceptional Children*, Vol. 51, 1985, pp. 479–486. Copyright 1985 by The Council for Exceptional Children. Reprinted with permission.

represents this expanded model. While the three bridges from the OSERS model (Will, 1984) were retained, the destination was expanded from employment only to community adjustment. Community adjustment rests on the three pillars of employment, residential environment, and social and interpersonal networks. These three pillars reflected the field's recognition of the fact that, to enjoy life, a person needs more than work.

Starting in the mid-1980s and continuing into the early 1990s, a series of studies were published that investigated the postsecondary outcomes of students with disabilities (Affleck, Edgar, Levine, & Kortering, 1990; Blackorby & Wagner, 1996; Frank, Sitlington, Cooper, & Cool, 1990; Hasazi, Gordon, & Roe, 1985). These studies, conducted in different states, geographic areas (i.e., urban, suburban, rural) with almost all types of students with disabilities, found that (a) while an average of 50% to 60% of students with disabilities were employed, only 20% to 30% were employed full time; (b) about 50% earned a salary at or above minimum wage; and (c) few held jobs that provided fringe benefits. These findings clarified the fact that although students with disabilities had been receiving a free, appropriate public education since 1975, their postschool outcomes were dismal. It was clear that something had to change.

Fortunately, help was on the way when P.L. 101–476, the Individuals with Disabilities Education Act (IDEA), was signed into law on October 30, 1990. These landmark amendments to P.L. 94–142 defined transition services and added a transition component to the individualized education program (IEP; Storms, DeStefano, & O'Leary, 1996). While IDEA was the culmination of the three historical transition movements from 1960 to 1990 just described, it was also part of a legislative context for transition.

LEGAL MANDATES FOR TRANSITION

While the educational movements described in the previous section are one piece of the historical background leading to the legislative mandate for transition services, an equally important piece is the legislative context. Understanding both the historical background and current laws related to transition will ultimately help improve services to students, since educators will be more knowledgeable about the rights of their students and the responsibilities of others. To help you understand the transition-related legislation, we have divided the following section into three parts: rehabilitation-related legislation; educational legislation; and employment-related legislation, which includes vocational, general, and special education legislation. Figure 1.3 provides a chronological list of this legislation.

Rehabilitation-Related Legislation

The Vocational Rehabilitation Act, P.L. 93–112 (1973).   This important law extended civil rights to people with disabilities by mandating equal opportunity (Section 503) and nondiscrimination (Section 504) in public workplaces and educational settings. Not surprisingly, much of this act was modeled after the Civil Rights Act of 1964, which prohibited discrimination based on race, color, or national origin (Heward, 2003). The Vocational Rehabilitation Act laid the foundation for later transition-related legislation in a number of ways. First, Section 504 included the statement that

> no otherwise qualified handicapped individual in the United States, as defined by Section 7(6) shall, solely by reason of his handicap, be excluded from participation in, be denied the benefits of, or be subjected to discrimination under any program or activity receiving Federal financial assistance.

As a result, this act affirmed the civil rights of people with disabilities.

Second, this act required the development of an individualized written rehabilitation plan (IWRP). The IWRP had to include a statement of long-range rehabilitation goals, types of rehabilitation, dates of services to be provided, and evaluation procedures. As such, the IWRP appeared to be a forerunner of the IEP mandated in P.L. 94–142 in 1975 (Sitlington, Clark, & Kolstoe, 2000).

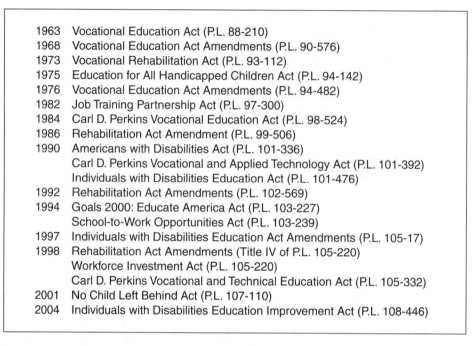

Figure 1.3
Chronology of Transition-Related Legislation

Third, state rehabilitation programs were required to give priority to persons with the most severe disabilities. This recognition of the rights of people with severe disabilities by Congress paved the way for future legislation to strengthen the employment rights for this population.

Finally, the act recognized that living in the community and getting help with daily living activities is just as important as working, and that people with disabilities should have primary control over what services they receive and how they are provided. This legislative recognition of the fact that there is more to a person's life than his or her job foreshadowed the emphasis in Halpern's (1985) transition model on the three areas of community adjustment, not just work.

Rehabilitation Act Amendments, P.L. 99–506 (1986).   While not directly related to transition, this act defined supported employment for state vocational rehabilitation programs. This continued congressional recognition of the right of persons with the most severe disabilities to be employed, as well as their need for ongoing employment support. First, the act redefined the concept of *employability* to include both part-time and full-time employment with supported employment services. Second, it provided funds (called Title VI, Part C, money) specifically designed to provide supported employment. Finally, it encouraged interagency cooperation between vocational rehabilitation agencies, which were mandated to provide time-limited services, and other state agencies that were expected to provide long-term support services. The emergence of supported employment services for adults with disabilities was a major impetus for establishing community-based employment training programs in school systems across the nation.

Americans with Disabilities Act, P.L. 101–336 (1990).   Signed on July 26, 1990, the Americans with Disabilities Act (ADA) extended civil rights protection from public sector employment (provided in the 1973 Vocational Rehabilitation Act, P.L. 93–112) to private sector employment and all public services, including transportation, public accommodations, and telecommunications.

In the area of *employment,* the ADA required that by July 26, 1994, no employers with 15 or more employees could refuse to hire or promote a person with a disability when the person was qualified to perform the job. In addition, employers were required to make "reasonable accommodations" for a person with a disability if it would allow the person to perform the essential functions of the job. "Reasonable accommodation" meant that if, by modifying a job's requirements or structure a person with a disability could perform a job, and the modification did not cause the employer undue hardship, the accommodation must be made. Although many businesses felt that making accommodations would cause them financial hardship, it quickly became evident that most reasonable accommodations cost relatively little.

In *transportation,* the ADA required that new vehicles purchased by public transit authorities, new buses by private transportation providers (such as Trailways and Greyhound), and new and existing rail stations be accessible to people with disabilities. Paratransit service for people with disabilities who cannot use the mainline transportation system was required unless provision would result in an undue financial burden.

In terms of *public accommodations,* ADA made it illegal to exclude or refuse services to people with disabilities. This meant that businesses and services that are used every day by all people, such as restaurants, grocery stores, schools, parks, and motels, must be accessible to people with disabilities. In addition, this required the provision of auxiliary services such as large-print materials, captioning, and tape-recorded materials to enable people with disabilities to use and enjoy the goods and service provided by public accommodations.

Finally, *telecommunication* companies were required to provide telephone relay services for the deaf (TDDs) 24 hours a day, 7 days a week, at regular rates.

DID YOU KNOW?

The Office of Disability Employment Policy of the U.S. Department of Labor offers a free website called the Job Accommodation Network (http://www.jan.wvu.edu/) to help people with disabilities and employers find suitable job accommodations.

Clearly the ADA was more than a piece of rehabilitation legislation. We included it here, however, because it expanded the employment possibilities of students and adults with disabilities by making communities and public services more accessible to everyone.

Rehabilitation Act Amendments, P.L. 102–569 (1992). The 1992 Amendments continued legislative recognition that

> individuals with disabilities, including individuals with the most severe disabilities, are generally presumed to be capable of engaging in gainful employment and the provision of individualized vocational rehabilitation services can improve their ability to become gainfully employed. (Section 100. (a) (3) (A))

This introduced the concept of "presumption of benefit," which is the assumption that all individuals can benefit from vocational rehabilitation services unless the agency can demonstrate by "clear and convincing" evidence that an individual cannot benefit from employment because of a disability.

While this act continued to energize the national supported employment movement, it also reinforced the growing transition movement by removing barriers to interagency cooperation between school systems and vocational rehabilitation programs. First, the definition of transition services in this act was the same definition as that used in the Individuals with Disabilities Education Act of 1990 (P.L. 101–476). The fact that the definition and key provisions were the same for both acts is evidence of the influence of the same consumer and professional advocacy organizations that were involved in amending both laws.

Second, the act made it easier for high school students with disabilities to gain access to vocational rehabilitation services by: (a) allowing vocational rehabilitation counselors, in their intake procedures, to use existing assessment data provided by an individual with a disability, the family, an advocate, or an education agency if the report had been completed in the past year and (b) requiring that the IWRP be coordinated with a student's IEP.

Rehabilitation Act Amendments, Title IV of P.L. 105–220 (Workforce Investment Act of 1998). In 1998, the Rehabilitation Act Amendments were included in workforce development legislation to signal the integration of employment and training programs at the local, state, and federal levels. Title IV reinforced the notion of "presumption of benefit." Title IV also empowered individuals with disabilities by emphasizing the need for people with disabilities to have "informed choice" throughout the rehabilitation process. This effort to increase informed choice also led to increases in promoting self-determination for students with disabilities. Next, the IWRP was renamed the *individualized plan for employment (IPE)*. Finally, the act expanded employment outcomes to include self-employment and telecommunications.

Employment-Related Legislation

Job Training Partnership Act, P.L. 97–300 (1982).   The Job Training Partnership Act (JTPA) of 1982 was designed to replace the Comprehensive Employment and Training Act (CETA) of 1973. CETA was originally designed to provide job training for economically disadvantaged youths and adults in urban settings. The JTPA of 1982 permanently authorized job training programs for economically disadvantaged individuals as well as other individuals who face serious barriers to employment. The act required that each state identify designated service delivery areas (SDAs) where JTPA programs would be established and administered by local private industry councils. These councils were to be comprised of representatives from both business and education.

Workforce Investment Act, P.L. 105–220 (1998).   In 1998 Congress passed the Workforce Investment Act (WIA) to replace JTPA. WIA was based on the belief that all youths deserve access to career skills and training. One of the key principles of WIA was universal access through one-stop career centers. One-stop career centers are designed to provide seamless access to a variety of workforce development programs. While a number of federally funded programs are mandated as one-stop partners, the only mandated disability partner is the public vocational rehabilitation system. Services available at the one-stop centers are divided into three categories: core, intensive, and training (Hoff, 2002).

Core services focus on providing basic assistance in finding employment. *Intensive* services are typically provided on a one-to-one basis to individuals who need more than core services. *Training* services are designed for individuals for whom core and intensive services were not successful. Training services are provided through individual training accounts and can include occupational skills training, skills upgrading, and customized training for employers (Hoff, 2002).

While WIA mandated one-stop centers for all, it also called for combining traditional youth employment and training services. To be eligible for WIA youth services, an individual must be between the ages of 14 and 21, be low income, and meet at least one of the following six employment barriers:

1. Have a basic skills deficiency.
2. Be a school dropout.
3. Be homeless, a runaway, or a foster child.
4. Be a pregnant teen or teen parent.
5. Be an offender.
6. Require additional assistance to complete an educational program or to find and keep employment (University of Minnesota, 1999).

WIA also replaced private industry councils (from JTPA) with workforce investment boards. These boards are required to establish youth councils, which must include representatives of youth service agencies (including juvenile justice), public housing authorities, Job Corps, parents, youths who were formerly program participants, and other persons who have experience related to youth activities. The workforce investment boards and youth councils must provide, at least, the following activities:

1. Tutoring, study skills training, and dropout prevention strategies.
2. Alternative secondary school services.
3. Summer employment opportunities that are linked to academic and occupational learning.
4. Paid and unpaid work experiences, including internships and job shadowing.
5. Occupational skill training.
6. Leadership development activities, including community service and peer-centered activities.
7. Adult mentoring for the period of participation and a subsequent period, for a total of not less than 12 months.
8. Follow-up services for not less than 12 months after the completion of participation.
9. Comprehensive guidance and counseling, which may include drug and alcohol abuse counseling and referral as appropriate. (University of Minnesota, 1999, p. 2)

School-Related Legislation

In this section we discuss legislation that was designed to impact directly on school-based programs. These include vocational education, general education, and special education programs.

Vocational Education Legislation   **Vocational Education Act and Amendments, P.L. 88–210 (1963), P.L. 90–576 (1968), and 94–482 (1976).**   The original Vocational Education Act (P.L. 88–210) was passed in 1963 with the intent of moving away from programs in specific occupations such as agriculture and home economics to meet a more diverse and rapidly changing labor market. The act contained funds for retraining adults, as well as vocational training for special populations. These special populations included persons with academic, social, or other challenges that prevented them from being successful in general vocational education programs. Thus, the act opened the door for students with disabilities to receive vocational education. However, no funds were directly set aside for students with disabilities.

This was remedied in 1968 with the amendments enacted in P.L. 90–576. These amendments directed states to spend a minimum of 10% of their federal vocational education funds for students with disabilities and 15% for students who were socially, economically, or academically disadvantaged. However, in spite of increased funding, few students with disabilities actually received vocational education services. Congress attempted to remedy this situation further by passing the Vocational Education Amendments of 1976 (P.L. 94–482). These amendments required states to match the 10% of federal monies required to be set aside for students with disabilities with state and local dollars, thereby increasing the amount of money directly targeted to providing vocational education to students with disabilities. Together, these acts provided the impetus for making vocational education programs accessible to students with disabilities.

The Carl D. Perkins Vocational Education Act, P.L. 98–524 (1984), P.L. 101–392 (1990), and 105–332 (1998).   With the passage of the Carl D. Perkins Vocational Education Act of 1984 (P.L. 98–524), Congress again affirmed the fact that high-quality vocational education programs were essential to our nation's future as a free and democratic society. The act had two basic goals. The first goal was to improve the work skills of the labor force, and the second goal was to provide equal opportunities for adults in vocational education. The Carl D. Perkins Act also affirmed that individuals with disabilities were entitled to participate in any program funded through the act. As stated in Section 2 (2) of P.L. 98–524, one of the purposes of the act is:

> to assure that individuals who are inadequately served under vocational education programs are assured equal access to quality vocational educational programs, especially individuals who are disadvantaged, who are handicapped.

In addition, Section 204 stated that vocational education program activities would be provided in the least restrictive environment and, whenever appropriate, vocation education services should be included in a student's IEP.

The Carl D. Perkins Vocational and Applied Technology Act of 1990 (P.L. 101–392) amended and extended the 1984 act and authorized the largest amount of funds ever for vocational education. The act was again designed to make the United States more competitive in the world's economy, and a major goal was to provide greater vocational opportunities for disadvantaged persons. Basic state grants were exclusively targeted to so-called special populations. Special populations were divided into three categories. The first category was Disadvantaged Students; it included students who were academically disadvantaged, those who were economically disadvantaged, students from migrant populations, limited English proficiency, drop-outs, and potential drop-outs. The second category was Disabled/Handicapped Students and included students covered by IDEA and Section 504. The third category was Other Categories and included sex equity programs, foster children, and individuals in correctional institutions (North Carolina Department of Public Instruction, 2002). Chapter 7 provides more detail on the assurances guaranteed to students who participate in vocational education services provided under the Carl D. Perkins Act (see Figure 7.2 for a list of these assurances).

Finally, the Carl D. Perkins Vocational and Technical Education Act of 1998 (P.L. 105–332) removed set-asides for special populations, giving local school systems greater control over how funds were spent. However, at the same time the act called for more precise accountability by states. It required states to integrate academic and vocational competence and include them in accountability measures.

General   Education   Legislation **School-to-Work   Opportunities   Act,   P.L. 103–239 (1994).**   On April 20, 1994, Congress passed the School-to-Work Opportunities Act (STWOA). Similar to the goals of the transition provisions in IDEA (1990) (described in the next section), this law mandated that the secretaries of education and labor work collaboratively to improve postschool outcomes of secondary and postsecondary education. Many of the provisions outlined in legislation were parallel to those delineated in the transition provisions of IDEA. Key elements of STWOA included the following:

♦ Collaborative partnerships.

♦ Integrated curriculum.

♦ Technological advances.

♦ Adaptable workers.

♦ Comprehensive career guidance.

♦ Work-based learning.

♦ A step-by-step approach.

The goal was to encourage schools to integrate academic and vocational coursework. To do this, the basic elements of STWOA were divided into three major components: school-based learning, work-based learning, and connecting activities.

School-based learning involved providing students with instruction and experiences based on academic and occupational skill standards. Activities in this component included career awareness activities, career counseling, selection of a career major, applied academics, and regular evaluations to track student progress.

Work-based learning involved developing student learning activities to prepare students for the world of work. Activities in this component included workplace experiences, structured training, mentoring, and apprenticeships at job sites.

Finally, *connecting activities* were designed to build and maintain bridges between school, work, and other adult environments. The activities in this component included matching students with employers, establishing liaisons between education and work, job placement, further training assistance, linkages with youth development activities and industry, participation of business in a large variety of school-based and work-based activities, and postprogram outcome analysis.

The School-to-Work initiative was designed to be implemented by local partnerships consisting of representatives from local businesses and employer organizations, secondary and postsecondary institutions, community-based organizations, rehabilitation agencies, labor organizations, parent organizations, teacher organizations, rehabilitation agencies, student organizations, private industry councils, and other relevant parties. Local partnerships were responsible for determining activities under the work-based learning, school-based learning, and connecting activities components, determining measurable program goals and outcomes, establishing a plan for including all students in the area, providing paid work experiences, determining types of employer involvement, and providing opportunities for students to be involved in industries and occupations that offer high-skill, high-wage employment opportunities. Although this law was not reauthorized by Congress, 6 months after STWOA expired 48 states continued to implement programs and services begun as a result of the act ("States Continue STW," 2002).

Goals 2000: Educate America Act, P.L. 103–227 (1994). Signed into law on March 3, 1994, this act provided resources to states and communities to ensure that all students reached their full potential. Goals 2000 established a framework to identify world-class academic standards, measure student progress, and provide support to help students meet the standards. To do this, Section 102 put forth the following eight national education goals:

By the Year 2000-

1. All children in America will start school ready to learn.

2. The high school graduation rate will increase to at least 90 percent.

3. All students will leave grades 4, 8, and 12 having demonstrated competency over challenging subject matter including English, mathematics, science, foreign languages, civics and government, economics, the arts, history, and geography, and every school in America will ensure that all students learn to use their minds well, so they may be prepared for responsible citizenship, further learning, and productive employment in our nation's modern economy.

4. United States students will be first in the world in mathematics and science achievement.

5. Every adult American will be literate and will possess the knowledge and skills necessary to compete in a global economy and exercise the rights and responsibilities of citizenship.

6. Every school in the United States will be free of drugs, violence, and the unauthorized presence of firearms and alcohol and will offer a disciplined environment conducive to learning.

7. The nation's teaching force will have access to programs for the continued improvement of their professional skills and the opportunity to acquire the knowledge and skills needed to instruct and prepare all American students for the next century.

8. Every school will promote partnerships that will increase parental involvement and participation in promoting the social, emotional, and academic growth of children. http://www.ncrel.org/sdrs/areas/issues/envrnmnt/stw/sw0goals.htm

No Child Left Behind Act, P.L. 107–110 (2001). The No Child Left Behind (NCLB) Act made a bold commitment that every child, regardless of race, family background, or disability status would learn. Some of the major provisions include the following:

© Establishing accountability for results.

© Creating flexibility at the state and local levels and reducing red tape.

© Expanding options for parents of children from disadvantaged backgrounds.

© Ensuring that every child can read with the Reading First initiative.

© Strengthening teacher quality.

♦ Confirming progress.

♦ Promoting English proficiency.

In addition, the President's Commission on Excellence in Special Education was convened to make recommendations on applying the principles of NCLB to IDEA. Among the recommendations set forth by the commission were the need for better intra-agency and interagency coordination and a call to redefine transition services as a results-oriented process. Both sets of recommendations require teachers to have increased knowledge about transition from school to adulthood.

Special Education Legislation **The Education for All Handicapped Children Act, P.L. 94–142 (1975).** Signed in 1975, P.L. 94–142 mandated that all children with disabilities between the ages of 3 and 21 shall receive a free, appropriate public education. P.L. 94–142 consisted of six principles that have stood the test of time:

1. Zero reject.
2. Nondiscriminatory testing.
3. An appropriate education designed to meet individual student needs and stated in the IEP.
4. Least restrictive environment.
5. Due process.
6. Parent participation (Heward, 2003)

While P.L. 94–142 is not considered transition-related legislation, it did lay the foundation for many future laws that were. For example, while IDEA created the IEP as a blueprint for a child's future, the Carl D. Perkins Act (1984) stated that vocational services should be included in a student's IEP when appropriate.

The Individuals with Disabilities Education Act, P.L. 101–476 (1990). On October 30, 1990, P.L. 101–476 was signed into law. This legislation changed the title of the Education for All Handicapped Children Act to the Individuals with Disabilities Education Act. The original P.L. 94–142 mandated five components for the IEP:

1. The student's present level of performance.
2. Annual goals and short-term objectives for reaching the goals.
3. Specific special education and related services to be provided and the extent of participation in general education.
4. Projected dates for initiation of services and the anticipated duration of the services.
5. Appropriate objective criteria, evaluation procedures, and schedules for determining (at least on an annual basis) whether the short-term objectives have been met.

IDEA 1990 added a sixth component to the IEP for students 16 years and older (younger if needed)—the transition component (Storms, DeStefano, & O'Leary,

1996). The act included the first formal definition of transition as well as describing who should be included in transition meetings.

In addition to defining transition, IDEA 1990 mandated that a transition component of the IEP be in place by the time the student reached age 16 and that transition services for youths with disabilities be coordinated with the school and other service providers within the community. As a result, IDEA 1990 has become known as the "transition law." Because this law had such impact on the IEP process and interagency collaboration, we will discuss the requirements in more detail in Chapters 4 and 5.

The Individuals with Disabilities Education Act Amendments, P.L. 105–17 (1997). IDEA was amended again in 1997. The 1997 amendments included several changes designed to strengthen the delivery of transition services, as well as to change the focus of special education from concentrating on process to emphasizing educational and transition postschool outcomes (Flexer, Simmons, Luft, & Baer, 2001).

The following changes were made that impacted transition either directly or indirectly. First, related services was added to the list of possible transition services. Related services may include, to name a few, speech and language therapy, psychological services, physical therapy, rehabilitation counseling, therapeutic recreation, social work, occupational therapy, and/or transportation. Second, the definition of special education was broadened to include educational activities designed specifically to prepare students for transition, including vocational education and applied technology education. Third, a statement of transition service needs that focuses on the student's course of study must be present in the IEP beginning at age 14. In the 1990 version of the law, a transition statement was mandated for students beginning at age 16 (or younger, when appropriate); however, the IEP team did not need to address the student's course of study at that time. Finally, the 1997 amendments stated that at least 1 year before the student reaches the age of majority in his or her state, there must be a statement in the IEP indicating that the student has been informed that his or her rights will transfer when that age of majority is reached.

In addition, while not designed to directly impact transition services, an important change in 1997 was the emphasis of access to the general education curriculum. Some of the highlights of this new focus are as follows:

1. There must now be a statement about how the student's disability "affects involvement and progress in general curriculum."
2. There must be a statement identifying services that will help students to "be involved and progress in general curriculum."
3. There must be an "explanation of [the] extent to which [the] child will not participate in [the] regular class." This represents a shift from the 1990 amendments, which required an explanation of the "extent to which [the] child will participate in regular educational programs." The assumption now is that all children will participate in general education, and the IEP team must explain when a child is *not* participating in general education.

4. Children with disabilities must be included in state-and district-wide assessments, with accommodations as needed. If a child cannot participate in such assessments, he or she must participate in an alternate assessment.

5. A general education teacher must now participate in every IEP meeting if the child participates, or will participate, in general education.

Together, the focus on access to the general education curriculum impacted the delivery of transition services in at least three ways:

1. The IEP team has to address each student's course of study beginning at age 14. Determining a student's course of study is directly related to determining the extent to which a child will be involved in the general education curriculum as well as what transition services will be received.

2. The course of study through which a child progresses determines, in many states, what type of diploma or other exit document students are awarded upon completing or leaving school.

3. Teachers who work with transitioning students must not sacrifice academics for teaching transition skills. As a result, teachers, students, and families must seek creative ways to allow students access to the general curriculum while at the same time, teaching students the skills they need to successfully achieve their desired adult outcomes.

The Individuals with Disabilities Education Improvement Act, P. L. 108–446 (IDEA 2004).   On December 3, 2004, P. L. 108–446 was once again amended. IDEA 2004 contains a number of changes to the transition provisions. First, the definition of "transition services" was changed to emphasize that services must be designed "within a results-oriented process" that focuses on "improving the academic and functional achievement" of students. In addition, "vocational education" was added to the list of potential transition services and each student's strengths as well as preferences and interests must now be taken into account when considering his or her transition needs. The current definition of transition services can be found in Figure 1.4.

Second, IDEA 2004 clarifies that the purpose of each student's free, appropriate public education is to "prepare them for further education, employment, and independent living". Third, IDEA 2004 eliminates all references to transition activities beginning at age 14 by mandating that all transition requirements are to be followed no later than the first IEP in effect when a student turns 16 years old. However, it does not preclude a state or school system from starting transition services at an earlier age. As you will read later, beginning transition services as early as possible is a recommended best practice.

Fourth, schools are now required to include transition goals beyond high school in IEPs by including appropriate measurable postsecondary goals based on age-appropriate transition assessments and describe the transition services—including courses of study—needed to reach a student's goals. Fifth, as students with disabilities graduate from high school, they must be provided with a summary of their accomplishments and transition needs.

Finally, while IDEA 2004 is designed to more closely align IDEA with the No Child Left Behind Act, it also modifies requirements regarding individualized student planning, transition, and litigation; due process protections, monitoring, and enforcement; and federal funding. While the full impact of the changes will not be known until the rules and regulations are completed, any of the following Web sites can provide current information: www.cec.sped.org; http://thomas.loc.gov/; www.wrightslaw.com/law/idea/; www.ncset.org

STRATEGIES FOR ADDRESSING COMMON CHALLENGES

Teaching Transition Content and Skills Within a High-Stakes Assessment Environment

Too often we hear teachers say that they cannot provide transition services because they have to prepare students for local and state exams. Fortunately, we have found that it does not have to be an either/or proposition if one takes a **transition perspective** of education (Kohler, 1996). The following are some suggestions for providing transition services within today's standards-based, high-stakes assessment school environments:

1. *Make transition planning the foundation for a student's educational program.* In addition to being legally mandated, the process systematically coordinates a student's course of study (curriculum), assessment strategies and accommodations, and school and community supports and services to foster both immediate and long-range successful student outcomes.

2. *Help students access the general education curriculum.* Wehmeyer, Sands, Knowlton, and Kozleski (2002) identified four action steps for gaining access to the general curriculum:
    a. Writing standards and curriculum that are open-ended and that incorporate principles of universal design (Orkwis & McLane, 1998).
    b. Using the IEP process to ensure that a student's educational program is based on the general curriculum.
    c. Grouping students based on instructional needs to ensure progress in the curriculum.
    d. Designing individual instructional interventions for students who are not progressing by other means.

3. *Teach applied academics (Patton & Trainor, 2002) and use authentic assessment (Braden, Schroeder, & Buckley, 2001).* Applied academics are skills and knowledge typically associated with core academic content areas that are applied to real-life contexts and situations. For example, instead of calculating percentages on a worksheet, a student might be able to figure the amount of sales tax on an item to be

Part A: General Provisions

Section 601: Short Title; Table of Contents; Findings; Purposes

(d)   PURPOSES. The purposes of this title are–

(1)   (A) to ensure that all children with disabilities have available to them a free appropriate public education that emphasizes special education and related services designed to meet their unique needs and prepare them **for further education**, employment, and independent living;

Section 602: Definitions

(34)   TRANSITION SERVICES: The term "transition services" means a coordinated set of activities for a **child** with a disability that–

(A)   is designed to be **within a results**-oriented process, **that is focused on improving the academic and functional achievement of the child with a disability to facilitate the child's** movement from school to postschool activities, including postsecondary education, vocational **education**, integrated employment (including supported employment), continuing and adult education, adult services, independent living, or community participation;

Part B: Assistance for Education for All Children with Disabilities

Section 614: Individualized Education Programs

(C)   ADDITIONAL REQUIREMENTS FOR EVALUATION AND REEVALUATIONS

(5)   EVALUATIONS BEFORE CHANGE IN ELIGIBILITY–

(A)   IN GENERAL – **Except as provided in subparagraph (B),** a local educational agency shall evaluate a child with a disability in accordance with this section before determining that the child is no longer a child with a disability.

(B)   Exception–

(i)   IN GENERAL – **The evaluation described in subparagraph (A) shall not be required before the termination of a child's eligibility under this part due to graduation from secondary school with a regular diploma, or due to exceeding the age eligibility for a free appropriate public education under State law.**

(ii)   SUMMARY OF PERFORMANCE – **For a child whose eligibility under this part terminates under circumstances described in clause (i), a local education agency shall provide the child with a summary of the child's academic achievement and functional performance, which shall include recommendations on how to assist the child in meeting the child's postsecondary goals.**

Section 614, INDIVIDUALIZED EDUCATION PROGRAMS

(d)   INDIVIDUALIZED EDUCATION PROGRAMS

(1)   DEFINITIONS

(A)   INDIVIDUALIZED EDUCATION PROGRAM

(VIII) **beginning not later than the first IEP to be in effect when the child is 16, and updated annually thereafter–**

(aa) **appropriate measurable postsecondary goals based upon age appropriate transition assessments related to training, education, employment, and, where appropriate, independent living skills;**

Figure 1.4
Summary of Key Changes on Transition in IDEA, 2004

(bb) **the transition services (including courses of study) needed to assist the child in reaching those goals; and**

(cc) beginning **not later than** 1 year before the child reaches the age of majority under State law, a statement that the child has been informed of the child's rights under this title, if any, that will transfer to the child on reaching the age of majority under section 615 (m).

(ii) RULE OF CONSTRUCTION–**nothing in this section shall be construed to require–**

(I) **that additional information be included in a child's IEP beyond what is explicitly required in this section; and**

(II) **the IEP Team to include information under 1 component of a child's IEP that is already contained under another component of such IEP.**

[Note: The following text appears in Part B, Section 614 (d) (1) (A) (i), as part of the definition of what an IEP includes.]

(II) a statement of measurable annual goals, including **academic and functional goals,** designed to–

(**aa**) meet the child's needs that result from the child's disability to enable the child to be involved in and **make** progress in the general education curriculum; and

(bb) meet each of the child's other educational needs that result from the child's disability;

(III) a description of how the child's progress toward meeting the annual goals described in subclause (II) will be measured and when periodic reports on the progress the child is making toward meeting the annual goals (such as through the use of quarterly or other periodic reports, concurrent with the issuance of report card) will be provided;

(3) DEVELOPMENT OF IEP –

(A) IN GENERAL – In developing each child's IEP, the IEP Team, subject to subparagraph (C), shall consider –

(i) the strengths of the child;

(ii) the concerns of the parent of enhancing the education of their child;

(iii) the results of the initial evaluation or most recent evaluation of the child; and

(iv) the academic, developmental, and functional needs of the child.

(7) CHILDREN WITH DISABILITIES IN ADULT PRISONS–

(A) IN GENERAL – The following requirements shall not apply to children with disabilities who are convicted as adults under State law and incarcerated in adult prisons:

(i) The requirements contained in section 612 (a) (16) and paragraph (1) (A) (i) (VI) (relating to participation of children with disabilities in general assessments).

(ii) The requirements of items (aa) and (bb) of paragraph (1) (A) (i) (VIII) (relating to transition planning and transition service), do not apply with respect to such children whose eligibility under this part will end, because of **such children's age, before such children** will be released from prison.

Note. Bold text indicates changes from IDEA 1997. Adapted from *Key Provisions on Transition: IDEA 1997 Compared to H.R. 1350 (IDEA 2004).* Retrieved February 18, 2005, from http://www.ncset.org/idea.asp.

(continued)

Where Can Families Find Out More Information About Transition?

National Center on Secondary Education and Transition
www.ncset.org

The National Center on Secondary Education and Transition (NCSET) was established to create opportunities for youths with disabilities to achieve successful futures. Headquartered at the Institute on Community Integration, University of Minnesota, NCSET provides technical assistance and disseminates information focused on four major areas of national significance for young people with disabilities and their families:

1. Providing students with disabilities with improved access and success in the secondary education curriculum.
2. Ensuring that students achieve positive postschool results in accessing postsecondary education, meaningful employment, independent living, and participation in all aspects of community life.
3. Supporting student and family participation in educational and postschool decision making and planning.
4. Improving collaboration and system linkages at all levels through the development of broad-based partnerships and networks at the national, state, and local levels.

National Information Center for Children and Youth with Disabilities
www.nichcy.org

NICHCY is a central source of information on the following topics:

1. Disabilities in infants, toddlers, children, and youth.
2. The Individuals with Disabilities Education Act, which is the law authorizing special education.
3. No Child Left Behind (as it relates to children with disabilities).
4. Research-based information on effective educational practices.

On-Campus Outreach
www.education.umd.edu/ocol

The purpose of On-Campus Outreach (OCO) is to provide information and support to programs and personnel that provide services to public school students ages 18 to 21 with significant disabilities in postsecondary settings such as colleges, universities, or other community locations.

PACER Center
www.pacer.org

The mission of the PACER Center is to expand opportunities and enhance the quality of life of children and young adults with disabilities and their families, based on the concept of parents helping parents. Through its ALLIANCE and other national projects, PACER, a national center, responds to thousands of parents and professionals each year. PACER provides assistance to individual families, workshops,

> *materials for parents and professionals, and leadership in securing a free and appropriate public education for all children*
>
> Transition Coalition
> www.transitioncoalition.org
> *The mission of the Transition Coalition is to maximize professional development in secondary school reform and transition at the national, state, and local levels. The coalition supports best practices and creates professional development forums using face-to-face and online training and technical assistance.*

purchased. By extending this example, one can see that if applied academics are taught, then authentic assessment will easily follow. In addition, the School-to-Work Opportunities Act and the Secretary's Commission on Achieving Necessary Skills (SCANS) Competencies both offer applied career skills, competencies, and instructional strategies needed by competent and successful employees.

4. *Involve families in the planning and instructional process.* Morningstar (2002) suggested two ways families can become involved. First, they can help interpret the results from standards-based assessments as they relate to future goals; second, they can help balance the individual transition outcome needs for their sons and daughters with the standards-based education reforms. The balancing act will occur primarily around the areas of assessment including recommendation for accommodations, alternative approaches, or in some cases opting out of high stakes assessment.

CASE STUDY

ANDY

Beginning the Planning Process

Andy lives at home with his mother and four brothers and sisters. He is labeled as trainable mentally disabled and his major goal was to complete high school and graduate with a diploma. Andy's transition planning process began in the eighth grade when he and his mother were provided information on the course-of-study options and Andy chose to participate in a course of study designed to prepare him for a career. Information on Andy was gathered from Andy and his mother through student dream sheets and mapping forms.

Conducting the Individual-Level Team Meeting

After Andy chose his course of study, his team helped him prepare his IEP. His coursework included employment English, job skills math, life skills science, career preparation, music, and physical education. Because Andy wanted to live at home, his residential needs appeared to be taken care of. He was able to get work experience in the community using enclaves in custodial, retail, restaurant, industrial, and yard work. He was a member of the honors chorus and participated in many local and state performances. He also participated in Special Olympics teams playing soccer, softball, and basketball. During the second semester of his sophomore year, Andy and his mother were invited to a panel presentation by the school-level team, where they were provided with information on the array of possible adult services and met the key players Andy might become involved with over the next few years.

Planning the School-Level Team Meeting

Since Andy decided to pursue an occupational course of study, he began meeting with the school-level team during the second semester of his sophomore year. Prior to the meeting, a transition assessment was conducted. A checklist and an informational form were prepared to assist Andy when meeting with the school-level transition team. The transition teacher rehearsed with Andy through role-playing prior to the initial school-level team meeting.

Conducting the School-Level Team Meeting

Andy's first school-level transition meeting was held at the end of his sophomore year. Andy and the other team members decided that his major postgraduate goal was to attend a community college compensatory education program and enroll in adapted art classes. He also expressed an interest in continuing his recreation program at the YMCA and his participation in Special Olympics, obtaining a driver's license, and becoming a productive citizen. He wanted to be fully independent in the future. He was beginning to visualize what it would be like to live on his own.

During the school-level team meeting, Andy talked about having extra time on his hands and said he wanted to seek a part-time job. During that school year, he participated in several on-campus jobs and worked in the school-based enterprise, where he received excellent evaluations.

Andy stated that during his junior year he wanted to participate in an on-campus job as a work station supervisor in the school-based enterprise. He also wanted to job shadow at six different businesses. The team determined that at the end of his junior year he would become eligible for vocational rehabilitation services and receive a vocational evaluation. Andy also stated that he wanted to participate in driver's education at the end of his junior year.

During his senior year, he wanted to complete his job placement portfolio, participate in sports, and complete requirements for receiving the occupational diploma.

As the school year progressed, Andy began to talk more about moving out of his mother's home, but he knew he needed a job first. He and his mother were provided information on residential options, and he visited several group homes in the area.

He got a part-time job at the YMCA during his senior year and received good work evaluations. He continued to lean toward getting his own apartment.

Andy continued to meet with both the school-level team and individual teams as needed. As an outcome of the school-level meetings, Andy's vocational rehabilitation counselor and case manager were invited to his individual transition team meetings.

The Exit Meeting

Prior to graduation, the school-level team conducted an exit meeting in which Andy discussed his final plans. With job coach support, he was able to get a full-time job prior to graduation earning $7.73 per hour. He wanted to continue working full time, get his driver's license, and move into an apartment in approximately 3 months. At the exit meeting, Andy was reminded that he would continue to receive supported employment follow-up services from his job coach and that the school would also follow up on his progress for 3 years. He planned to enroll in compensatory education classes during the day since he would be working third shift. Andy stated that he would like to continue his family membership at the YMCA. Both Andy and his mother stated that they believed that the early interagency collaboration through the school-level team had helped him make a successful transition to living in his community.

One Year Later

Andy continues to work in his full-time job and has received a raise to $9.25 per hour. Through his membership at the YMCA he has started to date, and he and his partner are considering either moving into a supported living setting or purchasing a home of their own. Andy is currently enrolled in compensatory education classes at the local community college, but he still has not passed the driver's test to get his license.

STUDY GUIDE QUESTIONS

1. What is disturbing about postschool outcomes for students with disabilities?
2. Why can transition be thought of as "old wine in a new bottle"?
3. How does Halpern define transition?
4. Differentiate between the OSERS transition model and Halpern's transition model.
5. Describe the importance of the following pieces of legislation:
   a. Vocational Rehabilitation Act of 1973, 1986, 1992, and 1998.
   b. Americans with Disabilities Act.
   c. Job Training Partnership Act.
   d. Workforce Investment Act.
   e. Vocational Education Act Amendments of 1963, 1968, and 1976.
   f. Carl D. Perkins Vocational Education Act of 1984, 1990, and 1998.
   g. School-to-Work Opportunities Act.

h. Goals 2000.
i. No Child Left Behind Act.
j. Education for All Handicapped Children Act.
k. Individuals with Disabilities Education Act.
6. What is the "presumption of benefit"?
7. How is transition defined in IDEA 1990? What changes are made in IDEA 1997 and IDEA 2004?

REFERENCES

Adelman, P. B., & Vogel, S. A. (1993). Issues in program evaluation. In S. A. Vogel & P. B. Adelman (Eds.), *Success for college students with learning disabilities* (pp. 323–343). New York: Springer-Verlag.

Affleck, J. Q., Edgar, E., Levine, P., & Kortering, L. (1990). Post-school status of students classified as mildly mentally retarded, learning disabled, or nonhandicapped: Does it get better with time? *Education and Training in Mental Retardation, 25,* 315–324.

Blackorby, J., & Wagner, M. (1996). Longitudinal post-school outcomes of youth with disabilities: Findings from the National Longitudinal Transition Study. *Exceptional Children, 62,* 399–413.

Bound, J., & Johnson, G. (1995). What are the causes of rising wage inequality in the United States? *Economic Policy Review, 1*(1), 9–17.

Braden, J. P., Schroeder, J. L., & Buckley, J. A. (2001). *Secondary school reform, inclusion, and authentic assessment* (Brief No. 3). Madison, WI: Research Institute and Secondary Education Reform for Youth with Disabilities.

Brolin, D. (1983). Career education: Where do we go from here? *Career Development for Exceptional Individuals, 6,* 3–14.

Cegelka, P. (1979). Career education. In M. Epstein & D. Cullinan (Eds.), *Special education for adolescents: Issues and perspectives* (pp. 155–184). Upper Saddle River, NJ: Merrill/Prentice Hall.

Coley, R. J. (1995). *Dreams deferred: High school dropouts in the United States.* Princeton, NJ: Educational Testing Service, Policy Information Center.

Collett-Klingenberg, L. L. (1998). The reality of best practices in transition: A case study. *Exceptional Children, 65,* 67–78.

Flexer, R. W., Simmons, T. J., Luft, P., & Baer, R. M. (2001). *Transition planning for secondary students with disabilities.* Upper Saddle River, NJ: Prentice Hall.

Frank, A. R., Sitlington, P. L., Cooper, L., & Cool, V. (1990). Adult adjustment of recent graduates of Iowa mental disabilities programs. *Education and Training in Mental Retardation, 25,* 62–75.

Gottesman, B. (1994). The big picture: The South Carolina collaborative to renew teacher education. *Record in Educational Leadership, 14*(2), 67–76.

Halpern, A. (1973). General unemployment and vocational opportunities for EMR individuals. *American Journal of Mental Deficiency, 80,* 81–89.

Halpern, A. (1985). Transition: A look at the foundations. *Exceptional Children, 51,* 479–486.

Halpern, A., (1992). Transition: Old wine in new bottles. *Exceptional Children, 58,* 202–211.

Hasazi, S. B., Furney, K. S., & DeStefano, L. (1999). Implementing the IDEA transition mandates. *Exceptional Children, 65,* 555–566.

Hasazi, S., Gordon, L., & Roe, C. (1985). Factors associated with the employment status of handicapped youth exiting high school from 1979–1983. *Exceptional Children, 51,* 455–469.

Heward, W. L. (2003). *Exceptional children: An introduction to special education* (7th ed.). Upper Saddle River, NJ: Merrill/Prentice Hall.

Hoff, D. (2002). Workforce Investment Act and one-stop career centers: Opportunities and ongoing challenges. *TASH Connections, 28*(9/10), 23–26.

Hoyt, K. (1982). Career education: Beginning of the end? Or a new beginning? *Career Development for Exceptional Individuals, 5,* 3–12.

Kohler, P. (1996). *A taxonomy for transition programming: Linking research and practice.* Champaign: University of Illinois, Transition Research Institute.

Kohler, P. D. (1998). Implementing a transition perspective of education: A comprehensive approach to planning and delivering secondary education and transition services. In F. R. Rusch & J. G. Chadsey (Eds.), *Beyond high school: Transition from school to work* (pp. 179–205). Belmont, CA: Wadsworth.

Kortering, L., & Braziel, P. (1999). School dropout from the perspective of former students: Implications for secondary special education programs. *Remedial and Special Education, 20,* 78–83.

Love, L., & Malian, I. (1997). What happens to students leaving secondary special education services in Arizona? Implications for education program improvement and transition services. *Remedial and Special Education, 18,* 261–269.

McMillan, M., Kaufman, P., & Klein, S. (1997). *Dropout rates in the United States: 1995.* Washington, DC: National Center for Education Statistics.

Morningstar, M. E. (2002). The role of families of adolescents with disabilities in standards-based educational reform and transition. In C. A. Kochhar-Bryant & D. S. Bassett (Eds.), *Aligning transition and standards-based education: Issues and strategies.* Arlington, VA: Council for Exceptional Children.

Murnane, R. J., Willett, J. B., & Boudett, K. P. (1997). Does a GED lead to more training, postsecondary education, and military service for school dropouts? *Industrial and Labor Relations Review, 51,* 100–116.

National Council on Disability. (2000). *Transition and post-school outcomes for youth with disabilities: Closing the gaps to post-secondary education and employment.* Washington, DC: National Council on Disability and Social Security Aministration.

North Carolina Department of Public Instruction (NCDPI). (2002). *Special populations challenge handbook.* Raleigh: NCDPI Career-Technical Education.

Orkwis, R., & McLane, K. (1998, Fall). *A curriculum every student can use: Design principles for student access* (ERIC/OSEP Topical Brief). Arlington, VA: Council for Exceptional Children. (ERIC Document Reproduction Service No. ED423654.

Patton, J. R., & Trainor, A. (2002). Using applied academics to enhance curricular reform in secondary education. In C. A. Kochhar-Bryant & D. S. Bassett (Eds.), *Aligning transition and standards-based education: Issues and strategies* (pp. 55–75). Arlington, VA: Council for Exceptional Children.

Schelly, C., Sample, P., & Kothe, J. (1995). *Vocational support strategies for students with emotional disorders.* Arlington, VA: ERIC Clearinghouse on Disabilities and Gifted Education, Council for Exceptional Children. (ERIC/EC Digest No. E534)

Sitlington, P., Clark, G., & Kolstoe, O. (2000). *Transition education and services for adolescents with disabilities* (3rd ed.). Needham Heights, MA: Allyn & Bacon.

Sitlington, P., & Frank, A. (1993). Dropouts with learning disabilities: What happens to them as young adults? *Learning Disabilities Research and Practice, 8,* 244–252.

Special education dropout rate remains stagnant. (1997) *Special Education Law Reporter, 23*(1), 1–2.

States continue STW and federal role phases out. (2002). *Vocational Training News, 33* (8), 4–5).

Storms, J., DeStefano, L., & O'Leary, E. (1996). *Individuals with Disabilities Education Act: Transition requirements—a guide for states, districts, schools, and families.* Stillwater: Oklahoma State University, National Clearinghouse on Rehabilitation.

Swaim, R. C., Beauvis, F., Chavez, E. L., & Oetting, E. R. (1997). The effect of dropout rates on estimates of adolescent substance abuse among three racial/ethnic groups. *American Journal of Public Health, 87,* 51–55.

University of Minnesota. (1999). *Workforce Investment Act. What's Working in Transition.* St. Paul: University of Minnesota, Collaborative Interagency Project, Institute on Community Integration.

U.S. Department of Education. (2001). *Twenty-third annual report to Congress on the Implementation of the Individuals with Disabilities Education Act.* Washington, DC: Author.

Wehmeyer, M. L., Sands, D. J., Knowlton, H. E., & Kozleski, E. B. (2002). *Teaching students with mental retardation: Access to the general curriculum.* Baltimore: Brookes.

Westberry, S. J. (1994). A review of learning strategies for adults with learning disabilities preparing for the GED exam. *Journal of Learning Disabilities, 27,* 202–209.

Will, M. (1984). *OSERS programing for the transition of youth with disabilities: Bridges from school to working life.* Washington, DC: U.S. Department of Education.

Best Practices and Future Issues in Transition

Chapter 2

Introduction

The goal of this chapter is to introduce educators to current best practices in providing transition using the Taxonomy for Transition Programming (Kohler, 1996). This taxonomy establishes the foundation for the strategies and methods described in the remaining chapters. The chapter then concludes with a discussion of future trends and issues that can impact the delivery of transition services. We provide an example of how a common challenge is being addressed, along with a case study demonstrating the impact of providing a full array of transition services on student postschool outcomes.

Key Terms

Taxonomy for Transition Programming
student-focused planning
student development
family involvement
interagency collaboration
self-determination movement

A Personal Perspective on the Importance of Self-Determination

Aimee Gravette

College Student, Ithaca College

The clock on the wall of the high school counseling office read 7:10 A.M. There I sat nervous, with palms sweaty, and staring at the methodical jolt of the clock's red second hand. Each tick pounded in my head, reminding me of the weeklong migraine I had after this same type of meeting just 6 months before. On my right sat my dad, staring straight ahead in his pressed business suit. On my left sat my mom, who couldn't seem to do anything but shake her leg impatiently. I watched the second hand hit the 12, marking exactly 7:15 A.M. I always dreaded 7:15 A.M. because it meant the beginning of the school day.
Prompt as always, the counselor glided into the room and asked me sympathetically whether I was ready. Well, ready or not I thought, here I come. We walked up the hall to the small conference room, where I saw the intimidating faces of my new ninth-grade teachers.

The reason I was having this meeting was because just 6 months before I had been diagnosed with attention deficit disorder. Ever since second grade I had struggled. Every night I was forced to sit at my desk and study with my dad. I would work with him for hours on homework, crying through every problem. I was confused about why it took me longer to understand and get through my studies than my friends. If I had not had such wonderful parents, or had been in any number of other school districts across the country, my chances of making it to high school graduation would have been slim.

Fortunately, I attend a proactive and progressive high school that started a class called LEAD (Learning and Educating About Disabilities). I became a member of the class in my freshman year. LEAD taught me and many other students about our disabilities and how we should advocate for ourselves and take ownership of our lives.

I calmed down and gathered my thoughts, knowing that this was my first chance to prove myself. For the next few minutes I shocked my parents and teachers with my knowledge and confidence about my disability. My parents sat there with their mouths shut and tears in their eyes. This was a side of me they had never seen. I finally under-stood my particular needs and was able to speak with confidence about them.

By the end of the meeting my teachers and parents knew my goals and had a roadmap for how we would work to achieve them. I am proud to say that I reached the goals set in that meeting and surpassed them long ago. I have continued to be an avid spokesperson for students with learning disabilities. By giving numerous presentations in my commu-nity and speaking at several international learning disability conferences, I work to dispel the stereotypes that students with learning disabilities face. I now look forward to the start of the school day, and I want other students like me to feel the same.

Note: This was Aimee's essay for her application for admission.

BEST PRACTICES IN TRANSITION

What Are "Best Practices"?

One of the most interesting challenges facing educators who wish to develop and implement transition programs that will improve the postschool outcomes of their students is trying to determine what constitutes "best practice." Fortunately, researchers in the field of transition have been trying to provide this answer since the introduction of Will's (1984) model of three bridges to transition.

Promising transition practices were first identified in some of the early transition outcome studies (Hasazi, Gordon, & Roe, 1985; Kortering & Edgar, 1988; Mithaug, Horiuchi, & Fanning, 1985; Sitlington & Frank, 1990; Wehman, Kregel, & Seyfarth, 1985). Among these original studies, which documented poor postschool outcomes for students exiting high school programs, were a set of studies that also investigated the relationship between improved postschool outcomes and the components of these students' high school program.

Hasazi and colleagues (1985) conducted a study of 462 youths from nine Vermont school districts who exited high school between 1979 and 1983. Their results indicated that 55% were in paid jobs but only 67% of these were full time. Of those who graduated from high school, 72% earned less than $5.00/hour, while of those who dropped out, more than 84% earned less than $5.00/hour. One important finding was that students who received work experiences while in high school had better postschool employment outcomes than students who did not.

Overall, these studies found a positive relationship between taking vocational education classes, participating in paid job experiences, and receiving transition programming and better student postschool employment outcomes. These early findings are still being supported by research (see Baer et al., 2003).

Following the 1990 Individuals with Disabilities Education Act (IDEA) revisions mandating transition services, the compilation of lists of best practices accelerated. These lists, summarized in Table 2.1, were developed based on a variety of analyses including the following:

- ◆ Exemplary transition programs (Kohler, DeStefano, Wermuth, Grayson, & McGinty, 1994).
- ◆ School-to-work components (Benz, Yovanoff, & Doren, 1997).
- ◆ Three exemplary states (Furney, Hasazi, & DeStefano, 1997).
- ◆ Five model and four representative local school systems (Hasazi, Furney, & DeStefano, 1999).
- ◆ The research literature (Hughes, Eisenman, et al., 1997; Karge, Patton, & de la Garza, 1992).
- ◆ Empirical validation from transition teachers (Hughes, Kim, et al., 1997).
- ◆ Follow-up study data (Johnson & Rusch, 1993).

Table 2.1

Summary of Best Practice Suggestions

Reference	Data Source	Data Source
Benz, Yovanoff, and Doren (1997)	Students with disabilities in Oregon and Nevada	Listed eight suggestions based on school-to-work framework of school-based, work-based, and connecting activities
DeStefano, Heck, Hasazi, and Furney (1999)	1997 Policy Forum on Transition	Listed 23 recommendations in 7 areas: 1. Considering transition as a Pre-K–16 issue 2. Promoting schools responsibility for all students 3. Cultivating leadership 4. Working effectively with students and families 5. Addressing issues of collaboration and the holistic nature of transition 6. Appreciating local contexts 7. Continuing research and dissemination
Furney, Hasazi, and DeStefano (1997)	Three exemplary states	Identified seven themes: 1. The role of shared values 2. Using direct policy approaches 3. Paving the way for change by uniting leadership and advocacy 4. Building collaborative structures 5. Using research results 6. Building capacity 7. Linking to other restructuring efforts
Hasazi, Furney, and DeStefano (1999)	Comparison of five model and four representative local education agencies	Identified six factors: 1. System-wide student- and family-centered strategies 2. Effective interagency collaboration 3. Systematic professional development 4. Visionary leadership 5. Integrated reform efforts 6. Connections with local and federal transition initiatives
Hughes, Eisenman, et al. (1997)	Special education, psychology, rehabilitation, community, integration, and employment literature (1990–1993)	Identified 268 outcomes in 8 categories: 1. Social interaction 2. Employment 3. Community adjustment 4. Self-determination 5. Recreation and leisure 6. Physical and material well-being 7. Civic responsibility 8. Psychological well-being

Hughes, Hwang, et al. (1997)	Transition teachers	Empirically and socially validated 8 support strategies and 592 procedures in two areas: 1. Develop support in environment 2. Increase student's competence
Hughes, Kim, et al. (1997)	National survey of researchers	Identified 10 strategies that support transition: 1. Teach social skills 2. Teach self-management 3. Identify independence objectives 4. Assess social acceptance 5. Identify coworker, peer, and family support 6. Identify student choices 7. Monitor social acceptance across time 8. Identify environment support 9. Match support to needs 10. Teach choice making/decision making
Johnson and Rusch (1993)	Twenty-four follow-up studies (1984–1991)	Made recommendations in seven areas: 1. Drop-out prevention 2. Student–parent involvement 3. Transition planning 4. Curriculum and instruction 5. Best practices 6. Transition policy 7. Future research and demonstration
Karge, Patton, and de la Garza (1992)	Research literature	Identified 12 functional curriculum areas: 1. Job search 2. Job maintenance 3. Job-related functional academics 4. Mobility and transportation 5. Plan and access recreation activities 6. Paid jobs in the community before graduation 7. Counseling for postsecondary options 8. Referral to adult agencies before graduation 9. Self-advocacy for job and community 10. Parent training and self-advocacy 11. Individual transition plan (ITP) 12. Participation in ITP planning and meetings
Kohler et al. (1994)	Analysis of exemplary programs	Identified 107 key elements grouped into 14 categories: 1. Career and vocational training 2. Interdisciplinary transition planning 3. Life and work skills curricula

(continued)

Table 2.1
(*Continued*)

Reference	Data Source	Data Source
		4. Appropriate integration
		5. Interagency collaboration
		6. Support services
		7. Staff development
		8. Public and employer relations
		9. Academic instruction
		10. Social/independent living skills training
		11. Program evaluation
		12. Instructional issues and strategies
		13. Funding
		14. Early intervention
Kohler (1996)	Concept mapping	Created transition taxonomy involving five areas:
		1. Student development
		2. Student-focused planning
		3. Family involvement
		4. Interagency collaboration
		5. Program structure and attributes

♦ Transition researchers (Hughes, Hwang, et al., 1997).

♦ The 1997 Policy Forum on Transition (DeStefano, Heck, Hasazi, & Furney, 1999).

Taxonomy for Transition Programming

As shown in Table 2.1, many lists of transition best practices are available and many are grounded in research. However, the **Taxonomy for Transition Programming** (Kohler, 1996) is the only model based on both empirical and validation studies as well as outcomes from the Office of Special Education and Rehabilitation Services (OSERS)-funded model demonstration transition projects. As such, the Taxonomy provides a user-friendly conceptual framework based on practices associated with improved postschool outcomes for thousands of students with disabilities. Figure 2.1 provides a diagram of the Taxonomy for Transition Programming. It includes a comprehensive set of strategies organized into five categories including (a) student-focused planning, (b) student development, (c) family involvement, (d) interagency collaboration, and (e) program structures.

Student-Focused Planning.   This category focuses on using student assessment data and promoting student self-determination skills to help students develop individualized education programs (IEPs) based on their chosen postschool goals. The transition planning process provides the cornerstone for providing effective

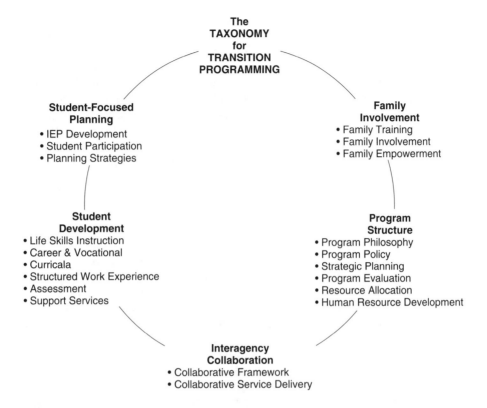

Figure 2.1
The Taxonomy for Transition Programming.

Note. From *A Taxonomy for Transition Programming: Linking Research and Practice* by P. D. Kohler, 1996, Champaign: University of Illinois, Transition Research Institute.

transition services (Grigal, Test, Beattie, & Wood, 1997; Halpern, Yovanoff, Doren, & Benz, 1995; Sale, Metzler, Everson, & Moon, 1991; Zhang & Stecker, 2001). Two of the most critical competencies for transition educators are knowledge of IDEA's transition planning requirements (P.L. 105–17 and amendments), and the skills to involve students in the IEP process. For example, transition personnel must know the definition of transition (P.L. 105–17, Section 300.29), the content of the IEP relative to transition planning (P.L. 105–17, Section 300.347), and the IEP requirements for students beginning at ages 14 and 16 (P.L. 105–17, Section 300.347(6)). Educators also need to know proven best practices in transition (Grigal et al., 1997), such as student involvement in the transition process. Although IDEA (2004) no longer requires involvement by age 14, this best practice was originally recommended in P.L. 94–142, the Education for All Handicapped Children Act of 1975 (Martin & Marshall, 1995), promoting shared responsibility and self-determination.

Although research indicates that to date not all students are involved in their transition planning process (deFur, Getzel, & Kregel, 1994; Everson, Zhang, &

Guillory, 2001; Grigal et al., 1997; Williams & O'Leary, 2001; Zhang & Stecker, 2001), numerous examples of empirically validated strategies for increasing student self-determination skills, including involvement in transition planning, are available (Allen, Smith, Test, Flowers, & Wood, 2001; Cross, Cooke, Wood, & Test, 1999; Powers, Turner, Westwood, et al., 2001; Van Reusen & Bos, 1994; Van Reusen, Deshler, & Shumaker, 1989) and must be strategically shared.

Recently, Test and colleagues (2004) reviewed the literature to identify strategies for promoting student involvement in the IEP process. Results indicated that students with widely varying disabilities can be actively involved in their IEP process. In addition, these researchers' results indicated that both published curricula designed to teach students skills to enhance their IEP participation and person-centered planning strategies were effective in increasing students' involvement in the IEP meeting. In other words, students can be taught to take charge of their future. Chapter 4 provides more information on this topic.

Student Development.   Determining, evaluating, and supporting individual achievement in the academic, life, employability, and occupational skills needed for successful transitions provides the foundation for the **student development** category of the Taxonomy for Transition Programming. Student development activities help students acquire and apply self-determination skills as well as academic, living, social, and occupational skills; career awareness; and work-related behaviors in both school-based and work-based settings as set forth by the School to Work Opportunities Act of 1994.

Student development includes teaching students a variety of skills including daily living skills, functional academics, independent living and personal living skills, and self-determination and self-advocacy skills. These skills can be taught using locally developed functional curricula or by using commercially available materials such as *Life Centered Career Education* (Brolin, 1997). Chapters 7 through 10 provide more information on how to teach these critical skills.

Next, students need to develop employment skills. Employment skills can be taught using a variety of strategies including school- and community-based work experiences (paid or nonpaid) and through vocational education coursework. Training can be conducted by teachers, occupational therapists, physical therapists, peers, job coaches, and/or mentors in community businesses. Chapters 7 and 8 provide more detail on strategies for teaching employment skills.

Assessment plays a key role in determining what skills need to be taught as well as what skills students have learned. While traditional vocational assessments have not proved to be consistently useful for these purposes, Chapter 3 provides readers with information about student-friendly vocational assessment strategies.

Family Involvement.   Strategies in this category are designed to encourage parents and families to become involved in planning and delivering transition services for their sons and daughters. Family-focused training and empowerment activities should be developed to help family members collaborate effectively with educators and other service providers. For this to be accomplished, educators must learn to communicate effectively with families to create a supportive environment for their participation in transition planning, since their involvement in the transition process is mandated by IDEA (P.L. 105-17; Section 300.345), is desired by students (Morningstar, Turnbull, & Turnbull, 1995), and has been shown to be key to successful postschool transition (Greene, 1996; McNair & Rusch, 1991; Sample, 1998).

Families should be encouraged to participate in the range of transition activities from assessment and planning to implementation and evaluation. For many parents this will require training (by educators or other parents) in such issues as parents' transition-related roles (Wehman, 1996), their participation in the IEP process (Miner & Bates, 1997), the variety of adult services and supports available in their community, and strategies families can use to promote student self-determination (Abery, 1994; Curtis & Dezelsky, 1986; Field, Martin, Miller, Ward, & Wehmeyer, 1998).

At the same time, educators must be taught not to impose their own values and cultural biases on families by learning strategies for understanding and working with culturally and linguistically diverse families (e.g., Gersten, Baker, & Marks, 1999; Greenan, Powers, & Lopez-Vasquez, 2001; Harry, Kalyanpur, & Day, 1999; Kalyanpur & Harry, 1999; Lynch & Hanson, 1998).

Finally, transition personnel should be trained in strategies to help empower families (deFur, Todd-Allen, & Getzel, 2001). Chapter 4 provides strategies for increasing family involvement in the transition process.

Interagency Collaboration. **Interagency collaboration** refers to key people, businesses, and agencies joining together in their efforts to promote students' pursuit of successful outcomes during the transition process. Educators can learn to foster collaborative service delivery by using interagency agreements that clearly articulate roles, responsibilities, communication strategies, and other cooperative actions that enhance curriculum and program development and service delivery.

Another major vehicle for collaborating with potential partners is the planning meeting. Therefore, transition personnel must know about the IDEA requirements for agency notification and participation (Section 300.344) and agency responsibilities (Section 300.348), as well as specific information on various adult service agencies, including their eligibility requirements and the types of services offered. This means that transition personnel will need to have knowledge and skills related to (a) the multiple levels of transition planning teams, (b) possible membership and responsibilities of interagency teams, and (c) how to successfully implement collaborative service delivery.

Empirically-supported interagency collaboration processes, such as the TASSEL transition model (Aspel, Bettis, Quinn, Test, & Wood, 1999) exemplify the multilevel approach by advocating community-level, school-level, and individual-level teams as well as specific processes for facilitating team accomplishments. Chapter 5 provides more detail on this important area.

Parent's Timeline for Transition from School to Life

Student Age	Action Needed
11–14	◆ Make sure your child's IEP (individualized education program) includes social skills, communication, and self-help skills with at least functional math and functional reading within inclusive settings (if appropriate).
By 14	◆ Begin transition planning as part of the IEP process (focus on student's course of study).
	◆ Learn about exit options to ensure that your child will be able to reach his or her goals (e.g., going to college or entering military service).
No later than 16	◆ Continue transition planning (focus on interagency responsibility or any needed linkages).
	◆ Identify job interests and abilities.
	◆ Include activities such as career exploration, job sampling, and some job training.
	◆ Begin to identify community services that provide job training and placement.
	◆ Prepare a job placement file with references and skills the student has acquired.
	◆ Begin application to adult service agencies.
	◆ Consider summer employment or participation in volunteer experiences.
16–18*	◆ Contact adult services programs:
	◆ Colleges, vocational or technical schools.
	◆ Social Security Administration.
	◆ Residential or independent living services.
	◆ Recreation/leisure groups.
	◆ Medical services.
17–18*	◆ Begin to consider and research guardianship.
	◆ Continue to review and update the transition plan.
	◆ Have the student take ACT or SAT tests.
	◆ Visit colleges and their disabilities services offices.
	◆ Register with the disability service office of the student's preferred school by the end of the senior year.
18–21*	◆ Continue to review and update the transition plan.
	◆ Establish needed health benefits.
	◆ Develop a long-term financial support plan (e.g., SSI).

*Depending on the extent of their disability, some students may remain in school and continue working on transition goals through age 21 or as defined by state law.

Note. Adapted from *Full Life Ahead: A Workbook and Guide to Adult Life for Students and Families of Students with Disabilities.* Montgomery, AL: Southeast Regional Resource Center, Auburn University–Montgomery.

Program Structures and Attributes.   Program structures are features that relate to efficient and effective delivery of transition-focused education and services, including philosophy, planning, policy, evaluation, and resource development. These structures and attributes represent many of the systems change targets that educators must be equipped and motivated to address in order to implement all the other practices featured in Kohler's (1996) Taxonomy.

Transition personnel must develop knowledge and skills to address systemic problems with coordination among schools, adult services agencies, and employers. In addition, the information generated to evaluate a school system's transition practices has direct implications for continuous program improvement, as well as for ensuring that students are achieving their goals. Chapter 11 provides more detail on how to develop a thorough transition program evaluation plan.

FUTURE ISSUES AND TRENDS

What makes the field of transition from school to adulthood so exciting and at the same time so exasperating, is the fact that requirements and best practices are constantly evolving. This section introduces the reader to a few of the issues and trends that currently impact how transition services are implemented.

Adolescent Milestones

The first issue is the fact that while transition personnel are attempting to provide quality transition services within an ever-shifting educational environment, the students who are receiving these services are undergoing their own internal rite of passage called *adolescence*. For example, between the ages of 13 and 20, students undergo many fundamental changes including the onset of puberty, developing an identity separate from their parents, developing advanced reasoning abilities, and reaching the age of majority (Steinberg, 1999). The adolescent transition carries with it many new rights, privileges, and responsibilities, including the opportunities to drive, marry, and vote. As a result, as transition programs for students with disabilities are developed and refined, we must consider the fact that our students will not always want to do as we say. It is imperative, then, that we promote self-determination skills and abilities for all of our students.

Gender Differences

Unfortunately, research has documented that young women with disabilities experience poorer outcomes when compared to men with disabilities (Baer et al., 2003; Benz et al., 1997; Fulton & Sabornie, 1994; Hasazi, Johnson, Hasazi, Gordon, & Hull, 1989). These outcomes appear to be related to the fact that young women with disabilities often do not have access to the full array of transition services while in high school. For example, numerous studies have documented that young women are less likely to be enrolled in work-study and vocational education programs (Baer et al., 2003; Blackorby & Wagner, 1996; Van Beaver, Kohler, & Chadsey, 2000). While the field is calling for research designed to help promote better transition services and outcomes for young women, school systems and transition personnel need not wait. What is needed is to make sure that all students, including young women with disabilities, have equal access to all the transition services they need to become successful adults.

Self-Determination

The **self-determination movement** is one of the most important initiatives in the fields of special education and rehabilitation today. The right to make one's own decisions about one's life and future is viewed as an inalienable right by American adults without disabilities and yet has only recently been recognized for adults with disabilities. Evidence of this belated recognition is present in key pieces of disability legislation that have been passed or reauthorized since 1990, including the Americans with Disabilities Act of 1990, the Individuals with Disabilities Education Act of 1990 and its 1997 and 2004 amendments, and the Rehabilitation Act Amendments of 1992. These laws have all stressed the right of individuals with disabilities to choose where and with whom they want to live, what jobs they want, and by what means they want to achieve their personal goals.

The U.S. Department of Education has identified self-determination as an important outcome of the educational process for children and adults with disabilities and has committed significant resources promoting this concept by funding initiatives on self-determination (Wehmeyer & Schwartz, 1998a; Wehmeyer & Ward, 1995). The Rehabilitation Services Administration has also committed agency resources to increasing consumer choice by funding seven choice demonstration projects following the passage of the 1992 Rehabilitation Act Amendments. Choice and self-determination are also encouraged for funding within the grants program of the Administration on Developmental Disabilities (ADD).

Self-determination might be viewed as the culmination of the normalization and deinstitutionalization movements that started in the early 1970s. We have been trying to restore the rights of U.S. citizenship to individuals with disabilities since the inception of the deinstitutionalization movement with an ongoing succession of values-driven movements and paradigm shifts (e.g., from developmental to chronologically age-appropriate functional life skills instruction; from institutionalization to community integration and inclusion; from segregated sheltered employment to supported employment in integrated jobs for real pay).

Because of our country's history of having other people (i.e., professionals) make most major life decisions for people with disabilities, actualizing the concept of self-determination now requires that we spend considerable effort to teach children, youths, and adults with disabilities how to be self-determining citizens. At the same time, we must retrain citizens without disabilities to respect and honor the choices and decisions of individuals with disabilities. Therefore, actualizing self-determination for our citizens with disabilities requires a two-way paradigm shift that involves both teaching and encouraging citizens with disabilities to self-determine and teaching citizens without disabilities to honor their choices and decisions.

Many of the changes written into the 1997 IDEA amendments encouraged a focus on promoting self-determination skills. For example, (a) delivering a set of coordinated activities based on student needs, preferences, and interests and (b) the requirement to notify students as to the rights, if any, that will transfer to them upon reaching the age of majority both focus on a need to promote self-determination skills and knowledge for students with disabilities. As a result, the Division on Career Development and Transition published a position statement supporting self-determination for persons with disabilities (Field et al., 1998). This position statement emphasized the importance of self-determination to career development and transition for all students. In addition, it suggested "exemplary educational activities that encourage student self-determination" (p. 119) including student involvement in assessment and IEP transition planning and implementation.

The concept of self-determination was defined by consensus by Field and colleagues (1998) as

> a combination of skills, knowledge, and beliefs that enable a person to engage in goal-directed, self-regulated, autonomous behavior. An understanding of one's strengths and limitations together with a belief in oneself as capable and effective are essential to self-determination. When acting on the basis of these skills and attitudes, individuals have greater ability to take control of their lives and assume the role of successful adults. (p. 2)

To aid teachers in promoting self-determination in their classrooms, the concept of self-determination has been divided into a number of teachable components. The components most commonly identified in the literature (e.g., Field & Hoffman, 1994; Mithaug, Campeau, & Wolman, 1992; Ward, 1988; Wehmeyer, 1996) are choice/decision making, goal setting/attainment, problem solving, self-evaluation/management, self-advocacy, person-centered IEP planning, relationships with others, and self-awareness.

Further support for the importance of promoting self-determination for students with disabilities can be seen in the results of several studies that have found a positive relationship between people with higher levels of self-determination and a better quality of life (Wehmeyer & Palmer, 2003; Wehmeyer & Schwartz, 1997; Wehmeyer & Schwartz, 1998b).

In another study, Algozzine, Browder, Karvonen, Test, and Wood (2001) reviewed the literature to investigate what self-determination interventions have been studied, what groups of individuals with disabilities have been taught self-determination, and what levels of outcomes have been achieved using self-determination interventions. While Algozzine and his colleagues located more than 450 articles on self-determination, only 51 were actually studies designed to evaluate the effects of an intervention or teaching strategy specifically designed to promote a self-determination skill. Based on their findings, they concluded that:

1.   The components of self-determination that were most often taught were self-advocacy and choice making. In terms of teaching self-advocacy skills to students with disabilities, Algozzine and colleagues found that self-advocacy skills were typically taught to students with learning disabilities and that choice-making skills were taught to students with mental retardation. In fact, most research on self-determination has been conducted with students with either learning disabilities or mental retardation. Only a few studies were found that included students with sensory impairments, behavioral and emotional disabilities, or traumatic brain injury. Finally, the least studied components of self-determination were self-advocacy and self-efficiency.

2.   Self-determination skills have been taught using a variety of instructional methods including large-group instruction, individual conferences, and one-to-one instruction with systematic prompting and feedback. While most interventions have directly taught self-determination skills, self-determination has also been enhanced through the use of preference assessments to promote choice making and person-centered planning to promote goal setting. In addition, while more than 60 self-determination curricula were identified, only 12 studies have been conducted to evaluate the effects of these materials empirically. Although many of the 12 studies were researcher implemented, some presented results from teacher or direct service staff field tests.

In conclusion, it appears that self-determination is an important and teachable skill. Since the concept of self-determination is not new, why do we include it as a future issue? Unfortunately, while recent research has indicated that special education teachers view self-determination skills as important (Agran, Snow, & Swaner, 1999; Mason, Field, & Sawilowsky, 2004), teachers do not write self-determination skills into student IEPs (Wehmeyer, Agran, & Hughes, 2000; Wehmeyer & Schwartz, 1998a). As a result, the need still exists for transition methods to incorporate strategies that promote self-determination for all students. Finally, because transition and self-determination are so interwoven, we offer Figure 2.2, Transition and Self-Determination Pitfalls to Avoid, as a reminder that while the focus is on each student's desired postschool outcomes, the process is still full of difficult issues that must be overcome through collaboration and teamwork.

High-Stakes Assessment

With the current push for student accountability expressed in the 1997 IDEA amendments and the 2002 No Child Left Behind Act, many students find themselves in general education classes that stress academics and meeting performance standards (Blalock et al., 2003). While this does not necessarily mean that students will not have access to needed transition services, it does complicate the situation. As Johnson, Stodden, Emanuel, Luecking, and Mack (2002) pointed out, the challenge now is to ensure that students with disabilities have access to the full range of general education curricular options while at the same time ensuring access to full participation in postsecondary education, employment, and independent living opportunities.

This balance can be achieved if the content-based standards and increased expectations for skill learning are both embedded in the transition process. Kohler (1996) has argued that this is possible if education will adopt a "transition perspective." For example, the post-high school (or future) outcomes focus of the IEP transition planning process requires students to select a course of study appropriate to their educational goals. Thus, all coursework taken by a student would be determined appropriate only if it moved the student closer to his or her desired postschool outcomes.

Next, high-stakes assessments can be infused into the transition process if they are used to obtain a snapshot of how students are doing relative to accessing content standards and other educational opportunities (Blalock et al., 2003). These assessments can be accomplished by use of alternative measures. As part of the IEP transition planning process, students, teachers, and families can advocate for the types of accommodations that will promote the use of alternative assessments designed to measure mastery of skills in real-life environments.

Finally, teachers can look for state standards that overlap career and academic skills. For example, Williams (2002) identified 17 states that have already developed performance standards for all students in the areas of career readiness, career preparation, and workplace competencies. Still other states (e.g., New Jersey, Massachusetts) have incorporated workplace competencies into their academic standards.

Diploma Options

Another current issue involves the lack of consistent graduation requirements (e.g., credits, exams) and exit options (e.g., standard diploma, IEP diploma, graduation certificate) across states and sometimes within states. Pankaskie and Webb (1999) found that the number of states requiring an exit exam for graduation increased from 15 in 1984 to 17 in 1996 and to 22 in 1998. At the same time, the average number of Carnegie Units required for graduation has increased by 2.5 points since 1996. To compound this issue, Guy, Shin, Lee, and Thurlow (2000) found that at least one third of the states were considering making changes to their current systems. The confusion surrounding exit criteria and documents raises a major concern that students can become frustrated by repeated failure on state graduation tests and their related requirements and simply drop out of school to avoid the confusion (Johnson et al., 2002).

Approximately 80% of the states provide an alternative exit document, usually a certificate or alternative diploma that verifies the student's attendance in school but does not document the student's level of skill attainment or require the completion of a specified course of study. The real worth of these exit documents is questionable when it comes to future education and career opportunities.

Only a little more than 10% of the states allow students with disabilities to obtain a standard high school diploma by demonstrating the completion of IEP goals and objectives or an alternative course of study. Without the options of

Pitfall One: Defining Successful Transition as a Specific Set of Outcomes

As professionals we must not define someone else's life goals for them. For example, equating a successful transition program with specific outcomes such as living independently or finding a full-time job is contradictory to self-determination because it takes away the person's freedom of choice. Honoring self-determination means respecting individuals' choices about how to spend their lives (Wehmeyer, 1998). For example, some people choose not to work outside the home, but to contribute to the family unit in other ways (e.g., homemaking, childrearing) or to pursue a self-directed vocation (e.g., art, music). Other individuals choose not to move out of their parents' home upon reaching adulthood. In some cultures, multigenerational families living in the same household are both typical and valued. When planning for specific transition outcomes with adolescents, educators need to remember that promoting self-determination means respecting student choice, not achieving outcomes valued by someone else.

Pitfall Two: Not Considering Cultural Diversity

If multicultural values are not considered, teachers may not realize that they are imposing their own cultural values on students. Successful transition and self-determination outcomes can easily be confused with the individualism that has traditionally been valued by Anglo-American culture. In collectivist cultures (e.g., Asian, Native American, Latino), a sense of self is understood in relationship with others, whereas in individualistic cultures the focus is more on an independent sense of self. Gudykunst and colleagues (1989) questioned goals that encourage individuals to assume an individualistic focus. For example, in Asian cultures, young adults' decisions about their future are often focused on how to bring honor to their families versus focusing on what is best for themselves. *The Road to Personal Freedom* (Ludi & Martin, 1995), a self-determination curriculum developed to incorporate Native American values, has a unit entitled "How Interdependence Is Consistent with Being Self-Determined." Turnbull and Turnbull (1996) described an example of cultural diversity in encouraging self-determination based on their work with Latino American families. They discovered that young adults, with and without disabilities, typically live with families for an extended period of time. For young adults, even when married, moving out is considered a breakdown in family ties.

While it is important to consider cultural differences, it would be equally insensitive to assume that an individual's goals can be ascertained simply by knowing his or her culture. For example, it would be inappropriate to assume that all young adults who are Latino want to live with their families. By listening carefully and honoring the students' and families' values, educators can respect diverse viewpoints about what constitutes desirable outcomes.

Pitfall Three: Not Collaborating with Families

In their qualitative study, Morningstar, Turnbull, and Turnbull (1995) found that most adolescents with disabilities want their families involved in making transition

Figure 2.2
Transition and Self-Determination Pitfalls to Avoid

decisions. Families often are the most important resource in the lives of students with and without disabilities. It would be unfortunate if the concept of self-determination were misunderstood to mean that adolescents do not need parental guidance and nurture.

Encouraging transition and self-determination should not involve "siding with students" to help free them of parental influence. Teachers need to respect the parents' authority in the life of their child. Good parenting sometimes requires overruling minor children's decisions that are unsafe or unwise. In contrast, when students turn 18 they have the legal right to make decisions for themselves and are held legally accountable for them unless the courts remove this right through guardianship assignment. In preparation for this adult role, teachers and parents need to work together to help students learn to make wise decisions.

To collaborate with parents, teachers can make IEP planning activities both family and student centered. Miner and Bates (1997) found that having a person-centered planning meeting in preparation for the IEP meeting encouraged family involvement in the planning process. Sometimes parents of adolescents need help understanding how to transfer control of decision making to their children as they mature. Some self-determination curricula and related materials include resources for parent involvement (Abery, 1994; Curtis & Dezelsky, 1986; Field et al., 1998; Matuszewski, 1998). Teachers might also consider providing parents with an inservice session or other resources on promoting self-determination. For example, The Arc publishes a pamphlet that suggests 10 steps parents can follow to encourage their children's self-determination at home (Davis & Wehmeyer, 1991).

Pitfall Four: Requiring Prerequisites for Transition and Self-Determination

Another potential pitfall is to assume that there are prerequisite skills that need to be mastered for a person to be self-determined. Assuming that self-determination applies only to individuals who will achieve independent living as adults is a misinterpretation of the concept (Wehmeyer, 1998). All individuals have the right to be self-determined. While high-quality skill instruction can help students exercise this right to the fullest extent possible, the lack of prerequisite skills does not negate a person's right to be self-determining. For example, students with severe disabilities can take charge of their lives through making their preferences known even when they rely on others for assistance. Sometimes teachers will need to use systematic methods to understand the preferences of individuals who do not have symbolic communication (Lohrmann-O'Rourke & Browder, 1998). Once these preferences are recognized, they can be honored in planning for transition support needs.

Pitfall Five: Ignoring the Social Environment in Encouraging Transition and Self-Determination

Learning skills related to transition and self-determination is important, but it is meaningless if the students' environments do not allow the use of these skills (Abery & Stancliffe, 1996; Field & Hoffman, 1999). An important part of the environment for self-determination is the students' social relationships with others. In contrast, many

(continued)

people are confused about how self-determination and interdependence can co-exist. In a *New York Times* survey, Cherlin (1999) found evidence of this confusion in American society in general. In this survey, "Being able to stand up for yourself" and "Being able to communicate your feelings" were rated as among the most important personal values by more than 75% of respondents. In contrast, only about a third valued "Being involved in the community" and "Having lots of friends." Cherlin noted that not many see that if everyone puts the highest priority on his or her own interests, family and community ties may be weakened. Educators need to be careful not to encourage a shallow form of self-determination that focuses only on what "I want" without consideration of others (i.e., "selfishness"). Students need to develop social skills to have the kind of social relationships they value. Being in a relationship requires responding to the other person's needs and wishes as well as expressing one's own. Students also need opportunities to learn altruism, in which they place someone else's needs and interests above their own preferences. For example, in their self-determination curriculum for students with spina bifida, Denniston and Enlow (1996) encourage participants to discover ways to contribute to their community as a volunteer in a unit called "There Is a Larger Meaning Than Self."

Note. Adapted from "Reviewing resources on self-determination: A map for teachers by D. M. Browder, W. M. Wood, D. W. Test, M. Karvonen, and B. Algozzine, 2001, *Remedial and Special Education, 22,* 233–244. Copyright 2001 by PRO-ED, Inc. Reprinted with permission.

Figure 2.2
Continued

modified coursework and alternate testing policies, students with disabilities may never progress to postsecondary education settings even at the community college level. They may miss career opportunities despite their ability to do certain jobs, simply because they are unable to meet their state's uniform standard for a high school diploma (Guy et al., 2000).

During the transition planning process, students and their families must receive honest and clear advisement regarding curriculum options and exit documents so that they can make informed decisions regarding the choice of a pathway to graduation. High school personnel should be fully informed about the acceptance of alternative exit documents by the military, postsecondary educational institutions and vocational education programs so they can share this information during transition planning to ensure that postschool goals are realistic.

Programs for Students Ages 18 to 21

Given the need for students with disabilities to master both academic and transition skills as well as meet the variety of requirements for diplomas and other options, some students with disabilities may need to stay in high school beyond age 18, when the majority of their peers will graduate. However, to counter the stigma of remaining in high school after age 18, some school systems have begun to provide what are being called "18-to-21-year-old programs." These programs are often located away from the high school campus at either community colleges, 4-year colleges and universities, or other community sites (Grigal, Neubert, & Moon, 2002), but they are designed and staffed by public school personnel. The goal of such programs is to provide students aged 18 to 21 with age-appropriate settings in which to receive their final transition services. Specific goals and services are typically designed through a person-centered planning strategy. Grigal and colleagues suggested that students' goals can focus on obtaining full-time or part-time employment, participating in college classes, increasing community mobility, accessing the support of adult services, improving social and communication skills, promoting self-determination skills, developing friendships, and learning leisure and recreation skills.

Placing these programs on college campuses or in the community provides students with disabilities ready access to classes, resources, and supports that are available to other young adults. For example, students receiving "18 to 21" services at a community college might be able to take or audit classes and use the cafeteria, fitness center, computer lab, and library just like other students their age.

STRATEGIES FOR ADDRESSING COMMON CHALLENGES

How Do I Develop an Off-Campus Program for 18- to 21-Year-Olds?

Grigal (2002) developed a fact sheet designed to provide a step-by-step procedure for school personnel interested in developing off-campus programs for 18- to 21-year-old students with disabilities. What follows is a summary of the information provided in the fact sheet. For more detail visit: http://www.education.umd .edu/oco/resources/factsheet.html.

Step 1: Visit other programs. By visiting and talking to personnel who are already providing these services you can get ideas for resources, curriculum, and strategies that have already worked. Visiting existing programs will also help you get a feel for the logistics and see what you like and do not like. If you are planning to provide services at a community or 4-year college, invite a representative to accompany you so that person, too, can see first hand how the pieces fit.

Step 2: Identify a population of students. Identify the age, employment experience, and instructional support needed for students to be successful in your program.

Step 3: Identify planning partners. Partners should include high-level administrators at both the high school and community location who have the authority to make financial and personnel decisions. In addition, consider including local adult service providers, department of vocational rehabilitation and developmental disabilities personnel, parents, and employers. Be sure to create a process for ensuring ongoing communication among all partners.

Step 4: Identify possible funding needs and resources. Funding needs will vary based on program goals and students served. Local school systems typically fund personnel, transportation, office, and instruction space. Other necessary equipment will include computers; desks; filing cabinets; telephones or cell phones; and access to fax machines, e-mail and photocopiers. Be sure to get written agreements from all parties as to who will be paying for what.

Step 5: Identify access issues. If you want to access college resources you will have to find out how. Do students need to apply to the college? Is there an activity fee? Can students take courses for credit or must they audit? Can students receiving supplemental security income (SSI) have their tuition waived? Which instructors are more responsive to having students with disabilities in their class? These are all questions to consider when determining how to access resources.

Step 6: Deal with school system logistics. Make sure you plan for success by considering transportation requirements, free and reduced-price lunch availability, how medication is dispensed, liability insurance, access to mail and e-mail, attendance policies, student participation in the high school graduation ceremony, and differences between the high school's calendar and the college's calendar.

Step 7: Establish a referral process. Clearly communicate the process in writing to all people who might make referrals. Ideally the process should begin 1 year in advance so that students, families, and teachers have an opportunity to make an informed choice about the appropriateness of services. Remember, this may not be the right service for all students.

Step 8: Create a daily schedule of activities. Most programs combine classroom and community-based instruction in functional and life skills, paid and unpaid work experiences, participation in college courses, use of campus facilities, and participation in campus and/or community clubs. Posting individual weekly schedules will help encourage student independence.

Step 9: Don't get discouraged; relationships take time. Since "18 to 21" programs are not typical, it will take time for all parties to understand how the program works and why it is necessary. Focus on developing relationships with key individuals, and remember to communicate regularly.

Step 10: Be an asset and learn to barter. Find out how your students, you, and your staff can help others at your site. If you give a little, you may get much in return.

Step 11: Create opportunities for peers to become involved. Can college students work with your program for field experience credit? Talk to instructors in education; social work; physical education; and occupational, speech, and physical therapies to learn whether their students could benefit from working with your students. Also, see if your campus has a Best Buddies or other peer-related program.

Step 12: Think outside the box. If there is no college available, consider contacting local adult service agencies, employers, libraries, and shopping malls. If space at the local college is the only limitation, consider locating your program someplace else but get an agreement with the college to access its resources.

Step 13: Evaluate your program from day one. Collect data on goals achieved, program costs, customer satisfaction (including students, families, businesses, college personnel, adult services personnel, and others), and outcomes of students who have graduated from your program. All may be necessary to justify continuation or expansion funding.

CASE STUDY

MARY

Beginning the Planning Process

Mary was adopted at the age of 5 and lives at home with her parents, three brothers, and a sister. During her school career, she was labeled as both educable mentally disabled and trainable mentally disabled. She enjoyed talking on the telephone to friends and collecting "Gone with the Wind" memorabilia and teddy bears. At the end of eighth grade, Mary and her parents were invited to a panel presentation on high school options. Later that year she began meeting with her individual-level team.

Conducting the Individual-Level Team Meeting

Mary's initial transition planning process began with student dream sheets and mapping forms completed by both Mary and her mother. Through her dream sheet Mary stated that she wanted to live with her family or in very near proximity. She said that she would like to obtain a job in child care, cafeteria services, or custodial services. She also dreamed of obtaining a driver's license. She had plans to continue special trade classes after graduation and dancing for recreation. Based on Mary's input, the individual-level team prepared an IEP with a transition component. Mary's class schedule consisted of employment English, job skills math, life skills science, career preparation, physical education, music, and vocational education.

Planning the School-Level Team Meeting

A transition assessment, checklist, and informational form were prepared to assist Mary with conducting her school-level team meeting. Mary prepared for the meeting through self-advocacy classes and role playing.

Conducting the School-Level Team Meeting

At the first meeting, Mary spoke for herself and expressed her desires and concerns for her future. Mary stated that her major postgraduate goals were becoming competitively employed, living at home, attending special trade classes at the community college, and continuing a recreation activity in the community. The school-level team members then helped Mary develop a set of activities to assist her in reaching her goals. At later meetings, Mary stated that she had participated in an on-campus job in the school-based enterprise and job shadowing. She had received good evaluations and stressed that she wanted to get a part-time job. As a result, the individual-level team revised her IEP.

When Mary became eligible for vocational rehabilitation services, the counselor and transition teacher began assisting her with job searches. She was employed part time as a housekeeper for a nursing center in the summer prior to her senior year. She received job coach services through vocational rehabilitation. After 200 hours, the job coach services faded and follow-along services began. After the 60-day evaluation was completed, Mary's employment was increased to full time.

Other individual- and school-level team meetings were held as issues arose that needed to be addressed. As an outcome of the school-level meetings, Mary's vocational rehabilitation counselor was invited to her individual transition team meetings. Finally, as Mary neared graduation, plans were developed for her exit meeting.

The Exit Meeting

Mary conducted her own exit meeting with the school-level team members to discuss her present and future plans. Mary talked about her plans to continue to live at home with her parents and attend community college, enrolling in classes in child care and food service. She also talked about the possibility of getting a driver's license. She stated that she wanted to continue to participate in dance lessons and collect "Gone with the Wind" memorabilia and teddy bears. She stated that her major goal was to continue saving money until she could purchase a place to live independently. Her plans were to put a mobile home near her parents so she would have assistance when needed.

The vocational rehabilitation counselor provided information on paying for special trade classes at the community college as long as Mary was able to maintain a C average. Since Mary had been successful, the vocational rehabilitation counselor had planned to close her case; however, he decided to keep her case open to provide assistance with the postsecondary education process. The transition teacher stated that she would follow up for 3 years. Mary will also continue to receive continuous follow-along on her job through a community rehabilitation agency. She credits the transition services provided by her school for helping her to achieve her goals to prepare for adulthood and, more important, to become a productive member of society.

One Year Later

Mary continues to work full time at the nursing center. However, she is enrolled in child care classes at the local community college and is beginning to look for jobs at day care centers. Mary and her family have calculated that if she continues to save at the same rate she has been, they will be able purchase a trailer for her to live in within the next 5 years. Mary's hobbies have led her to join her church's women's circle, and she now attends weekly meetings.

STUDY GUIDE QUESTIONS

1. Name five best practices in transition based on the literature.
2. Briefly describe the *Taxonomy for Transition Programming* (Kohler, 1996) including:
   a. student-focused planning
   b. student development
   c. family involvement
   d. interagency collaboration
   e. program structures
3. Name and describe three future issues or trends in transition.
4. What changes in IDEA 1997 encouraged self-determination?
5. How is self-determination defined? What are its components?
6. Develop a plan for starting a program for students ages 18 to 21.
7. What is the relationship between transition and self-determination?

REFERENCES

Abery, B. (1994). A conceptual framework for enhancing self-determination. In M. F. Hayden & B. H. Abery (Eds.), *Challenges for a service system in transition* (pp. 345–380). Baltimore: Brookes.

Abery, B., & Stancliffe, R. (1996). The ecology of self-determination. In D. J. Sands, & M. Wehmeyer (Eds.), *Self-determination across the life-span: Independence and choice for people with disabilities* (pp.111–145). Baltimore: Brookes.

Agran, M., Snow, K., & Swaner, J. (1999). Teacher perceptions of self-determination: Benefits, characteristics, and strategies. *Education and Training in Mental Retardation and Developmental Disabilities, 34,* 293–301.

Algozzine, B., Browder, D., Karvonen, M., Test, D. W., & Wood, W. M. (2001). Effects of interventions to promote self-determination for individuals with disabilities. *Review of Educational Research, 71,* 219–277.

Allen, S. K., Smith, A. C., Test, D. W., Flowers, C., & Wood, W. M. (2001). The effects of Self-Directed IEP on student participation in IEP meetings. *Career Development for Exceptional Individuals, 24,* 107–120.

Aspel, N., Bettis, G., Quinn, P., Test, D. W., & Wood, W. M. (1999). A collaborative process for planning transitional services for all students with disabilities. *Career Development for Exceptional Individuals, 22,* 21–42.

Baer, R. M., Flexer, R. W., Beck, S., Amstutz, N., Hoffman, L., Brothers, J., et al. (2003). A collaborative followup study on transition service utilization and post-school outcomes. *Career Development for Exceptional Individuals, 26,* 7–25.

Benz, M. R., Yovanoff, P., & Doren, B. (1997). School-to-work components that predict post-school success for students with and without disabilities. *Exceptional Children, 63,* 151–165.

Blackorby, J., & Wagner, M. (1996). Longitudinal post-school outcomes of youth with disabilities: Findings from the National Longitudinal Transition Study. *Exceptional Children, 62,* 399–413.

Blalock, G., Kochhar-Bryant, C., Test, D. W., Kohler, P., White, W., Lehmann, J., et al. (2003). The need for comprehensive personnel preparation in transition and career development: DCDT position statement. *Career Development for Exceptional Individuals, 26,* 207–226.

Brolin, D. (1997). *Life-centered career education: A competency-based approach* (5th ed.). Arlington, VA: Council for Exceptional Children.

Cherlin, A. J. (1999, October 17). I'm O.K., you're selfish. *New York Times Magazine,* pp. 44–65.

Cross, T., Cooke, N. L., Wood, W. M., & Test, D. W. (1999). Comparison of the effects of MAPS and ChoiceMaker on student self-determination skills. *Education and Training in Mental Retardation and Developmental Disabilities, 34,* 499–510.

Curtis, E., & Dezelsky, M. (1986). *New hats for letting go.* Salt Lake City, UT: New Hats.

Davis, S., & Wehmeyer, M. L. (1991). *Ten steps to independence: Promoting self-determination in the home.* Arlington, TX: The Arc of the United States.

deFur, S., Getzel, E. E., & Kregel, J. (1994). Individual transition plans: A work in progress. *Journal of Vocational Rehabilitation, 4,* 139–145.

deFur, S. H., Todd-Allen, M., & Getzel, E. E. (2001). Parent participation in the transition planning process. *Career Development for Exceptional Individuals, 24,* 19–36.

Denniston, S., & Enlow, C. (1996). *Making choices: A journal/workbook for teens with spina bifida that provides opportunities for making choices about their lives.* Louisville, KY: Spina Bifida Association.

DeStefano, L., Heck, D., Hasazi, S., & Furney, K. (1999). Enhancing the implementation of the transition requirements of IDEA: A report on the Policy Forum on Transition. *Career Development for Exceptional Individuals, 22,* 85–100.

Everson, J. M., Zhang, D., & Guillory, J. D. (2001). A statewide investigation of individualized transition plans in Louisiana. *Career Development for Exceptional Individuals, 24,* 37–49.

Field, S., & Hoffman, A. (1999). The importance of family involvement for promoting self-determination in adolescents with autism and other developmental disabilities. *Focus on Autism and Other Developmental Disabilities, 14*(1), 36–41.

Field, S., Martin, J., Miller, R., Ward, M., & Wehmeyer, M. (1998). Self-determination for persons with disabilities: A position statement of the Division on Career Development and Transition. *Career Development for Exceptional Individuals, 21,* 113–128.

Fulton, S. A., & Sabornie, E. J. (1994). Evidence of employment inequality among females with disabilities. *The Journal of Special Education, 28,* 149–165.

Furney, K. S., Hasazi, S. B., & DeStefano, L. (1997). Transition policies, practices, and promises: Lessons from three states. *Exceptional Children, 63,* 343–355.

Gersten, R., Baker, S. K., & Marks, S. U. (1999). *Teaching English-language learners with learning difficulties: Guiding principles and examples from research-based practice.* Arlington, VA: Council for Exceptional Children.

Greenan, S., Powers, L. E., & Lopez-Vasquez, A. (2001). Multicultural aspects of parent involvement in transition planning. *Exceptional Children, 67,* 265–282.

Greene, G. (1996). Empowering culturally and linguistically diverse families in the transition planning process. *The Journal for Vocational Special Needs Education, 19*(1), 26–30.

Grigal, M. (2002). *OCO fact sheet: How to start a program for students with significant disabilities in a postsecondary setting.* Retrieved March 11, 2003, from University of Maryland, On-Campus Outreach Web site: http://www .education.umd.edu/oco/ resources/factsheet .html

Grigal, M., Neubert, D. A., & Moon, M. S. (2002). Postsecondary options for students with significant disabilities. *Teaching Exceptional Children, 35*(2), 68–73.

Grigal, M., Test, D. W., Beattie, J., & Wood, W. M. (1997). An evaluation of transition components of individualized education programs. *Exceptional Children, 63,* 357–372.

Gudykunst, W. B., Nishida, T., Leung, K, Gao, G., Bond, M. H., Wang, G., et al. (1989). A cross-cultural comparison of self-monitoring. *Communication Research Reports, 6,* 7–12.

Guy, B., Shin, H., Lee, S., & Thurlow, M. (2000). State graduation requirements for students with and without disabilities. In D. R. Johnson & E. J. Emanuel (Eds.), *Issues influencing the future of transition programs and services in the United States* (pp. 85–110). Minneapolis: University of Minnesota, National Transition Network.

Halpern, A., Yovanoff, P., Doren, B., & Benz, M. R. (1995). Predicting participation in post-secondary education for school leavers with disabilities. *Exceptional Children, 62,* 151–164.

Harry, B., Kalyanpur, M., & Day, M. (1999). *Building cultural reciprocity with families: Case studies in special education.* Baltimore: Brookes.

Hasazi, S. B., Furney, K. S., & DeStefano, L. (1999). Implementing the IDEA transition mandates. *Exceptional Children, 65,* 555–566.

Hasazi, S., Gordon, L., & Roe, C. (1985). Factors associated with the employment status of handicapped youth exiting high school from 1979–1983. *Exceptional Children, 51,* 455–469.

Hasazi, S. B., Johnson, R. E., Hasazi, J. E., Gordon, L. R., & Hull, M. (1989). Employment of youth with and without handicaps following high school: Outcomes and correlates. *The Journal of Special Education, 23*, 243–255.

Hughes, C., Eisenman, L. T., Hwang, B., Kim, J. H., Killian, D. J., & Scott, S. V. (1997). Transition from secondary special education to adult life: A review and analysis of empirical measures. *Education and Training in Mental Retardation and Developmental Disabilities, 32*, 85–104.

Hughes, C., Hwang, B., Kim, J., Killian, D. J., Harmer, M. L., & Alcantara, P. R. (1997). A preliminary validation on strategies that support the transition from school to adult life. *Career Development for Exceptional Individuals, 20*, 1–14.

Hughes, C., Kim, J., Hwang, B., Killian, D.J., Fischer, G.M., Brock, M.L., et al. (1997). Practitioner-validated secondary transition support strategies. *Education and Training in Mental Retardation and Developmental Disabilities, 32*, 201–212.

Johnson, J. R., & Rusch, F. R. (1993). Secondary special education and transition services: Identification and recommendations for future research and demonstration. *Career Development for Exceptional Individuals, 16*, 1–18.

Johnson, D. R., Stodden, R. A., Emanuel, E. J., Luecking, R., & Mack, M. (2002). Current challenges facing secondary education and transition services: What research tells us. *Exceptional Children, 68*, 519–531.

Kalyanpur, K., & Harry, B. (1999). *Culture in special education: Building reciprocal family–professional relationships.* Baltimore: Brookes.

Karge, B. D., Patton, P. L., & de la Garza, B. (1992). Transition services for youth with mild disabilities: Do they exist, are they needed? *Career Development for Exceptional Individuals, 15*, 47–60.

Kohler, P. (1996). *A taxonomy for transition programming: Linking research and practice.* Champaign: University of Illinois, Transition Research Institute.

Kohler, P. D., DeStefano L., Wermuth, T. R., Grayson, T. E., & McGinty, S. (1994). An analysis of exemplary transition programs: How and why are they selected? *Career Development for Exceptional Individuals, 17*, 187–202.

Kortering, L., & Edgar, E. (1988). Special education and rehabilitation: A need for cooperation. *Rehabilitation Counseling Bulletin, 31*, 178–184.

Lohrmann-O'Rourke, S., & Browder, D. (1998). Empirically based methods to assess preferences of individuals with severe disabilities. *American Journal of Mental Retardation, 103*, 146–161.

Ludi, D. C., & Martin, L. (1995). The road to personal freedom: Self determination. *Intervention in School and Clinic, 30*, 164–169.

Lynch, E. W., & Hanson, M. J. (Eds.). (1998). *Developing cross-cultural competence: A guide for working with young children and their families* (2nd ed.). Baltimore: Brookes.

Martin, J. E., & Marshall, L. H. (1995). Choice-Maker: A comprehensive self-determination transition program. *Intervention in School and Clinic, 30*, 147–156.

Mason, C., Field, S., & Sawilowsky, S. (2004). Implementation of self-determination activities and student participation in IEPs. *Exceptional Children, 70*, 441–451.

Matuszewski, J. (1998). *TAKE CHARGE for the future: A guide for parents.* Portland: Oregon Health Sciences University.

McNair, J., & Rusch, F. (1991). Parent involvement in transition programs. *Mental Retardation, 29*, 93–101.

Miner, C. A., & Bates, P. E. (1997). The effects of person centered planning activities on the IEP/transition planning process. *Education and Training in Mental Retardation and Developmental Disabilities, 32*, 105–112.

Mithaug, D., Campeau, P., & Wolman, J. (1992). *Research on self-determination in individuals with disabilities.* Unpublished manuscript.

Mithaug, P., Horiuchi, C., & Fanning, P. (1985). A report on the Colorado Statewide Follow-Up Survey of Special Education Students. *Exceptional Children, 51*, 397–404.

Morningstar, M., Turnbull, A., & Turnbull, R. (1995). What do students with disabilities tell us about the importance of family involvement in the transition from school to adult life? *Exceptional Children, 62*, 249–260.

Pankaskie, S., & Webb, K. (1999, October). *A comparison of graduation requirements.* Paper presented at the meeting of the Division on Career Development and Transition, Charleston, SC.

Powers, L. E., Turner, A., Westwood, D., Matuszewski, J., Wilson, R., & Phillips, A. (2001). TAKE CHARGE for the future: A controlled field-test of a model to promote student involvement in transition planning. *Career Development for Exceptional Individuals, 24*, 89–104.

Sale, P., Metzler, H., Everson, J. M., & Moon, M. S. (1991). Quality indicators of successful vocational transition programs. *Journal of Vocational Rehabilitation, 1*(4), 47–63.

Sample, P. L. (1998). Postschool outcomes for students with significant emotional disturbance following best-practice transition services. *Behavioral Disorders, 23,* 231–242.

Sitlington, P., & Frank, A. (1990). Are adolescents with learning disabilities successfully crossing the bridge to adult life? *Learning Disabilities Quarterly, 13,* 97–111.

Steinberg, L. (1999). *Adolescence* (5th ed.). Boston: McGraw-Hill.

Test, D. W., Mason, C., Hughes, C., Konrad, M., Neale, M., & Wood, W. M. (2004). Student involvement in individualized education program meetings. *Exceptional Children, 70,* 391–412.

Turnbull, A. P., & Turnbull III, H. R. (1996). Self-determination within a culturally responsive family systems perspective: Balancing the family mobile. In L. E. Powers, G. H. S. Singer, & J. Sowers (Eds.), *On the road to autonomy: Promoting self-competence for children and youth with disabilities* (pp. 195–220). Baltimore: Brookes.

Van Beaver, S. M., Kohler, P. D., & Chadsey, J. G. (2000). Vocational education enrollment patterns of females with disabilities. *Career Development for Exceptional Individuals, 23,* 87–103.

Van Reusen, A. K., & Bos, C. S. (1994). Facilitating student participation in individualized education programs through motivation strategy instruction. *Exceptional Children, 60,* 466–475.

Van Reusen, A. K., Deshler, D. D., & Schumaker, J. B. (1989). Effects of a student participation strategy in facilitating the involvement of adolescents with learning disabilities in the individualized education program planning process. *Learning Disabilities, 1,* 23–34.

Ward, M. J. (1988). The many facets of self-determination. *NICHCY transition summary: National Information Center for Children and Youth with Disabilities, 5,* 2–3.

Wehman, P. (1996). *Life beyond the classroom: Transition strategies for young people with disabilities* (2nd ed.). Baltimore: Brookes.

Wehman, P., Kregel, J., & Seyfarth, J. (1985). Transition from school to work for individuals with severe handicaps: A follow-up study. *Journal of The Association for Persons with Severe Handicaps, 10,* 132–136.

Wehmeyer, M. L. (1996). Self-determination in youth with severe cognitive disabilities: From theory to practice. In L. E. Powers, G. H. S. Singer, & J. Sowers (Eds.), *On the road to autonomy: Promoting self-competence for children and youth with disabilities* (pp. 17–36). Baltimore: Brookes.

Wehmeyer, M. L. (1998). Self-determination and individuals with significant disabilities: Examining meaning and misinterpretations. *Journal of The Association for Persons with Severe Handicaps, 23,* 5–16.

Wehmeyer, M., Agran, M., & Hughes, C. (2000). A national survey of teachers' promotion of self-determination and student-directed learning. *Journal of Special Education, 34*(2), 58–68.

Wehmeyer, M. L., & Palmer, S. B. (2003). Adult outcomes for students with cognitive disabilities three years after high school: The impact of self-determination. *Education and Training in Developmental Disabilities, 38,* 131–144.

Wehmeyer, M. L., & Schwartz, M. (1997). Self-determination and positive adult outcomes: A follow up study of youth with mental retardation or learning disabilities. *Exceptional Children, 63,* 245–255.

Wehmeyer, M. L., & Schwartz, M. (1998a). The self-determination focus on transition goals for students with mental retardation. *Career Development for Exceptional Individuals, 21,* 75–86.

Wehmeyer, M. L., & Schwartz, M. (1998b). The relationship between self-determination and quality of life for adults with mental retardation. *Education and Training in Mental Retardation and Developmental Disabilities, 33,* 3–12.

Wehmeyer, M. L., & Ward, M. (1995). The spirit of the IDEA mandate: Student involvement in transition planning. *Journal of Vocational Special Needs Education, 17*(3), 108–111.

Will, M. (1984, March/April). Bridges from school to working life. *Programs for the Handicapped.* Washington, DC: Clearinghouse on the Handicapped.

Williams, J. (2002). Using school-to-career strategies, workplace competencies, and industry skill standards to enhance the transition process in standards-based education. In C. A. Kochhar-Bryant & D. S. Bassett (Eds.), *Aligning transition and standards-based education: Issues and strategies.* Arlington, VA: Council for Exceptional Children.

Williams, J. M., & O'Leary, E. (2001). What we've learned and where we go from here. *Career Development for Exceptional Individuals, 24,* 51–71.

Zhang, D., & Stecker, P. M. (2001). Student involvement in transition planning: Are we there yet? *Education and Training in Mental Retardation and Developmental Disabilities, 36,* 293–303.

Assessing for Transition

Chapter 3

Introduction

Given the link between self-determination and improved postschool outcomes, it is imperative that transition assessment be student centered. Student-centered transition assessment could be considered the foundation for all transition planning and instruction. As you will discover in this chapter, transition assessment is reflected in four parts of the Taxonomy for Transition Programming *(Kohler, 1996). First, Student-Focused Planning cannot take place without assessing students' strengths, needs, interests, and preferences. Second, assessment is key to the instructional planning and decision making that must take place in the area of Student Development. Finally, valuable information must be gathered from others to help in the planning and instructional process, so the areas of Interagency Collaboration and Family Involvement also include transition assessment.*

This chapter introduces educators to the concept of transition assessment, the purpose of assessment, what should be assessed, methods for assessing, and who is involved in the assessment process. The chapter concludes with a discussion of strategies for addressing common challenges and case studies.

Key Terms

transition assessment
curriculum-based vocational assessment
career assessment
APIE model
vocational assessment
ecological assessment
situational assessment

A Personal Perspective on Community-Based Transition Assessment in Action

Sharon Fish

Transition Specialist, Worthington City Schools

Margo Vreeburg Izzo

Nisonger Center, The Ohio State University

One aspect of transition assessment that helps students make informed choices about their careers is exposing them to multiple school- and community-based work experiences. Kevin, a 20-year-old young adult who recently graduated from high school, is an excellent example of how this process can work.

In high school Kevin participated in a 5-year continuum of transition courses and services, including in-school work experiences, community-based exploration, situational assessments, supervised summer jobs, vocational education, and on-the-job training. His classroom coursework included curricula that focused on career exploration, self-advocacy, following directions, problem solving, getting along with peers, and communication skills.

The process began in 8th grade when he took an internship that helped him practice employability skills by working in a school business, the Bagel Shop, and earning his first paycheck. In this experience he practiced serving and preparing bagels, taking orders, ringing up orders on the cash register, maintaining inventory, customer service, getting along with coworkers, taking directions from a supervisor, and cleaning. In addition to practicing employability skills, Kevin learned math skills by managing a bank account. His parents collaborated with the school in performing banking activities with him at a local bank on paydays. During this experience, Kevin was assessed on each of the skills he was taught, and he used these experiences to consider various possible jobs.

During 9th and 10th grades, his career exploration opportunities moved to the community, and during his 11th and 12th years of school, Kevin received specific vocational training in his areas of choice. Throughout the process, his guidance counselors and teachers continued to work with him on career planning.

During his high school program, Kevin participated in the school Bagel Shop, enclaves at both grocery and retail stores, and a hotel job. During the summer, he participated in a Parks and Recreation Department vocational camp, worked at a restaurant and day care center, and worked in a summer community-based hospital program—with support from his mother—and a local mental retardation/developmental disabilities agency.

Due to the experiences Kevin received from the school and family and agency supports, today he is successfully employed as a dietary aide at an assisted-living center. Kevin works approximately 30 hours per week and lives by himself in a one-bedroom apartment. He has chosen to move twice since moving from his mother's home in 2002 because he wanted an apartment complex with more amenities. To do this, Kevin hired a private provider to provide 30 hours per week of support to assist him with budgeting, paying bills, and maintaining his apartment. Everyone involved with Kevin attributes his current success to the many school- and community-based work experiences and assessments he had while in high school.

DEFINING TRANSITION ASSESSMENT

Surprisingly, the term **transition assessment** was not included in the Individuals with Disabilities Education Act's description of transition services until the 2004 reauthorization, the Individuals with Disabilities Education Improvement Act (IDEA 2004). However, IDEA 2004 now states that transition assessments are needed to develop a coordinated set of activities within a results-oriented process based on student needs and taking into account student strengths, preferences, and interests and that a student's IEP must include "appropriate measurable postsecondary goals based upon age-appropriate transition assessments related to training, education, employment, and where appropriate, independent living skills" (P.L. 108-446, Section 614). IDEA 2004 also states that the coordinated set of activities includes instruction, related services, community experiences, the development of employment and other postschool objectives, and, when appropriate, acquisition of daily living skills and functional vocational evaluation. Since the IDEA 2004 rules and regulations have not yet defined what is meant by transition assessment we will use the Division on Career Development and Transition (DCDT) of the Council for Exceptional Children definition, which defined transition assessment as:

> the ongoing process of collecting data on the individual's needs, preferences, and interests as they relate to the demands of current and future working, educational, living, and personal and social environments. Assessment data serve as the common thread in the transition process and form the basis for defining goals and services to be included in the individualized education program. (Sitlington, Neubert, & Leconte, 1997, pp. 70–71).

DCDT's definition considers transition assessment as an umbrella term that covers **career assessment** (which relates to lifelong career development for all life roles), **vocational assessment** (which relates to work and employment), and ecological or functional assessment (which involves assessing students in the environment where a skill typically occurs). Greene and Kochhar-Bryant (2003) further differentiated transition assessment from traditional assessment, stating that transition assessment is ongoing, future focused, and person centered whereas traditional assessment is typically an annual process, focuses on current strengths and weakness, and is skill centered.

GOALS OF TRANSITION ASSESSMENT

While transition assessment encompasses a wide range of assessment possibilities, it focuses on three interrelated goals or purposes.

Goal 1: Helping Students Make Informed Choices

The first goal of transition assessment is to enable students to make informed choices that will enhance their postschool lives (Sitlington et al., 1997). This means that students must be provided with information and experiences that will assist them in determining their interests, needs, and preferences related to desired postschool outcomes in the areas of employment, postsecondary education, community housing, and community participation.

Goal 2: Helping Students Take Charge of the Process

The second goal of transition assessment is to have students assume the responsibility of coordinating their own assessment and transition process (Sitlington et al., 1997). This goal also requires students to become aware of their own interests, needs, and preferences, as well as desired postschool outcomes, but it also requires use of other self-determination skills such as problem solving, decision making, and self-advocacy.

Goal 3: Helping Students Understand Skills Needed for Postschool Environments

The final goal of transition assessment is to ensure that students and other team members have a thorough understanding of skills related to postschool adult-living domains that will lead to more appropriate choices when setting transition goals and selecting a course of study that will help achieve desired postschool outcomes (National Information Center for Children and Youth with Disabilities [NICHCY], 1993). This final goal draws attention to the all-inclusive nature of transition assessment. Not only is transition assessment critical for helping students make plans and choices, but it also plays a crucial role in assessing students' ongoing performance in coursework and community experiences that are designed to help them achieve their desired postschool outcomes.

CHARACTERISTICS OF TRANSITION ASSESSMENT

Six characteristics must be considered when conducting a transition assessment.

DID YOU KNOW?

"Transition assessment and planning has expanded its focus beyond employment and careers to include community living, daily living skills, recreation/leisure, social skills, transportation, and financial skills" (Thoma, Held, & Saddler, 2002, p. 248).

DID YOU KNOW?

Thoma, Held, and Saddler (2002) found that special educators are not using transition assessment practices that facilitate student involvement and self-determination in the assessment process.

Transition Assessment Is Student Centered

First, transition assessment is student centered and self determined. For example, if a student states that he wants to attend a 4-year university but his parents want him to attend a local community college, then his team should help him develop a plan to enroll in a 4-year university. It is important to remember that it is the student's life that is being discussed, not the teacher's or the parent's. It is the educator's job to help students become self-aware, for self-awareness and knowledge of rights and responsibilities lead to self-advocacy (Test, Fowler, Wood, Brewer, & Eddy, 2005).

Transition Assessment Is Continuous

Second, transition assessment is an ongoing process. It typically begins with gathering information to help develop the transition component of the individualized education program (IEP; see Chapter 4) and continues throughout a student's high school career. A good transition assessment will help students and others both plan an appropriate course of study and evaluate performance based on instruction designed to help them achieve their desired postschool outcomes.

Transition Assessment Occurs in Many Places

Third, the ongoing process of transition assessment requires that assessment take place in a variety of natural environments focusing on future postschool outcomes. As students move toward making choices and learning the skills required to achieve each choice, there will be a need to evaluate their performance in employment situations, as well as in the other community settings (e.g., in restaurants, on buses, in theaters). In addition, exposing students to a variety of options in employment (Chapter 8), postsecondary education (Chapter 6), community housing (Chapter 9), and community participation (Chapter 10) will help them make informed choices and refine their desired postschool outcomes.

Transition Assessment Must Involve Other People

Fourth, transition assessment must be collaborative and interdisciplinary. Getting an accurate picture of students' strengths requires collecting information from parents, friends, employers, and case managers, to name just a few (Sitlington & Clark, 2001). Collecting ongoing information in natural environments also necessitates the assistance of several individuals, including the student. Thus, interagency collaboration (Chapter 5) is a must for high-quality transition assessment to occur.

Transition Assessment Data Must Be Understandable

Fifth, data gathered as a result of transition assessment must be useful and understandable to all people involved. In many cases, the use of ongoing, naturally occurring data is useful and understandable; however, there are times when students must be taught how to interpret the results of standardized vocational, interest, and intelligence tests (Pocock et al., 2002).

Transition Assessment Must Be Sensitive to Cultural Diversity

Finally, the transition assessment process must be sensitive to cultural diversity. To do this, teachers and others must (a) understand their own cultural and ethnic identities; (b) identify their own values that underlie their interpretation of each student's assessment data; (c) determine the "fit" between their cultural values and assumptions and those of the student and his family; (d) attempt to explain any differences between "mainstream" societal values and the values of the student's family; and (e) work collaboratively to reconcile differences to help achieve desired postschool outcomes (Owens & Blanchett, 2004). In addition, Sitlington and Clark (2001) have suggested some "commonsense guidelines" to help ensure fairness:

1. Be ready to respond to any past experiences with discrimination in assessments.
2. Consider using selected members of a family's cultural community if misunderstandings arise.
3. Talk with the student and family about the best way to communicate with them.
4. If a translation is necessary, spend time beforehand making sure the translator understands the purpose and context of any assessment.

DID YOU KNOW?

"The focus on compliance and bureaucratic imperatives in the current system, instead of academic achievement and social outcomes, fails too many children with disabilities. Too few successfully graduate from high school or transition to full employment and postsecondary opportunities, despite provisions in IDEA providing for transition services. Parents want an education system that is results-oriented and focused on the child's needs–*in school and beyond*." (President's Commission on Excellence in Special Education, 2002, p. 8)

THE APIE MODEL FOR TRANSITION ASSESSMENT

Transition assessment aims to help students (a) make informed choices, (b) take charge of the assessment process, and (c) understand the skills needed for postschool environments. To meet these goals, effective transition assessment must (a) be student centered, (b) be continuous, (c) occur in many places, (d) involve other people, (e) produce understandable data, and (f) be culturally sensitive. Therefore, it is clear that transition assessment must be an ongoing process that uses a variety of methods to gather many different types of information.

One assessment model that can be adapted to meet these needs is the **APIE Model**. The APIE model for transition assessment used in this chapter is adapted from the directive teaching process (Stephens, 1977) and the model for systematic instruction (Heward, as cited in Cameira, 1987). As shown in Figure 3.1, the APIE model consists of four basic steps: Assess, Plan, Instruct, and Evaluate. By following this model, educators should be able to design and implement a systematic process for transition assessment that meets the needs of all students.

Step 1: Assess for Planning and Instruction

The first step is to assess each student to determine his or her individual needs, preferences, and interests in terms of desired postschool outcomes. This initial assessment must take into account the current resources available and future resources needed to achieve the student's postschool outcomes. To be effective, information must be collected from many individuals using a variety of assessment strategies.

The information gathered in Step 1 will be used for both planning the transition component of the IEP and a student's course of study, which specifies the instruction the student will need to receive in order to reach the desired postschool outcomes. Figure 3.2 provides a summary of some of the key questions that need to be answered during Step 1. Another question that must be answered is, What is needed to help each student achieve these goals in terms of (a) new student skills, (b) environmental supports needed, and (c) current resources available and future resources needed?

Guidelines for Selecting Transition Assessment Strategies.   Since assessment plans are tailored to meet students' individual needs, Sitlington and colleagues (1997) suggested nine guidelines for selecting strategies to be used in the transition assessment process:

1. Assessment methods must be tailored to the types of information needed and the decisions to be made regarding transition planning and various postsecondary outcomes.
2. Specific methods selected must be appropriate for the learning characteristics of the individual, including cultural and linguistic differences.

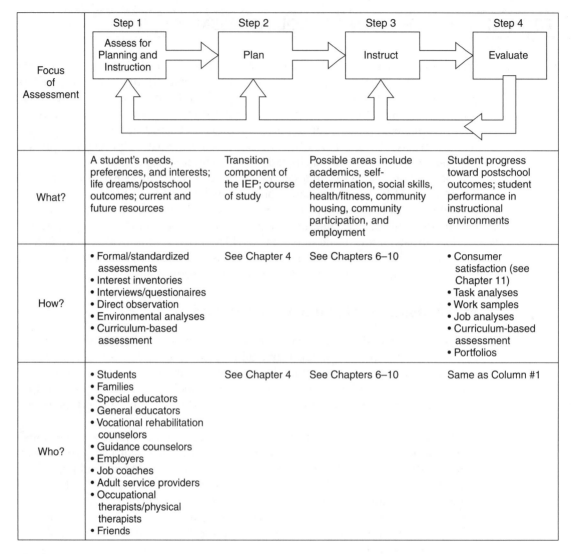

Focus of Assessment	Step 1	Step 2	Step 3	Step 4
	Assess for Planning and Instruction →	Plan →	Instruct →	Evaluate
What?	A student's needs, preferences, and interests; life dreams/postschool outcomes; current and future resources	Transition component of the IEP; course of study	Possible areas include academics, self-determination, social skills, health/fitness, community housing, community participation, and employment	Student progress toward postschool outcomes; student performance in instructional environments
How?	• Formal/standardized assessments • Interest inventories • Interviews/questionaires • Direct observation • Environmental analyses • Curriculum-based assessment	See Chapter 4	See Chapters 6–10	• Consumer satisfaction (see Chapter 11) • Task analyses • Work samples • Job analyses • Curriculum-based assessment • Portfolios
Who?	• Students • Families • Special educators • General educators • Vocational rehabilitation counselors • Guidance counselors • Employers • Job coaches • Adult service providers • Occupational therapists/physical therapists • Friends	See Chapter 4	See Chapters 6–10	Same as Column #1

Figure 3.1
Summary of APIE Model for Transition Assessment

3. Assessment methods must incorporate assistive technology or accommodations that will allow an individual to demonstrate his or her abilities and potential.

4. Assessment methods must occur in environments that resemble actual vocational training, employment, independent living, or community environments.

5. Assessment methods must produce outcomes that contribute to ongoing development, planning, and implementation of "next steps" in the individual's transition process.

- *Life Dreams*
  What are your hopes, aspirations, and life dreams?
- *Relationships/Belonging*
  Who are the key people who will be involved and what will your relationships
  be like?
  Where and how will you find a life partner?
  What future do you envision for your family life?
- *Home*
  Where do you want to live?
  Who do you want to live with?
  What kind of home, neighborhood, and community would you enjoy?
  What lifestyle do you prefer?
- *Career*
  How will you support your lifestyle?
  What kind of work interests you?
  What kind of work are you good at?
  What jobs do you enjoy?
  What is your career goal and how can you get there?
  How much money do you need and want to earn?
  What kind of setting do you want to work in?
  What kind of people do you want to work with?
- *Recreation*
  What kind of leisure would you like to be involved in?
  What and how can you make friends you enjoy?
- *Personal Growth*
  What kinds of knowledge do you wish and need to learn to realize your goals?
- *Health*
  How can you maintain a healthy lifestyle?
- *Education*
  How can you continue to develop skills you want or need?

Figure 3.2
Key Questions for Transition

Note. From *Where Did the Time Go? Transition to Adult Life* (p. 5) by D. Dileo, 2002, St Augustine,
FL: Training Resource Network, Inc. Reprinted with permission.

6. Assessment methods must be varied and include a sequence of activities that sample an individual's behavior and skills over time.

7. Assessment data must be verified by more than one method and by more than one person.

8. Assessment data must be synthesized and interpreted to individuals with disabilities, their families, and transition team members.

9. Assessment data and the results of the assessment process must be documented in a format that can be used to facilitate transition planning (p. 75).

How Can Data Be Collected to Assess for Planning and Instruction?   Transition assessments can be grouped into two categories called *formal* and *informal* (Flexer & Luft, 2001) or *standardized* and *nonstandardized* (Clark, 1996). Formal assessment procedures typically involve using a standardized procedure for administering, scoring, and interpreting an assessment. By clearly defining how an assessment is administered, scored, and interpreted, this allows a student's score to be interpreted relative to those of other students (e.g., norms), although not all standardized assessments are norm referenced. On the other hand, informal assessment procedures are less structured and do not allow comparison with other students. However, because informal procedures allow assessment of student performance over time, they are useful in designing and evaluating the effects of instructional interventions. In addition, they allow data to be collected from a variety of individuals using a variety of nonstandardized methods.

Standardized Transition Assessments.   Clark (1996) listed 13 types of formal, standardized assessment procedures that might be used in transition assessment:

1. Learning style inventories.
2. Academic achievement tests.
3. Intellectual functional assessment.
4. Adaptive behavior scales.
5. Aptitude tests.
6. Interest inventories.
7. Personality scales.
8. Quality-of-life scales.
9. Social skills inventories.
10. Prevocational/employability scales.
11. Vocational skills assessments.
12. Transition knowledge and skills inventories.
13. Medical laboratory procedures.

It is important to keep in mind that formal assessments are designed to provide data about a student, relative to others, at a single point in time. Therefore, it is useful to supplement findings from formal transition assessments with information gathered from informal transition assessment procedures. Figure 3.3 lists some of the more widely used transition assessments.

Informal Transition Assessment Methods.   Because transition assessment is an ongoing process that is student centered and student determined, collaborative, and future oriented, informal methods are used most often. These include interviews and questionnaires, direct observation of students in various settings (e.g., at worksites, in class, in the community, at home), environmental analysis, and curriculum-based assessment (CBA).

Comprehensive Assessments

1. *Life Centered Career Education* [LCCE] *Mild Curriculum Assessment System* (Brolin, 1997). This system includes four instruments: (a) The Competency Rating Scale is a teacher rating scale based on the 22 competencies and 97 subcompetencies in the LCCE: Mild Curriculum Guide; (b) the Knowledge Battery is a criterion-referenced assessment consisting of 200 multiple-choice questions covering the three LCCE: Mild Curriculum domains; (c) the Performance Battery contains a combination of open-ended questions, role-playing scenarios, card sorts, and hands-on activities to assess functional performance on the first 21 LCCE: Mild Curriculum competencies; and (d) the LCCE Self-Determination Scale is a 40-item self-report measure.
2. *Life Centered Career Education Moderate Curriculum Assessment System* (Loyd & Brolin, 1997). This system includes three instruments: (a) the Competency Rating Scale-M is a teacher rating scale based on 20 competencies and 75 subcompetencies in the LCCE Moderate Curriculum; (b) the Pictorial Knowledge Battery is a reading-free, criterion-referenced assessment consisting of 150 multiple-choice questions covering the first 18 LCCE Moderate Curriculum competencies; and (c) the Performance Assessment Battery is another reading-free, criterion-referenced instrument consisting of a combination of open-ended questions, role-playing, card sorts, and hands-on activities.
3. *Transition Planning Inventory* [TPI] (Clark & Patton, 1998.) This inventory is designed to provide educators with a comprehensive method for determining perceived transition needs in the following domains: employment, future education, daily living, leisure activities, community participation, health, self-determination, communication, and interpersonal relationships. The TPI includes three levels of assessment: (a) a general needs assessment of each domain; (b) a comprehensive informal inventory of more than 600 items; and (c) select informal assessment instruments corresponding to the nine domains.

Self-Determination Assessments

1. *AIR Self-Determination Scale and User Guide* (Wolman, Campeau, DuBois, Mithaug, & Stolarski, 1994). The main purpose of the AIR Self-Determination Scale and User Guide is to "provide an easy-to-use tool to assess and develop strategies for improving a student's level of self-determination" (p. 9). The scale was designed to be used with all school-age students, grades K through 12+. It can be used to (a) assess and develop a profile of a student's level of self-determination, (b) determine strengths and areas for improvement to increase self-determination, (c) identify goals and objectives, and (d) develop strategies to increase a student's capacities and opportunities. The scale measures *capacity* (i.e., ability, knowledge, and perceptions) and *opportunity* (at school and at home) related to three components of self-determination: *thinking, doing,* and *adjusting.* A five-point Likert-type scale (1 = never; 5 = always) is used to rate students and environments on self-determination components. There are three forms of the scale. The educator form is intended for use by teachers. The

Figure 3.3
Sample Transition Assessments

(continued)

student form can be used by students who have the requisite reading and comprehension skills. The parent form is intended for use with parents who could benefit by considering the self-determination of their sons or daughters. The forms were field-tested with students between the ages of 6 and 25.

Further information about the AIR Self-Determination Scale can be obtained from American Institutes for Research, P.O. Box 1113, Palo Alto, CA 94302. Telephone: 650.493.3550 csef@air-ca.org

2. *The Arc's Self-Determination Scale* (Wehmeyer & Kelchner, 1995). The Arc's Self-Determination Scale is a student self-report measure of self-determination designed for use by adolescents with disabilities, particularly students with mild cognitive and learning disabilities. The 72-item scale measures overall self-determination and the domain areas of autonomy, self-regulation, psychological empowerment, and self-realization. The scale includes four-point Likert-type scale items, story completion items (i.e., the beginning and ending of a story are provided and the student writes the middle section), items that require the student to identify goals and break the goals into smaller steps, and items that require students to make a choice between two options. The scale can be completed by the student independently or it can be read to the student. The scale can be administered to 15 students at one time, provided students' reading abilities warrant this and there are enough persons to provide necessary support to students during scale administration.

For further information on The Arc's Self-Determination Scale, contact The Arc of the United States, 500 East Border Street, Suite 300, Arlington, TX 76010. Telephone: 817.261.6003. This scale may also be ordered from The Council for Exceptional Children, 1920 Association Drive, Reston, VA 20191-1589. Telephone: 888.232.7323.

3. *ChoiceMaker Self-Determination Assessment* (Martin & Marshall, 1996). The ChoiceMaker Self-Determination Assessment is a curriculum-based assessment and planning tool intended for use with middle to high school students with emotional or behavior disabilities and mild to moderate learning problems. It may be adapted for older elementary students or for students with more severe learning problems. The ChoiceMaker assessment measures student skills and opportunities at school in three areas: choosing goals, expressing goals, and taking action. The assessment has three parts. The first part is a rating scale of student skills related to self-determination and opportunities at school to perform each of the self-determination-related skills. Student skills and opportunities are rated on a scale from 0 to 4. The second part of the assessment is an assessment profile. The student skills and school opportunities ratings are recorded on a profile where differences in scores are more readily apparent. The third part of the assessment, the ChoiceMaker Curriculum Matrix, provides objectives and corresponding goals for consideration as teaching priorities.

Further information on the ChoiceMaker Self-Determination Assessment can be obtained from Sopris West Publishers, 1140 Boston Avenue, Longmont, CO 80501. Telephone: 800.547.6747.

Figure 3.3
Continued

4. *The Self-Determination Assessment Battery* (Hoffman, Field, & Sawilowsky, 2004). The Self-Determination Assessment Battery measures cognitive, affective, and behavioral factors related to self-determination. These factors are assessed from the perspectives of the student, teacher, and parent. The battery is based on the Field and Hoffman model of self-determination. The model focuses on those variables related to self-determination that are within the individual's control and are potential targets for instructional intervention. The model contains five components: Know Yourself, Value Yourself, Plan, Act, and Experience Outcomes and Learn. There are five instruments in the battery:

(a) The Self-Determination Knowledge Scale (forms A and B; Hoffman, Field, & Sawilowsky, 1996) is a multiple-choice and true/false format instrument designed to assess students' cognitive knowledge of self-determination skills as taught in the *Steps to Self-Determination* (Field & Hoffman, 1996) curriculum.

(b) The Self-Determination Observation Checklist is a 38-item behavioral checklist designed to be used by classroom teachers. Students are observed over a class period, and behaviors that have been found to be correlated with self-determination are checked.

(c) The Self-Determination Student Scale is a 92-item self-report instrument completed by the student that measures both affective and cognitive aspects of self-determination. The items contain a brief stimulus to which the student marks "That's me" or "That's not me."

(d) and (e) The Teacher Perception Scale and the Parent Perception Scale are 30-item questionnaires on which teachers or parents rate their student or child on a five-point Likert-type scale on a variety of behaviors, abilities, and skills associated with self-determination. The instruments in the battery can be used separately or together to assess student variables associated with self-determination.

Further information about the Self-Determination Knowledge Scale can be obtained from Pro-Ed, 8700 Shoal Creek Boulevard, Austin, TX 78757-6897. Telephone: 512.451.3246. It is also available from the Council for Exceptional Children. Telephone: 888.232.7733. Information about the Self-Determination Assessment Battery is available from the Self-Determination and Transition Projects Office, 469 Education Building, College of Education, Wayne State University, Detroit, MI 48202. Telephone: 313.577.1638.

5. *The Self-Determination Profile: An Assessment Package.* (Curtis, 1996). This package is one of the New Hats curriculum sets designed to help youths and adults determine their preferences, activities, relationships, and routines as they are now as well as into the future. Students use card decks composed of illustrations to show what their life is now like and what they would like to do in the future. Various summary sheets are provided for student use, along with facilitator instructions.

The Self-Determination Profile: An Assessment Package is available from New Hats Inc., P.O. Box 57567, Salt Lake City, UT 84157. Telephone: 435.259.9400.

Interviews and Questionnaires.   Interviews and questionnaires can be conducted with a variety of individuals. However, they all have a central goal—to gather information that can be used to determine each student's needs, preferences, and interests relative to anticipated postschool outcomes. In other words, What is currently known about the student and the student's family that can be used to help develop postschool outcomes and plan a course of study that will help the student reach his or her goals? Figures 3.4 and 3.5 provide examples of different questions that can be asked of students and their families to gather assessment information for planning and instruction. An important part of this data-collection process involves gathering information about the student's and family's current and future resources. For example, if a student's education choice requires enrolling in postsecondary education, it is helpful to know as soon as possible what financial resources the family might have or need. A second example might involve current and future transportation needs to get to work or to various activities and locations in the community. Finally, families can often suggest current and future employment options for their sons and daughters or other students in a high school program.

Direct Observation.   Direct observation of a student should be conducted within the natural or school employment, postsecondary, or community setting (Sitlington et al., 1997). Sometimes called **situational assessment** (Sitlington & Clark, 2001), direct observations are often done by an expert in the environment such as a job coach, coworker, recreation specialist, and/or general or vocational educator. However, in keeping with a philosophy of self-determination students should be taught to record their own observational (or self-recording) data. Direct observation data typically include task-analytic data of steps in completing a task, work behaviors (e.g., on task, following directions, getting along with coworkers), and affective information (e.g., is the student happy, excited, frustrated, or bored?). For example, if, when observing at a worksite, a student quickly and accurately completes his tasks, interacts well with coworkers, and appears happy, this could provide evidence that this type of job is one that the student likes. However, if, after visiting a community residential setting, a student appears withdrawn, this may be an indication that the particular situation may not be suitable.

Environmental Analysis.   Environmental analysis, sometimes referred to as **ecological assessment** and/or *job analysis*, involves carefully examining the environment in which an activity normally occurs. For example, a student may express an interest in attending karate classes at the local YMCA. In this case an environmental analysis could be conducted of the transportation needs and the expectations at the YMCA for attending (e.g., being a member, using the locker room, taking a shower). In a second example, if a student expressed interest in a specific type of job, an environmental job analysis could be conducted. The purpose of a job analysis is to compare the requirements of a specific job to the job seeker's skills (Griffin & Sherron, 1996). A critical part of the job analysis would be to help identify the types of accommodations that could be provided to help

Student Dream Sheet

Student Name: *Ernest Lee*
Initial Date: _____
School: *Shelby High School*   Teacher: *Mr. Howard*

Review Dates: _____

Anticipated Date of Graduation: *May 2005*

The following questions will be used to assist in transition planning activities and to determine postschool goals.

1. Where do you want to live after graduation? *In Shelby by myself*
    What kind of housing? *An apartment*
2. How do you intend to continue learning after graduation? *Go to college*
    What types of things do you want to learn after graduation? *Agriculture, reading*
    Where do you want this learning to occur? *A community college or technical school*
3. What kind of job do you want now? *Part-time job, earn a few bucks, just a teenage kind of job*
4. What kind of job do you want when you graduate? *Full-time job building things or working with wood, possibly truck driving*
5. Where do you want to work? *Anywhere near Shelby*
6. What type of work schedule do you want? *Anytime – any shift, weekends are OK*
7. What type of pay and benefits do you want from your future job? *$20.00 an hour, insurance, lots of good benefits like winning trips and stuff*
8. What types of chores do you do at home? *Whatever I need to do but I hate to cook and do dishes.*
9. What equipment/tools can you use? *Lawn care equipment, power tools, woodworking tools*
10. Do you have any significant medical problems that need to be considered when determining postschool goals? *No.*
11. What choices do you make now? *Almost everything*
12. What choices are made for you that you want to take charge of? *When to eat, curfew, how to spend my money*
13. What kind of transportation will you use after graduation? *A car that I own*
14. What do you do for fun now? *Ride around with my cousin, listen to music, hunt, fish, camping out in the woods*
15. What would you like to do for fun in the future? *Same stuff I do now, deep-sea fishing, big game hunting, races*

Figure 3.4   *(continued)*
Sample Student Dream Sheet and Student Mapping Form Completed by Family

Student Mapping Form for Parents

Student Name: *Ernest Lee*
Initial Date: _____
Review Date: _____

Parent(s)/Guardian Name: *Grandparents*

Anticipated Date of Graduation: *May 2005*

What are your dreams for your child? List them no matter how big they are.
Good job, marriage, kids

What are you fears for your child?
Drinking and doing drugs
Dropping out of school
Getting a girl pregnant

What are your child's needs?
Job skills

List at least three things that you would like your child to work on during the time he or she is in high school.
Carpentry skills, personal finance management, job-seeking skills

What one thing could we teach your child at school that would make life easier at home?
Cooking skills, clean his room, come in at his curfew time

What do you see as postschool goals for your child in each of the following areas?
Employment: *A good job that he likes in a place that will be patient with him and train him*
Education: *Trucking school or carpentry classes*
Residential: *Live with us (grandparents). Maybe live by himself if one day he has a good job*
Recreation: *Whatever he wants*

Figure 3.4
Continued

Note. From Shelby City Schools/Cleveland County Schools (revised, 2001). Reprinted with permission.

General Questions for Assessment Planning
1. What are your greatest dreams or goals?
2. What are your greatest fears?
3. How can school/agency resources help you to reach your goals?
4. Is there anything the school/family/agencies are doing for you now that you could/should be doing for yourself?

Educational Questions
1. Why do you think you're successful in some classes?
2. Why are you experiencing difficulty in other classes?
3. What modifications do you need in your classes to succeed?
4. How do you learn best?
5. What specific skills are you lacking that could be taught to you in school?
6. What further educational training do you wish you could get?
7. How will you pay for further educational training?

Career Questions
1. What would you like to be doing 2–5–10 years from now?
2. What skills will you need to get the job you want?
3. What kinds of things do you think you're good at? What are you not good at?
4. What kind of vocational training/education would you like to have after high school?
5. What would your ideal job be?
6. What kinds of information/classes/training do you need to have in order to reach your career goals?
7. What hobbies, interests, recreation activities do you have that you could use in a career?
8. What job shadowing or job try-outs would you like to try in order to explore possible careers?
9. What kind of work experience have you had?

Community/Residential Questions
1. Where do you want to live after you graduate?
2. What kind of transportation will be available to you after graduation?
3. What kinds of chores/jobs do you do at home that will help you as an independent adult?
4. What kinds of domestic skills do you need help with (cooking, household management, etc)?
5. If you moved to a new community, how would you locate housing, recreational opportunities, transportation, medical, and legal resources, etc.?
6. How will you manage your money after you graduate?
7. What money/banking skills do you have?

Medical/Legal Questions
1. Do you have a family doctor/dentist?
2. Do you have any medical needs that will require support beyond high school?
3. If you run into a legal problem, how will you handle it? Who will you go to for help?

Figure 3.5
Student Transition Assessment

(continued)

4. Who would you contact in case of emergency?
5. What would you need to know about first aid if help wasn't readily available?
6. If you don't understand the terms of a contract, who can you go to for help?
7. What kinds of insurance will you need, and how will you pay for it?

Recreation/Leisure Questions

1. What do you like to do for fun?
2. What are your hobbies and interests?
3. Is there anything you wish you could learn how to do that you don't know now?
4. Are there any school activities you think you might like to get involved in?
5. What recreation opportunities are offered in your community that might interest you?
6. What recreation resources might you look for if you moved to a new community?
7. Would you rather spend leisure time alone or with others?

Social/Interpersonal Questions

1. How do you handle conflicts or solve problems?
2. Who do you/would you like to go to when you have a problem or need help at home? at school? in the community?
3. Do you have someone you trust to talk with when things aren't going well?
4. Who do you include in your circle of friends?

Figure 3.5
Continued

Note. From North Dakota Transition Project (1995). Bridging the Gap: Charting a Successful Transition from School to Living and Working Independently Within the Community: North Dakota Transition Guide. Minot, ND: Minot State University. Reprinted with permissions.

the student perform the necessary functions of the job (e.g., job restructuring, modifying equipment, acquiring an adaptive device, reorganizing the work space, hiring a personal assistant; Griffin & Sherron).

Curriculum-Based Assessments. Curriculum-based assessments (CBA) are typically designed by educators to gather information about a student's performance in a specific curriculum (McLoughlin & Lewis, 2005). The purpose of a CBA is to develop instructional plans for a specific student. To gather data for use in determining specific instructional needs, an educator might use a task analysis, work sample analysis, portfolio assessment, and/or criterion-referenced tests. In fact, in the area of transition to adulthood, as early as 1988 Albright and Cobb introduced the concept of **curriculum-based vocational assessment** (CBVA) to encourage the field of vocational education to begin to use informal assessment procedures. CBVA was described as a continuous process designed "to answer questions about instruction and special services needs of individual students as they enter into the [sic] progress through specific vocational education programs" (p. 14). Albright and Cobb argued that the CBVA process should be based on

Transition Assessment for Parents

Dear Parents,

As your son or daughter moves closer to graduation, it is important to begin to plan for his/her future. At the next meeting we will develop a transition plan. The transition plan will identify future goals for your son/daughter and ways to support him/her in reaching these goals. We would like to see all our students become productive members of society. Your input and involvement is critical. Please take a few minutes to complete this transition assessment. Think of your son/daughter as an adult after graduation and identify your dreams and goals for him/her.

Employment:

I think my son/daughter could work in:

_____ A full-time regular job (competitive employment).

_____ A part-time regular job (competitive employment).

_____ A job that has support and is supervised, full or part time (supported employment).

_____ Military service.

_____ Volunteer work.

_____ Other: _____

My son's/daughter's strength(s) in this area are:

My son/daughter seems to be interested in working as:

When I think of my son/daughter working, I am afraid that:

To work, my son/daughter needs to develop skills in:

Education:

Future education for my son/daughter will include (check all that apply):

_____ College or university.	_____ Adult basic education classes.
_____ Community college.	_____ Compensatory education classes.
_____ Vocational training.	_____ Life skills classes.
_____ On-the-job training.	_____ Other: _____

My son's/daughter's educational strengths are:

To attend postsecondary training, my son/daughter will need to develop skills in:

Residential/Living:

After graduation my son/daughter will live:

_____ On his/her own in a house or an apartment.

_____ With a roommate.

_____ In a supervised living situation (group home, supervised apartment).

_____ With parents.

_____ With other family members.

_____ Other: _____

(continued)

My son's/daughter's strength(s) in this area are:

When I think about where my son/daughter will live, I am afraid that:

To live as independently as possible, my son or daughter needs to develop skills in:

Recreation and Leisure:

When my son/daughter graduates, I hope he/she is involved in (check all that apply):
_____ Independent recreational activities.

_____ Activities with friends.

_____ Organized recreational activities (club, team sports).

_____ Classes (to develop hobbies, and explore areas of interest).

_____ Supported and supervised recreational activities.

_____ Other: _____

During free time, my son or daughter enjoys:

My son's/daughter's strength(s) in this area are:

When I think of the free time my son or daughter will have after graduation, I am afraid that:

To be active and enjoy leisure time, my son or daughter needs to develop skills in:

Transportation:

When my son/daughter graduates, he/she will (check all that apply):
_____ Have a driver's license and a car.

_____ Walk, or ride a bike.

_____ Use transportation independently (bus, taxi, train).

_____ Use supported transportation (family, service groups, car pool, special program).

_____ Other: _____

My son's/daughter's strength(s) in this area are:

When I think of my son/daughter traveling around the community I worry about:

To access transportation my son/daughter needs to develop skills in:

Review items in the following three areas. Please identify areas in which your son or daughter needs information/support.

Social/Interpersonal

_____ Making friends   _____ Communicating needs/wants

_____ Setting goals   _____ Relationships with the opposite sex

_____ Family relationships   _____ Counseling

_____ Handling legal responsibilities   _____ Other: _____

_____ Handling anger

Personal Management

_____ Hygiene   _____ Money management/budgeting

_____ Safety   _____ Time/time management

_____ Mobility/transportation   _____ Personal care

_____ Domestic skills   _____ Other: _____

Health

_____ Ongoing care for a serious   _____ Information on drug/chemical
      medical condition   abuse

_____ Sex education   _____ Other: _____

_____ AIDS awareness

Note. From _The Colorado Transition Manual_ by S. J. McAlonan, 1993, Denver; Colorado Department of Education. Reprinted with permission.

student needs and be integrated into ongoing instruction. They viewed CBVA as a novel application of the "assess–teach–assess–teach" feedback loop, much like the APIE model used in this text.

**Who Can Be Involved in Assessing for Planning and Instruction?**   A wide variety of people can be involved in this process. Figure 3.1 provides a starting point for determining which people to gather data from as well as people who can gather data for you. Sitlington and colleagues' (1997) nine guidelines for selecting assessment methods, described earlier, can help you decide who to involve in this step of the transition assessment process. For example, Guideline 4 requires assessing in actual environments. If this is going to happen, who is the best person to get to help collect data? If it is at a worksite, you might want to use a coworker, the supervisor, or the job coach. If it involves postsecondary education, it might involve high school guidance counselors or college-level disability services personnel. If it involves community housing, you might want to involve the family and a realtor.

Guideline 7 requires that data be verified by more than one person. For example, family members might be able to verify whether or not a student likes a specific job or housing option, while a friend might be able to verify a student's interest in visiting local art galleries and museums during monthly "gallery crawls."

In conclusion, remember that the APIE model is designed to be ongoing, which allows other individuals to be invited into the assessment process at any time once the student and team identify a need for a particular person. For example, a student who has been planning to live at home for a few years after graduating now decides that he would like to explore community housing alternatives. As a result, information must be gathered from a representative from the local public housing authority.

Step 2: Plan

Once enough information has been gathered to determine a student's needs, preferences, and interests related to postschool outcomes and current and future resources have been established, it is time to move on to the second step in the APIE model. If Guidelines 8 (i.e., synthesizing and interpreting assessment data to students, families, and teams) and 9 (i.e., documenting assessment data in a format that can be used to facilitate transition planning), have been followed, the information has been synthesized and interpreted so that all members of the planning team understand them and the results are in a format that will facilitate planning. The planning that now occurs will be written into the transition component of the student's IEP, along with the course of study. For more information on how this planning process works and who should be involved, see Chapter 4.

Step 3: Instruct

Once the second step of the APIE model is completed and the transition component of the IEP, the IEP goals and objectives, and the course of study have been determined, the next step is to provide instruction to the student. This instruction will be designed to help the student attain the skills needed to achieve the postschool outcomes stated in the IEP. Possible areas for instruction could include self-determination, social skills, health and fitness, community housing, community participation, and employment. For more information on how to teach and assess student performance in these areas, as well as who should be involved, see Chapters 6 through 10.

Step 4: Evaluate

While Step 4 is the last step in the APIE model, it is not the last step in the transition assessment process. Remember that a key characteristic of transition assessment is that it is an on-going process. As shown in Figure 3.1, the information gathered in Step 4 feeds back to all the earlier steps making the process cyclical and thus ongoing. Step 4 allows the educator, student, and family to take stock of where they are with respect to the student's achieving the desired postschool outcomes. As a result, evaluation will take place at regular intervals. To determine whether adequate progress is being made on transition activities and IEP goals and objectives, evaluation might occur semiannually, but it must occur annually.

To determine a student's performance in instructional environments, brief weekly or monthly progress reports could be developed and shared with the student and his or her family. As students are taught to self-evaluate, they could be given the task of sending home their own monthly reports. These reports could simply be a self-report checklist of tasks completed and current performance. A student who is currently involved in a community-based work experience might complete a self-graphing task analysis for his or her job (or a job task) each Friday, and at the end of the month (or week), these analyses would be sent home for the family to see.

How Can Data Be Collected to Evaluate?   All of the strategies described for Step 1 can also be used in Step 4. However, instead of gathering information to begin planning and instruction, the educator collects data to guide ongoing planning and instruction. Therefore it is important that students and families be given multiple opportunities to revisit desired postschool outcomes and revise them as needed. It should be expected that, as a student has opportunities to try out and learn more about different jobs, community housing options, and postsecondary educational opportunities, his or her plans may change entirely (e.g., from getting a job to attending college) or become more precise (e.g., from wanting a job to wanting a job working with computers).

An additional set of data that needs to be collected once students get involved in their transition programs is consumer satisfaction data. It is important to collect these data from students and families to ensure that everyone is satisfied with the instruction, services, and supports being provided. In addition, this information can be used to make changes to the transition program to ensure that transition services are being provided at the highest possible level of quality. For more detail on what consumer satisfaction data to collect and how to collect it, see Chapter 11.

STRATEGIES FOR ADDRESSING COMMON CHALLENGES

What to Do If a Student Has Been Referred to Vocational Rehabilitation for an Evaluation

At some point in high school, students with disabilities will probably be involved in what is often called a traditional vocational evaluation. While the traditional vocational evaluation process typically includes four steps—clinical assessment, work evaluation, work adjustment, and job site evaluation—students may not be involved in all four steps. The first thing to do is to find out exactly which steps will be involved in each student's vocational evaluation. Once this is known, educators can help prepare the students by describing the process in advance.

The first step in traditional vocational evaluation process is called *clinical assessment*. Clinical assessment usually involves collecting medical, social, educational, and psychological information. Social, educational, and psychological information is typically gathered using standardized adaptive behavior, academic, and intelligence tests. All clinical assessment data should focus on a student's strengths and how these abilities relate to different vocational opportunities. The 1992 Rehabilitation Act Amendments (P.L. 102–569), mentioned in Chapter 1, states that vocational rehabilitation (VR) counselors are allowed to use existing assessment data if the report was completed in the past year. This means that the educator should find out what clinical assessment information the VR counselor will need and, if it is available from the past year, help the counselor get access to the data. (You will learn more about VR counselors and their role in the transition process in Chapter 5.) This also means that students will not have to retake a set of tests that they have recently taken for school.

The second step in the traditional vocational evaluation process is *work evaluation*. Because clinical assessment data often are not a good predictor of vocational success, work (real or simulated) has been used more often. There are three basic types of work evaluations: standardized interest and aptitude tests, work/job samples, and situational assessments.

Standardized interest and aptitude tests come in written formats, pictorial formats, and CD formats. CDs typically include video clips of people performing actual jobs. Standardized tests have limited usefulness because students often need work experience to make choices, must have the ability to make choices, and, at times, need good reading skills. The use of video clips and pictures is an attempt to avoid these problems. However, there is no real substitution for actual on-the-job experience to help students decide on their interests. Examples of standardized interest and aptitude tests include the Strong Interest Inventory (Strong et al., 1994), Digital Pictorial Inventory of Careers (Talent Assessment, Inc., 2000), and The Wide Range Interest and Occupation Test (Glutting & Wilkinson, 2003).

The other two types of work evaluation involve having students perform either simulated or real work tasks. Work samples involve having a student perform a real or simulated task (e.g., sorting mail, collating, fixing a drain), while situational assessments involve observing individuals doing entire jobs. Both work samples and situational assessments typically include collecting task-analytic data on specific job tasks as well as data on general work skills (e.g., following directions, getting along with coworkers, attitude). Educators can share any data they have from any on-campus or off-campus work experiences a student has participated in. The more data that are available to help make recommendations, the more realistic they will be.

The third step in a traditional vocational evaluation is called *work adjustment*. This process is similar to the APIE model in that it consists of a period of work experience followed by a planned sequence of instruction to remediate specific vocational weaknesses, which is then followed by another work experience and more skill instruction. Historically this process has taken place in sheltered workshops or other rehabilitation facilities. Today, however, best practice involves conducting work adjustment at community-based sites. As a result educators should be ready to offer, or recommend, the use of the school's community-based training sites (see Chapter 8) and the data collected, as the work adjustment step.

The final step in a traditional vocational evaluation is *job site evaluation*. In a true job site evaluation, students have an opportunity to try out a paid, competitive job as the final step in their vocational evaluation. This is probably the best way to tell whether or not an individual is both interested in and capable of performing a specific job. Educators may be able to volunteer the use of their community-based training sites for this step. One limitation of this is that jobs performed in many community-based training sites are unpaid.

To summarize, armed with an understanding of what is going to occur during a student's vocational evaluation, educators can assist by (a) supplying existing testing data (provided it was gathered within the past year), (b) sharing any existing data on the student's performance on work tasks and at on-campus or community-based training sites, and (c) offering on-campus or community-based training sites for use in the evaluation process.

What to Do When Students and Families Disagree

Educators should try to be aware of, and prepared for, any potential areas of disagreement between students and families. Comparing student and family responses to Student Dream Sheets and Parent Mapping Forms (see Figure 3.4 for examples) is an excellent way to be alerted early to possible disagreements. What follows are ideas for dealing with some common areas of disagreement. In addition, see Chapter 5 for strategies to help resolve conflicts.

Disagreements About Postschool Goals.   This situation might occur if a student wants to move out and the family wants him or her to stay at home. One suggestion is to develop a long-range plan for how the student can be "free" while the parents still feel that he or she is safe.

Disagreement also occurs around the type of job the student wants and/or the job hours. Both students and families can have preconceived notions about what jobs are acceptable (e.g., sometimes a white-collar family will have issues with a blue-collar job). Another reason why a family may not want their son or daughter to get a job is loss of income and healthcare benefits if the student can no longer receive supplemental security income (SSI). In this case the family and student will need to be educated about new Ticket-to-Work requirements and social security work incentives such as the Plan for Achieving Self-Support (PASS) and impairment-related work expenses (IRWE). A good starting point is to have a local social security expert work with the family. For more detail, see Chapters 5 and 8. The suggestion here is to create a long-term plan for employment that includes as many opportunities as possible for a student to try out a variety of jobs.

Fear of Risk Taking.   Typically this involves families who feel that their child is not ready for a specific job or community participation experience. Overcoming this fear requires providing students with as many experiences as possible while they are still in school to prove to families that their sons and daughters will be successful in different situations. If possible, the family should be involved in planning for each experience and should be educated about the safeguards in place for each community-based training experience.

Differences in Expectations.   This is another issue that will require long-range planning, but it also has to be overcome early or it will get in the way of the student's having any community-based experiences. Many things can be done to prove to parents that their sons and daughters are capable of doing more than the parents believe they can. The more students are involved in leadership roles in team meetings, the more their parents will see them as being in charge. Self-determination training is important to help students stand up for what they want in life.

Begin by conducting a thorough interview with a student to help identify the areas in his or her personal life over which he or she wants more control (e.g., finances, free time, TV time, curfew). Next, help the student develop an action plan for assuming more responsibility and present the plan to the student's parents. Students must understand that for their parents to stop treating them like children, they must stop acting like children. This can be accomplished by doing their own laundry, keeping a calendar so they don't have to be reminded of everything, and/or taking care of the family pet. Often students can do a trade-off with parents; if the students will start doing certain chores at home, the parents will allow more independence.

Inability to Provide Support for Students.   When a family cannot, for whatever reason, provide financial, transportation, and/or emotional support, it may be possible to access community agency supports through the interagency team (see Chapter 5) and/or access natural supports such a grandparents, siblings, or friends. Start by identifying the areas in which the student needs support (e.g., getting up on time, banking, transportation). Once these areas are identified, begin to get the needed supports in place. This will probably involve both teaching students new skills (see Chapter 10) and organizing interagency and natural supports (see Chapter 5).

SUMMARY

Transition assessment can take many forms, occur in a multitude of environments (e.g., school, community, occupational training sites), and involve a number of school personnel (e.g., career guidance counselors, special education teachers, vocational education teachers) and adult service providers (e.g., vocational rehabilitation counselors, job coaches, case managers). Areas appropriate for assessment during the transition planning process include academic skills; communication skills; social skills; personal hygiene and grooming; work behaviors, habits, and skills; learning styles; career interests; medical and health status; and self-determination.

Transition assessment is directly tied to transition planning. First, transition assessment must occur prior to the actual development of the transition component of the IEP in order to assist students in achieving the self-awareness needed to establish postschool goals linked to the life-style and interests they want to pursue after graduation. Second, transition assessment must be ongoing during all aspects of transition service delivery so that transition components can be updated based on the changing interests and needs of students as they mature and gain additional life experiences. Third, transition assessment must occur prior to the exit from high school to ensure access to any needed adult service delivery systems.

Transition activities should routinely include determining the types of transition assessments needed and making arrangements for these assessments to occur. There must also be a systematic method of sharing the results with the student, his or her family, and relevant school personnel and adult service providers and ensuring that the results are used with the student in self-determination training and in designing all transition activities and experiences.

During all phases of transition assessment, the goal should be to conduct assessments in a manner that will provide specific information related to each student's desired postschool outcomes. In other words, information from assessments must be based on input from the student and those who know the student, and from direct observation of the student in real-life situations.

CASE STUDIES

SAMPLE TRANSITION PLANS

Table 3.1 provides an example of a transition assessment plan for a student who has chosen to get a full-time job as a postschool goal. Table 3.2 provides an example of a transition assessment plan for a student who has chosen to go to college as one of his postschool goals. Both assessment plans require ongoing assessment to enable the student and the student's team to have access to information needed to ensure access to the high school-based supports and services needed to achieve the desired postschool outcomes.

STUDY GUIDE QUESTIONS

1. What is transition assessment?
2. How is transition assessment different from traditional assessment?
3. What are the three goals of transition assessment?
4. What are the five characteristics of transition assessment?
5. Describe the steps of the APIE model for transition assessment.
6. What can an educator do to help with a traditional vocational evaluation?
7. How does student self-determination fit into the transition assessment process?

Table 3.1

Example of Transition Assessment Plan for a Student Who Chose to Enter Employment

School Year	Assess	Plan	Instruct	Evaluate
Freshman Year	• Initial student dream sheet • Initial parent dream sheet • Review standardized test scores from student file	• Write postschool goals • Establish course of study	• Self-recording task analyses collected in school-based enterprise (SBE) • Supervisor evaluations in SBE • Student grades on tests and assignments	• End-of-year student satisfaction surveys • End-of-year parent satisfaction surveys • Student course grades • State portfolio assessment scores
Sophomore Year	• Update all dream sheets	• Update post-school goals and course of study	• Self-recording task analyses collected at community-based training site • Supervisor evaluations • Student grades on tests and assignments	
Junior Year	• Update all dream sheets	• Vocational evaluation through Vocational Rehabilitation • Update post-school goals and course of study		
Senior Year	• Update all dream sheets	• Update post-school goals and course of study		

Table 3.2

Example of Transition Assessment Plan for a Student Who Chose to Attend College

School Year	Assess	Plan	Instruct	Evaluate
Freshman Year	• Initial student dream sheet • Initial parent dream sheet • Review standardized test scores from student file	• Write postschool goals • Establish course of study • Extracurricular activities	• Student grades on tests and assignments	• End-of-year student satisfaction surveys • End-of-year parent satisfaction surveys • Student course grades • End-of-grade test scores/state competency tests
Sophomore Year	• Update all dream sheets	• Take Pre-SAT • Update postschool goals and course of study • Update extracurricular activities	• Student grades on tests and assignments	
Junior Year	• Update all dream sheets • Conduct formal needs assessment	• Take SAT/College Boards • Update postschool goals and course of study • Update extracurricular activities	• Student grades on tests and assignments	
Senior Year	• Update all dream sheets • Update financial assessment	• Vocational evaluation through Vocational Rehabilitation • Update postschool goals and course of study • Update extracurricular activities • Apply to colleges	• Student grades on tests and assignments	

REFERENCES

Albright, L., & Cobb, R. B. (1988, winter). Curriculum based vocational assessment: A concept whose time has come. *Journal for Vocational Special Needs Education, 10*(2), 13–16.

Brolin, D. E. (1997). Life Centered Career Education Mild Curriculum Assessment System. Arlington, VA: Council for Exceptional Children.

Cameira, A. J. M. (1987). Some thoughts on the development and delivery of systematic teaching: An interview with William L. Heward. *Jornal de Psicologia, 6*(1), 20–24.

Clark, G. M. (1996). Transition planning assessment for secondary-level students with learning disabilities. *Journal of Learning Disabilities, 29,* 79–92.

Clark, G., & Patton, J. (1998). Transition Planning Inventory. Austin, TX: PRO-ED.

Curtis, E. (1996). *The Self-Determination Profile: An assessment package.* Salt Lake City, UT: New Hats.

DiLeo, D. (2002). *Where did the time go? Transition to adult life.* St. Augustine, FL: Training Resource Network.

Field, S., & Hoffman, A. (1996). *Steps to self-determination: A curriculum to help adolescents learn to achieve their goals.* Austin, TX: PRO-ED.

Flexer, R. W., & Luft, P. (2001). Transition assessment and post-school outcomes. In R. W. Flexer, T. J. Simmons, P. Luft, & R. M. Baer (Eds.), *Transition planning for secondary students with disabilities* (pp. 197–226). Upper Saddle River, NJ: Merrill/Prentice Hall.

Glutting, J. J., & Wilkinson, G. (2003). Wide Range Interest and Occupation Test (2nd ed.). Austin, TX: PRO-ED.

Greene, G., & Kochhar-Bryant, C. A. (2003). *Pathways to successful transition for youth with disabilities.* Upper Saddle River, NJ: Merrill/Prentice Hall.

Griffin, C., & Sherron, P. (1996). Finding jobs for young people with disabilities. In P. Wehman (Ed.), *Life beyond the classroom: Transition strategies for young people with disabilities* (2nd ed., pp. 163–187). Baltimore: Brookes.

Hoffman, A., Field, S., & Sawilowsky, S. (1996). Self-Determination Knowledge Scale. Austin, TX: PRO-ED.

Hoffman, A., Field, S., & Sawilowsky, S. (2004). Self-Determination Assessment Battery and User's Guide. Detroit, MI: College of Education, Wayne State University.

Kohler, P. (1996). *A taxonomy for transition programming: Linking research and practice.* Champaign: University of Illinois, Transition Research Institute.

Loyd, R. J., & Brolin, D. E. (1997). Life Centered Career Education Moderate Curriculum Assessment System. Arlington: VA: Council for Exceptional Children.

Martin, J. E., & Marshall, L. H. (1996). The Choice-Maker Self-Determination Assessment. Longmont, CO: Sopris West.

McAlonan, S. J. (1993). *The Colorado transition manual.* Denver, CO: Colorado Department of Education.

McLoughlin, J. A., & Lewis, R. B. (2005). *Assessing students with special needs* (6th ed.). Upper Saddle River, NJ: Merrill/Prentice Hall.

National Information Center for Children and Youth with Disabilities. (1993). *Transition services in the IEP.* Retrieved January 23, 2004, from http://www.nichcy.org/pubs/outprint/ts8txt.htm.

North Dakota Transition Project. (1995). *Bridging the gap: Charting a successful transition from school to living and working independently within the community: North Dakota transition guide.* Minot, ND: Minot State University.

Owens L., & Blanchett, W. J. (2004, April). *Providing culturally relevant transition planning for students with disabilities: Perceptions of general and special education teachers.* Paper presented at the annual conference of the Council for Exceptional Children, New Orleans, LA.

Pocock, A., Lambros, S., Karvonen, M., Test, D. W., Algozzine, B., Wood, W., et al. (2002). Successful strategies for promoting self-advocacy among students with LD: The LEAD group. *Intervention in School and Clinic, 37,* 209–216.

President's Commission on Excellence in Special Education. (2002). *A new era: Revitalizing special education for children and their families.* Jessup, MD: U.S. Department of Education.

Sitlington, P. L., & Clark, G. M. (2001). Career/vocational assessment: A critical component of transition planning. *Assessment for Effective Intervention, 26*(4), 5–22.

Sitlington, P. L., Neubert, D. A., & Leconte, P. J. (1997). Transition assessment: The position of the Division on Career Development and Transition. *Career Development for Exceptional Individuals, 20,* 69–79.

Stephens, T. M. (1977). *Teaching skills to students with learning and behavioral disorders.* Upper Saddle River, NJ: Merrill/Prentice Hall.

Strong, E. K., Campbell, D. P., Harmon, L. W., Hansen, J. I. C., Borgen, F. H., & Hammer, A. L. (1994). Strong Interest Inventory. Palo Alto, CA: Consulting Psychologists Press.

Talent Assessment, Inc. (2000). Digital Pictorial Inventory of Careers. Jacksonville, FL: Author.

Test, D. W., Fowler, C. H., Wood, W. M., Brewer, D. M., & Eddy, S. (2005). A conceptual framework of self-advocacy for students with disabilities. *Remedial and Special Education, 26,* 43–54.

Thoma, C. A., Held, M. F., & Saddler, S. (2002). Transition assessment practices in Nevada and Arizona: Are they tied to best practices? *Focus on Autism and Other Developmental Disabilities, 17,* 242–250.

Wehmeyer, M. L., & Kelchner, K. (1995). The Arc's Self-Determination Scale. Arlington, TX: The Arc.

Wolman, J. M., Campeau, P. L., DuBois, P. A., Mithaug, D. E., & Stolarski, V. S. (1994). AIR Self-Determination Scale. Washington, DC: American Institutes of Research.

Planning for Transition

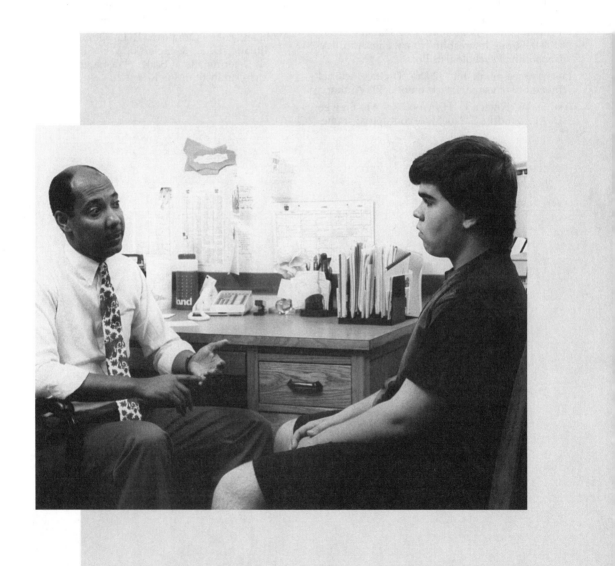

Chapter 4

Introduction

Student-focused planning, a component of Kohler's Taxonomy of Transition Programming, encourages the development of postschool outcomes that are based on student choice and input, thus increasing the likelihood of a productive and satisfying life after graduation. This process can be improved through student-focused planning that ensures family involvement, interagency collaboration, and the development of self-determination skills (Kohler, Field, Izzo, & Johnson, 1997).

This chapter is designed to assist educators in understanding this process. It explains how the transition mandates of the Individuals with Disabilities Education Act (IDEA) apply to a realistic and achievable transition component of a student's individualized education program (IEP). Emphasis is placed on meeting the spirit of the mandates for interagency collaboration and student and parent involvement, particularly in the areas of self-determination and person-centered planning. The chapter also provides strategies for overcoming common challenges. Case studies show how the transition planning process differs for various students based on their disabilities and their postschool goals.

Key Terms

postschool goals
transition planning process
transition component of the IEP
transition activities
age of majority
person-centered planning

A Personal Perspective on Transition Planning

Freda M. Lee

Exceptional Children Division, North Carolina
Department of Public Instruction

Every day I read new journal articles and research studies that highlight the need for comprehensive transition planning for students with disabilities, but, unfortunately, they only tell a small part of a very complex story. To truly understand why comprehensive transition planning is so important, you need to talk with students and their families on a personal level. As the state-level consultant for transition in North Carolina, I have had the opportunity to listen as parents share their concerns and fears about their sons' and daughters' future. Their concerns are the same concerns all parents have. They want their sons and daughters to live rich, full lives and be contributing members of society. To accomplish this goal, many students with disabilities must overcome challenges that sometimes appear to be insurmountable and often are exacerbated by systems that place even more obstacles in their way.

At the state level, the obstacles come in the form of stringent graduation standards, curricula that are academically rigorous, and accountability measures that may be very narrow and rigid. The obstacles cited are not inherently bad for students with disabilities; they promote inclusion and ensure that high expectations are held for all students. The big challenge for educators is striking a balance between the need to provide an educational experience for students with disabilities that meets their unique needs while still preparing them to meet the demands of society.

The transition needs of most students with disabilities can be met by providing access to the general curriculum, comprehensive school and career counseling, opportunities to participate in career-technical education and individualized education programs (IEPs) that thoroughly address transition issues. However, for a small number of students with disabilities these things are not enough; they need a curriculum framework that focuses on applied academics and acquisition of work-related skills before exiting high school. To meet this need in North Carolina, a new transition-focused curriculum framework was developed that requires students to participate in community-based vocational training and paid competitive employment in an integrated setting while still in high school. The new course of study is referred to as the occupational course of study (OCS). The OCS is one of four courses of study students with disabilities may choose to follow that lead to a high school diploma recognized by the state.

The implementation of the new course of study has required extensive systems change, and it has not always been easy for local school systems. They have had to deal with increased transportation costs, the need for better interagency collaboration, staffing shortages, parental concerns, and a fluctuating unemployment rate. The big question is, Has it all been worth it?

Three recent OCS graduates who addressed the North Carolina State Board of Education in July of 2004 answered this question quite eloquently. The students shared with the Board transition activities that they had participated in and told about their plans for the future. One student, with support from the Department of Vocational Rehabilitation, is starting her own business, and the other two are competitively employed and thinking positively about the future. In fact, one student said, "I feel like I am driving off into the future and there are no brakes on my car and nothing to stop me."

As a career educator, I can think of nothing more important for all students than comprehensive transition planning that emphasizes self-determination, problem solving, and career planning. As we all know, sometimes there are bumps in the road and we will need to apply brakes and navigate around them. Good transition planning provides students an internal roadmap to use when they have to make a detour or apply the brakes. The positive outcomes of these three students exemplify what can happen when students, parents, and professionals work together to plan for the future.

Comprehensive transition planning is the vehicle that ensures that each student reaches his or her **postschool goals.** The final outcome of this planning process should be a life that includes employment, postsecondary education, a place to live, community involvement, financial stability, transportation, and ample medical services (Virginia Commonwealth University Rehabilitation Research and Training Center on Supported Employment, 1994). To achieve this result, the transition planning process should begin with helping students determine their desired postschool goals.

DETERMINING POSTSCHOOL GOALS AND COURSE OF STUDY

The **transition planning process** assists students and their families in establishing long-range goals and making the service connections necessary to accomplish these goals. Students must be assisted in developing the self-determination skills needed to fulfill their role as a key member of the transition team. A well-organized transition team that is student focused must play a primary role in supporting the delivery of transition services if meaningful change is to occur in the student's life (Blalock, 1996).

Beginning Early

Since 1990 local education agencies have had the primary responsibility for coordinating all aspects of the transition planning process. When transition services were first mandated in 1990, special educators were required to begin transition planning with students no later than age 16 but were encouraged to begin earlier. The 1997 Individuals with Disabilities Education Act amendments (IDEA 1997) changed the minimum age for beginning the transition process to age 14, with the provision that services could still begin earlier if needed.

With the reauthorization of IDEA in 2004 as the Individuals with Disabilities Education Improvement Act, school systems are now directed to ensure that transition services are in place by the time a student reaches his or her 16th birthday, requiring that a transition component be added no later than the first IEP in effect when the child turns 16. IDEA 2004 requires that IEPs for this age group include "appropriate measurable postsecondary goals based upon age appropriate transition assessments related to training, education, employment, and where appropriate, independent living skills." In addition "the transition services (including courses of study) needed to assist the child in reach these goals" must also be addressed (Section 614, (D) (1) (A) (VIII) (aa-bb)).

Although the age at which transition must be addressed has been raised, it is important that special educators realize that nothing in IDEA 2004 precludes beginning transition services for a student earlier than age 16 if needed. In some cases age 16 will be too late to begin the transition planning process. Students who are at high risk for dropping out of school, have significant disabilities, need extensive vocational training, are pregnant or parenting, have unstable home situations, are involved in the juvenile justice system, or otherwise require the involvement of multiple adult service agencies need to have comprehensive transition components developed and agency linkages established beginning at age 14 or younger. As discussed in Chapter 3, each student should be assessed individually to determine the appropriate time to initiate the transition planning process. The final decision regarding when to develop a full transition component for a student younger than age 16 is left up to the IEP team, but it can be expected that some students will need the process to begin prior to the minimum age required by law.

Beginning the transition planning process early can be considered best practice for a large portion of students with disabilities. By beginning early to determine realistic postschool goals, educators can ensure that students have the opportunity to access curriculum and participate in community experiences to develop the skills needed for future environments. Also, early planning increases the time that students and their families have to familiarize themselves with and develop relationships with the adult service system (Center on Community Living and Careers, 2003).

Beginning by Age 16

At this point in a student's educational career, he or she should be assisted in determining postschool goals along with an appropriate course of study, specific transition services, and the adult service linkages needed to support the student's efforts to achieve postschool plans for employment, education, and community participation.

Since 16-year-olds who are on target to graduate at age 18 are only 2 years from completing high school, and the students who will remain in school until age 21 are often those with the most significant disabilities requiring multiple service linkages, it is important for IEP teams to have a clear focus regarding the child's future as soon as possible. Establishing clear and realistic postschool goals matching student strengths, needs, and interests that are supported by a comprehensive course of study and a broad array of transition activities can help make the best use of the time available for service delivery.

Understanding the Vision: Postschool Goals

Regardless of when the transition planning process begins, all involved parties need to understand the student's postschool vision. Postschool goals can articulate this vision and help paint a mental image of where the student wants to work, live, and learn and the types of community activities in which the student will be involved. A comprehensive transition planning process requires that everyone become a detective, willing to ask the questions that will uncover the essence of the vision for the student's life after graduation. Questions should focus on the student's present abilities, needs, and interests, available services both on the school campus and in the community, and what is needed to assist the student in getting from where he or she is now to where he or she needs to be at graduation. School personnel should not hesitate to dig deep for the information even if the answers uncover the school's need to change service delivery strategies, add additional services, or try new ideas. Figure 4.1 lists examples of questions that could be asked of the student and family members to ensure that the transition process is truly student driven.

1. What is the student's dream job? If the student does not have a specific career interest, what transition activities are needed to assist the student with career awareness and determining vocational interests?
2. If the student could live anywhere, with anyone, in any residential setting, what would his or her first choice be?
3. What are the student's strengths and capabilities? How have these assets been used in the educational setting? What can be done to ensure that the student's skills are used to increase future success?
4. What type of exit document does the student desire, and which course of study best matches the student's postschool plans? If necessary, is the student willing to remain in school past the age of 18 to complete a specific course of study?
5. In what types of extracurricular activities and community activities is the student participating? What can be done to facilitate greater involvement in activities related to the student's future goals?
6. What barriers might hinder the student's achievement of postschool goals? What solutions are there to these barriers, and how can they be implemented effectively?
7. What types of accommodations and modifications will be needed to ensure that the student achieves a high level of success?
8. What types of personal resources and natural supports (e.g., transportation, job leads, adaptive equipment) does the student have access to that might assist in accomplishing postschool goals? (deFur, 2000; Morningstar, 1995).

Figure 4.1
Examples of Questions to Ensure a Student-Driven Transition Planning Process

IDEA 2004 requires that all transition services be designed

"within a results-oriented process, that is focused on improving the academic and functional achievement of the child with a disability to facilitate the child's movement from school to postschool activities, including postsecondary education, vocational education, integrated employment (including supported employment), continuing and adult education, adult services, independent living, or community participation (Section 602(34) (A)).

The postschool areas noted in IDEA can be consolidated into four domains:

1. *Employment* (integrated employment including supported employment);
2. *Postsecondary education* (continuing and adult education/vocational education);
3. *Residential* (independent living); and
4. *Community participation* (adult services).

Postschool goals describe the student's desired status after graduation and should be developed prior to any other component of the IEP. The outcome goals should drive the development of the IEP through a backward planning process. Beginning with the student's postschool goals ensures that the remainder of the IEP supports the student's desires regarding life after graduation (Flexer, Simmons, Luft, & Baer, 2001). Transition planning requires teams to plan several years ahead—a much broader vision for student achievement than looking at a single school year (deFur, 1999).

Postschool outcomes should reflect high but realistic expectations for student achievement. Students who have been involved in an appropriate course of study, community experiences, and self-determination training will have the self-knowledge needed to understand their abilities and limitations. Most adolescents struggle with future career decisions, and it is the responsibility of parents/guardians and transition staff to assist them in holding onto their dreams while establishing attainable postschool goals.

Initially postschool goals may be less specific, increasing in detail as students move closer to graduation. In all cases, goals should reflect measurable outcomes so that a child's progress toward accomplishing post-high-school plans can be accurately determined. A measurable postschool goal can assist team members in making needed adjustments in the quality or quantity of transition activities in which the student is involved if the student is not making progress.

The chances of developing achievable postschool goals can be increased if students are supported in exploring their interests and abilities through vocational education, academic coursework, community participation, and career awareness activities. The greater the range of experiences, the more prepared a student will be to make decisions about the future. Failure to provide such support can result in a student's not receiving the transition services needed by the conclusion of high school, resulting in a period of instability after graduation.

Students and those supporting them in transition planning must be aware that postschool outcomes will change from year to year as they mature and gain additional knowledge. Sometimes postschool goals can change drastically for a student due to unexpected events. A student planning to live at home and attend a local university may receive a scholarship and decide to attend a university away from home, thus needing skills required for dorm life. A student who plans to live at home may have to pursue a group home placement due to the sudden illness of an elderly caregiver. The process of transition planning must be flexible enough to accommodate students' expected and unexpected changing desires, needs, situations, and dreams.

DETERMINING A COURSE OF STUDY

Once postschool goals are determined, students must be assisted in choosing a course of study that best matches their future plans. Course-of-study descriptions should be clear enough so that all parties involved understand the specific courses that are being recommended along with the sequence in which these courses should be completed. Since failure to see the relevance of high school coursework to future goals can be a contributing factor in dropping out of school, clearly aligning a course of study with future goals can motivate a student to obtain a high school diploma.

Pathways to a high school diploma are often preestablished, and students should be guided in choosing the pathway that best meets their abilities, interests, and future dreams. Care should be taken to ensure that students are encouraged to pursue a rigorous course of study that results in obtaining a viable high school exit document. All planning documents required for general education students (e.g., career development plans, 4-year plans) should also be used when determining the transition needs of students with disabilities in order to ensure alignment of these documents with the **transition component of the IEP.** Once postschool goals are developed and a course of study is chosen, the IEP team must look at what will be needed to encourage and support the student in achieving his or her goals for life after graduation.

DETERMINING TRANSITION ACTIVITIES

Postschool outcome goals comprise major life accomplishments or milestones, and a wide range of activities must be provided to ensure their accomplishment. IDEA 2004 requires that these transition activities be delivered in a coordinated fashion and states that it be:

> based on the individual child's needs; taking into account the student's strengths preferences and interests; and includes instruction, related services, community experiences, the development of employment and other post-school adult living objectives, and when appropriate, the acquisition of daily living skills and functional vocational evaluation. (Section 602 (34) (B-C))

What Transition Activities Are

Transition activities are the steps leading to accomplishing postschool goals. An array of activities and services must be planned and implemented for each postschool goal. Some students will not need activities in all postschool goal areas, but it is important that the IEP team thoroughly evaluate each student's desired goals to ensure that all necessary activities are provided. Since the school's legal responsibility for a student ends when the student exits from high school, all transition activities should be planned to ensure their completion by the time of graduation. Any support that will be needed after graduation should be clearly indicated as a responsibility of the appropriate adult service provider. Beginning with postschool goals, the IEP team should assist the student in outlining the steps from the goals back to the present to determine what activities need to occur before graduation.

Categories of Transition Activities

IDEA 2004 indicates the areas of transition activities that should be considered, including instruction, related services, community experiences, employment, postschool adult living activities, and, if needed, daily living skills, as well as functional vocational evaluation. More than likely, these activities will be linked to more than one of the student's postschool goals. IDEA does not provide definitions for the various categories of transition activities, allowing greater latitude and fewer boundaries in the transition planning process. Storms, O'Leary, and Williams (2000) have provided descriptions for each of the categories that can be helpful in explaining the areas to transition team planning members who may not be familiar with some of the terminology.

Instruction.   Instruction involves formal strategies designed to teach a skill or set of skills. Instruction can be provided in school through a variety of modes (e.g., tutoring, general education classes, career/technical education classes, academic classes) or in other locations by various agencies (e.g., a community college). Transition activities that are instructional in nature can range from assisting a student in attaining high scores on a college entrance exam to improving daily living skills in preparation for living in a supported apartment.

Related Services.   Related services include supportive and therapeutic services and activities that students will need during and after high school to achieve and maintain their goals. This area can include services such as transportation, physical therapy, occupational therapy, rehabilitation counseling, parent counseling and training, orientation and mobility training, and speech therapy. Transition planning teams must not confuse this section of the IEP with the portion that speaks to the delivery of related services within the school environment. It is important to ensure that students receive all necessary related services while in school, but planning must also address needs outside the school environment and postschool needs. Many students and their families will need assistance in connecting with the agencies that will ensure continuation of needed supports throughout adult life.

Community Experiences.   Community experiences provide students the opportunity to practice skills in the actual settings in which they will be used (e.g., vocational education, shopping, transportation, banking, recreation and leisure activities). These activities can be incorporated into a student's curricular experiences or conducted by adult service providers through various training programs during or after school hours.

Employment.   Employment activities prepare a student for a future career. This area incorporates career awareness, career exploration, career preparation, and career assimilation. Employment activities can assist students in choosing appropriate postsecondary training or education or for entering the workforce immediately upon graduation.

Postschool Adult Living Activities.   Adult living activities foster skills needed to function at a high level of independence (e.g., registering to vote, filing insurance claims, obtaining medical care, obtaining legal assistance, buying furniture, renting an apartment). These activities enhance the quality of a student's life as an adult because the skills, although not necessarily used on a daily basis, eliminate the need to rely on others for assistance.

The two areas of transition activities that IDEA 2004 proposes to be applied "when appropriate" are acquisition of daily living skills and functional vocational evaluation. Although some students may appear not to require these activities, transition team members should help students analyze their individual needs to ensure that areas of need are not overlooked.

Daily Living Skills.   Daily living skills involve activities that are required for day-to-day functioning within the home and community. These are activities that are done routinely by self-sufficient adults (e.g., cleaning, bill paying, personal hygiene, home maintenance, cooking, shopping for groceries). Daily living skills can also include activities that will encourage increased independence (e.g., assisting in physical care, self-feeding, assisting with food preparation).

Functional Vocational Evaluation.   The assessment of a student's interests, aptitudes, and vocational skills can help determine appropriate vocational training and educational placements. Vocational evaluation can take many forms, but the key to obtaining a realistic picture of the student is observation in real vocational settings. Since students with disabilities often experience difficulty with traditional forms of assessment or may not have the life experiences necessary to make informed decisions about their interests, it is important to expose them to a variety of real and simulated work environments. Vocational assessment can be performed by school personnel (e.g., special populations coordinators, transition coordinators, guidance counselors) or by outside agencies (e.g., Vocational Rehabilitation, college/university testing services). More information about assessment can be found in Chapter 3.

Transition planning includes the areas that are mandated by IDEA, but care should be taken to include any additional areas critical to a successful adult life.

Areas such as health and medical issues, transportation, and financial planning, although not specifically designated as categories of transition activities under IDEA, should be addressed during the planning process (Everson, Zhang, & Guillory, 2001). For example, learning to make transportation arrangements, use of public transit, or obtaining a driver's license are vital to success in employment, community participation, and postsecondary education. Likewise, accessing medical services and maintaining one's health are considered adult postschool activities that promote a better quality of life.

DID YOU KNOW?

♦ People with disabilities are much more likely than those without disabilities to consider inadequate transportation to be a problem (30% versus 10%, respectively)—a gap of 20 percentage points.

♦ People with disabilities are three times as likely as those without disabilities to not have received necessary health care on at least one occasion in the previous year (19% versus 6%, respectively). Similarly, people with disabilities are much more likely than those without disabilities to postpone or put off seeking needed health care because they cannot afford it (28% versus 12%, respectively; National Organization of Disability, 2000).

GETTING IT DONE

There must be depth and breadth to the planning process. It is not enough to simply list activities and services that are routinely provided or readily available. The transition component must contain activities specific to the postschool goals of the individual student. Those involved in transition planning must be willing to brainstorm, problem solve, and make arrangements for services that typically might not be considered. In a study conducted by McGill and Vogtle (2001), it was discovered that although students with physical disabilities felt that learning to drive would increase their independence and life choices, participation in high school driver's education classes often was not even presented as an option. Those involved in planning must avoid limiting options and access to services even if a student desires to participate in something in which students with disabilities have not traditionally been involved. Systems change within a school system can result by illuminating student needs that are not being met and offering options for meeting these needs. The availability of options and opportunities can increase the achievement and stability of postschool goals (Lindstrom & Benz, 2002).

There may be cases when a student does not need services in one of the transition domains. This is usually the result of the student's possessing all the skills and/or having access to all the postschool resources needed to accomplish his or her postschool goals. IDEA '97 removed the requirement that the IEP contain a justification statement for any transition domain that was not addressed; however, it is still imperative that the IEP team consider all areas to ensure that the final plan is comprehensive.

Think Outside the Box

Transition activities can and should occur in a variety of environments, including those in which the student will be expected to function after graduation. These environments can include the school campus, vocational training sites, adult living skill training sites, postsecondary campuses, home, and local neighborhoods. Within each of these settings there will be various individuals, including school staff, family members, adult service providers, friends, and employers, who will oversee the implementation of the transition activities. To ensure coordination, a single activity may be the responsibility of more than one person or agency. This requires that care be taken when assigning responsible persons for each transition activity.

Although students should be given multiple opportunities to demonstrate their independence, school personnel and adult service providers should not make assumptions about a student's ability that result in a lack of follow-through. Members of the transition team must strive to balance the need for student independence with comprehensive service delivery. In situations in which a student lacks emotional and financial support, closer monitoring of the implementation of the transition plan may be needed (Taylor-Ritzler et al., 2001).

Consider Timelines

When selecting transition activities, the time span needed for completion should be considered and each activity should designate the date by which the activity will be accomplished. Some activities will involve a one-time event while others might continue over several months or throughout an entire school year. The complexity of activities will determine the amount of time needed for planning and implementation.

Provide Students with Multiple Experiences

Determining the activities needed to accomplish a student's postschool goals requires input from a variety of individuals over a number of years. During the early phases, the activities may serve as a means of assisting students in finalizing their plans for life after graduation. For example, students must have the opportunity to refine their interests and experiment with matching their abilities and desires to various career pathways (McBride & Stitt-Godhes, 1994). By choosing appropriate employment-related transition activities, students can be exposed to an array of services and experiences needed to finalize their postschool employment goals. The same is true in all domains of transition planning. Students cannot be expected to make informed decisions regarding where they want to live, postsecondary education, or other community activities unless they have the experience upon which to base these decisions.

One of the keys to successful transition planning is to ensure the availability of a wide range of activities that are individualized to each student's specific needs and desires. Figure 4.2 provides examples of various transition activities that are relevant to the domains of employment, residential living, postsecondary education, and community participation. While Figure 4.2 lists transition activities for middle school and high school students, it is never too early to start preparing students for the transition planning process. Therefore, Figure 4.3 lists some activities that can be done by both teachers and families that will help younger students be better prepared to participate in their transition from school to adult life.

Get Students Involved

Students, parents, and adult service providers can increase the quality of the transition component dramatically through effective involvement. Regulatory guidelines for the implementation of IDEA mandates have been clear regarding the intent for students upon reaching transition age to be actively involved in developing their IEPs. Professional organizations recommend that the previous regulations in the area of student involvement be retained and strengthened in this area. It is best practice for students to both attend their team meetings and be a contributing member of the team using self-determination skills obtained through guided instruction and practice (Division on Career Development and Transition, 2005).

Age of Majority.   IDEA also recognizes that most students will reach the **age of majority** while in high school and requires schools to notify students and their parents or guardians of the impending transfer of rights:

> Beginning not later than one year before a student reaches the age of majority under State law, a statement that the child has been informed of the child's rights under this title, if any, that will transfer to the child on reaching the age of majority. (Section 614 [VIII] [CC])

Educational rights that transfer to a student at the age of majority include those related to educational placement, evaluation, programming, mediation, and due process. Exceptions for transferring all rights to a child upon reaching the age of majority can be made if the child is not capable of making informed decisions regarding his or her education.

Postsecondary Education

- Referral to Vocational Rehabilitation for tuition assistance
- Assistance with applications/financial aid forms
- Assistance with selecting an educational institution
- Assistance in understanding the criteria for admission and deadlines for application
- Contacting the student support services personnel at a college and learning about services for students with special needs
- Effectively expressing limitations and needs
- Information about civil rights, confidentiality, and personal rights as they relate to postsecondary education
- Training in budgeting skills
- Remedial classes in academic areas
- Information about residential options for postsecondary education
- Visits to campus(es)
- Arranging transportation to postsecondary education
- Preparation for college admission tests
- Assistance in arranging for accommodations/modifications for admission tests
- Self-advocacy training
- Study skills training
- Test-taking skills training

Employment

- Off-campus vocational experiences (e.g., job shadowing, paid community-based training)
- On-campus vocational experiences (e.g., school-based enterprise, small business, on-campus jobs)
- Vocational education courses
- Workforce Investment Act (WIA)-related activities (e.g., work experience, summer employment, leadership training, mentoring)
- Work adjustment activities
- Referral to Vocational Rehabilitation for supported employment services
- Referral to state Medicaid waiver program
- Referral to Mental Health for case management services
- Establishment of case management services for long-term follow-up through Medicaid reimbursement for supported employment
- Training in job-seeking skills
- Training in job-maintenance skills
- Training in employment-related social skills
- Vocational training in the skills required for a specific vocational area
- Work behavior and work habit training
- Registration at Employment Security Commission
- Vocational evaluation/assessment
- Assistance in understanding the results of vocational evaluations/assessments

(continued)

Figure 4.2
Examples of Transition Activities by Domains

- Assistance in understanding work-related forms/paperwork
- Training in functional academic skills related to employment settings
- Self-advocacy skills
- Career counseling
- Establishment of natural supports on the job site
- Training in employment-related laws and legislation related to persons with disabilities
- Training in employment goal setting
- Plan for Achieving Self-Support (PASS) or Impairment-Related Work Expenses (IRWE) development and approval
- Transportation arrangements
- Tour of a technical school
- Attendance at a job fair

Residential (Independent Living)

- Assistance in understanding social security benefits
- Training in clothing care
- Training in household maintenance (e.g., cleaning, simple repairs, contacting a repairman)
- Cooking skills training
- Menu planning
- Training in money-related skills (e.g., opening a bank account and using banking services, budgeting, comparison shopping, checkbook management, use of coupons, credit and loans, purchasing major items, paying bills)
- Yard care
- Simple first-aid training
- Training in obtaining medical/health care services
- Training in budgeting skills
- Choosing a financial institution that meets personal financial needs
- Community service use training
- Telephone usage training
- Touring residential living options
- Referral to Mental Health for assistance in locating residential placement
- Learning about criteria for subsidized housing

Community Participation (Recreation)

- Taking community-based classes in a hobby or area of special interest
- Exposure to and training in community recreational activities
- Assistance in enrolling/joining community recreational organization
- Social skills training
- Training in social amenities
- Arranging for a recreation buddy
- Training in budgeting for recreation and leisure activities
- Training in how to make and keep friends

Figure 4.2
Continued

- Evaluating personal recreational interests
- Participating in school sports
- Joining a community sports team
- Participating in a church-related activity
- Administering recreational/leisure assessments and surveys
- Joining a hobby club
- Joining the YMCA
- Touring community recreation sites

Figure 4.2
Continued

Sources: Aspel, 1997; Fairfax County Public Schools, 1998.

Making Informed Decisions.   Making an informed decision requires the ability to consider multiple options and understand the consequences of various decisions, ultimately making a decision after synthesizing and analyzing all available information. The legal transfer of rights to students is a huge step in empowering students in their planning process. However, some students are not able to participate fully in the process due to the severity of their cognitive or emotional disabilities. IDEA recognizes this possibility and includes measures to ensure that the student's best interests will be protected. If a student has been declared incompetent through the court system, a guardian is appointed to make decisions for the individual. In some cases an individual under limited guardianship may maintain certain rights. In the case of limited guardianship, it is important for the school staff to obtain a copy of the guardianship papers and determine the extent to which the student will legally be involved in the educational decision-making process.

Some students, although they have not legally been declared incompetent, will exhibit such severe cognitive or emotional disabilities that they will be unable to participate meaningfully in making educational decisions. In these instances, IDEA allows school systems to appoint someone (often a parent or relative) to act in the best interest of the student when educational decisions and plans are being made.

School systems should use the age-of-majority ruling to adopt a philosophy that promotes self-determination instruction beginning in elementary school. If a school system meets only the requirement of notification without proper education, family members may become worried that their decision-making authority will be undermined. Parents and students must be prepared far in advance for the transfer of rights in order to prevent parents from seeking unnecessary guardianship or misunderstanding their role as a partner in the transition planning process (Lindsey, Wehmeyer, Guy, & Martin, 2001).

Why Student Involvement Is Important.   It is best practice for students to be active members of their IEP team to ensure that the transition component accurately reflects their abilities, preferences, and interests. Previous IDEA regulations have

- Begin as early as possible to assist students in thinking about life after graduation by teaching self-determination, social skills, academic skills, and daily living skills beginning in elementary school.
- Help students develop an understanding of their disability and the impact it may have on adult life.
- Show students their educational records and provide guidance in understanding the forms and terminology. Educate students about legal rights in the areas of special education, vocational education, postsecondary education, employment, and the adult service system.
- Teach specific skills related to student participation in the IEP process.
- Teach students how to set goals and objectives. Develop a personal action plan that allows students to see the connection between setting long-range goals and following a plan to achieve those goals (e.g., planning a party, learning a new hobby).
- Bring in as guest speakers older students or young adults with disabilities who have been successful in accomplishing their postschool goals.

Figure 4.3
Activities That Prepare Younger Students for the Transition Planning Process

Sources: ERIC/OSEP, 2000; Warger & Burnette, 2000.

reinforced this practice with requirements for student attendance at IEP meetings and the consideration of student interests, preferences, needs, and abilities in developing all transition components. A student's absence at the IEP meeting when transition is to be discussed should be a rare occurrence. Even if a student must miss the IEP team meeting, measures should be taken to ensure that the student's input is considered.

Wehmeyer, Palmer, Agran, Mithaug, and Martin (2000) recommended that student involvement in transition planning include focused, student-directed instruction involving problem solving, goal setting, decision making, self-advocacy, and opportunities to direct planning meetings. If postschool goals are to be achieved, each goal must focus on the desires of student and family and not simply be a reflection of what the professionals think is best (Wehman, 1992).

Involving Students in Team Meetings.   Inviting the student by extending a separate invitation to the IEP meeting encourages the student's presence during transition planning. However, simply inviting the student to attend does not guarantee active involvement and may not even guarantee attendance. The first step toward meeting the spirit of the law is ensuring that students are self-determined. Without sufficient self-determination skills it is very difficult for students to overcome fears and speak up for themselves regarding what they want in life and what is needed to get there.

Special educators must first work with students to ensure that they understand the importance of attending meetings. Fostering of this awareness should begin prior to high school by educating students about the importance of future

DID YOU KNOW?

In a study of nearly 5,000 adults with mental retardation, Wehmeyer and Metzler (1995) found that

◆ Only 6.3% indicated they had a choice in where they lived.

◆ Only 9.4% indicated they had chosen their roommate.

◆ Only 11.3% indicated they had selected where they worked or their daytime activities.

---

planning. Students should understand their role as a consumer of services and the school's responsibility in assisting them in achieving postschool dreams. If needed, a school system should put supports in place such as providing transportation to the meeting or offering incentives for student attendance and active participation.

The presence of the student at meetings will assist team members in staying focused and allow adult service providers to become familiar with the student, thereby increasing the soundness of decisions concerning current and future service delivery. Effective transition planning can come about only if a student leads his or her transition planning team meetings or at the very least is a contributing member of the team. Countryman and Schroeder (1996) discovered that family members had a better understanding of their child's abilities and interests when school conferences and meetings were student led.

Self-determination training should begin at an early age, with opportunities for students to learn about their personal traits (e.g., learning styles, abilities, interests, needed accommodations, modifications, future life-style preferences, natural supports) in order to ensure their readiness for participation in transition planning by the time they reach high school. For more information on commercial self-determination curricula that can be used to provide direct instruction to students in the area of self-determination, visit www.uncc.edu/sdsp. In addition, examples of *PowerPoint* presentations used by students to lead their IEP meetings, as well as teacher training materials, are available at www.studentledieps.org.

Helping Students Guide Their Futures. To make informed decisions, students must have an understanding of what they want and need in life. As discussed in Chapter 3, self-awareness can be enhanced through transition assessment.

The goal for all students is to ensure that transition planning decisions are truly based on their desires and interests even if they are not able to communicate this information through traditional means. Life experiences are also important to students when making decisions related to their future. Both parents and school personnel should provide exploratory activities in the home and community that will provide a base of experience upon which to make decisions regarding a future career and life-style.

Making clear to students the importance of transition planning to their future is also necessary. A commitment should be obtained from each student to participate in all transition planning activities. This commitment may be verbal or may even involve a written statement. Students also must be taught about how the transition process works, including how and when meetings are conducted, possible team members, what IDEA mandates, their individual rights, and available services. Prior to actual participation in a transition planning meeting, students should be given multiple opportunities (i.e., small-group activities and role playing) to identify appropriate postschool goals and to practice expressing these goals, requesting services, and discussing their personal traits.

A student's participation can be hampered by fear of the unknown or an intimidating situation, so it is helpful if the student can actually observe another student's meeting, watch a videotape of a meeting prior to attending for the first time, and/or meet the members who will be in attendance. It is also helpful for students to spend time with transition professionals in activities such as completing transition surveys, interviews, and/or dream sheets. A sample of a student dream sheet can be found in Figure 3.4.

Test and colleagues (2004) conducted a review of the literature to investigate interventions designed to increase students' involvement in their IEP process. Their findings suggested that students with widely varying abilities could be actively involved in the IEP process. Results also indicated that both published curricula designed to teach students skills to enhance their participation prior to IEP meetings and person-centered planning strategies are effective in increasing students' involvement in their IEP meetings.

Encourage Others to Support Student Participation

The level of student participation in transition meetings can also be enhanced or hindered by the actions of team members (Timmons & Whitney-Thomas, 1998; Whitney-Thomas & Timmons, 1998). Members should receive training in encouraging behaviors and actions that can facilitate a greater comfort level for the student while establishing an atmosphere of openness and acceptance. For example, team members should take care to talk *to* the student rather than *about* the student, directing comments, suggestions, and questions to the student even if he or she has limited communication skills. This may be a change for many adult service providers who are used to "staffing" clients who may not be present at the meetings and for special educators who are used to holding dialogues with parents or guardians.

Team meetings should be conducted in a manner that is flexible enough to accommodate a wide range of communication levels and modes. Team members should refrain from using professional jargon or making assumptions about the comprehension level of the student. Students may need to use an augmentative communication device, be assisted by an interpreter, have statements clarified, be given additional time to respond to questions, or be prompted to participate in team discussions.

During transition planning it is imperative that students feel that their desires and dreams are being taken into consideration and that their opinions are valued. Team members should ensure that student input is not met with negativity or disdain even if students' suggestions appear unrealistic. It is the team members' responsibility to guide and assist students in achieving their postschool goals even if these goals are not what the team members would have chosen. No decision or conclusion should be reached during the transition planning that does not receive the student's approval. In the end, ensuring student involvement will pay off in increased commitment by the students to accomplishing their postschool goals and a greater awareness of the final vision—independent and productive involvement in the community after graduation.

Get Parents Involved.   Although the student is the focus of all transition-related activities, the parent is also a vital player (Hanley-Maxwell, Pogoloff, & Whitney-Thomas, 1998; Wehmeyer, Morningstar, & Husted, 1999). Federal regulations have long required parent participation in the IEP process, but if the purpose of the meeting is to discuss transition issues, the parent invitation should indicate this purpose, the adult service agencies that will be invited, and the student's involvement. Of course, long before the student's parents receive an invitation to a transition meeting, educators should have provided information to them concerning laws, transition planning, adult services, promising practices, goal setting, advocacy, and any other information relevant to their child's transition needs.

Successful transition is dependent on the support network available to the student after graduation. Since many students, with and without disabilities, are often dependent on their families for emotional and financial support, getting parental input into the transition planning process increases the chances of future success. Parents who participate in transition planning prior to graduation will be better equipped to assist their sons and daughters in navigating the adult service provider system after graduation. For example, after graduation a student might not qualify for the level of services provided while he or she was in school, and therefore parents would be required to help with tasks such as case management (Thorin & Irvin, 1992).

DID YOU KNOW?

In a study conducted by Salembier and Furney (1997):

♦ 30% of parents interviewed "didn't like" or "really didn't like" their level of participation in IEP/transition planning meetings.

♦ 69% reported listening more than talking during meetings.

♦ 40% indicated that their son's or daughter's plans did not reflect individual interests and needs.

Importance of Parent Participation. Parental support can facilitate a smooth transition to adult life by encouraging good school attendance, increased academic achievement, and high self-esteem. The information parents possess about their sons and daughters (e.g., abilities and skills in environments outside the school, natural supports, likes and dislikes, social skills in the community) can increase the chances of a good match between students and their postschool goals (Furney, Hasazi, & DeStefano, 1997; Solembier & Furney, 1998; Wittenstein, 1993), and the influence parents possess can assist in the accomplishment of these goals.

Parents can serve as powerful role models for work ethic, community involvement, and good citizenship. Parents can also provide the stable and secure environment needed as their young adult practices advocacy skills, takes risks, tries out new things, makes mistakes, and even flounders a bit before settling on a definitive life path. Parents who serve as active and knowledgeable participants in the transition process can advance their son's or daughter's progress toward postschool goals, often more effectively than school personnel, due to their history and relationship with their child.

Ensuring Active Parent Participation. Parent involvement can be enhanced through trusting, caring, and open relationships. Educators must spend time with family members formally and informally discussing the desired vision they have for their young adult. Taking the time to assist family members in understanding high school curricular options, adult services the student can access, educational, vocational and rehabilitation laws and regulations, transition terminology, the transition planning process, and advocacy strategies can enhance communication with the family during the transition planning process (Salembier & Furney, 1997). Although parent education is vital to ensuring effective participation, a national survey administered by Johnson and Sharpe (2000) to special education administrators across the nation indicated that 76% of the respondents reported that they did not provide formal parent workshops. Parents must be assisted in comprehending the full range of possibilities for their child. It is helpful to pair them with other parents whose children have had successful transition experiences so success stories can be shared and fears alleviated.

Just as the students, family members must be made to feel that they are full partners in the transition planning process. All team members should understand the importance of effective family involvement and exhibit behaviors and attitudes that sincerely convey the value placed on family participation. Team members should be open to family involvement in transition team meeting agenda setting, implementation of transition activities, and measures that ensure the inclusion of family members in all communications that normally occur between team members.

The quality of the relationship between service providers and family members can be a key factor in the quantity and quality of family involvement. deFur, Todd-Allen, and Getzel (2001) reported that families view the transition experience as more positive if service providers take the time to understand the family dynamics and culture, become personally involved, and share information freely. Family members desire a collaborative partnership, but they view issues related to bureaucracy, cultural differences, trust, equality, and attitudes as barriers to participation in transition planning activities.

The entire transition process will be smoother if both parents and students are prepared early for the future. Parents can have an enormous impact on their children through their actions and words. During the early years of development, parents can begin to talk with the student about his or her future, model a good work ethic, assist the student in learning about the jobs of family members, and encourage risk taking appropriate to the student's future dreams. Even in the best of situations, however, the transition years require changes not only for the student but also for the family, and both educators and outside agencies should be available to provide the resources and emotional support needed so that families can be equipped to handle the changes. Educators must be sensitive to the family situation and take into consideration the family's needs when facilitating involvement in the transition planning process (deFur et al., 2001).

Get Agencies Involved.   By now it should be clear that school systems cannot conduct effective transition planning without the involvement of students and families. But school systems also need the support and assistance of the adult service system. The magnitude, intricacy, and complexity of transition require educators to look outside the school system for assistance in ensuring that all students' transition needs are met. Invitations to IEP meetings at which transition is going to be discussed should be extended to any agency or individual who can be expected to be involved in assisting in the delivery of transition services. It is important for students and their parents to be properly informed of adult services and supports so that they can assist in deciding which representatives should attend transition meetings.

Even if adult service providers are included at team meetings and indicate their willingness to deliver services, there may be incidences when agencies do not follow through with commitments. In these situations special educators should be prepared to make other plans to ensure that students receive needed services to accomplish their postschool goals. This may require reconvening the IEP team to discuss alternative options for obtaining services for the high school and post-high-school years. Adult service agencies should not be relieved of the responsibility for delivering services if a student meets eligibility guidelines simply because of the school system involvement in the transition process.

The collaboration and coordination of service delivery between the school system and adult service providers is important if service integration is to occur. Students can receive a greater benefit from the transition service delivery process if there is an array of service providers involved in planning and implementing transition activities (see Chapters 1 and 5).

Bringing all parties together for transition planning will assist in obtaining information needed to develop a realistic and comprehensive IEP. This information

---

Strategies for Effective Family Involvement

Parents should be encouraged to:

♦ Involve the child in household chores and allow the child to take responsibility for as many age-appropriate life activities as possible. For example, involve the child in his or her medical care with a focus on the child's understanding medical needs and obtaining the skills needed to access medical and health care. Share information regarding the child's performance in these areas at transition planning meetings.

♦ Attend all meetings related to transition, and ensure that family members have input in determining who is invited and the content of the agenda. If assistance is needed for family members to attend the meeting (e.g., transportation, day care) it should be provided.

♦ Arrange for the child to learn about the jobs of family members, and take advantage of opportunities to talk with the child about his or her career goals. Help the child understand the importance of goal setting and completing the steps needed to achieve those goals.

♦ Observe the child on occasion in work-based vocational training settings so that transition planning discussions regarding these experiences can include family member input.

♦ Verbally assure the child that he or she is supported in decisions regarding life after graduation. Prior to transition planning meetings, role-play strategies that can be used for self-advocacy to clarify the lead role that the child is expected to assume. Let the child know that family members will be there to provide back-up support as needed.

♦ Require school personnel and adult service providers to share the results of transition assessments in a manner that is functional and relevant to the planning process.

♦ Request information about the high school curriculum, adult services, and postsecondary education.

♦ Make arrangements to spend some time talking with other children and their family members who have been through transition planning. Find out about their experiences, and ask for tips about obtaining needed services.

---

can consist of the student's abilities, interests, and needs; supports naturally available to the student; eligibility for adult services; family needs; and access to curriculum in addition to a wide range of other issues relevant to the child. A unified vision of postschool outcomes and support needs is required to chart the course for students as they move through high school toward their dreams. The relationship between student needs and desires, parental input, and the content of the transition component must be clearly observable (Thompson, Fulk, & Piercy, 2000).

PUTTING IT IN WRITING

One of the results of transition planning should be a document that concisely and accurately reflects the information derived from the planning process in a format that is friendly to both the student and service providers. The transition component should be based on the student's present level of performance and his or her interests and desires. The format in which these items are included as a component of the IEP varies widely from state to state and even from district to district if the state does not have a mandated format. What is important is that the transition component be individualized and linked to the other components of the IEP. Instead of trying to fit all students to a single transition planning process, there should be a process in place that focuses on designing an appropriate array of services and curricular options designed to fit the individual student's needs.

Transition teams should avoid using predetermined checklists or listings of standard transition objectives and activities (although some commercial curricula can certainly help with ideas). The format of the transition component should not hinder creativity or flexibility in meeting individualized needs. Schools must take care not to equate technical compliance (e.g., completing a form that meets legal mandates for use during program audits) with program quality (e.g., comprehensive transition planning and services; Grigal, Test, Beattie, & Wood, 1997; Johnson et al., 1993).

Link Transition Components to Other Parts of the IEP

The transition component must also be linked to the other sections of the IEP. It is a mistake to treat the transition component as a separate plan or document. Remember, the transition component steers the remainder of the IEP toward the student's desired destination for life after high school. Once the student's postschool goals are determined, each transition activity and all instructional goals and objectives should be steps that support these goals. Linking the transition component and the other sections of the IEP will enhance the continuity and delivery of transition services. For example, a student who is pursuing a career in manufacturing with plans to work part time after graduation and enroll in manufacturing coursework at the local community college would have transition activities aimed at vocational training and work experience in the student's chosen career along with tasks associated with college enrollment. Instructional goals and objectives would be focused on developing academic skills needed for high school graduation and success in a postsecondary education setting paired with the employability skills and any adult living skills needed for future independence in college or at work.

Use a Dynamic Planning Process

IEP team members must change the way planning has traditionally been accomplished. In addition to increasing the time frame for which planning is occurring, the team must ensure that the planning process is ongoing and involves many formal and informal avenues throughout the year. Transition planning cannot be considered just an annual event for the purpose of ensuring compliance. Instead, it must be viewed as encompassing everything in which students with disabilities participate during their high school years (Kohler, 1998). In fact, since the true test of the effectiveness of special education services can be judged only by the real-world success of its graduates, then the case can be made that students' entire educational career from the time they enter public school should consist of activities aimed at preparing them for life after graduation.

Use a Portfolio

With the number of people involved in transition planning and the need to design an individual transition component for each student, it is imperative that there be structure and organization to the planning process. However, the process should not be so standardized that it ceases to be flexible and dynamic. The framework by which transition planning occurs should specify the tasks to be accomplished before, during, and after the transition planning meeting. Although the transition component of the IEP requires an annual review, revisiting postschool goals and transition activities only one time a year may not be often enough for some students. Ideally there will be close monitoring of student progress toward postschool goals by a designated staff member (e.g., transition coordinator or special education teacher) and a system for documenting progress.

One method that can be used to track student progress is to develop a career portfolio in which students accumulate information related to career interests, vocational training evaluations, work experience history, participation in extracurricular activities, achievement of transition-related skills, and completed coursework (North Carolina Department of Public Instruction, 2000; Sarkees-Wircenski & Wircenski, 1994). The portfolio can serve as a starting point for team planning sessions, can be used to document the completion of program requirements, and can be used by the student after graduation as a reference tool for obtaining services or job searches. School personnel may also consider using a service referral or transition activity checklist to assist in coordinating the transition responsibilities assigned to school personnel and outside agencies. The method of documenting progress can involve a combination of several strategies, but the key point is that there must be a systematic and manageable approach to routinely monitoring each student's progress.

Use a Person-Centered Planning Process

Transition planning teams should use some form of person-centered planning to encourage and facilitate student and family involvement. **Person-centered planning** is a term describing a collection of techniques—such as personal futures planning, essential life-styles planning, whole life planning, group action planning, and MAPS, among others—with defined assessment and planning features (O'Brien & O'Brien, 2002). Person-centered planning models and tools have been suggested as appropriate transition assessment and planning tools (Wehman, Everson, & Reid, 2001) because they attempt to position people with disabilities in more self-determined roles on planning teams.

The goal of all person-centered approaches is to learn about people with disabilities in more effective and efficient ways to create supports that can assist them in participating in and experiencing more self-directed lives in their communities. A related goal is to place individuals with disabilities in respected positions, even leadership positions, during the assessment, planning, and service delivery process. Therefore, there is a clear alignment between the goals of individualized transition planning and person-centered planning.

A team may choose to mix and match various elements of different approaches to person-centered planning. Regardless of the specific person-centered elements used, the goal is to create an environment that encourages the student to dream, supports the student, creates possibilities, solves problems, and enhances the student's overall present and future quality of life. The use of person-centered planning can also increase parental participation by helping parents feel more comfortable in taking an active role in meetings (Miner & Bates, 1997). If transition team members receive training in person-centered planning strategies, there is a greater chance that there will be increased community support for transition activities by a wider range of individuals and that team members' satisfaction with the process will be higher (Flannery et al., 2000).

Transition teams can provide a great deal of support to students and their families. Trusting relationships between students and service providers can result in the level of support needed for postschool goal accomplishment. Important roles for team members include being available to discuss problems, providing specific support for the accomplishment of transition goals and educational activities, problem-solving barriers and real-life issues, and helping with a wide range of issues that may arise during the transition years (Benz, Lindstrom, & Yovanoff, 2000). For more information, see Chapter 5.

OVERCOMING BARRIERS

There are a variety of factors that can impact the transition planning process. Each school system has its own unique culture and system of policies and procedures related to delivering services to students with disabilities. What is a barrier in one school system or even in one school may not be an issue in another educational setting. Each transition team must be given the latitude to design planning strategies and procedures based on student population, available resources, personnel, and cultural diversity.

Develop a Transition Planning Process That Is Both Systematic and Flexible

Striving toward a comprehensive transition planning process that is standardized in some aspects yet allows the flexibility needed to ensure individualization is an ongoing challenge for a school system. Because of the number of participants in the planning process, there must be some formality to the manner in which individuals and agencies are invited to meetings and are prepared for participation. The complexity of transition planning requires leadership. School systems should designate a transition coordinator, program specialist, or transition teacher to oversee the transition planning process in the areas of interagency and intra-agency coordination, student and family involvement, follow-up on the implementation of transition activities, and monitoring of student progress toward postschool goal accomplishment. School systems lacking the funds to hire someone specifically for these responsibilities should consider shifting roles among already existing staff to ensure that transition issues are addressed sufficiently (Hasazi, Furney, & Destefano, 1999).

Get All Participants Actively Involved

Participant attitudes can also serve as a barrier to achieving postschool outcomes through the planning process. As stated previously, parents and students must be included in a meaningful manner and the preparation necessary for this to occur should begin many years prior to high school. A school system should strive to help all educators understand that student achievement can be increased through the use of student-directed IEPs, person-centered planning, and by providing the resources parents need to be actively involved. Training and monitoring procedures should be implemented that encourage the internalization of these concepts by all staff.

A lack of interagency collaboration can result in many postschool outcomes not being accomplished or being only partially accomplished because a school system simply cannot provide the wide range of community experiences and services needed by many students. A similar barrier can result from a lack of intra-agency (i.e., within the school system) collaboration. School systems should evaluate how well school personnel from different departments (e.g., vocational education, special education, general education) work together within the school setting to deliver transition services. Consumer satisfaction surveys such as those described in Chapter 11 can help determine areas that need strengthening. Students should be able to access the full range of services at their school along with the services in the community necessary to facilitate effective transition from school to adult life.

Many of the barriers related to intra-agency and interagency collaboration can be eliminated through strong administrative leadership. All those involved must cease to think of transition as an add-on to an already existing program or an exercise in paperwork to meet legal mandates. Transition must be viewed as the foundation of each student's educational experience and the focus of the student's education throughout his or her years in school. Program evaluation must be conducted to determine what services are in place, what services are needed, how program resources can be redirected, and how service delivery can be reformatted to achieve a full menu of options for all students with disabilities. Transition teams will have a difficult time conducting individualized transition planning if the curricular and service options are limited due to a school system's failure to restructure the educational program or if transition planning is conducted in a vacuum.

SUMMARY

Comprehensive transition planning and the subsequent delivery of appropriate and timely services is not an easy task. Educators and adult service providers must be committed to the long haul. There must be cooperation within the school, collaboration with outside service providers, and a strong emphasis on student and family involvement. Creativity, perseverance, patience, and strong advocacy skills are required. The process requires never giving up on a student and his or her dreams. The final pay-off for all involved will be a student who is ready to take a place in the community as an independent and contributing citizen.

CASE STUDY

COMPREHENSIVE TRANSITION PLANNING IN ACTION

The following case study describes the transition planning process from the 8th grade through the 12th grade for Jamalia Adams (a pseudonym), who has a learning disability in math. Following the case study are a sample transition component and sample IEP objectives related to her postschool goals.

Jamalia is a girl with a learning disability in math who has received special education services since the third grade. She lives at home with her mother, who works 12-hour shifts at a local furniture factory. Jamalia has two older brothers.

Prior to entering *eighth grade*, Jamalia and Mrs. Adams, her mother met with Jamalia's IEP team. Jamalia had attended her IEP meeting the previous year, and her teachers had talked with her about her objectives and asked questions about what types of help she needed in order to learn best. When Jamalia's special education teacher, Mrs. Greene, invited her to this year's meeting, they talked about what Jamalia wanted to do after graduation and helped her come up with some ideas. Mrs. Greene also talked with Jamalia about the importance of participating in her transition planning meetings and how various people and agencies would be able to help her pursue her goals.

The IEP meeting began with the transition issues facing Jamalia as she approached high school age. Jamalia would turn 14 years old in January, so it was decided that her IEP have a transition component that at the very least contained a statement of transition needs focusing on her projected course of study. The team members determined that a number of factors warranted developing a full transition component with postschool goals, transition services, and agency linkages. Mrs. Adams had concerns that her son, who had dropped out of high school, might influence Jamalia to do the same. Mrs. Greene felt that Jamalia would need supports to pass the required high school exit exams. Jamalia expressed her fears regarding high school, which included failing to make passing grades and not being able to obtain a diploma.

When asked about her future plans, Jamalia told the team that she wanted to get a job after graduation but wasn't sure about going to college. When questioned about where she might like to live after graduation, Jamalia stated that she definitely wanted to live in her own place someday but knew that would require money. Jamalia was satisfied with her level of participation in school activities and the community. She played basketball on the school team, was a member of the school drama club, and had several good friends. Jamalia also played basketball and swam at the community recreation department after school and during the summer months. She attended the AME Zion Methodist Church and sang in the choir. Jamalia shared with her team that she enjoyed collecting dolls and would like to learn to play the guitar.

After establishing postschool goals for Jamalia in postsecondary education, employment, community living, and community participation, the team discussed what types of transition activities and services would be appropriate for the upcoming year. Her special education teacher suggested some transition assessment activities to determine Jamalia's vocational interests. Also, she suggested an after-school study skills class to improve her note-taking, test-taking, outlining, and study skills. Jamalia agreed to both of these ideas after learning that the class would not interfere with basketball or drama. Jamalia's mother requested some assistance in learning more about high school course offerings, and Jamalia agreed that she needed help in making course selections. Meeting with the guidance counselor and attending the high school scheduling sessions held for all eighth graders were suggested.

After the team reviewed Jamalia's previous coursework and grades, it was decided that Jamalia would continue to be included in general education classes for all subjects, with one period a day in the resource lab for remediation and assistance with homework and projects. Since it was clear to the team that Jamalia had very limited experience on which to base future career decisions the special populations coordinator suggested that she take a vocational exploratory class and a keyboarding class. Jamalia liked these suggestions, and the classes were included in her eighth-grade schedule. Jamalia's mother felt that her involvement with the basketball team and drama club at the middle school had had a positive influence on her life. Plans were made for Jamalia to further investigate extracurricular options at the high school. (See Figures 4.4 and 4.5 at the end of the case study for more details.)

In preparation for Jamalia's *ninth-grade* IEP meeting, her mother completed a written interview form regarding her dreams and transition needs for Jamalia. Jamalia completed a student dream sheet to focus her dreams for after graduation. Jamalia had the opportunity to practice expressing her postschool dreams and requesting various services through role-playing sessions with her teacher and classmates. Jamalia requested that her teacher and the transition coordinator assist her in leading the meeting by prompting her with questions, making suggestions, and helping to summarize discussions.

In addition to the IEP team members who had attended Jamalia's eighth-grade meeting, a high school special education teacher and the vocational rehabilitation counselor were also invited to Jamalia's ninth-grade IEP meeting. The vocational rehabilitation counselor was invited because Jamalia's mother requested information about vocational services. At the meeting, Jamalia, with the assistance of her special education teacher, took a partial lead role. She called the meeting to order and, after asking the members to introduce themselves, she reviewed her activities from the previous year.

Jamalia presented her employment interests based on the results of her vocational interest assessments and career development activities. After completing activities in a vocational exploration class, Jamalia had decided that she would probably need to consider classes at the community college. The team discussed postsecondary options for Jamalia that would match her interest in a business career. Team members felt it was important for Jamalia to enroll in a high school pathway that would ensure her enrollment in college preparation courses. The decision was made for Jamalia to pursue the state's career preparation pathway, requiring Jamalia take academic courses needed for admission to a community college but also allowing her to take a sequence of vocational pathway courses. Mrs. Adams was very supportive of Jamalia's future career goals. She was committed to helping her get a good job so her daughter would not have to struggle the way she had.

Jamalia was happy with her living arrangements for now, but she looked forward to living independently some day. She also felt that she was involved as much as she could be with school and community activities because of her schoolwork. She was looking forward to taking driver's education and getting her license. Additional discussion during the meeting focused on identifying and clarifying the specific transition activities Jamalia needed during the upcoming year. (See Figures 4.4 and 4.5 for more specific details.)

By the end of the ninth grade, Jamalia felt more comfortable taking a lead role in her transition planning. She received approval for her best friend Sherritta to attend her *10th grade* IEP meeting for support. Jamalia approved the transition coordinator's sending invitations to her computer teacher, her special education teacher, the vocational rehabilitation school counselor, the diagnostician, the special populations coordinator, the basketball coach, and her minister. Jamalia spent time with the transition coordinator outlining the meeting and deciding what types of information she wanted to share with the team.

Jamalia brought her report cards, a completed computer applications project, her job-shadowing evaluations, and a certificate of commendation from her church to share with the team members. After two job-shadowing experiences at Wal-Mart and Office Max and completing the Introduction to Marketing course, Jamalia wanted a career in retail, expressing interest in customer service, inventory, and sales. She also had developed a keen interest in technology and was very interested in getting a home computer and taking more technology courses. The vocational rehabilitation counselor suggested that additional vocational assessment might assist Jamalia in further narrowing her career choices.

Jamalia remained interested in independent living, but she felt that her college goals would require her to remain living at home. Jamalia indicated concerns about taking physical science in the 10th grade, and the team discussed the accommodations that had been the most helpful to her along with ideas for making sure she received the support she needed in the physical science class. Jamalia's minister suggested a church member who might be interested in tutoring Jamalia if needed.

When asked about community activities, Jamalia shared with the team that the church youth director was giving her guitar lessons. Her participation in the church choir meant a great deal to her, and she continued to enjoy playing on the high school basketball team. She was also still involved with the recreation department and was coaching a junior basketball team at her church. Jamalia had successfully completed driver's education and passed the driver's examination, and she was anxious to get her license in January. Jamalia's mother added that she had been saving money and hoped to afford car insurance by the time Jamalia earned her license.

During the IEP meeting, Jamalia needed her special education teacher to assist with summarizing suggestions that had been made and finalizing some of the plan's details. Following the meeting, Jamalia met with her special education teacher and transition coordinator to clarify some of the specific tasks that would need to be accomplished. (See Figures 4.4 and 4.5 for more specific details.)

Prior to her entering the *11th grade,* Jamalia's IEP team reconvened. Several adult service providers were invited to this meeting, including the special student services coordinator from the local community college, the vocational rehabilitation counselor, and the Workforce Investment Act (WIA) coordinator. Also present were Jamalia's special education teacher, the transition coordinator, the guidance counselor, the marketing teacher, a diagnostician, the basketball coach, and the youth director from her church. Jamalia came prepared to talk to the team members about her revised goals. She and her mother agreed that her high school grades were good and that she should seek summer employment. A summer internship at one of the area's larger retail stores was suggested, and the WIA coordinator agreed to make a referral to the program for the upcoming summer. In addition, Jamalia would be eligible for an adult mentoring program that might provide her with a role model and direction with her future employment plans. Jamalia's church youth director voiced interest in helping obtain mentoring for her from a church member who had taken a special interest in Jamalia after tutoring her the previous year.

Jamalia asked the special student services coordinator from the community college to review her preparedness for admission to the community college. The team also discussed accommodations Jamalia presently received to determine whether these same options would be available to her at the community college. This led to a discussion about the various tasks that Jamalia would need to accomplish in order to gain admission to the college. (For more detail on preparing students for community college, see Chapter 6.)

When the discussion moved toward Jamalia's community living plans, she indicated that she was interested in living in an apartment some day but recognized that she would need a steady source of income to live independently. She requested some help in developing a budget to see whether living away from home after graduation was really a feasible goal. Mrs. Adams told the team that Jamalia also needed some instruction in cooking and cleaning. Although Jamalia didn't totally agree, she did admit needing some help taking care of her own clothes.

In the area of community participation, Jamalia was frustrated by not having access to a car when she wanted. The guidance counselor shared information about a new program, Wheels for Work, sponsored by the Salvation Army, the United Way, and the Department of Social Services (DSS). This program provided used cars at no cost to individuals with transportation barriers to employment as long as the recipient purchased insurance, tags, and licenses. Everyone agreed that more information about this program would be pertinent to Jamalia's situation.

Prior to concluding the meeting, the transition coordinator spent some time discussing the legal rights that would transfer to Jamalia when she turned 18 years of age. Both Jamalia and her mother felt this was an appropriate step toward adulthood. Some written information was provided for Mrs. Adams about age of majority and its educational implications. The transition coordinator noted that Jamalia would be involved in a two-part training session she would be conducting for juniors who would be reaching the age of majority within the next year. (See Figures 4.4 and 4.5 for more specific details.)

For Jamalia's last transition planning meeting before entering the *12th grade,* she had the confidence and skills needed to oversee the meeting. The team members were the same as those who attended her 11th grade meeting with the addition of a DSS representative who was invited to share information about the Wheels for Work program.

The meeting began with Jamalia expressing concerns about the exit exam requirement for graduating with a high school diploma. Because Jamalia failed the math section of the exam on her first attempt, after-school remediation classes and a before-school peer-tutoring program were suggested. The special services coordinator from the community college assisted Jamalia in reviewing the tasks that had been accomplished toward enrolling in the community college along with the remaining tasks.

Jamalia shared her employment goals. After working at Lowe's the previous summer as a stock clerk, she talked with the store manager, who supported Jamalia's desire to work part time during the school year and to try out new positions. The special populations coordinator suggested that an internship at Lowe's might be arranged for vocational credit. Jamalia asked whether there was any on-the-job training assistance, and the vocational rehabilitation counselor suggested a referral for short-term job coaching, if Jamalia was promoted to a position requiring advanced skills.

Jamalia also wanted to talk to her team members about the application she planned to submit through Wheels for Work. The DSS representative confirmed that Jamalia was approved to receive a car but that she needed at least three recommendations and someone to cosign the application for her.

Jamalia continued to be satisfied with her level of community participation. She was excited about her senior year on the basketball team and would be coaching a junior basketball team at the recreation department on Saturdays. (See Figure 4.4 for more specific details.)

Jamalia's exit transition meeting was held 4 weeks prior to graduation. Everyone who had been involved with Jamalia's planning meetings throughout high school was present. After discussion with the transition coordinator, Jamalia decided to use her exit meeting to share her progress toward accomplishing her goals and to thank the team members for the support she had received during the last 4 years.

First, Jamalia and her special education teacher told the team that she had obtained passing grades on her exit exams, was on track for completion of all graduation requirements, and would receive a high school diploma in May, along with a concentration in the marketing/business pathway.

Jamalia told the team that she had been working part time at Lowe's for almost a year and had been appointed to a new position in the kitchen design center. A recent meeting between Jamalia, the human resource manager, and the transition coordinator resulted in a full-time employment placement once she completed high school. Jamalia reported that she had also been told that she could apply for the management trainee program at Lowe's after she had been employed full time for 1 year.

Jamalia also planned to move to an apartment with her cousin, promising her mother that she would work full time for at least 3 months and complete a semester at the community college before moving out on her own. She had been approved for the Wheels for Work program, and by July she hoped to have saved enough money for all the associated fees and received her car.

Jamalia reported that she had completed an application to the community college and planned on pursuing an associate's degree in business administration. She knew that she was going to miss her high school basketball teammates, but she planned to play softball on the Lowe's team and to continue her involvement in church activities.

Toward the end of the meeting, Jamalia proudly shared her career portfolio with the team and thanked everyone for the support she had received in reaching her dreams. The transition coordinator described the high school's postschool follow-up program, and all of the team members indicated that Jamalia could contact them any time she needed assistance. She was given a list of names and contact information to include in her career portfolio.

Transition Component of the IEP for Jamalia Adams

Student: Jamalia Adams
School: M. S. Turner High School
Course of Study: Career Preparation Pathway
Desired Exit Document: Diploma
Schedule Format: Traditional six-period day
Statement of Needed Transition Services: Jamalia will be enrolled in the career preparation pathway and will take the following courses (24 credits required for graduation):

9th Grade	10th Grade
English I	English II
Pre-Algebra	Algebra I
World Studies	Government/Economics
Health/PE	Computer Applications II
Computer Applications I	Physical Science
Introduction to Marketing	Principles of Business

11th Grade	12th Grade
English III	English IV
U.S. History	Marketing Management
Earth/Environmental Science	Biology
Business Technology	Technical Math II
Technical Math I	Family and Consumer Science
Theater I	Career/Technical Education Marketing Internship

Student Needs and Preferences: Indicate how the information related to student needs, preferences, interests, and course of study selection was obtained and used in the development of postschool goals and transition activities. Check all that apply.

From Whom?

Student	_____
Interest and skill inventories	_____
Parents and family members	_____
Formal Assessments	_____
Peers and friends	_____
Ratings	_____
Adult service agency(ies)	_____
Interviews	_____
School staff	_____
Observations	_____
Others (Please specify) _____	_____
Situational assessments	_____

Postschool Goals

Employment *(Vocational Training, Integrated Employment, Supported Employment)*
8th Grade: Jamalia will work after graduation in an occupational area that matches her life-style preferences and vocational interests.

Figure 4.4
Transition Component of the IEP for Jamalia Adams

(continued)

125

9th Grade: Jamalia will work in an occupational area that involves customer service, retail sales, and some business/clerical skills.

10th Grade: Jamalia will work full time in a retail setting (e.g., grocery store, department store, homebuilding supply store).

11th Grade: Jamalia will work full time at Lowe's, Home Depot, Wal-Mart, Kmart, or a local grocery store in a position with career advancement potential.

12th Grade: Jamalia will work full time at Lowe's and will apply for the management trainee program.

Postsecondary Education *(Continuing and Adult Education)*

8th Grade: Jamalia will pursue postsecondary education opportunities that can enhance her career opportunities.

9th Grade: Jamalia will take courses at the community college in an area related to her interests.

10th Grade: Jamalia will enroll in part-time courses at the community college to advance her computer skills.

11th Grade: Jamalia will enroll in courses at the community college to advance her computer and business skills.

12th Grade: Jamalia will enroll in courses at the community college leading to a 2-year business degree and will apply for the management trainee program at Lowe's.

Residential *(Independent Living)*

8th Grade: Jamalia will live at home until sufficient funds have been obtained to support an independent living arrangement.

9th Grade: Jamalia will live at home until sufficient funds have been obtained to support an independent living arrangement.

10th Grade: Jamalia will live at home until sufficient funds have been obtained to support an independent living arrangement in an apartment.

11th Grade: Jamalia will live at home while attending the community college and advancing in her career with plans to move into an independent living arrangement with a roommate within 3 years of graduation.

12th Grade: Jamalia will live in an apartment with a roommate while attending college and move into an independent living setting within 1 year of graduation.

Community Participation

8th Grade: Jamalia will participate in sports and hobbies related to her interests.

9th Grade: Jamalia will participate in sports and hobbies related to her interests.

10th Grade: Jamalia will play team sports and will pursue her hobbies of collecting dolls and playing the guitar.

11th Grade: Jamalia will play team sports and pursue her hobbies of collecting dolls, playing the guitar, and learning more about computers.

12th Grade: Jamalia will play team sports through the local recreation department, collect dolls, play the guitar, and participate in a college computer club.

Figure 4.4
Continued

Transition Activity Area	Transition Service/Activity	Responsible Person or Agency/Support Personnel	Timeline
Instruction	Receive 1 hour a day resource support and identified accommodations and modifications in general education classes	Special education and general education staff	8th grade
	Small-group instruction in self-determination skills and personal rights	Transition coordinator	8th grade
	Participate in after-school study skills club (Community in Schools)	Community in Schools staff	8th grade
	Receive guidance counseling regarding high school course offerings	Middle school guidance counselor/special education staff	8th grade
	Participate in scheduling high school classes	High school guidance counselor/special education staff	8th grade
	Enroll in vocational education semester courses: keyboarding and vocational exploratory lab	Special populations coordinator/career technical education staff	9th grade
	Enroll in the career preparation pathway to pursue a high school diploma	High school guidance counselor/special education staff	9th grade
	Pursue a vocational concentration in the business and marketing vocational education pathway: Computer Applications I, Introduction to Marketing, Computer Applications II, Principles of Business, Business Technology, and Marketing Management	Special populations coordinator/career technical education staff	9th grade–12th grade

(continued)

Transition Activity Area	Transition Service/Activity	Responsible Person or Agency/Support Personnel	Timeline
	Enroll in driver's education and obtain a learner's permit	Jamalia/driver's education instructor	9th grade
	Receive tutoring in physical science	Jamalia/Reverend Brown	10th grade
	Obtain "recycled" computer for home use through Community in Schools program	Community in Schools staff/Jamalia/Mrs. Adams	10th grade
	Participate in Age of Majority seminar	Transition coordinator	11th grade
	Attend an orientation session at the community college to investigate curriculum programs available in the area of computers and business	Jamalia/Mrs. Adams/ transition coordinator	11th grade
	Investigate possible sources of financial assistance for college expenses	Jamalia/Mrs. Adams/ high school guidance counselor	11th grade
	Meet with vocational rehabilitation counselor to update individual plan of employment (IPE) to include college attendance and complete financial needs assessment to determine eligibility for assistance with college expenses	Jamalia/vocational rehabilitation counselor/ Mrs. Adams	12th grade
	Complete applications for college admission and financial aid	Jamalia/Mrs. Adams/ high school guidance counselor/transition coordinator	12th grade
	Provide appropriate evaluation information to the student special	Jamalia/transition coordinator	12th grade

Figure 4.4
Continued

Transition Activity Area	Transition Service/Activity	Responsible Person or Agency/Support Personnel	Timeline
	services coordinator and make arrangements for necessary accommodations		
Community Experiences	Participate in extracurricular activities (middle school): basketball and drama	Jamalia	8th grade
	Use services at the community recreation department (basketball and swimming)	Jamalia/Mrs. Adams	8th grade–12th grade
	Take guitar lessons with youth director at AME Zion Methodist Church	Jamalia/Mr. Dickens	10th grade–12th grade
	Participate in the AME Zion Methodist Church youth choir	Jamalia/Mrs. Adams	8th grade–12th grade
	Tour the high school and meet with the basketball coach	Jamalia/transition coordinator	8th grade
	Participate in extracurricular activities (high school): basketball	Jamalia/Coach Ledford	9th grade–12th grade
	Assist in coaching junior basketball team at the Recreation Department	Jamalia/Mr. Dickens	9th grade
Employment	Attend the career fair at the community college	Transition coordinator/special populations coordinator	8th grade
	Complete career portfolio	Special populations coordinator/transition coordinator/career guidance counselor	9th grade–12th grade
	Participate in two job-shadowing experiences in retail settings	Special populations coordinator/transition coordinator	9th grade

(continued)

Transition Activity Area	Transition Service/Activity	Responsible Person or Agency/Support Personnel	Timeline
	Complete situational assessment in retail settings	Transition coordinator/vocational rehabilitation counselor/vocational evaluation counselor	10th grade
	Tour various retail stores within the community and obtain information regarding possible job openings	Jamalia/Mrs. Adams	11th grade
	Refer to Workforce Investment Act (WIA) youth program for summer employment and the adult mentoring program	Special populations coordinator/transition coordinator/WIA representative	11th grade
	Participate in summer youth leadership summit	Special populations coordinator/transition coordinator/WIA representative	12th grade
	Obtain part-time job at Lowe's and receive vocational education credit for internship	Special populations coordinator/transition coordinator	12th grade
	Meet with Vocational Rehabilitation counselor to update individual plan of employment (IPE) to include community-based work adjustment services (e.g., job coaching)	Jamalia/Vocational Rehabilitation school counselor	12th grade
	Participate in mock interviews conducted by the Rotary Club	Jamalia/transition coordinator/Rotary Club members	12th grade
Activities of Adult Living and Daily Living Skills	Obtain driver's license	Jamalia/Mrs. Adams	10th grade
	Investigate the "Wheels for Work" program through the Salvation Army	Jamalia/Mrs. Adams/transition coordinator	11th grade
	Training in budgeting for living expenses and	Transition coordinator/technical math teacher	11th grade

Figure 4.4
Continued

Transition Activity Area	Transition Service/Activity	Responsible Person or Agency/Support Personnel	Timeline
	completion of a personal budget plan		
	Training in clothing care	Jamalia/Mrs. Adams	11th grade
	Investigate possible independent and affordable living arrangements within the community	Jamalia/Mrs. Adams/ transition coordinator	11th grade
	Set up savings account for expenses related to obtaining a car	Jamalia/Mrs. Adams	11th grade
	Complete application process for the "Wheels for Work" program	Jamalia/Mrs. Adams/ transition coordinator	11th grade
Functional Vocational Evaluation	Participate in transition assessments to identify vocational interests and learning style	Transition coordinator	8th grade
	Referral to Vocational Rehabilitation for vocational assessment and evaluation	Transition coordinator/ Vocational Rehabilitation school counselor	10th grade
Related Services	Transportation as needed to all transition-related activities that occur during school hours	Transition coordinator/ transportation director	9th grade– 12th grade

Figure 4.4
Continued

Following are sample pages of Jamalia's IEP demonstrating the relationship between IEP goals and objectives and the transition component.

Individualized Education Program

Student Name: Jamalia Adams

Grade: 10th

Present Level of Education Performance: Jamalia has participated in some career awareness activities through vocational education that exposed her to the basic steps involved in obtaining employment. Her career exploration activities involving job shadowing and transition assessments have assisted her in identifying occupational interests. Jamalia has never completed a job application, developed a résumé, or participated in a job interview. She possesses the written and verbal communication skills needed for these activities but needs specific instruction related to process and content. The successful completion of job-seeking skill objectives will prepare Jamalia for future employment goals.

Annual Goal: Jamalia will exhibit job-seeking skills needed to secure employment in her chosen career pathway.

Short Term Objectives:

1. Jamalia will successfully conduct a job search based on career interests and abilities using all of the following: want ads, Yellow Pages, Internet sources, Employment Security Commission job listing, and friends and relatives.
2. Jamalia will develop a one-page résumé using a computerized résumé generator.
3. Jamalia will complete five different application forms with 100% accuracy.
4. Jamalia will compose a letter of introduction/cover letter to accompany an application or résumé.
5. Jamalia will demonstrate the ability to answer eight common interview questions correctly and confidently and give examples of three appropriate questions for a job applicant to ask during an interview.

Figure 4.5
Sample Individualized Education Program (IEP) Pages

Individualized Education Program (IEP)

Student Name: Jamalia Adams
Grade: 10th
Present Level of Education Performance: Although Jamalia has participated in various aspects of her transition planning process, she has not developed the skills needed to assume total leadership of her team. Jamalia has completed dream sheets, practiced setting postschool goals, and role-played various transition meeting scenarios. She has also assisted the transition coordinator in setting the agenda and determining team participants. At meetings Jamalia has provided information to the team regarding her goals and high school experiences. At this point, Jamalia has very limited knowledge regarding her rights and the various services that are available to her from various adult service providers. Also, Jamalia needs to take a more active leadership role at her transition team meetings.

Annual Goal: Jamalia will exhibit the self-determination skills needed to participate in transition planning and successful adjustment to adult life.

Short Term Objectives:

1. Jamalia will be able provide an operational definition of "age of majority" and describe how the age-of-majority ruling will affect her role in making educational decisions.
2. Jamalia will identify basic rights related to her disability under IDEA, the Americans with Disabilities Act, Section 504 of the Rehabilitation Act of 1973, and the Workforce Investment Act.
3. Jamalia will identify five adult service providers, five services offered by each agency, and the process for accessing the services of each agency.
4. Jamalia will demonstrate active participation in the transition planning process by setting postschool goals, identifying appropriate transition activities for accomplishing goals, identifying appropriate agencies and persons to invite to a team meeting, establishing an agenda for a transition meeting, and chairing a meeting.

(continued)

Individualized Education Program (IEP)

Student Name: Jamalia Adams

Grade: 11th

Present Level of Education Performance: Through participation in the standard course of study, Jamalia has achieved the basic math skills needed for personal budgeting. However, Jamalia has never had the opportunity to apply these skills to the actual development of a budget relevant to her postschool goals of living independently and owning a car. Up to this point Jamalia's mother has assisted her in managing her finances, which have primarily consisted of an allowance, money earned from mowing grass in the neighborhood, and cash gifts from relatives on special occasions. Jamalia requested assistance in learning budgeting skills at her last transition team meeting.

Annual Goal: Jamalia will develop basic budgeting skills applicable to independent living situations.

Short Term Objectives:

1. Jamalia will correctly identify important sections of bills, statements, and invoices and correctly interpret the information contained in these sections.
2. Jamalia will identify four methods of paying bills and correctly identify the steps involved in paying bills using these four methods.
3. Jamalia will correctly define terms associated with banking, list the considerations for choosing a bank, and identify the steps involved in establishing a savings account and a checking account.
4. Jamalia will prepare an independent living budget that incorporates fixed and variable monthly expenses and planned and unplanned expenses.
5. Jamalia will calculate the cost of owning an automobile and develop a budget that incorporates costs associated with licenses, taxes, tags, insurance, fuel, and maintenance.

Figure 4.5
Continued

Individualized Education Program (IEP)

Student Name: Jamalia Adams

Grade: 11th

Present Level of Education Performance: Jamalia has had no experience in locating or obtaining housing. She has lived with her mother up to this point but has a postschool goal of future independent living. Jamalia also has little knowledge of the expenses involved in obtaining or maintaining a house or apartment. Jamalia has the written and verbal communication skills and math skills needed to identify housing, complete the process for obtaining housing, and develop a budget associated with these tasks. However, she needs instruction and guidance in the real-life activities that will be required to achieve her postschool goal of independent living.

Annual Goal: Jamalia will develop the skills needed to locate and obtain residential housing.

Short Term Objectives:

1. Jamalia will determine the availability and location of five residential options that match her budget and life-style preferences.
2. Jamalia will correctly complete two rental applications for housing and obtain all accompanying documentation needed to complete the rental process.
3. Jamalia will develop a spreadsheet that lists the costs associated with independent living, including moving, utilities, rent/house payment, furnishings, deposits, and insurance.

Figure 4.5
Continued

STUDY GUIDE QUESTIONS

1. What is required in the area of transition planning for students at 14 years of age? At 16 years of age?
2. What occurs in the educational process when a student reaches the age of majority?
3. What does IDEA say about student involvement in the transition planning process? Why is student involvement important?
4. How does a lack of family involvement affect the transition planning process? What are some practical strategies for increasing family involvement?
5. What are the domains for postsecondary goals that should be addressed in the transition component of the IEP?
6. What transition activity areas should be addressed during transition planning? Give an example of a transition activity in each area.
7. What should school systems do in the area of adult service involvement in the transition process? What should happen if an adult service agency fails to follow through on a promised service?
8. Why is it important for transition to be a component of the IEP instead of a separate document? What should be the connection between the transition component and the rest of the IEP?
9. What role does student self-determination play in the transition planning process?
10. Referring to the case study, identify the strategies used to ensure that Jamalia was involved in her transition planning process.
11. Identify the adult agencies involved and the services provided by each agency in the case study.
12. What role did vocational education play in the process of preparing Jamalia for a future career?
13. Identify any barriers you think might impede Jamalia's successful transition to adult life. What types of supports were put in place to overcome these barriers?
14. Identify specific situations during the transition planning process in which Jamalia's preferences, interests, and needs were taken into account. How were these addressed in the actual transition component?
15. What types of natural supports are in place for Jamalia? How can these supports be enhanced to ensure future success for Jamalia?
16. Describe the changes observed in the development of Jamalia's postschool goals as her high school career progressed. How were these changes reflective of Jamalia's changing preferences, interests, and needs?
17. After reviewing the transition component, can you think of any other transition activities that could be added to increase Jamalia's chances of achieving her postschool goals?

REFERENCES

Aspel, N. (1997). *North Carolina transition manual.* Raleigh: North Carolina Department of Public Instruction.

Benz, M., Lindstrom, L., & Yovanoff, P. (2000). Improving graduation and employment outcomes of students with disabilities: Predictive factors and student perspectives. *Exceptional Children, 66,* 509–529.

Blalock, G. (1996). Community transition teams as the foundation for transition services for youth with learning disabilities. *Journal of Learning Disabilities, 29,* 148–159.

Center on Community Living and Careers. (2003, March). *Transition to adult life: A shared responsibility.* Retrieved September 24, 2003, from http://www.iidc.indiana.edu/cclc/transition1 .htm.

Countryman, L. L., & Schroeder, M. (1996). When students lead parent–teacher conferences. *Educational Leadership, 53,* 64–68.

deFur, S. H. (1999). Transition planning: A team effort. *Transition summary.* Washington, DC: National Information Center for Children and Youth with Disabilities.

deFur, S. H. (2000). *Designing individualized education program (IEP) transition plans* (ERIC Digest No. E598). Arlington, VA: ERIC Clearinghouse on Disabilities and Gifted Education.

deFur, S. H., Todd-Allen, M., & Getzel, E. E. (2001). Parent participation in the transition planning process. *Career Development for Exceptional Individuals, 23,* 19 –36.

Division of Career Development & Transition. (2005). *Comments on regulations for IDEA 2004.* Retrieved February 1, 2005, from http:// www.udel.edu/dcdt.

ERIC/OSEP Special Project. (2000, Spring). *New ideas for planning transitions to the adult world* (Research Connections No. 6). Reston, VA: Author.

Everson, J., Zhang, D., & Guillory, J. D. (2001). A statewide investigation of individualized transition plans in Louisiana. *Career Development for Exceptional Individuals, 24,* 31–49.

Fairfax County Public Schools. (1998). *Transition planning manual.* Fairfax, VA: Author.

Flannery, K. B., Newton, S., Horner, R. H., Slovic, R., Blumberg, R. & Ard, W. R. (2000). The impact of person centered planning on the content and organization of individual supports. *Career Development for Exceptional Individuals, 23,* 123–137.

Flexer, R. W., Simmons, T. J., Luft, P., & Baer, R. M. (2001). *Transition planning for secondary students with disabilities.* Upper Saddle River, NJ: Merrill/Prentice Hall.

Furney, K., Hasazi, S., & DeStefano, L. (1997). Transition policies, practices, and promises: Lessons from three states. *Exceptional Children, 63,* 343–355.

Grigal, M., Test, D. W., Beattie, J., & Wood, W. M. (1997). An evaluation of transition components of individualized education programs. *Exceptional Children, 63,* 357–372.

Hanley-Maxwell, C., Pogoloff, S. M., & Whitney-Thomas, J. (1998). Families: The heart of transition. In F. R. Rusch & J. G. Chadsey (Eds.), *Beyond high school: Transition from school to work* (pp. 234–261). Belmont, CA: Wadsworth.

Hasazi, S. B., Furney, K. S., & Destefano, L. (1999). Implementing the IDEA transition mandates. *Exceptional Children, 65,* 555–566.

Johnson, D. R., & Sharpe, M. N. (2000). Analysis of local education agency efforts to implement the transition service requirements of IDEA of 1990. In D. R. Johnson & E. J. Emanuel (Eds.), *Issues influencing the future of transition programs and services in the United States* (pp. 31–48). Minneapolis: University of Minnesota.

Johnson, D. R., Thompson, S. J., Sinclair, M., Krantz, G. C., Evelo, S., Stolte, K., et al., (1993). Considerations in the design of follow-up and follow-along systems for improving transition programs and service. *Career Development for Exceptional Individuals, 16,* 225–238.

Kohler, P. (1998). Implementing a transition perspective of education: A comprehensive approach to planning and delivering secondary education and transition services. In F. R. Rusch & J. G. Chadsey (Eds.), *Beyond high school: Transition from school to work* (pp. 159–205). Belmont, CA: Wadsworth.

Kohler, P., Field, S., Izzo, M., & Johnson, J. (1997). *Transition from school to life*. Arlington, VA: Council for Exceptional Children.

Lindsey, P., Wehmeyer, M. L., Guy, B., & Martin, J. (2001). Age of majority and mental retardation: A position statement of the Division on Mental Retardation and Developmental Disabilities. *Education and Training in Mental Retardation and Developmental Disabilities, 36*, 3–15.

Lindstrom, L. E., & Benz, M. R. (2002). Phases of career development: Case studies of young women with learning disabilities. *Exceptional Children, 69*, 67–83.

McBride, M. V., & Stitt-Godhes, W. (1994). Career development: Issues of race, class, and gender. *The Journal for Vocational Special Needs Education, 23*, 62–67.

McGill, T., & Vogtle, L. (2001). Driver's education for students with physical disabilities. *Exceptional Children, 67*, 455–466.

Miner, C. A., & Bates, P. E. (1997). The effect of person centered planning activities on the IEP/transition planning process. *Education and Training in Mental Retardation and Developmental Disabilities, 32*, 105–112.

Morningstar, M. (1995). *Planning for the future: A workbook to help young adults with disabilities, their families, and professionals to plan for living, working and participating in the community.* Lawrence: University of Kansas, Department of Special Education.

National Organization on Disability. (2000). *Louis Harris survey of Americans with disabilities.* Washington: DC: Author.

North Carolina Department of Public Instruction. (2000). *Occupational course of study career portfolio.* Retrieved February 25, 2005, from http://education.uncc.edu/transition/combined.pdf.

O'Brien, C. L., & O'Brien, J. (2002). The origins of person-centered planning: A community of practice perspective. In S. Holburn & P. M Vietze (Eds.), *Person-centered planning: Research, practice, and future directions* (pp.3–28). Baltimore: Brookes.

Salembier, G., & Furney, K. S. (1997). Facilitating participation: Parents' perceptions of their involvement in the IEP/transition planning process. *Career Development for Exceptional Individuals, 20*, 29–42.

Salembier, G., & Furney, K. S. (1998). Speaking up for your child's future. *Exceptional Parent, 28*, 62–64.

Sarkees-Wircenski, M., & Wircenski, J. (1994). Transition planning: Developing a career portfolio for students with disabilities. *Career Development for Exceptional Individuals, 17*, 203–214.

Storms, J., O'Leary, E., & Williams, J. (2000). *Transition requirements: A guide for states, districts, schools, universities, and families.* Minneapolis: University of Minnesota, Institute on Community Integration.

Taylor-Ritzler, T., Balcazar, F. E., Keys, C. B., Hayes, E., Garate-Serafini, T., & Espino, S. (2001). Promoting attainment of transition-related goals among low-income ethnic minority students with disabilities. *Career Development for Exceptional Individuals, 24*, 147–167.

Test, D. W., Mason, C., Hughes, C., Konrad, M., Neale, M. & Wood, W. M. (2004). Student involvement in individualized education program meetings. *Exceptional Children, 70*, 391–412.

Thompson, J. R., Fulk, B. M., & Piercy, S. W. (2000). Do individualized transition plans match the postschool projections of students with learning disabilities and their parents? *Career Development for Exceptional Individuals, 23*, 3–25.

Thorin, E. J., & Irvin, L. K. (1992). Family stress associated with transition to adulthood of young people with severe disabilities. *Journal of the Association for Persons with Severe Handicaps, 17*, 31–39.

Timmons, J. C., & Whitney-Thomas, J. (1998). The most important member: Facilitating the focus person's participation in person centered planning. *Research to Practice, 4*(1), 3–6.

Virginia Commonwealth University Rehabilitation Research and Training Center on Supported Employment. (1994, September). *Planning for quality life outcomes: Transition to adulthood.* Richmond, VA: Supported Employment Telecourse Network.

Warger, C., & Burnette, J. (2000). *Planning student-directed transitions to adult life* (ERIC/OSEP Digest No. E593). Arlington, VA: ERIC Clearinghouse on Disabilities and Gifted Education.

Wehman, P. (1992). *Life beyond the classroom: Transition strategies for young people with disabilities.* Baltimore: Brookes.

Wehman, P., Everson, J. M., & Reid, D. (2001). Beyond programs and placements: Using person-centered practices to individualize the transition processes and outcomes. In P. Wehman (Ed.), *Life beyond the classroom: Transition strategies for young people with disabilities* (3rd ed., pp. 91–124). Baltimore: Brookes.

Wehmeyer, M. L., & Metzler, C. (1995). How self-determined are people with mental retardation? The national consumer survey. *Mental Retardation, 31,* 111–119.

Wehmeyer, M., Morningstar, M., & Husted, D. (1999). *Family involvement in transition planning and implementation.* Austin, TX: Pro-Ed.

Wehmeyer, M., Palmer, S., Agran, M., Mithaug, D., & Martin, J. (2000). Promoting causal agency: The self-determined learning model of instruction. *Exceptional Children, 66,* 439–453.

Whitney-Thomas, J., & Timmons, J. C. (1998). Building authentic visions: How to support the focus person in person centered planning. *Research to Practice, 4*(3), 3–4.

Wittenstein, S. H. (1993). A parent–professional collaboration model of transitional planning. *Journal of Visual Impairment and Blindness, 87,* 227–229.

Interagency Collaboration and Teamwork

Chapter 5

Introduction

For many years, human services professionals have recognized the important roles that teams may play in planning and delivering quality services. As a result, teamwork is considered a best practice in early intervention, assistive technology, workforce development, affordable housing, family support, as well as in many other human services areas. Thus, it is not surprising that teamwork is also considered a best practice in high-school-to-adult-life transition services and is an essential component of Kohler's (1996) taxonomy. In fact, interagency collaboration may very well be the glue that holds together Kohler's components of student-focused planning, student development, program structure, and family involvement. Attention to collaborative interagency practices enables educators to foster effective relationships not only with other agencies, but also with families. Furthermore, collaborative interagency practices enable educators to model effective practices with students and ultimately enable students to plan, communicate, and engage in more self-determined behaviors.

Arguably, however, even with all the attention that it has received, interagency collaboration remains among the least researched and thus the least understood of all suggested transition practices (Johnson & Emanuel, 2000). What do we know for certain about effective interagency collaboration and how it can enhance transition services? This chapter responds to this question by providing examples of effective teamwork models and strategies that may be used across disciplines, agencies, and organizations to develop and provide more comprehensive and outcome-oriented transition services for individual students and their communities. The chapter begins with definitions of key concepts, along with a rationale for the use of collaborative teams. It continues with suggestions for building effective teams, including strategies for increasing the involvement of students, their families, and adult services providers. Throughout, case study examples of teams effectively addressing an array of transition issues in various and diverse communities illustrate key points.

Key Terms

team
interagency
collaboration
transition specialist
goal
action planning
effective communication

Personal Perspective on Interagency Planning

A Family Member

Rose A. Gilbert

Executive Director, Families Helping Families of Greater New Orleans

There are advantages and disadvantages of using interagency teams to address transition services and outcomes. If the team is strong and cohesive, then members can truly focus on the needs of the students they serve. They can put aside their individual concerns, becoming flexible and creative in how they plan for specific students and for the community at large. A team approach will allow the opportunity to communicate and combine the best resources of each team member and agency. Remember, the outcomes for the student are the best confirmation that your transition team has done a great job, especially if team members are willing to think outside of the box.

There are also disadvantages of interagency transition teams and services. It takes time, sometimes months or even years, for teams to become teams. Many times, the interagency transition team cannot function because of a lack of structure and training. People move or are promoted, and there is nothing to ensure that the member replacing them comes to the table with the same level of understanding and experience. Team members' lack of respect for the family and self-advocate role in the teaming process is another issue that must be considered and, if evident, must be addressed.

If I could tell educators and transition specialists one thing about family and self-advocate roles on interagency teams, it would be to put aside your individual roles and focus on the goal of becoming a strong team. Recognize that team members have a variety of unique strengths and experiences. Allow family members and self-advocates to function as equal members of the team. These people are not in this process as a job; they are in it for a lifetime.

B eginning in the early 1980s, and continuing into the present, collaborative interagency teamwork has been suggested consistently in legislation and in professional literature as a promising transition practice (e.g., Everson & Guillory, 2002; Johnson & Emanuel, 2000; Kohler, 1993; Phelps & Hanley-Maxwell, 1997). Practical applications of collaborative interagency teamwork in transition services have taken many forms (e.g., Aspel, Bettis, Quinn, Test, & Wood, 1999; Certo et al., 2003; Everson, Guillory, & Ivester, 2005).

For example, without argument, collaboration among students, their families, and the numerous education and related services professionals involved in a student's individualized education program (IEP) has been identified as a necessary component of comprehensive transition assessment and service delivery while a student is in high school (deFur & Patton, 1999). Likewise, collaboration between teams of school personnel and adult services personnel has been suggested as a promising practice for accomplishing the seamless transition of paperwork and services as a student prepares to exit special education services and enter adult services (Wehman, 2001).

The membership of collaborative teams has been expanded to include students and their families, the business community, affordable housing organizations, institutions of postsecondary education, the health and medical community, public and private transportation providers, and other social services agencies and organizations (Everson & Guillory, 2002). In addition, the functions of these collaborative interagency teams have been expanded to include local program development, program management, and program monitoring and evaluation (Aspel et al., 1999; Certo et al., 2003; Everson et al., 2005). There can be little doubt that interagency collaboration is viewed by professionals and public policymakers, as well as by students and their families, as a critical component of comprehensive transition models and a promising practice in improving an array of postsecondary outcomes for students with disabilities.

DEFINITION OF KEY CONCEPTS

Teamwork is a familiar if somewhat fuzzy term to most educators and social services personnel. Federal legislation mandating special education, vocational rehabilitation, and other social services frequently includes language promoting

---

DID YOU KNOW?

Transition studies indicate that collaborative interagency teamwork can enhance employment and other postsecondary outcomes among young adults with disabilities (Aspel et al., 1999; Certo et al., 2003; Everson et al., 2005).

teamwork. Lectures, and sometimes entire courses, are dedicated to the importance of teamwork in most university personnel preparation programs for future educators and social services personnel. Professional conferences and other continuing education forums dedicate sessions, and even entire events, to the importance of teamwork. Book chapters and textbooks on teamwork fill the shelves of university libraries. Teaming is consistently rated one of the most requested training and technical assistance needs among practicing human services professionals.

With all of this information about teamwork readily available, why don't we do a better job of collaborating with our fellow team members? The simple answer may be that while we agree on the *importance* of teamwork, we do not truly understand the *concept* or the *process* of teamwork. If we do not understand the concept and process, then we cannot begin to apply teamwork knowledge, skills, and behaviors to transition practices, or indeed, to any of our social services mandates and models. And if we can not systematically apply teamwork abilities, then we will never be able to achieve the seductive promises of teamwork that lurk behind every university class, conference presentation, book chapter, and federal and state mandate.

What Is a Team?

An often-quoted adage states, "Agencies don't collaborate, people do." In truth, collaborative teamwork is largely about individual people—not agencies—working together. A **team** may be defined as a group of two or more people who agree to come together and work interdependently to address common needs and pursue common goals (Everson & Guillory, 2002). The group becomes a team if, and only if, its members (a) identify shared needs and values, (b) agree upon common goals, (c) define roles and processes that enable members to know how to behave, and (d) agree upon team regulating and evaluating procedures (Everson & Guillory, 2002). Similarly, Varney (1989) noted that a successful team embraces four concepts:

1. Members' roles are clear to each individual as well as to other team members.
2. Individuals have goals, and the sum of individual goals adds up to the team's goals.
3. Structure and practices are understood and agreed to by all team members.
4. Working relations are viewed as an essential part of the team.

As these definitions indicate, teamwork is not magical. It is hard work, and it is serious work. A team may be initiated when a defined group of people agrees to meet together for a common goal or purpose, but it takes much more than an agreement to meet for the group to function as a team. Consider the commonly held myths about teams listed in Figure 5.1.

The term *team* is generally assigned to any group of people—even if their membership and roles vary—when they are charged with working together for any length of time in order to pursue any goal, even if it is poorly defined. But

♦ A team is a group of people who all work in the same department or are employees of the same business.

♦ A team is a group of people who are all assigned to serve on the same task force and are charged with accomplishing the same impossible task within an impossibly short time frame with no identifiable resources.

♦ A team is a group of people who all wear the same color hat or the same tee shirt and who play the same game or sport.

♦ A team is a group of people who claim the same academic credentials and who understand and use the same mysterious terminology and acronyms.

♦ A team is a group of people who all provide services and supports to the same student or client.

♦ A team is a group of people who come together once or twice a year for a 2- to 3-hour meeting to write an individualized education program (IEP).

Figure 5.1
Common Myths About Teamwork

many of these groups are not truly teams. Groups must, by definition, exhibit the characteristics and behaviors described earlier in order to be defined as teams. A group of people who meet together once or twice a year to develop or monitor an IEP is not a team unless these defining characteristics and behaviors are evident. Similarly, a group of people who meet quarterly to address a community's employment services for citizens with disabilities is not a team unless these defining characteristics and behaviors are evident.

Most important, if these groups do not behave as teams, then they cannot be expected to achieve the outcomes expected of teams. As this chapter will show, teamwork behavior requires all team members to demonstrate knowledge, skills, and behaviors in three areas: defining goals, establishing roles, and following processes.

What Is Meant by *Interagency?*

Interagency is an adjective used to describe the relationships between two or more agencies or organizations and between the representatives of these agencies and organizations. The term is typically used to describe a team whose membership consists of various agencies and organizations, each of which plays some defined role in planning and delivering services to a specified target population. In the arena of transition services, the word *interagency* may describe a team that is composed of numerous education and adult services personnel. Education personnel may represent one agency—the student's school system—but they may also represent numerous disciplines—special educators, general educators, vocational educators, school nurses, occupational therapists and physical therapists, speech and language therapists, orientation and mobility specialists, school counselors and social workers, audiologists, and psychologists. Similarly, adult services personnel may represent several different agencies as well as several different disciplines. Among others, these may include vocational rehabilitation counselors, case managers, personal care assistants, Social Security Administration representatives, job coaches and other employment services representatives, community college and university personnel, personnel from affordable housing agencies and organizations, and staff from centers for independent living (CILs).

When applied to transition services, *interagency* also describes a team that includes students, their immediate families, and sometimes potential employers and other family members and friends. By definition, a transition planning team must have interagency membership. That is, a transition planning team will always include one or more educators, a student, one or more family members, and one or more adult services providers.

What Is Collaboration?

Collaboration is another concept that is frequently used in the arena of transition services. Typically, *collaborative* is used as an adjective to describe the manner in which a team of people organize themselves, communicate among themselves, and accomplish tasks. **Collaboration** may be defined as a relationship between two or more people, agencies, or organizations that is well defined and mutually beneficial (Everson & Guillory, 1998). The purpose of such a relationship is to achieve common goals by pursuing mutually agreed-upon actions and roles.

Specific to the planning and delivery of effective transition services, collaboration demands coordination and communication among multiple team members who may represent differing agencies and organizations, differing mandates and policies, differing cultures, differing languages, differing professional disciplines, and differing needs and goals. Thus, to be collaborative, a transition team will need to articulate common goals and values, agree upon operating structures, share roles and responsibilities, share resources, and share accountability for successes and failures. Just like teamwork itself, developing collaboration within a team requires time and is serious work.

Putting It All Together: Collaborative Interagency Teamwork

Specific to high-school-to-adult-life transition services, Everson and Guillory (1998) defined a collaborative interagency team as

> a group of individuals and organizations who come together to address a common need and agree to pursue a common goal. Over time and with much effort, the group becomes a team if its members agree to common values and a mission, set clear goals and objectives, design an organizational structure and operating procedures, develop common communication patterns, and pursue agreed-upon roles and activities. (p. 301)

DID YOU KNOW?

In planning and delivering transition services, collaborative interagency teams typi-cally are convened at different levels to accomplish distinctly different goals. First, by Individuals with Disabilities Education Improvement Act (IDEA 2004) mandate, student-level IEP teams must be convened for every student with a disability. Their goal is to develop, implement, and monitor an IEP for individual students. Second, community-level teams may be convened by cities, counties, or regions that are in-terested in pursuing systems change. Their goal is to identify the transition service needs of a defined group of high school students and to mobilize community re-sources to address those needs. Third, state-level teams may be convened by state-level agency administrators to address legislative, policy, and funding needs. Their goal is to address the statewide transition needs of students through legislative, pol-icy, and fiscal responses.

BUILDING EFFECTIVE INTERAGENCY COLLABORATION

The remainder of this chapter offers examples of effective teamwork strategies that may be used to convene and build student-, community-, and state-level teams. Strategies are suggested for building student-level teams across agencies, disciplines, and organizations whose purposes are to develop, implement, and monitor individual students' IEPs, as well as for building community- and state-level teams whose purposes are to promote more comprehensive and outcome-oriented services. Strategies are also suggested for encouraging students' self-determination abilities both as members and as leaders of these teams.

Rationale for Using Collaborative Interagency Teams

Transition services are complex for a number of reasons. First, they demand the involvement and expertise of multiple disciplines, agencies, and organizations. At the very least, special educators and general educators need to collaborate with students and their families. More typically, these players need to collaborate not only with each other, but also with a host of educational support personnel and adult services personnel. Thus, identifying common values and goals is es-sential. Second, transition services demand adherence to a number of IDEA edu-cational mandates as well as to a host of adult services mandates covering postsecondary education, housing, employment, transportation, legal services, and medical services. Thus, communication about roles is essential to avoid gaps in service delivery and to ensure nonduplication of services. Finally, transition services frequently must be accomplished within limited timelines and with lim-ited resources. Thus, effective meeting and action planning processes are essential to make best use of scarce resources.

Collaborative interagency teamwork, when used effectively, brings all available resources together so that teams may assess, plan, implement, monitor, and evaluate individualized services and outcomes for students and their communities.

Key Collaborators in Transition Services

The cornerstone of effective transition planning is collaborative interagency teamwork between educators and adult services personnel and between professionals, students, and families. Although the specific agencies and team players are by necessity defined by state legislative mandates and local priorities, as well as by the level and goals of the team, most transition planning teams consist of the key collaborators and roles summarized in Figure 5.2.

Transition Specialists: Essential Team Members

Who is a "transition specialist"? Unfortunately, in many school systems, the answer may be simply "whoever is assigned responsibility for transition services!" In practice, school systems assign one or more school personnel responsibility for all aspects of transition services within a defined geographic area and to a defined population of students. That is, depending upon the size of the school district, transition personnel may be responsible for an entire school district, or they may be responsible for all transition-age students within multiple high schools within the school district. Within their assigned area, they may be responsible for all transition-age students, or different personnel may be assigned to students with specific educational classifications. They may be assigned full time to transition services, or they may be responsible for transition services along with other administrative or teaching duties. In some cases, systems may even assign high school teachers responsibility for coordinating all aspects of transition services for the students assigned to their classrooms.

The term **transition specialist** is used in this chapter to refer to any educator who is assigned responsibility for any aspect of transition services. Regardless of the approach adopted by a school system, the person (or persons) assigned responsibility for transition services functions as a transition specialist and must be prepared to play a number of roles.

A Fact Sheet developed by the Council for Exceptional Children, Division on Career Development and Transition (DCDT) defines a transition specialist as

an individual who plans, coordinates, delivers, and evaluates transition education and services at the school or system level, in conjunction with other educators, families, students, and representatives of community organizations. (Council for Exceptional Children, 2000, p. 1)

This Fact Sheet further suggests that a transition specialist should possess competencies in the following eight core areas:

1. Foundations of special education.
2. Characteristics of learners.

Education personnel may include among others: special education teachers, general education teachers, vocational educators, school nurses, occupational therapists and physical therapists, speech and language therapists, orientation and mobility specialists, school counselors and social workers, audiologists, and psychologists.

♦ As appropriate, conduct educational, psychological, speech and language, motor, behavioral, vocational, and adaptive skill assessments and evaluations of students.
♦ Provide functional interpretations of assessment and evaluation data.
♦ Identify appropriate members to serve on teams and represent the respective agencies and disciplines.
♦ As appropriate, convene and participate in individualized education program (IEP) and other team meetings by communicating meeting goals, roles, and processes.
♦ Engage in effective discussion, manage conflict, and summarize decisions and action steps during meetings.
♦ Support students' self-determination abilities before, during, and between meetings.
♦ Communicate with family members and promote family involvement before, during, and between meetings.
♦ Coordinate development and implementation of IEPs, including transition requirements.
♦ Provide interdisciplinary skill instruction according to IEP requirements.
♦ Assist with job development and job placement goals and outcomes.
♦ Assist with postsecondary education goals and outcomes.
♦ Assist with community living goals and outcomes.
♦ Assist with other community participation goals and outcomes.
♦ Participate in staff development activities.
♦ Share information with other agencies, disciplines, and team members.
♦ Assist with program evaluation
♦ Participate in development and implementation of interagency agreements.

Adult services personnel may include: vocational rehabilitation counselors, case managers, personal care assistants, Social Security Administration representatives, job coaches and other employment services representatives, community college and university personnel, personnel from affordable housing agencies and organizations, and staff from centers for independent living.

♦ As appropriate, conduct vocational, financial, medical, psychological, behavioral, and adaptive skill assessments and evaluations of students.
♦ Provide functional interpretations of assessment and evaluation data.
♦ Identify appropriate members to serve on teams and represent the respective agencies and disciplines.

(continued)

Figure 5.2
Key Collaborators and Their Roles

149

◆ Engage in effective discussion, conflict management, and decision making during meetings.
◆ Support students' self-determination abilities before, during, and between meetings.
◆ Communicate with family members and promote family involvement before, during, and between meetings.
◆ Implement agreed-upon transition action steps between meetings.
◆ Oversee job development and job placement goals and outcomes.
◆ Oversee postsecondary education goals and outcomes.
◆ Oversee community living goals and outcomes.
◆ Oversee other community participation goals and outcomes.
◆ Participate in staff development activities.
◆ Share information with other agencies, disciplines, and team members.
◆ Assist with program evaluation.
◆ Participate in development and implementation of interagency agreements.

Figure 5.2
Continued

3. Assessment, diagnosis, and evaluation.
4. Instruction.
5. Planning and managing the teaching and learning environment.
6. Managing student behavior and social interaction skills.
7. Communication and collaborative partnerships.
8. Professionalism and ethical practices.

Competency 7, "communication and collaborative partnerships," requires a transition specialist to be able to demonstrate a variety of collaborative interagency teamwork abilities. A transition specialist may be called upon to demonstrate this competency in many ways. For example, a transition specialist may be asked to convene and facilitate student-level IEP teams, or to convene and facilitate community-level teams, or, just as critically, to represent the school district on one of these teams. A transition specialist may be asked to serve as a member of a state-level team.

A transition specialist may be asked to form a new team, lead an existing team, guide a struggling team, manage a team in conflict, implement activities identified by the team, or evaluate a team's activities and accomplishments. Regardless of the team's level, its goals, or the transition specialist's role, transition specialists who use teamwork practices will be able to maximize scarce resources, individualize plans and services, and effect quality student outcomes more effectively than those who do not.

Strategies for Building Teams

A transition specialist charged with forming new teams and/or leading existing teams needs to be able to respond to a number of planning questions (see Figure 5.3). For example, an IEP team's membership and goals, as well as the frequency and even the structure and process of its meetings, are dictated to a large extent by IDEA and district mandates and policies. Likewise, a community- or state-level team's membership and goals may be defined by local and/or state policies. The team may be encouraged or supported by special grants and technical assistance endeavors. At the other extreme, team-forming ideas and activities may be left almost entirely to the vision and resources of a transition specialist charged with forming the team.

In all cases, a transition specialist, as the person charged with organizing and convening a team, has responsibility for some initial planning and decision-making tasks that can help a new or existing team organize and operate itself effectively at every meeting. Being able to answer the questions posed in Figure 5.3 will help a transition specialist form and convene both new and existing teams.

1. Confirm the need for a team.
   ◆ Has a team's existence been mandated?
   ◆ If not, what factors support or hinder a team's development?
   ◆ What will a team accomplish that individuals cannot?
2. Define the team's goals.
   ◆ What is the team's goal or goals?
   ◆ What are the goals of the meeting that is to be scheduled?
3. Establish roles.
   ◆ Who needs to be invited?
   ◆ Who will be the team's facilitator?
   ◆ What roles will each agency and discipline and participant play?
   ◆ What information and resources do invited members need to bring to the team?
4. Follow processes.
   ◆ How should the agenda be structured to accomplish the goals?
   ◆ How much time is needed?
   ◆ How should the meeting flow from beginning to end? What paperwork, forms, and data need to be used during the meeting?
   ◆ How will communication be enhanced? How will conflict be managed?
   ◆ How will agreements be reached?
   ◆ What needs to occur after meetings end, and how will responsibilities be ensured?

Figure 5.3
Strategies for Forming New Teams and Convening Existing Teams

Define Goals.   The first planning task is to define the team's goals. Specifically, what is the goal of the new or existing team? And what is the goal of the meeting to be scheduled? A **goal** is a desired future state of affairs. Simply put, a goal describes where a team hopes to be by the end of a meeting and at the end of a series of meetings and actions. For example what is the goal to be attained at the end of a 2-hour IEP meeting? Or 12 months from now, once a county-wide affordable housing task force has written and implemented its new rental housing guidelines for citizens with disabilities? Goals should be behavioral, measurable, attainable, and have timeframes. Goals define a team's work scope and should be used to develop an agenda for every meeting.

For example, in the case of a community-level team convened to address employment services and outcomes for special education students in a specific community, an appropriate set of community-specific annual goals might read as follows:

The 2005–2006 goals for Jefferson County Transition Team are to:

1. *Conduct two focus groups with local employers to determine current and upcoming workforce needs.*

2. *Convene a business advisory task force twice annually to advise the teachers and staff at Jefferson High School and Lakeview High School about vocational programming for students with disabilities.*

3. *Use a request for proposals (RFP) process to establish three new employment providers to serve students exiting the two county high schools.*

4. *Secure employment placements for 125 students (55%) of the 227 students with disabilities scheduled to exit the two county high schools this year with occupational diplomas.*

Alternatively, an IEP team convened for a specific student should set annual goals that are more student centered while still adhering to behavioral, measurable, attainable, and timeframe components. For example:

Because Lincoln Anderson wants to complete an associate's degree in information services at Highview Community College, he will enroll in and complete two introductory computer courses and one English composition course at the community college during his senior year of high school. He will enroll in and complete CS 100 on Mondays and CS 110 on Tuesdays and ENG 150 on Mondays and Tuesdays. Lincoln will ride the high school bus from his home to the community college, and he will use the bus schedule and telephone to plan and make reservations to ride the accessible bus from the community college to the high school in the afternoons after his classes end.

Determining goals is not as simple as it may seem at first. In Lincoln's example, what goals need to be accomplished by the IEP team to support Lincoln's dreams of attending community college? What goals need to be accomplished by Lincoln himself? What are the goals of the IEP meeting?

A transition specialist may reply that the goal of Lincoln's IEP meeting is to update Lincoln's transition plan to include goals and activities associated with his recently articulated dreams to enroll in the local community college. Another team member, Lincoln's physical therapist (PT), may respond that the goal of the meeting is to develop a transition plan to enable Lincoln to use the accessible public bus system independently. An adult services team member, Lincoln's vocational rehabilitation (VR) counselor, may indicate that the goal of the meeting is to determine whether Lincoln is eligible for VR services and financial support to attend the community college once he completes high school, and if so, to provide the counselor with the information she needs to develop Lincoln's IPE (individualized plan for employment). Lincoln's grandmother may indicate that the goal of the meeting is to make sure Lincoln is prepared to use the bus service safely, while Lincoln may say that the goal of the meeting is to allow him more independence.

Certainly, all of these potential goals are related, and all may in fact be individual team members' goals for Lincoln's upcoming meeting. However, the transition specialist needs to reach agreement on team goals before the meeting in order to determine who needs to be at the meeting, what information members should bring with them and expect to leave with, and the expected length and outcomes of the meeting.

Whenever possible, a transition specialist should define the goal or goals of the meeting with team members before the meeting. This may be accomplished by talking with team members ahead of time, reviewing notes from the previous meeting, writing the goals in an invitational letter for the meeting, or telephoning participants to invite them to or remind them of a meeting. For example:

You have been asked to attend Lincoln Anderson's IEP meeting on April 21st from 2:00 P.M. to 4:00 P.M. in room 117 of Lakeview High School. At last month's preliminary meeting with Lincoln and his grandmother, we agreed that the goal of this meeting is to update Lincoln's transition plan and IEP for the upcoming school year. Specifically, the team's goals for this meeting are to: (1) write IEP objectives and activities to support Lincoln's enrollment in courses at Lakeview Community College; (2) write IEP objectives and activities to support Lincoln's use of the Lakeview transit system; and (3) discuss Lincoln's eligibility for vocational rehabilitation services and, if he is eligible, determine the necessary next steps to refer him to the vocational rehabilitation agency.

Another strategy is to begin the meeting by stating the meeting's goal or goals. When this strategy is used, the transition specialist must be prepared to revise or add additional goals or to negotiate postponing team members' goals to a follow-up meeting. For example:

"I understand from his English teacher that Lincoln recently wrote a paper expressing his dream of renting an apartment once he leaves high school. However, we only set aside 2 hours to address three specific goals. Can we postpone discussion on his independent living goal until our next meeting?"

In these situations, a transition specialist must also be prepared to address disagreement and conflict. For example:

> *"Ok, if you believe that it is essential to discuss Lincoln's independent living goals at this meeting, then I propose that we extend this meeting, perhaps by another 45 minutes. Raise your hand if you are willing to extend today's meeting to discuss Lincoln's independent living goal. Raise your hand if you are unable to extend today's meeting to discuss Lincoln's independent living goal."*

When goals are clarified before the meeting, or at the beginning of the meeting, all team members have a more accurate understanding of the expected outcomes of the meeting and their roles on the team during the meeting. As a result, the meeting will run more efficiently and productively.

Establish Roles.   Once goals have been articulated for a meeting, the transition specialist must consider each team member's unique roles on the team. This need is especially critical when a team convenes for the first time and when new members join the team. Again, the transition specialist should consider two questions. First, why is this specific member being invited to participate on this team? Second, what information or resources does this member bring to this meeting to help accomplish the meeting's goals? The transition specialist may consider several strategies to address these questions. Again, whenever possible, the transition specialist should define each team member's role with the team member ahead of time, by talking with team members in advance in person, by reviewing notes from the previous meeting, in writing, or by telephone.

When students and their families are involved in identifying people to invite to their IEP meetings, the transition specialist should ask them to help clarify responses to these two questions. For example:

> *"Tell me why you would like to invite Monique's vocational training site supervisor to her next transition planning meeting? How do you think he can help us find a permanent job for Monique?"*

An additional strategy, and one that is critical when a new member first joins a team, is to introduce the new member by describing the role that he or she is expected to play on the team and during the specific meeting. This should be done immediately following the statement of the meeting's goals. For example:

> *"Monique invited Mr. Richards, the evening manager from Farm Fresh, to attend today's meeting. Even though his store does not currently have any job openings, Mr. Richards does have some suggestions for additional skill training that Monique might benefit from, as well as some ideas for permanent job possibilities within the next 12 months."*

In some situations, especially during initial meetings of newly forming teams, it may be unclear to the transition specialist and other members of the team why a specific agency or member has been invited to join the team and attend a meeting. In these situations, it may be useful to begin the meeting by asking all members to briefly introduce themselves and describe the roles they might play.

When teams meet infrequently, membership changes between meetings, mandates dictate team membership, and/or goals are perceived by members as being adversarial, role clarification can be difficult. However, it is precisely in these cases that role clarification becomes most important. The transition specialist may need to encourage problem solving and decision making that will encourage members to take actions beyond their traditional and comfortable roles. For example:

> *"I understand that you provide Lincoln with his PT sessions on Tuesdays and Thursdays. However, if you and the principal can revise your weekly therapy schedule to address the issues you raised, would you be willing to meet with Lincoln and at the community college's office of disability affairs to assess his seating and positioning needs while using the college's computer lab?"*

Follow Processes.   Meeting processes include determining the agenda for a specific meeting, along with the meeting's organization and flow and the supporting paperwork, forms, or data that will be used during the meeting. The transition specialist is responsible for familiarizing all team members with the planned processes for every meeting. For example:

> *"At today's IEP meeting, we need to review Lincoln's IEP, and, as needed, revise goals and activities. Specifically, we agreed to discuss his plans for postsecondary education and the support services that he needs to pursue this goal. We are scheduled to begin now and adjourn at 4:00 P.M., so let's get started. Does anyone have any questions about today's agenda?"*

One simple process for planning meetings (Leadership Designs, n.d.) is to envision any meeting as having required actions that a transition specialist needs to attend to before, during, and after the meeting (see Figure 5.4). Attention to these items will help the transition specialist plan, facilitate, and follow upon interagency meetings, thereby maintaining the active participation of all team members.

Strategies for Facilitating Teams

Create Action Plans.   During team meetings, action planning is a strategy that many transition specialists find useful in helping teams attain their goals. **Action planning** is a flexible process that results in written planning documents such as an IEP, a team work plan, or an interagency agreement. Neither the title of the form nor the format used is important. What is important is that all action plans include these components: (a) the team's goals; (b) a list of actions or short-term steps necessary to accomplish each goal; (c) the names of team members responsible for accomplishing the actions; and (d) timelines for accomplishing the actions (Everson & Guillory, 2002).

Before a Transition Planning Meeting

♦ Determine the meeting's goals, roles, and processes.
♦ If possible, communicate the goals, roles, and processes to all team members before the meeting.
♦ Schedule the meeting date, time, and location, and notify all participants.
♦ Develop an agenda and, if possible, distribute it to all team members before the meeting.
♦ Arrange for assistive services and supports if needed.

During a Transition Planning Meeting

♦ Begin the meeting on time.
♦ Describe the goals of the meeting.
♦ Introduce any new members or visitors by name and by role.
♦ Summarize the agenda and meeting processes.
♦ Use effective communication skills to keep the meeting moving toward its goals.
♦ Manage conflict.
♦ Record action items for team members to accomplish.
♦ Complete the individualized education program (IEP) and/or any other paperwork. such as an action plan.
♦ Summarize discussions, decisions, and next steps.
♦ Develop draft agenda for the next meeting.

After a Transition Planning Meeting

♦ Evaluate the effectiveness of the meeting.
♦ Make contact with any team member(s) unable to attend the meeting.
♦ Distribute the IEP and/or any other paperwork, such as an action plan.

Figure 5.4
Effective Teaming Processes

Any team may use action planning to formalize the team's commitment to its goals and to define its work scope. Action plans are beneficial because they enable a team to break goals into the smaller, incremental steps necessary to accomplish the goals. Action plans also document the team's decisions, actions, and assignments during team meetings, thereby ensuring both forward movement toward goals and accountability.

When the transition specialist uses action planning, members feel positive about the time and other resources they are contributing to the team. Team members feel energetic and positive about the work they are accomplishing. They begin to develop relationships and trust with other team members. In sum, they begin to function as a team, and importantly, they develop and model a collaborative relationship for families and for students.

Practice Effective Communication Skills.   **Effective communication** strengthens all human relationships, including relationships among interagency team members.

There are literally dozens of examples of communication models described in teaming literature, and most models include strategies for (a) initiating communications with other team members; (b) listening to the communications of other team members; and (c) responding to the communications of other team members.

Leadership Designs (n.d.) suggests a communication model that many transition specialists have found useful when they are charged with facilitating interagency transition teams. Figure 5.5 summarizes this model.

The transition specialist may need to use some or all of these communication behaviors during interagency team meetings. For example, when a team is newly forming or when a student or family member has communication or language difficulties or is reticent to speak for other reasons, the transition specialist may need to use proposing, inquiring, or reflecting behaviors. For example, to bring in a reticent member the transition specialist might say:

"Monique, I would like to suggest that you begin today's meeting by sharing the dream map that you created in your English class with the rest of the team."

Or to reflect on an observed body language:

"Lincoln, do you have any concerns about attending the community college that you would like to share with the team today?"

Initiating Behaviors

- *Proposing:* proposing a new idea or action to the team.
- *Expanding:* expanding upon an idea or action previously proposed by another team member.

Active Listening Behaviors

- *Informing:* informing other team members about facts or information.
- *Inquiring:* inquiring of other team members about an idea, action, fact, or information previously communicated by another team member.
- *Reflecting:* reflecting upon the perceived emotion of another team member by commenting on an observed behavior or a communicated comment.
- *Testing for understanding:* asking a question of another team member in order to attempt to clarify one's understanding of a previous communication.
- *Summarizing:* summarizing previous discussion or decision making in order to conclude an agenda item.

Responding Behaviors

- *Agreeing:* agreeing with or supporting another team member's ideas
- *Disagreeing:* disagreeing with or expressing lack of support for another team member's ideas.

Figure 5.5
Effective Communication Competencies

To move discussion along, the transition specialist might find it useful to propose actionable ideas. For example:

"I propose that we postpone discussion about purchasing a new computer desk chair for Lincoln until his PT has visited the college campus and assessed what they have available for him to use."

Active listening and responding skills are most likely to be needed when goals and roles are unclear, when team members generate lots of exciting new ideas, and when there is little consensus about desired goals or action steps. For example, stating factual information limits aimless discussion:

"The school district's policies on transportation do support Lincoln's goal of using the public bus, including allowing us to purchase a bus pass for him."

There will be other times when a transition specialist will find it useful to test understanding of what has been stated by asking the speaker a question, for example:

"Mr. Richards, are you suggesting that Monique could be successfully employed as a bagger in a grocery store if she learned to look at customers, greet them, and smile?"

Acknowledging disagreement and keeping a team moving forward is sometimes difficult but always important for a transition specialist. For example:

"I understand that you disagree with postponing discussion about Lincoln's independent living goals until our next meeting, but if the rest of the team does support this decision, can you live with the decision?"

Or even:

"I disagree, and I cannot commit my agency's money to this project, but I am willing to continue working with the team on other goals."

Likewise, summarizing discussion and proposed actions is important:

"Let me summarize what we decided at today's meeting. Between now and our next IEP meeting, Lincoln will use his journalism class assignments to explore possible affordable apartments near the college campus. He will ask his cousin whether he can spend a weekend with him in his apartment to learn more about independent living. His journalism teacher will help him set up an interview with a representative from Neighborhood Housing Resources to learn about local housing services. And finally, Lincoln's PT will spend time with Lincoln evaluating his independent living skills. Did I leave anything out?"

STRATEGIES FOR INCREASING STUDENT INVOLVEMENT

During an IEP meeting, a transition specialist is responsible for ensuring that assessment, planning, and goal discussion begin from the point of view of the student. The transition specialist is also responsible for guiding the team into discussions about the student's preferences, needs, interests, talents, and goals. There are three broad strategies for a transition specialist to use to involve students more in their transition planning activities: (a) model effective communication; (b) use person-centered planning; and (c) develop students' self-determination abilities.

Model Effective Communication Behaviors

Modeling effective communication is useful in increasing an adolescent's involvement during meetings because it provides an organized, positive, and engaging environment. Specifically, a transition specialist might ask questions to encourage the student to participate and to encourage the team to listen. Inquiring can be used to prompt a student to share a story or an interest or to seek clarification on something the student has already shared. For example:

> *"Derek, would you tell your IEP team the story you told me about why you want to work at Frank's Sporting Goods Store?"*

Reflecting may also be used to encourage a student to participate in a discussion and to ensure that a student is comfortable with the content of a discussion. For example:

> *"Vong, how do you feel about Mr. Freeman's idea?"*

Testing for understanding by asking a question about what has previously been stated is a third strategy that a transition specialist can use to ensure that what a student says is understood by the team. For example:

> *"Lincoln, are you telling us that you would like someone to help you make that telephone call?"*

Each of these strategies will help the transition specialist and the rest of the team ensure the student's active involvement and understanding before the student agrees or disagrees with what has been shared.

Use Person-Centered Planning

Person-centered planning tools (see chapter 4) have been suggested as appropriate transition assessment and planning tools (Wehman, Everson, & Reid, 2001) because they attempt to position people with disabilities in more self-determined and leadership roles as members of their IEP teams. By encouraging young adults and their families to identify and express the young adult's wants and needs and to assume responsibility for goal setting and taking action, person-centered planning is clearly aligned with the goals of transition planning and interagency collaboration.

Develop Students' Self-Determination Abilities

Self-determination is a concept based on the belief that all individuals have the right to direct their own lives. It encompasses a broad set of knowledge, skills, and behaviors that enable an individual to set goals, make decisions, explore options, solve problems, speak up for himself or herself, understand what supports are needed for success, and evaluate outcomes (Martin & Marshall, 1996). Self-determination is a critical issue as a student approaches the age of majority and becomes legally responsible for control of and consent to his IEP. In addition, a small body of research is beginning to emerge supporting the relationship between self-determination abilities and positive transition outcomes among young adults with disabilities (e.g., Wehmeyer & Schwartz, 1997).

A transition specialist and other educators can support an adolescent's attainment of self-determination abilities as part of high school academic programming (Wehmeyer, Agran, & Hughes, 1998). Figure 5.6 summarizes best-practice strategies for building self-determination abilities in adolescents. In addition, there are a number of commercially available curricula and methodologies. For more information on these curricula, see Wood, Test, Browder, Algozzine, and Karvonen (2000), *A Summary of Self-Determination Curricula and Components*, available online at http://www.uncc.edu/sdsp/sd_curricula.asp.

STRATEGIES FOR INCREASING FAMILY AND COMMUNITY MEMBER INVOLVEMENT

The transition specialist is also responsible for ensuring that assessment, planning, and discussion incorporate the point of view of the student's family and, increasingly, the points of view and resources of other community members. The importance of family and community participation in transition planning at all team levels has been reinforced in recent legislation and in best-practices literature.

Family (including extended family members), along with neighbors, family friends, church members, and coworkers, can and should be active participants in person-centered planning activities. In addition, family must be involved in all IEP teams. These are the people who know the adolescent's experiences, preferences, dreams, hopes, and fears. They are also the people most connected to the adolescent, the ones most likely to witness and support the transition from educational services and experiences to adult services and experiences. Finally, they are the ones who are most frequently called upon to step up to the plate for the delivery of nonmandated adult services such as transportation, coordination of medical services, financial planning, and the promotion of social and recreation activities (see chapter 10).

Family members should also be involved, along with other community members, in community- and state-level teams, offering personal insight into how services and policies impact individuals with disabilities. As a team's goals are defined, the transition specialist will need to identify potential agencies and

♦ Ask students to define *self-determination,* and ask them to identify personal ex-amples of self-determined actions. Encourage them to identify how teamwork with others helped them in the past or could help them in the future.

♦ Develop case studies of teenagers in situations requiring them to evidence self-determination abilities in order to progress toward their desired goals, and ask students to discuss appropriate responses that the case study teenagers might evidence.

♦ Assign students group projects, and ask them not only to complete the project as a team, but also to identify both effective and ineffective teaming behaviors that they used.

♦ Have students develop person-centered planning "maps" illustrating their postschool goals. Have them share with their peers, and encourage group feed-back.

♦ Have students develop action plans of the steps and timelines they need to pur-sue in order to achieve their goals. Have them share with their peers and encour-age group feedback.

♦ Provide examples of potential challenges and setbacks to their goals, and have them identify alternative action strategies. Encourage them to identify how team-work with others helped them in the past or could help them in the future.

♦ Have students interview adults about their career goals and the actions they are undertaking to achieve them. Encourage them to identify how teamwork with others helped them.

♦ Invite guest speakers—especially successful adults with disabilities—to discuss their impressions of self-determination and personal goals and actions. Encour-age them to identify how teamwork with others helped them.

♦ Have students identify personal goals and actions, and ask them to self-evaluate their actions and the outcomes of their actions. Have them identify potential al-ternative action strategies.

Figure 5.6
Suggested Activities and Methods to Guide Self-Determination

organizations along with the specific community members who are most appro-priate to serve on teams. The transition specialist will also need to help these members understand and assume their roles as interagency team members.

Provide Family and Community Outreach and Support

Families can support adolescents' attainment of self-determination abilities in a number of ways. For example, families can encourage adolescents to make age-appropriate choices, take age-appropriate risks, and learn from the natural conse-quences of their choices. Families can encourage adolescents to learn about their disabilities and to assume an appropriate level of responsibility for managing their health and medical care and maintenance of their assistive devices and equipment. Families can also encourage adolescents to set goals for themselves and to plan the steps needed to accomplish the goals.

Valuable Family Supports

Parent training and information centers help families:

♦ Obtain special education services for a family member.

♦ Understand a family member's disabilities and abilities.

♦ Develop and use effective communication skills.

♦ Develop and use effective problem-solving and conflict-management strategies.

♦ Improve children's school and community behaviors.

♦ Obtain information from national, state, and local resources.

♦ Understand and use IDEA and other laws impacting disability services.

♦ Collaborate as team members with educational personnel and other professionals who assist families.

Parent training and information centers may provide:

♦ Workshops to help families develop knowledge, skills, and abilities.

♦ Dissemination of written and audiovisual information and materials.

♦ Individualized assistance targeted around specific family needs.

♦ Assistance in developing and nurturing family organizations.

♦ Public awareness of disability issues.

♦ Low-income/minority/at-risk family outreach.

To find out more about parent training and information centers in your area, visit the Technical Assistance ALLIANCE for Parent Centers at http://www.taalliance.org/Centers/PTIs.htm

Successful family and community involvement in transition planning depends on the identification of future, visionary goals for adolescents and the creation of clear and valued roles for family and community members. First, family members must be involved in the process of articulating goals for their transition-age children. This may be accomplished through person-centered planning, home visits, high school open houses, parent training and information centers (PTIs), and other family outreach and support groups. The transition specialist must encourage use of strategies that increase the participation of families in this process, especially families from diverse cultural backgrounds and those with low incomes.

The competencies needed by a transition specialist continue to evolve. Along with information on educational programming and mandates, a transition specialist must be able to share information with families about adult community options such as income maintenance programs, health and medical insurance programs, workforce development entities, affordable housing programs, specialized transportation programs, employment programs, and postsecondary education programs. A transition specialist must be able to identify and coordinate with these community resources and be able to provide students and families with contact people and agencies, telephone numbers, Web sites, and other resources to ensure that they are able to have their specific questions answered and their needs met.

Second, clear and valued roles for family and community members must be defined and promoted. Families are not only experts about their children; they are also experts in many other areas of adult life. For example, they may be employees and employers with connections to the local workforce. They may be homeowners, landlords, builders or contractors, or real estate agents with expertise about the real estate market, home maintenance, or budgeting. They may be members of local gyms, health clubs, or YMCAs with ideas about health, fitness, and social networks. They may be church members or civic leaders with connections to numerous people and groups. Families also have connections to their own network of friends, coworkers, employers, church members, and neighbors. Any one of these people may be the resource needed to secure a job, support a carpool, provide a helping hand at a health club, or serve as a real estate agent or landlord.

Like family involvement, community involvement may be accomplished in a number of different ways, including person-centered planning, PTI training and outreach activities, local interagency teams, and systematic outreach to civic and church groups.

STRATEGIES FOR INCREASING ADULT SERVICE AGENCY INVOLVEMENT

Involving adult service agencies in transition services requires interagency collaboration at all levels—student, community, and state. Although the participation of adult service agencies has been endorsed in recent IDEA legislation and in descriptions of effective transition models (e.g., Aspel et al., 1999; Certo et al., 2003, Everson et al., 2005), few states and communities have made a commitment to truly collaborative interagency teaming. To improve collaboration between education and adult service personnel at all levels, a transition specialist must join with others to aggressively pursue two components.

Encourage Teambuilding and Teamwork

First, teambuilding and teamwork, as illustrated in this chapter, must be viewed not as a desired practice, but as an essential practice. This means that a transition specialist must complete coursework in teaming as well as practica with interagency teamwork experiences. Classroom experiences must enable a transition specialist to complete role-play and case study assignments and be assigned to teams to practice and evidence teamwork skills. Practica experiences must enable the transition specialist to attend meetings and observe team leaders and members. Finally, for a practicing transition specialist, the educational environment must allow multiple opportunities to practice and refine teamwork abilities and have these skills monitored and evaluated by other professionals. This means, for example, that a school district's mission and policies must promote a culture of teamwork, and the transition specialist's job description and job duties must support opportunities to lead and serve on teams.

Develop Interagency Staff Development, Fiscal Resource Sharing, and Evaluation and Accountability Strategies

Interagency collaboration begins with an understanding of teamwork concepts and practices, and it continues with an opportunity to use these strategies in developing, implementing, and refining transition services at the student, community, and state levels. Communities and states must begin to encourage teamwork models, not just as a component of time-limited grants and model projects, but as an expected practice.

Community- and state-level teamwork models (e.g., Aspel et al., 1999; Certo et al., 2003; Everson et al., 2005) have been shown to improve communication and coordination of services and to improve consumer outcomes as a result of more efficient coordination of existing resources, interagency advocacy for new resources, removal of fiscal and policy disincentives and barriers, and collaborative evaluation and accountability for consumer outcomes (e.g., Everson et al., 2005). Figure 5.7 summarizes some of the promising interagency practices suggested by these other models. These practices have been used successfully and should be considered for use by interagency IEP teams addressing the goals and activities of individual students, by local interagency teams addressing a community's needs in a sparsely populated rural community, and by local interagency teams addressing a community's needs in heavily populated urban areas. The case study of Jackson illustrates the process, barriers, and outcomes of one community that embraced interagency teamwork. This case study is based on an actual community, but the name of the community and some of the descriptive information has been changed.

SUMMARY

Collaborative interagency teamwork is not a new concept in the arena of transition services, but it continues to be an underutilized one. This chapter provides transition specialists and others who are charged with organizing and facilitating teams with the knowledge they need to engage in more collaborative interagency transition practices. The concepts, practices, and strategies presented in this chapter may be used by transition specialists to initiate, build, and refine collaborative teams at the student, community, and state levels.

- Develop local and state interagency agreements or memorandums of understanding to formalize collaborative interagency relationships. These documents may be used to initiate and legitimize a team's goals and roles when it is first being formed. They may also be used to document and publicize a team's accomplishments once it has accomplished policy and procedural changes, funding coalitions, and/or shared service provisions.
- Include students, young adults, and family members on teams, and promote them into leadership positions. Consider establishing operating policies for cochairs that require one parent or family member and a professional to serve in these positions. Consider creative ways to include students and young adults in advisory capacities, evaluation activities, and/or provision of personnel training.
- Conduct community and state needs assessment to determine current and long-term needs of students and their families; current and long-term labor market needs; and current and long-term housing, transportation, and other community opportunities. Needs assessments do not need to be costly or time intensive. They may be as simple as holding annual community forums to identify needs and concerns; inviting representative members of the target population to attend focus groups to discuss needs and concerns; collecting follow-up or evaluation data from telephone or mail surveys; or preparing reports gleaned from extant data on service, waiting lists, and funding.
- Conduct self-evaluations or contract with third-party evaluators to conduct evaluations of educational programming and adult services to determine strengths and gaps.
- Develop strategic plans to address identified community and state needs. Ideally, plans should be developed to encompass a 3- to 5-year time period and updated annually. Strategic plans should be shared with and reviewed by key stakeholders, included elected officials, agency directors and personnel, consumer and advocacy groups, and local media. Annual reports documenting progress and barriers should be prepared and disseminated.
- Coordinate high school academic curricula and testing with vocational and occupational curricula and testing.
- Conduct family and community public education and outreach campaigns.
- Conduct cross-agency staff development. The best way to promote teamwork in practice is to promote it in staff development.
- Establish business and economic development advisory councils, steering committees, or other boards. Involve all key stakeholders, but be clear in defining how members will be used, how much time they are being asked to contribute, and how their feedback will be used in developing and implementing strategic plans.
- Seek to reduce paperwork burdens on professionals and families. Streamlined intake and referral processes, nonduplicative assessment methods, and shared fiscal streams and service provisions help to reduce gaps and duplications and generate positive involvement from families and individuals with disabilities.

(continued)

Figure 5.7
Promising Interagency Practices for Community- and State-Level Teams

- ◆ Establish single-point-of-entry systems ("one-stops") for eligibility and referrals to adult services. Designate one person or agency, one drop-in office, one form, one telephone number, and one Web site for individuals and families to contact.
- ◆ Establish procedures for early referral of students to adult services. Involving adult services agencies and personnel in meetings and including their brochures and eligibility forms in packets in the initial years of transition planning encourages questions and goal setting and reduces last-minute scrambling.
- ◆ Promote cross-agency resource sharing for staffing, program development, and operating costs.
- ◆ Coordinate with job development and job placement services.
- ◆ Coordinate with postsecondary transition programs, including early enrollment in community colleges and relationships with college and university offices of disability services.
- ◆ Coordinate with development of community housing development plans and community recreation and social service plans. Encourage transition specialists and other educators, students, and families to attend community hearings on city and county budgets and to review proposed state and local service plans.
- ◆ Promote and support innovative pilot or model programs and their maintenance and expansion. Address maintenance and expansion of these programs during the conceptualization process, not as an afterthought.
- ◆ Promote functional use of assistive technology for students while they are in high school and as they enter employment, housing, postsecondary education, and other community settings.
- ◆ Conduct local and state follow-up and follow-along studies of high school students.
- ◆ Disseminate outcomes and findings regionally and statewide.

Figure 5.7
Continued

CASE STUDY

COMMUNITY-LEVEL INTERAGENCY TRANSITION TEAM IN ACTION

Jackson is a small midwestern city of 28,000 residents. It is the county seat, and as a result, the primary employer is the county government. A regional hospital is also a major employer. Within the city there are several small shopping plazas and professional office buildings, a large auto parts manufacturing plant, three small furniture manufacturing plants, two automobile dealers, a community college, and a soft drink bottling plant. There are also two nursing homes and several medical practices associated with the hospital. Jackson has one high school, a middle school, and two elementary schools. There is a public bus system with limited routes and schedules, used almost exclusively by nondriving older people and people with disabilities for medical appointments and employment.

Many of Jackson's residents have lived in the community for several generations and have been part of the community's recent transition from a heavily manufacturing-based community into a more diversified service and health industries community. The median household income is $29,000, and the median educational level is a high school diploma or GED.

Approximately 10 years ago, Jackson's leaders established an interagency "healthy community" task force. The 14-member task force was initiated and originally led by hospital leaders. The goal of the task force is to bring citizens and elected officials together to discuss and address issues of concern to the larger community. Over the past few years, this task force has organized and sponsored civic events such as community health events, a summer leadership camp for high school youths, and fundraising events for the local school system.

Recently, the transition specialist at the high school, the county coordinator of services for senior citizens, and the director of the county's vocational/employment program for citizens with disabilities identified a pressing need for transportation options for nondriving citizens. Together, they approached the chair of the task force and asked for her assistance in pulling together a subcommittee of the task force to address the identified transportation need. After much discussion about the appropriate membership of such a subcommittee and how it should be structured, the task force agreed to support the establishment of a transportation subcommittee. Membership would be drawn from the larger task force, and the director of the vocational/employment program and the director of the public transportation program agreed to serve as cochairs of the subcommittee. The transition specialist agreed to serve as an active member of the subcommittee.

This subcommittee met twice to discuss the preliminary needs. As a result of these meetings, the subcommittee decided to hold two public forums—one at the high school and one at the hospital—to allow citizens to share their specific transportation needs and ideas. From these forums, the subcommittee determined that the county needed a more extensive, accessible, and flexible transportation option for nondrivers that citizens with disabilities and seniors could use for employment, errands, recreation activities, church, and other social activities. Next, the subcommittee spent several months and several meetings exploring options available in other, comparable communities.

The subcommittee's meetings during this time period were not always easy. Members disagreed about their agencys' roles, time commitment on the subcommittee, and the best solution. One cochair resigned his position, and his replacement had to be informed and nurtured by other subcommittee members. Although not every member agreed, eventually, the subcommittee selected one transportation option to pursue as the best match for their community—a church-run program with accessible vans and part-time drivers.

Over the next 6 months, the cochairs approached each of the auto dealers, who agreed to sell them two accessible vans at a discounted rate. They approached a private foundation that agreed to provide them with a $24,000 start-up grant. With the grant funds, they developed an operating budget, identified a local church to serve as the fiscal agent, and hired a part-time transportation coordinator. Next, they developed an interagency memorandum of understanding describing each subcommittee agency's responsibilities and a proposed timelines for activities. The subcommittee continued to meet monthly, and within 18 months the program was providing services at a prorated fee to approximately 45 of the county's citizens each month.

At the end of its first 12 months, the task force conducted a self-evaluation and, as a result, identified two nondriving citizens who were recent recipients of improved transportation services to join the subcommittee. They also approached the board of county commissioners and received a $15,000 annual appropriation that, along with program revenue, allowed them to sustain the program as their grant funds ended. During the team's self-evaluation process, the transition coordinator commented:

> If I had attempted to do this alone, just as an employee of the school system, I would have been overwhelmed. I wouldn't have had enough time, enough knowledge about transportation programs, or enough creativity and energy to envision a solution. This hasn't solved all of the transportation problems for students with disabilities in Jackson, but it has helped many of them find and keep jobs. And maybe, more importantly, it has shown me that joining with others ultimately makes everyone's job a little easier.

STUDY GUIDE QUESTIONS

1. Why are *collaborative, interagency,* and *team* all important defining features of comprehensive transition models?
2. What are the three broad functions of collaborative interagency teams at the student, community, and state levels? How are these functions distinct? How are they interrelated?
3. What interagency competencies should be possessed by a transition specialist? How do these competencies complement and expand the other roles of a transition specialist? How might a transition specialist work with a school district and his or her job description to promote and gain benefit for interagency practices?
4. Why are goals, roles, and processes so important in effective teamwork?
5. Provide an example of a scenario for each of the effective communication behaviors proposed in Figure 5.5. How might each of these behaviors be used to enhance teamwork with families? With students? With adult services agencies?
6. Provide an example of each of the interagency practices proposed in Figure 5.7.
7. Describe the relationship between a student's self-determination abilities and effective teamwork.

REFERENCES

Aspel, N., Bettis, G., Quinn, P., Test, D., & Wood, W. (1999). A collaborative process for planning transition services for all students with disabilities. *Career Development for Exceptional Individuals, 22*, 21–42.

Certo, N., Mautz, D., Pumpian, I., Sax, C., Smalley, K., Wade, H., et al., (2003). Review and discussion of a model for seamless transition to adulthood. *Education and Training in Developmental Disabilities, 38*, 3–17.

Council for Exceptional Children, Division on Career Development and Transition. (2000, March). *Transition specialist competencies* (Fact sheet). Arlington, VA: Author. http://www.dcdt.org

deFur, S. H., & Patton, J. R. (Eds.). (1999). *Transition and school-based services: Interdisciplinary perspectives for enhancing the transition process.* Austin, TX: Pro-Ed.

Everson, J. M., & Guillory, J. D. (1998). Building statewide transition services through collaborative teamwork. In F. R. Rusch & J. G. Chadsey (Eds.), *Beyond high school: Transition from school to work* (pp. 299–318). Belmont, CA: Wadsworth.

Everson, J. M., & Guillory, J. D. (2002). *Interagency teaming: Strategies for facilitating teams from forming through performing.* New Orleans: Louisiana State University Health Sciences Center, School of Allied Health Professions, Human Development Center.

Everson, J. M., Guillory, J. D., & Ivester, J. G. (2005). *Community development in Action: Illustrations from Communities in South Carolina and Louisiana.* Columbia: University of South Carolina School of Medicine, Center for Disability Resources.

Johnson, D. R., & Emanuel, E. E. (Eds.). (2000, November). *Issues influencing the future of transition programs and services in the United States. A collection of articles by leading researchers in secondary special education and transition services for students with disabilities.* Minneapolis: University of Minnesota, Institute on Community Integration, National Transition Network.

Kohler, P. (1993). Best practices in transition: Substantial or implied? *Career Development for Exceptional Individuals, 16*, 1–18.

Kohler, P. D. (1996). *A taxonomy for transition programming linking research and practice.* Champaign: University of Illinois, Transition Research Institute.

Leadership Designs, Inc. (n.d.). *Interactive behavior skills.* Longboat Key, FL: Author.

Martin, J. E., & Marshall, L. H. (1996). Infusing self-determination instruction into the IEP and transition process. In D. J. Sands & M. L. Wehmeyer (Eds.), *Self-determination across the lifespan: Independence and choice for people with disabilities* (pp. 215–236). Baltimore: Brookes.

Phelps, L. A., & Hanley-Maxwell, C. (1997). School-to-work transition for youth with disabilities: A review of outcomes and practices. *Review of Educational Research, 67*, 197–226.

Varney, G. H. (1989). *Building productive teams: An action guide and resource book.* San Francisco: Jossey-Bass.

Wehman, P. (Ed.). (2001). *Life beyond the classroom: Transition strategies for young people with disabilities* (3rd ed.). Baltimore: Brookes.

Wehman, P., Everson, J. M., & Reid, D. (2001). Beyond programs and placements: Using person-centered practices to individualize the transition processes and outcomes. In P. Wehman (Ed.), *Life beyond the classroom: Transition strategies for young people with disabilities* (3rd ed., pp. 91–124). Baltimore: Brookes.

Wehmeyer, M. L., Agran, M., & Hughes, C. (1998). *Teaching self-determination to students with disabilities. Basic skills for successful transition.* Baltimore: Brookes.

Wehmeyer, M. L., & Schwartz, M. (1997). Self-determination and positive adult outcomes: A follow-up study of youth with mental retardation or learning disabilities. *Exceptional Children, 63*, 245–255.

Wood, W. M., Test, D. W., Browder, D. M., Algozzine, B., & Karvonen, M. (2000). *Self-Determination Synthesis Project.* Available: http://www.uncc.edu/sdsp/sd_curricula.asp

Preparing Students for Postsecondary Education

Chapter 6

Introduction

This chapter focuses on information educators need to prepare students with disabilities for postsecondary education. Strategies are outlined for providing the supports students need to establish goals for postsecondary education and design a high school experience that ensures preparedness for enrollment in 4-year universities, community colleges, trade and vocational schools, alternative adult diploma programs, or other nontraditional types of lifelong learning environments. Emphasis is placed on student choice and the use of a team approach.

The chapter also provides information about postsecondary education-related resources available to educators and students regarding financial assistance, preparation for admission tests, the application process, accommodations, and modifications. A case study demonstrates the process of assisting a student with a disability in achieving her dream of postsecondary education.

For students with disabilities to enroll in postsecondary educational institutions and remain enrolled until completing their programs, multiple supports must be provided for them and their families. As Kohler's taxonomy of transition noted, student-focused planning and family involvement are essential to transition planning. The active participation of both students and their family members is particularly needed when plans are being formulated to pursue additional education or training after high school (Kohler, Field, Izzo, & Johnson, 1997). Students with disabilities entering a postsecondary educational environment discover quickly that a high level of self-determination is required to obtain needed services and navigate the postsecondary education system.

Personal Perspectives on Transition to Postsecondary Education for Students with Disabilities

Steven Eddy
Doctoral Student, University of North Carolina at Charlotte

As a student with a disability who has successfully made the transition from high school to postsecondary education, I wish that I had known more about the services offered to college students with disabilities before arriving on the college campus. Future college-bound students with disabilities will benefit if high school counselors provide access to information about college disability support services so students can consider that information in making their college choices.

I also wish I had known more about the differences between high school and college before I left high school. High school counselors can assist future students in making the transition to postsecondary education by specifically pointing out that the more rigorous courses and requirements in colleges or universities may necessitate that students access additional support services not needed in high school. Counselors should work closely with transition planning teams to help students determine what services they may need in college based on their postschool goals.

High school counselors should work to lessen any potential concern students may have about being labeled as a person with a disability if they register for college support services. Students may need to know that support services are based on students' needs rather than being blanket provisions for all students. Upon leaving high school, I was unaware that colleges and universities expected students with disabilities to self-advocate for needed services.

It would also be helpful if students visited disability support services offices of their top college choices during their junior or senior year so that they could begin to establish a rapport with support services personnel. Students who might be hesitant to identify themselves as having a disability would be more likely to do so if they already knew and trusted people at the college or university. Disability support personnel may need to make

172

*more frequent visits to high schools to explain documentation procedures directly to stu-
dents. High school students also need to know that they may be required to provide
medical documentation before receiving support services.*

*As someone who has made the transition to postsecondary education, I would encour-
age college-bound students with disabilities to learn about all services available to students with disabilities. In addition, I believe high school counselors should work with
college-bound students to help them practice self-advocacy skills. Students who already
know how to advocate for their needs are more likely to achieve their postsecondary goals.*

In 1978 only 2.6% of full-time first-year college students reported having any
type of disability (Henderson, 1995). By 2000, this percentage had grown to
17% (National Council on Disability, 2000). While this appears to be an extraor-
dinary advancement over the last 3 decades, in actuality Blackorby and Wagner
(1996) found that 3 to 5 years after graduating from high school only 27% of students with disabilities had attempted postsecondary education compared to 68%
of their peers without disabilities. Students with disabilities face many barriers to
attending college, including challenging high school coursework, limited accommodations and modifications, low expectations, lack of self-determination skills,
lack of role models, and learned dependence. In addition to these barriers, students with disabilities are often less qualified for college based on an index score
that includes grades, class rank, National Education Longitudinal Study (NELS)
composite test scores, and Scholastic Aptitude Test (SAT) or American College Test
(ACT) scores (National Center for Education Statistics [NCES], 1999a).

The Individuals with Disabilities Education Act (IDEA) states that transition
planning should include postschool goals for pursuing postsecondary education
and training. But despite federal legislation ensuring educational supports prior
to high school graduation and protecting the civil rights of students in postsecondary educational settings, few students with disabilities pursue a college degree. Obtaining a college degree is important because it can result in increased
employment options and financial stability.

THE IMPORTANCE OF POSTSECONDARY EDUCATION

For students who leave high school without a diploma, only about 15.6% obtain
employment, compared to 30.2% of students with a high school diploma and
45.1% of students who have had some college. For individuals with disabilities
who are able to obtain a 4-year degree, the employment rate rises to 50.3% (Yelin
& Katz, 1994). However, a college degree does not guarantee full-time employment, since fewer individuals with disabilities who hold bachelor's degrees work
full time than their counterparts without disabilities (National Center for the
Study of Postsecondary Educational Supports [NCSPES], 2002).

A college degree is a factor in the salary that can be commanded once an individual is in the labor market. Witte, Phillips, and Kakela (1998) reported that the

annual salaries of a sample of 72 college graduates with learning disabilities (1987–1994) ranged from $20,000 to $40,000 for 49% of the group, while 19% earned $40,000 and more annually. On the other hand, Blackorby and Wagner (1997) reported that 40% of students with learning disabilities who did not attend college earned an annual salary of approximately $12,000. Overall, college graduates can expect to have better health; greater self-confidence; increased career options; higher-level problem-solving skills; improved interpersonal relationships; a higher level of open-mindedness; and more involvement in politics, community affairs, recreation, and leadership activities than nongraduates have. Those graduating from a 4-year educational institution are also less dependent on parents and governmental benefits than individuals who do not pursue postsecondary education (Pascarella & Terenzini, 1991; Turnbull, Turnbull, Wehmeyer, & Park, 2003).

FACTORS AFFECTING POSTSECONDARY EDUCATION OUTCOMES

Given the significant impact that postsecondary education can have on the life of a student with a disability, it is imperative that transition planning in this area begin no later than middle school. The chance that a student with a disability will pursue a college education can be increased by educators and family members having the expectation that the student will attend college and by establishing college attendance as a postschool outcome on the transition component of the student's individualized education program (IEP'; Wagner, D'Amico, Marder, Newman, & Blackorby, 1992). Two major barriers that affect the possibility of students with disabilities enrolling in postsecondary education are (a) attitudes and expectations and (b) high school curriculum.

Attitudes and Expectations

The attitudes and expectations of parents and teachers can have a powerful impact on the path a student with disabilities will choose after graduation (Morningstar, Turnbull, & Turnbull, 1996). Since 1987 the number of parents of students with disabilities who expect their child to graduate from a 2-year college has increased from 2.6% to 12.7% (Wagner, 2003). However, there is a greater level of skepticism and doubt surrounding the achievement of postsecondary education goals than there is about employment goals among students with disabilities and their families.

The Half the Planet Foundation (2002) reported that people with disabilities often internalize the low expectations imposed on them by others. The study found that young people with disabilities are learning at an early age that the only two options they have in life are to work in a low-paying, menial job or to collect social security benefits. Maybe this is the reason that students with disabilities are twice as likely as their peers without disabilities to have no plans for pursuing any type of education past high school ("Roles for youth with Disabilities," 2002).

Although students and their parents do understand the connection between advanced training and obtaining a well-paying job, many students with disabilities do not perceive college to be a feasible option (Schuster, Timmons, & Moloney, 2003). Data from the National Longitudinal Transition Study-2 (Wagner, 2003) indicated that only about half of the students in the study (47%) had plans to go to college.

High School Curriculum Issues

Another barrier for students with disabilities transitioning into postsecondary educational settings is an IEP that does not include objectives addressing the skills needed to succeed in postsecondary education. As a result, students may not complete a course of study that prepares them for postsecondary education. Efforts to help students obtain the skills needed for success in pursuing advanced training and education should begin in elementary school. Students who plan on attending a 2-year college or 4-year university need to have a sound foundation in academic skills in order to complete the high school classes needed to meet college admission requirements. Figure 6.1 illustrates a sample college preparatory high school curriculum.

Many of the traditional instructional strategies and organizational frameworks common in high school academic programs can have a negative impact on students with disabilities (Gersten, 1998). The ability of students with learning

---

- ◆ **Four credits of English** (e.g., English literature, American literature, English composition, world literature)
- ◆ **Three credits of mathematics** (e.g., algebra I, algebra II, geometry, precalculus, trigonometry, calculus)
- ◆ **Three credits of science** (e.g., earth/environmental science, biology, chemistry, physics)
- ◆ **Three years of social studies** (e.g., United States history, government/economics, world history, world cultures, United States government)
- ◆ **Two to four credits of foreign language** (e.g., Spanish, French, German, Latin)
- ◆ **One credit of health and physical education**
- ◆ **One to three credits of challenging electives** (e.g., economics, computer technology, communications, psychology, statistics)
- ◆ **One or more arts education credits are usually recommended** (e.g., dance, music, theater arts, visual arts)
- ◆ **Vocational education credits** (appropriate for students pursuing any type of postsecondary education but vital to students entering a 2-year community college or vocational-technical training program)

Figure 6.1
Sample College/University Preparatory High School Curriculum

disabilities to learn effectively can be hindered by instruction delivered primarily through teacher lectures, student note-taking, and rote memorization of disconnected facts that have little or no relevance to their present or future life (Darling-Hammond, Ancess, & Falk, 1995). For some students with disabilities, failure to achieve a high level of academic achievement is directly related to the high school's inability to plan and deliver an appropriate curriculum (Berliner & Biddle, 1996; Hatch, 1998).

Educators must be careful to avoid pushing students with disabilities toward a general studies curriculum or encouraging course waivers, which might eliminate students from qualifying for admission to the college of their choice. Students with disabilities should be supported and encouraged to enroll in a college-preparatory course of study and, when appropriate, to take advanced placement (AP) courses, which can result in earning college credits while still in high school. For example, admission to a 4-year university usually requires that a student have high school foreign language credits, but data from the National Longitudinal Study-2 (Wagner, 2003) revealed that only 21% of the study's participants enrolled in foreign language courses. Having the expectation that students with disabilities will take challenging academic courses in the general curriculum was the intent of the 1997 reauthorization of IDEA.

Careful planning with active involvement by the student is required to ensure that at the conclusion of a 4-year high school program the student's academic credits, grade point average (GPA), and career exploration are in place for transition to a postsecondary educational institution. Guidance counselors can play a critical role in this process, since advising, schedule planning, and futures planning are typically part of their job responsibilities.

Students with disabilities should be assisted in obtaining the combination of courses that best matches their postsecondary education goals while simultaneously increasing their chances of academic success. Advance planning is needed to provide safety nets for students who might have difficulty in a course and need to make schedule changes or who might need to retake a course due to failure.

The type of scheduling used by a high school (e.g., block, six-period, A-B, seven-period), the number of course offerings, the state's pathways to a high school diploma, and the amount of time needed for special education support are all issues that must be considered when determining a 4-year high school plan. Certainly high schools that have classrooms, curriculum, courses, and programs that are universally accessible to all students and that provide the support staff needed for comprehensive planning will be more successful in graduating students prepared for continuing their education.

Additional issues that affect the ability of students with disabilities to transition successfully to postsecondary education include (a) the high drop-out rate of students with disabilities (NCSPES, 2002; U.S. Department of Education, 2002a), (b) the increased emphasis on high-stakes assessment (deFur, 2002; Langenfield, Thurlow, & Scott, 1997; Thurlow, Sinclair, & Johnson, 2002), and (c) students' possible confusion with the multiplicity of exit document options (e.g., certificates, diplomas) available (Guy, Shin, Lee, & Thurlow, 2002). For a more detailed discussion of these issues, see Chapter 2.

CHOOSING A POSTSECONDARY EDUCATION OPTION

The first step for a student in the transition process from school to postsecondary education is to decide between available options.

Colleges and Universities

It is the responsibility of the IEP/transition team to assist the student in getting ready for postsecondary education and training. This includes making decisions regarding the postsecondary educational setting most appropriate to the student's needs and future career goals, supporting the student through the process of choosing a college, and making necessary arrangements to attend the college of his or her choice. Traditionally, students focus on two types of postsecondary education—community colleges and 4-year universities—although there are other options such as vocational-technical schools, special training programs, and Internet-based learning. There are more than 3,000 colleges and universities in the United States (Reamer, 1997), and since services for students with disabilities vary widely among institutions, choosing an appropriate educational setting can be an enormous task for a student. The key is to ensure a good match between the student's unique needs, his or her career goal, and the characteristics of the college (McGuire & Shaw, 1987; Navicky, 1998).

One area that must be investigated when searching for an appropriate college is the level of services provided to students with disabilities. Although there are federal mandates covering issues related to postsecondary education of students with disabilities, there are still vast differences among institutions. Students and their families must be provided with information about what to expect at the college level regarding the delivery of special services. Figure 6.2 includes a list of questions that students can ask when choosing a college or university.

Community Colleges

The majority of students with disabilities who pursue postsecondary education enroll in 2-year **community colleges** or for-profit vocational training programs (NCES, 1999a). A community college setting is attractive to students with disabilities for a variety of reasons. Although community college standards vary from state to state, in general they have an open enrollment admission policy, meaning that any student with a high school diploma or general education diploma (GED) will be accepted. Community colleges typically require applicants to take a placement test such as the Assessment of Skills for Successful Entry and Transfer

- What are the requirements for admission? If the institution requires placement exams for math, English or reading, are special arrangements made for the student to take these exams?
- How many students with disabilities are on campus? What year are they in? Are they full time or part time? Residents or commuters? Traditional age or older? Men or women? Can they be contacted?
- Will the student be admitted into a general program of study as a "regular" student? If not, will this have any ramifications for financial aid and Vocational Rehabilitation benefits the student may receive?
- What are the goals and objectives of the programs for students with disabilities?
- What is the procedure for the student to follow in identifying his or her disability? Who are the persons on campus who should be notified?
- What are the special services provided? Is there a charge for these services? How does one obtain the services?
- What specialized training in disabilities do the professors have? In which disabilities have professors had experience?
- Is tutoring and/or counseling provided on a one-to-one basis or in a group? If in a group, how large is it? How frequently and intensively is it made available? Are there any costs?
- What supervision is provided for noncertified instructors or tutors?
- How is the duration of special services determined? Is it usually one semester? One year? Two years or longer? Who will be the student's academic advisor, and what training does this individual have with students with disabilities? How will academic advising (i.e., selection of courses) and registration be handled?
- Are students with disabilities required to take a full load of courses? If not, and if a student decides not to, does this decision affect financial aid or the ability to live in on-campus housing?
- Are any courses unavailable to students with disabilities?
- What modifications have faculty or administrators been willing to make for students with disabilities on the campus? Who is responsible for making the arrangements for accommodations?
- Are there offices on campus that can do further diagnostic testing, and if so, what type? Can they provide additional remedial services if necessary? Are there consultants on campus who specialize in teaching in the area of disabilities who can provide assistance if needed?
- Is there specialized equipment on campus available for use by students with disabilities? Is there a cost?
- Does the institution work closely with outside agencies such as Vocational Rehabilitation, Services for the Blind, and so forth?
- If mobility is a concern, how are arrangements made to assist students with physical disabilities? Are all buildings and dorms accessible?
- Are there any special support groups on campus for students with disabilities?
- Are there any types of financial aid or scholarships available for students with disabilities? If so, how do you apply for them?
- Are there courses required of students with disabilities? If so, do they carry college credit and does the credit count toward graduation credits?

Figure 6.2

Questions Students Can Use When Choosing a College or University

Note: Based on Barr, Hartman, and Spillane (1995), Higher Education Consortium on Learning Disabilities (1996), and Zaccarine and Stewart (1991).

(ASSET), but even if a student scores below the cut-off on admission tests they can still enroll in remedial classes or in vocationally oriented programs leading to a license, certificate, or credential (e.g., child care, food service, automotive repair, computer-assisted drafting) instead of pursuing an associate of science or associate of arts degree. Many community colleges have programs that are linked with local high schools (e.g., tech-prep, school-to-career, 2+2 programs) allowing students to take classes in a specific career pathway during the last 2 years of high school to better prepare them for college success. In some cases they allow students to obtain college credit prior to high school graduation.

Community colleges are usually located close to a student's home, and in many cases courses are offered at accessible times, with classes scheduled from 7:00 A.M. to 10:00 P.M. and some offered on weekends. Tuition costs are much lower at community colleges than those found in 4-year colleges and universities (Ignash, 1994). Students who experience difficulty obtaining sufficient financial aid may choose to attend a community college for 2 years, then transfer to a 4-year college or university, since community colleges typically have articulation agreements with 4-year colleges and universities. Students may also find the community college setting less threatening, since class sizes tend to be smaller, the student population is more reflective of the local community, and it is not unusual for community college students to attend college part time. Finally, some students may want to enter the workforce as soon as possible and feel that a 2-year degree or certification program is a more expedient path to a career (Cocchi, 1997).

Vocational-Technical Schools and Other Postsecondary Education Options

Not all students with disabilities will choose to attend a traditional educational or training program at a community college or 4-year university. Some students will desire educational opportunities such as a vocational-technical school or a specialized training program to obtain a better job. Options may include programs resulting in certification in areas such as child care, nursing assistance, cosmetology, secretarial work, or truck driving. Other students may want to take courses through adult education programs at community colleges aimed at improving a specific skill area (e.g.. reading, math), or they may wish to pursue an area of interest (e.g., cooking, gardening, computers) through continuing education courses offered in the community by various agencies. For students who are

---

DID YOU KNOW?

Two-year degrees in technical and occupational areas can result in high-paying careers and jobs equal to or greater than those obtained by graduates from 4-year colleges and universities (Gray, 1996).

eager to obtain employment immediately following graduation, programs offered through the Workforce Investment Act (WIA), designed to increase employability through training and education, might be an option.

The transition planning process should be used to ensure that students understand the wide variety of postsecondary educational options so that even those who feel that after high school graduation they "never want to go to school again" can begin to view adult learning in a different manner.

High School Diploma Alternatives

There may even be situations in which students decide to leave high school prior to completing the criteria for a high school diploma (e.g., no desire to remain in school past age 18) and want to enter the GED program or the adult high school diploma program at the local community college. A GED examination consists of six test sections: social studies, science, math, literature, arts, and writing. Passing scores for the GED are established by each state; however, all GED graduates must meet a standard that exceeds the performance of at least 33% of students receiving a high school diploma through the traditional high school route (American Council on Education, 2000). An adult high school diploma is earned through instruction offered cooperatively with local public school systems, usually follows a course of study identical to the high school curriculum, and results in the student's receiving a real high school diploma. Students who choose to pursue either of these paths toward a graduation credential should be well informed of the rigor involved in passing these tests—including the time commitment—and the skill levels that will be required so that they can make an informed decision regarding high school completion.

Postsecondary Education Programs for Students with Significant Disabilities

The disabilities most frequently reported by young people enrolled in postsecondary institutions are learning disabilities (LD) and/or attention deficit/hyperactivity disorder (ADHD; NCSPES, 2000a). Postsecondary education has only recently become an option for students with significant disabilities such as mental retardation, autism, or multiple disabilities. Some school systems are implementing programs to allow students who require educational services past the age of 18 to "graduate" with their peers and continue educational programming on the campuses of community colleges, universities, or vocational-technical schools. These programs are designed to provide a more age-appropriate learning environment in which students with significant disabilities can increase their independence through employment; community involvement; friendships with other college students; recreational activities; and the development of communication, social, and self-determination skills. Most programs offer a combination of college classes, basic or functional skills classes, and job experiences (Grigal,

Neubert, & Moon, 2002). See Chapter 2 for more information on programs for students ages 18 to 21.

PREPARING FOR POSTSECONDARY EDUCATION

To prepare students who choose to pursue postsecondary education, high schools should (a) provide rigorous programs designed to adequately prepare students, (b) promote self-determination skills, and (c) provide comprehensive and effective transition planning that begins early and focuses on the steps needed to successfully enroll in postsecondary education. In addition, students, families, and teams need to consider such issues as college admission tests, financial aid, differences between high school and postsecondary education environments, civil rights, accommodations and modifications, and technology.

Provide a Rigorous High School Program

Providing a rigorous high school program for students with disabilities that encompasses all of the experiences and instruction needed to ensure that they will achieve their desired postschool educational outcomes requires comprehensive instruction in a variety of areas, including self-determination, career awareness/ exploration, core academics, social skills, and study skills. It also requires student and family involvement, interagency collaboration, and the provision of supports students need to succeed in the least restrictive environment.

Regular academic course enrollment in high school is a significant predictor of future participation in postsecondary education (Baer et al., 2003). About 70% of students with disabilities who enroll in postsecondary education spend at least 75% of their time in general education classes while in high school (U.S. Department of Education, 1995). Enrollment in general education courses can result in students' being held to higher academic standards, similar to those they will experience at the postsecondary education level (Rojewski, 1996), and prepare them for an environment where they will be expected to participate in a regular course of study (Stodden, Galloway, & Stodden, 2003).

Exclusion from the general curriculum can result in lower expectations and stigmatization within the general student body (Rea, McLaughlin, & Walther-Thomas, 2002), and it does not promote mastery of academically challenging coursework (NCSPES, 2000b) such as algebra and geometry, which can increase the likelihood of postsecondary education attendance (U.S. Department of Education, 2000). Students who are enrolled in general education classes are generally viewed as more capable in all areas, including their personal decision making and goal setting, and this results in higher levels of self-determination.

It is unfortunate, but due to variables such as the shortage of financial and professional resources and conflicting philosophies, many high schools continue to use some form of tracking or ability grouping, resulting in unequal levels of curriculum (Oakes & Wells, 1998; Vough, Schumm, & Brick, 1998). If a high school focuses on students' academic weaknesses, using special education classes and modified curriculum to address individual learning needs instead of providing the general curriculum in a manner that addresses multiple learning styles and needs, students with disabilities will not only be ill-equipped academically, but will also be unprepared to meet the drastically different educational environment they will encounter on a college campus (Stodden & Jones, 2002).

High school special education programs must be open to incorporating a variety of innovative instructional strategies such as differentiated instruction, problem-based learning, metacognitive approaches, technological support, curriculum modifications, and graphic organizers into routine service delivery to support students in the general education program and facilitate their comprehension of course content (MacArthur, Schwartz, Graham, Molloy, & Harris, 1996; NCSPES, 2000b; Rose & Meyer, 2000; Tomlinson, 1999). High schools must take responsibility not only for expanding students' academic ability but also for ensuring the development of students as mature young adults capable of taking on the social challenges associated with the college experience.

Promote Self-Determination Skills

Self-determination is one of the most important skills for students with disabilities who wish to pursue postsecondary education. It is an area that permeates a young person's high school years, providing avenues for participation in planning, decision making, and self-advocacy. There must be sustained efforts by educators and family members to provide students with specific instruction in self-determination skills and opportunities for generalization (Zhang, Katsiyannis, & Zhang, 2002). Simply enrolling students in an isolated self-determination course is not sufficient. The high school environment must provide opportunities that allow students to practice self-determination skills on a daily basis. These practical application experiences should be reinforced with individualized instruction delivered through a structured self-determination curriculum (Field, Martin, Miller, Ward, & Wehmeyer, 1998).

Many researchers have noted that students can benefit from self-determination training (Algozzine, Browder, Karvonen, Test, & Wood, 2001). Involvement in self-determination training can increase a student's knowledge of available services, clarify future goals, and improve self-concept (Phillips, 1990). Students who have received self-determination training are able to generalize self-advocacy skills to a variety of school settings (Durlak, Rose, & Bursuck, 1994). Various curricula can be used in conjunction with individualized instruction and generalization opportunities to ensure that self-determination becomes a part of a student's repertoire of skills. Special educators should take advantage of curricula such as *TAKE CHARGE for the Future* (Powers et al., 2001) and *Whose Future Is It Anyway?* (Wehmeyer & Lawrence, 1995).

In addition to using commercial curricula, teachers should be encouraged to infuse self-determination training into the general curriculum. High-stakes testing has caused educators to struggle with the logistics of how, when, and where to teach self-determination skills due to what often appear to be conflicting academic expectations and pressures. Teachers should be trained to take advantage of routine events within the high school (e.g., scheduling, requesting accommodations and medication), augment curriculum, and infuse self-determination into classroom lessons. For example, increased self-awareness can result from the use of journaling in which students investigate and write about their own disabilities (Eisenman & Tascione, 2002), Instead of special education teachers' making all the arrangements for accommodations for students who are taking general education courses, students can participate in this process to improve their self-advocacy skills. Students can improve their decision-making skills by taking a lead role in managing their time for homework.

Although significant advancements have been made in increasing the self-determination of students with disabilities, research indicates that there is still work to be done by teachers and parents. For more information on self-determination, see Chapter 2.

Once a student is enrolled in college, self-determination skills will give him or her the foundation needed to handle social situations, obtain needed accommodations and modifications, and persevere through the many difficult situations that will be encountered on the path to an advanced degree. One of the major factors in succeeding in higher education is a student's inner strength (NCSPES, 2000c). Directors of postsecondary education disability support services report that students who have realistic goals, self-advocacy skills, and appropriate academic preparation have greater success in college programs than those who do not have these attributes (Kurtz & Hicks-Coolick, 1997).

Students who aspire to a postsecondary education and who want to be equipped to navigate the postsecondary educational environment must participate in self-determination activities that provide support in the following areas:

1. Investigating future career options and making decisions regarding the level of postsecondary education needed for a chosen career.

2. Using effective decision-making strategies regarding coursework, schedules, assignment completion, career training, postsecondary education, and employment.

3. Setting realistic and attainable short-term and long-term goals and accomplishing the goals by breaking them down into smaller objectives, establishing timelines, and identifying resources for helping them achieve the goals.

4. Solving problems by eliciting advice and assistance, alternating plans, demonstrating flexibility, and devising additional options for accomplishing goals or solving problems.

5. Conducting ongoing self-evaluation and monitoring of progress, which should include acknowledging ongoing problems, reflecting on past successes and failures, and devising solutions (Guillory, Brown, & Everson, 2001).

6. Fully understanding the impact of having a disability but viewing it as only part of what makes a person unique.

7. Being willing to take reasonable risks, trying new things, and disengaging themselves from dependent relationships with family members.

8. Effectively using emotional coping and stress-reducing strategies such as early identification of stress-producing situations, seeking counseling, seeking assistance when needed, using peer supports, developing a mentor, and planning ahead for difficult situations (Raskind, Goldberg, Higgins, & Herman, 2003).

9. Practicing conflict resolution skills when needed to work out differences with friends, family, and college personnel.

Get the Family and IEP Team Involved

It is important for educators and parents to assist students in understanding the importance of using their high school years to accumulate experiences that can help them in choosing and being successful in a future career. Students should be encouraged to take elective courses in many disciplines, master basic academic skills (e.g., writing composition, keyboarding, public speaking), join school clubs, do volunteer work, and, if possible, obtain a paid job while still in high school. To choose the proper course of study for postsecondary education, students must have access to career counseling supported by career awareness and career development activities that will provide realistic information about employment trends, educational requirements, and possible job accommodations (Hartman & Baker, 1986).

Although many students with disabilities are consumed with completing the academic credits needed for high school graduation and have little time leftover for elective courses and employability activities (Guy et al., 2002), participation in career-related experiences such as internships can be an asset in choosing the best match in both postsecondary education and future employment. Exposure to actual work settings allows students to understand the potential impact of their disability, practice self-advocacy related to disability issues, and test various accommodations and modifications (Stern, 2002). In general, students with disabilities who have access to vocational and occupational skill training will experience more positive outcomes associated with postschool employment and postsecondary education than those who do not have such access (Wagner, Blackorby, Cameto, & Newman, 1993).

As part of the transition planning process beginning in the late middle school and early high school years, educators and counselors should involve students in assessment activities and goal planning to assist them in making decisions regarding the types of postsecondary educational settings appropriate for their abilities, interests, and career goals. Pursuing postsecondary education and training must be the student's decision. Although family members and educators should ensure that students fully understand the career opportunities associated with a college degree and the other benefits of continuing their education, ultimately it is the student's choice to attend college.

DID YOU KNOW?

First-generation college students with disabilities face greater challenges since many are less academically and psychologically prepared for college than their peers from college-educated families (Mitchell, 1997).

The role that family members play in a young person's life also changes drastically as the young person advances from being a high school student to a college student. The Family Education Rights and Privacy Act of 1974 (FERPA) requires that postsecondary educational institutions treat all student information as confidential and maintain all disability-related information on separate forms in a secure location. Disability information is to be shared only on a limited basis with faculty and staff who have a compelling reason for accessing the information, such as planning accommodations or modifications. Since college students have reached the age of majority and are considered adults by legal standards, postsecondary educational institutions are unable to share information with a student's family or anyone else outside the college environment unless the student signs a release allowing the college to do so (Association on Higher Education and Disability [AHEAD], 1996).

During transition planning, activities and strategies should be developed that will help a student make the transition to a learning and social environment that is quite different from the one to which the student has been accustomed. A comprehensive transition component developed by a team that clearly establishes a postschool goal of postsecondary education can serve as the roadmap from high school to postsecondary education and/or training. The use of student surveys, interviews, and questionnaires can assist in determining the readiness of a student who desires postsecondary education and provide a systematic approach to identifying an overall picture of the student's strengths and needs (Babbit & White, 2002). Transition teams should work to discover answers to the following questions:

1. What knowledge and skills are needed to make the transition to a postsecondary academic or vocational-technical program a successful experience?
2. What knowledge and skills does the student possess at the present time?
3. What knowledge and skills does the student need to acquire? (NICHCY Transition Summary, 1993).

The key is to devise a plan that is holistic. It is true that a student must be academically successful to enter postsecondary education, but a narrow focus on academics can result in other transition need areas being overlooked or receiving limited attention (Hasazi, Furney, & DeStefano, 1999).

Strategies for Effective Family Involvement

1. Assist the young person in ensuring that all testing is updated and that copies of all documentation of disability have been obtained.

2. Support the young person in involving outside agencies such as Vocational Rehabilitation and the Social Security Administration.

3. Advocate for the young person to take college-prep courses in a fully inclusive learning environment and support the child in homework, test preparation, and assignments.

4. Allow the young person to take responsibility for independent living skills in the home environment, such as cleaning, cooking, and clothing care, that will transfer to a college dormitory.

5. Talk with the young person or have family members and friends talk with him or her about how college life differs from high school in areas such as course offerings, schedules, teacher expectations, and social opportunities.

6. Assist the young person in developing self-determination skills by encouraging goal setting, financial management, decision making, and risk taking. Give the young person opportunities for self-advocacy both at school and in the community.

7. Assist the young person in understanding how his or her disability is connected to social experiences with peers, teachers, and family members. Avoid "protecting" the young person from issues such as discrimination.

8. Assist the young person in completing applications for colleges and financial aid.

9. Encourage part-time employment or volunteer activities that will assist the young person in making career choices.

10. Allow the young person to establish a personal budget while still in high school and show him or her the additional expenses that can be expected after enrollment in postsecondary education.

11. Arrange for college tours and visits.

12. If possible, provide the opportunity for the young person to attend a special pre-session during the summer or at least attend a prospective student weekend at a college.

13. Arrange for all medical or health issues to be handled prior to attending college.

14. Encourage the young person to learn about various disability and advocacy organizations and become an active participant in any organizations that might provide assistance, advice, or information (Hart, Zimbeck, & Whelly, 2002; Sullivan, 1987).

Finally, having a student take a lead role in the transition planning process can contribute to independence and development of self-determination by allowing the student to describe his or her strengths, needs, and desires to the IEP team. Careful consideration should also be given during planning meetings to targeting goals that develop learning strategies related to studying, note-taking, test-taking, scheduling, communication, negotiation, assertiveness, memory, organization, time management, and assistive technology (Izzo & Lamb, 2002).

Many high school special education programs focus on remediation and/or maintenance in the general education program (e.g., assistance with homework, studying for tests, catching up on class assignments) and do not provide sufficient instruction in compensatory strategies needed for academic independence in a postsecondary setting. For example, students with learning disabilities report that they learn the majority of compensatory and learning strategies needed for postsecondary success after enrolling in college, even though they received special education services while in high school (Reis, Neu, & McGuire, 1997).

Teach Learning Strategies

Although many high school students have full schedules, time must be allotted to teach learning strategies that will transfer throughout the curriculum and assist in preparing for increasingly demanding academic tasks. Many learning strategies can easily be infused into general education classes. Learning strategies instruction can also be delivered in special education resource classes, during tutoring sessions, in after-school workshops, or in summer seminars. One approach that can be used by teachers at the high school or college level is the spontaneous teaching of skills in a structured format to help a student understand a strategy, its purpose, and how to use it. This process assists the student in internalizing the strategy, thereby increasing the likelihood that it will be added to the student's repertoire of learning techniques. Following is an outline for teachers to use when presenting a new strategy to students:

1. *What is the strategy?* The strategy is described or a definition is given in a manner that outlines the specific features of the strategy.

2. *Why should the strategy be learned?* Students are informed of why the strategy is being taught so they can develop an awareness of its importance in the learning process.

3. *How can the strategy be used?* The application of a strategy to a particular learning situation is outlined for students in a manner that provides a chronological, step-by-step breakdown of how the strategy should be applied.

4. *When and where should the strategy be used?* Students are given examples of situations in which the strategy could be used in an effective manner. This can involve verbal scenarios, role playing, and/or testimonials from students who have used the strategy effectively.

5. *How can the strategy be evaluated to determine its effectiveness for a student?* Students are taught how to judge the effectiveness of the strategy in relation to their specific needs (Seidenberg, as cited in Brinckerhoff, Shaw, & McGuire, 1993)

Take the College Admission Tests

Four-year universities look at several academic factors when determining admission, including GPA, rank in high school senior class, and **college admission test** (**SAT** or **ACT**) scores. A student's GPA and class rank can serve as indicators of consistency and performance over time. Test scores for the SAT or ACT serve as a measure of academic potential or aptitude and can serve as a predictor of success in a postsecondary education setting (Lissner, 1999). The majority of colleges and universities in the United States use one of these tests when making an admission decision.

For many students with disabilities, obtaining a satisfactory score on one of these tests serves as a major barrier to postsecondary education because the tests are time limited and require considerable reading. Without encouragement and support, some students with disabilities may avoid taking a college admission test due to test anxiety and/or a history of bad experiences in testing situations. The National Longitudinal Study-2 (Wagner, 2003) reported that only 26% of 11th- and 12th-graders in all disability categories take college entrance exams.

Determine the Need for Accommodations.   It is imperative that high school students with disabilities receive accurate and up-to-date information regarding testing accommodations for the SAT and ACT. About 2% of the 2 million students who take these tests each year receive accommodations. The majority of students requesting additional time have learning disabilities. As of fall 2003, the College Board stopped "flagging" the scores of students who take the test with extended time (Lewin, 2003). Both the SAT and ACT have specific rules for accommodations, referred to as the College Board's Eligibility and Documentation Guidelines. Section 504 of the Rehabilitation Act and the Americans with Disabilities Act require that testing accommodations be made available to students with disabilities unless the area of impairment is what is going to be measured, the test modification will fundamentally alter the assessment of the targeted skill, providing the accommodation will create undue hardship for the testing service, or the test applicant refuses the accommodation that is offered (Hishinuma, 2000).

Appropriate documentation regarding the student's disability is necessary not only to receive accommodations for admission tests but also, as will be discussed later, for the process of receiving accommodations once enrolled in a postsecondary education institution. The primary reasons for rejection of a requested accommodation by the College Board is the failure of documentation to accurately describe the testing and techniques used to determine the student's diagnosis or the functional limitations arising from the disability ("The SAT: Where It's At," 2004). Therefore, it is important for high school staff to assist students and their families in obtaining appropriate documentation of disability to secure accommodations in both college entrance examinations and college-level courses in order to prevent duplication of effort.

In general, a student must have a diagnosed disability, have documentation of the disability on file at the school (e.g., IEP, Section 504 plan, or appropriate evaluation), and have at least a 4-month history of receiving the same or similar accommodations in the high school program in order to receive accommodations on major college admission examinations (Fuller & Wehman, 2003).

Request an Accommodation.   All tests have similar guidelines and procedures for requesting accommodations. When requests are being reviewed, the student's prior academic performance, based on the specific accommodation being requested, will be considered. Also, approval of any request for testing accommodations will be based on the specific limitations of the student's disability, which makes the provision of supporting documentation regarding the disability very important. Test applicants requesting accommodations will need to provide a diagnostic testing report prepared by an appropriate professional that is based on reliable, valid, and standardized testing. It must address the functional limitations of the disability and how the accommodation being requested can alleviate the affect of the disability during a testing situation (American College Test [ACT], 2001).

Prepare for the Test.   Support and advice from high school guidance counselors and special education professionals as a student gets ready to take college admission tests can help the student become familiar with testing design, format, instructions, and general tips for obtaining higher scores. Ideally, a student should be provided with guidance in choosing testing accommodations that best fit the unique complexities of his or her specific disability and should have received extensive experience in using the accommodations during a variety of testing situations.

High school guidance counselors are an excellent source of information since they are knowledgeable about upcoming changes in test design and policies governing the administration of the tests. Inclusion of the guidance counselor on the IEP team can ensure that the student is informed in advance of issues that may impact test scores. For example, in 2005 an essay section was added to the SAT, which may pose an additional challenge for some students with learning disabilities ("The SAT: Where It's At," 2004).

To increase their likelihood of success, students can participate in a variety of activities prior to the college admission testing session. It has been noted that students who have practiced test-taking skills, learned relaxation strategies, and acquired techniques for dealing with test anxiety can obtain better scores than those who have not (Foster, Paulk, & Dastoor, 1999). It is also helpful for students to take the Preliminary Scholastic Aptitude Test (PSAT) during the early high school years to get a sense of how prepared they are to apply to a postsecondary education institution and to become familiar with the testing environment, test expectations, and test format. High school support staff should encourage students to think proactively about preparing for college admission tests since students can begin to take these tests as early as the 10th grade. Students should be encouraged to participate in test preparation classes and seminars and to use SAT or ACT preparation manuals and computer programs to prepare for taking the exam. Since states now require frequent end-of-grade and end-of-course examinations in public schools it is likely that students will be familiar with time-limited, group-administered, multiple-choice, comprehensive examinations.

Investigate Financial Assistance Options

The decision to attend college begins a complicated process of ensuring adequate preparation and completion of an array of tasks associated with applying for and being admitted to a postsecondary educational institution. Financial planning for college can never begin too early, and it is particularly important for students with disabilities. Variables such as the need to extend college attendance over a longer period of time, lack of scholarship eligibility (e.g., lower grades, lack of participation in athletics), and inability to take advantage of work–study programs or part-time employment because of a lack of job site accommodations and the impact on Supplemental Security Income (SSI) payments may complicate the process of obtaining financial assistance.

The National Center for Educational Statistics (1999a) found that only 48% of students with disabilities obtain financial aid compared to 59% of students without disabilities, and when aid is obtained it tends to be a lesser amount than that received by their peers without disabilities. If a student's family has not made plans for their child's future educational needs through a savings account or other financial resources, outside financial assistance will be needed to cover an assortment of college-related expenses such as tuition, fees, room and board, transportation, books, supplies, and campus activities. With annual tuition and fees (not including books, supplies, transportation, and room and board) ranging from $1,627 at a public 2-year college to $15,380 at a 4-year private university, many students can expect to graduate with some debt (Reisberg, 1999). The threat of debt may defer some students from pursuing loans because of the fear of not being able to pay them back if they do not complete college or they do not obtain employment soon after graduation. Other students may have unstable health conditions that create a sense of unpredictability in their life, making them hesitant to take out loans to pursue a degree they may be unable to complete.

Types of Financial Aid.   **Financial aid** for postsecondary education and training can be divided into four categories. The first category is *grants*. These do not have to be repaid. They are available to students based on financial need, which is determined by looking at the student's educational expenses and the amount of money the family is expected to contribute.

The second category is *college loans.* These allow a student to borrow money over a period of time for college expenses and, depending on the type of loan, may or may not take a student's financial need into consideration. College loans can usually be obtained at a low interest rate, and the student is not expected to begin making payment on the balance of the loan until after graduation.

Work-study programs are the third type of financial assistance. These programs allow a student to work in an on-campus job and apply the money earned to tuition costs. The final type of financial aid consists of *scholarships*, which are gifts and awards based on the student's academic performance, athletic performance, or some other criterion. There are a variety of unique situations that might qualify a student for a scholarship, such as disability type, ethnic or religious background, student's career goals, volunteer work, participation in extracurricular activities, or the parent's place of employment or type of job.

Two examples of institutions that make scholarships available specifically to individuals with disabilities are the Ethel Louise Armstrong Foundation (www.ela.org), which grants scholarships to women with physical disabilities who are already enrolled in college, and the American Council for the Blind (www.acb.org), which provides awards to students who are legally blind and who have been admitted to an academic or vocational training program.

Additional Sources of Financial Aid.   The HEATH Center provides a comprehensive listing of financial aid resources specific to students with disabilities in its publication *Creating Options: Financial Aid for Students with Disabilities* (updated annually), which can be downloaded from http://www.heath.gwu.edu/ Publicationspage.htm. In addition, Figure 6.3 lists Web sites with information about financial assistance and other college-related information.

Students may also want to pursue other options for obtaining funds for college, such as military service or AmeriCorps, that involve meeting a specific service obligation prior to receiving tuition funding. For example, in the AmeriCorps program students do community service full time for 1 year or part time for 2 years and receive educational funding awards of approximately $5,000. Individuals can serve for up to 2 terms in the AmeriCorps program, resulting in two separate educational awards. More information about AmeriCorps can be found at www.americorps.org.

Although students may be under the impression that at age 18 they are independent adults, for financial assistance a student can qualify for financial independence only if he or she is 24 years of age or older by December 31st of the award year, is a military veteran, is enrolling in graduate school, is an orphan or ward of the state, is married, has legal dependents, or is a student who the financial aid administrator has determined has a unique situation qualifying him or her for financial independence.

High school students with disabilities should be encouraged to notify all sources of possible financial assistance of the additional expenses incurred due to their disability, such as special equipment, medical expenses not covered by insurance, the cost of personal services (e.g., personal care assistant, tutors, interpreters), nutritional supplements, rehabilitation services, special housing needs, and special transportation, so these costs can be considered during the eligibility

Any College

www.anycollege.net

This site allows users to search for featured colleges.

Association of Higher Education and Disability (AHEAD)

www.ahead.org

This site provides information about the Association on Higher Education and Disability (AHEAD), which is an international, multicultural organization of professionals committed to full participation in higher education for persons with disabilities.

Campus Starter

www.campusstarter.com

This site provides resources for students exploring career opportunities and comparing undergraduate studies.

Careers and Colleges Magazine

www.careersandcolleges.com

This site is an online magazine that provides information about making career decisions and choosing the right college.

College Aid Sources for Higher Education (CASHE)

www.salliemae.com

This site provides information on Sallie Mae, which is the nation's leading provider of education funding. The company primarily provides federally guaranteed student loans originated under the Federal Family Education Loan Program (FFELP) and offers comprehensive information and resources to guide students, parents, and guidance professionals through the financial aid process.

College Board Home Page

www.collegeboard.com

This site provides information about college admission tests including preparation materials, online registration, test sites, and test dates, as well as information on choosing a college, planning for college, and financial aid.

College Degree Guide

www.collegedegreeguide.com

This site provides information about colleges throughout the United States along with information about various educational options (e.g., distance learning, online courses) and financial aid opportunities.

CollegeNet Mach 25

www.collegenet.com/mach25/

This site highlights more than 600,000 scholarships from 1,500 sponsoring organizations.

College Xpress

www.collegeexpress.com

This site allows users to search for colleges, scholarships, and loans.

Figure 6.3
Postsecondary Education Web Sites and Resources

Directory of State Higher Education Agencies

http://wdcrobcolp01.ed.gov/Programs/EROD/org_list.cfm?category_ID=SHE

This site provides information regarding the types of financial aid offered by the various states.

Disability Online Department of Labor (DOL) and Employment and Training Administration (ETA)

http://wdsc.doleta.gov/disability/default.cfm

This site includes information on grants for individuals with disabilities, success stories, informative articles, related government news, and a career center.

Expan Scholarship Search

www.collegeboard.com/clep

This site is an online scholarship search service outlining aid programs from more than 3,000 sponsors.

FAFSA on the Web (U.S. Department of Education)

http://www.fafsa.ed.gov/

This site provides the Free Application for Federal Student Aid from the U.S. Department of Education.

FastWeb

http://www.fastweb.com/

This site provides information on free scholarship and college searches plus financial aid tools.

Federal Student Financial Assistance

www.studentaid.gov

This site provides information on financial aid from the Department of Education.

Financial Aid Information

www.finaid.org

This site provides information on a variety of financial aid sources and options.

Interagency and Community Systems

http://transitioncoalition.org/ics/

This site has information for adolescents and young adults about topics such as education, health and human services, juvenile justice, employment, and social security.

LD In Depth: Postsecondary Education

http://www.ldonline.org/ld_indepth/postsecondary/

This site provides information on postsecondary education in the area of learning disabilities.

National Center on Secondary Education and Transition

www.ncset.org

This site provides information on the National Center on Secondary Education and Transition (NCSET), which coordinates national resources, offers technical assistance, and disseminates information related to secondary education and transition for young people with disabilities in order to create opportunities for them to achieve successful futures.

(continued)

Postsecondary Education Programs
www.pepnet.org
This site provides information about PEPNet, the Postsecondary Education Programs Network, which is the national collaboration of the four Regional Postsecondary Education Centers for Individuals who are Deaf and Hard of Hearing. The goal of PEPNet is to assist postsecondary institutions across the nation in attracting and effectively serving individuals who are deaf and hard of hearing.
Rehabilitation and Research Training Center
http://www.rrtc.hawaii.edu/
This site provides promising practices and up-to-date information for providing a system of educational supports for people with disabilities in the 21st century.
SRN Express
www.srnexpress.com
This site provides information regarding private, portable, non-need-based scholarships.
StudentLoans
www.StudentLoan.com
This site provides information on Citibank's student loan programs, links to college-related sites, and tools to assist in calculating the amount of money needed for college.
Transition and Post-School Outcomes for Youth with Disabilities: Closing the Gaps to Postsecondary Education and Employment (2000)
http://www.ncd.gov/newsroom/publications/2000/transition_11-01-00.htm
This site provides an online report about laws, research, and demonstration projects.
UNCF/The College Fund
www.uncf.org/scholarship/index.asp
This site provides information on scholarships available to students planning to attend historically black colleges that are members of the UNCF/The College Fund.

Figure 6.3
Continued

determination process. The Higher Education Act of 1998 allows financial aid officers to increase students' financial aid allotments to match their out-of-pocket expenses incurred due to disability.

Interagency Involvement with Financial Assistance.   As part of the financial planning process, it is important to involve outside agencies that might assist a student in making the transition from high school to postsecondary education.

Vocational Rehabilitation (VR) is an agency whose primary goal is to assist individuals with disabilities in obtaining employment, which can involve postsecondary education and training. If a student's educational plans align with future career goals and have the potential to increase the student's employability, then the student may be eligible for financial assistance. As with most other sources of

DID YOU KNOW?

Of postsecondary education institutions that enroll students with disabilities, 60% work either formally or informally with their state vocational rehabilitation agencies (NCES, 1998).

financial assistance, VR will base its assistance with college expenses on financial need and will require the student to apply for other sources of financial assistance prior to committing VR funds.

If a student is deemed eligible by VR, services may include help with tuition, books and supplies, room and board, reader services, interpreter services, assistive technology, medical services, and a variety of other goods and services that can ultimately result in the young person's completing his or her education and obtaining employment. Vocational rehabilitation services vary from state to state with regard to the amount of tuition assistance offered, participation in the Ticket-to-Work program, guidance counselors who follow the student from high school to higher education, and the type of educational setting for which financial assistance will be approved. Therefore, it is important for high school staff to make sure that accurate adult service information is provided to the student and the student's family during the transition planning process.

If a student is receiving social security benefits, work incentives such as a **Plan for Achieving Self Support (PASS)** might be applicable to a student's postsecondary education plans. A PASS can help a student save money for tuition and other education-related expenses. Chapter 8 provides additional information on SSI work incentives.

Recognize Differences Between High School and Postsecondary Educational Environments

A student's ability to recognize and be prepared for the differences between high school and postsecondary educational environments is critical to making a successful transition. These differences include academic expectations, performance monitoring, finding time to study, and social considerations.

Academic Expectations.   College instructors often have higher academic expectations for students by virtue of the fact that students have reached a higher-level learning environment. Although high expectations for student achievement is a desirable trait for teachers, in a college setting the level of expectation may result in instructional delivery strategies that reflect the instructors' expectations for a high level of independent learning. For example, in a college setting it is not unusual for an instructor to lecture for the entire class period, focusing on information that is not in the textbook, and to require independent reading and research outside of class time. Unlike high school teachers, who impart knowledge and facts using the textbook as a guide and provide both teacher-guided and independent practice, college instructors often expect students to integrate information from a variety of sources while monitoring their own progress. College instructors often provide a syllabus at the beginning of the semester outlining assignments, while high school teachers often provide step-by-step instructions for assignments and assistance with organization and time management.

Performance Monitoring.   Self-monitoring of performance, progress, and work quality is a skill that often is not encouraged with high school students. High school students usually have numerous quizzes, benchmark tests, and graded homework assignments, and students with disabilities usually have someone (e.g., a special educator) assigned to externally monitor their progress and assist them if they fall behind. Also, high school students with disabilities who are receiving modifications in their coursework may not be able to develop a full sense of where they stand in terms of achievement compared with their classmates.

In a postsecondary educational environment, all students are held to the same standards and semester grades may be based on just a few test scores or a major assignment. Tests in college may differ from high school tests in that they cover more material and often require extensive writing on essay questions that call for the students to synthesize or apply information from both lectures and reading materials. Without frequent signposts such as weekly grades and with no external monitoring of performance, the GPA of a student with a disability may drop below acceptable standards in one or two semesters.

Finding Time to Study.   Mixed in with all the differences in the instructional methodology, learning environment, and expectations, students at the postsecondary level also have much more responsibility for their actions both academically and personally than high school students do and a great deal more freedom in which to exert that responsibility. Free time must be balanced with study time. Outside assignments and homework in college may require twice as much time on a daily basis as high school assignments do. In addition, students may need to rewrite notes taken in class, spend time in the library, paraphrase information provided by the instructor, and link knowledge from a variety of sources. Study time must be balanced with social activities and any other obligations such as work-study or paid jobs. By the time students reach postsecondary education, they must make their own decisions regarding time management (Brinckerhoff, Shaw, & McGuire, 1992; Dalke & Schmitt, 1987; Shaw & Parker, 2003; Shaw, Brinckerhoff, Kistler, & McGuire, 1991).

Social Considerations.   All this responsibility comes at a time when students with disabilities are experiencing fewer externally exposed limits on their freedom. Some students may even perceive themselves as having more free time due to the manner in which college classes are scheduled. This new level of freedom, increased workload, lack of supports, and fear of failure can result in a high level of stress for many students.

Another source of stress for some students with disabilities is campus social life. The ability to assimilate into the campus environment and participate in clubs, organizations, departmental activities, and social gatherings can impact the student's satisfaction with the college experience and can have a greater impact on academic outcomes than other factors (Kezar, 1997). Peer support and friendship arising from social activities can impact a student's motivation to persevere in obtaining a college degree (Astin, 1993; Tinto, 1993).

Students with disabilities should be encouraged to prepare for the social side of college life while in high school by participating in clubs, organizations, and community activities involving their peers. If a student experiences problems in the social arena while in high school, these problems will more than likely continue into the postsecondary environment unless interventions such as social skill training and counseling are provided (Chadsey & Sheldon, 1998). Interpersonal relationships with peers can be a strong source of support for college students. College students rely on each other for assistance in studying, test preparation, information about courses and professors, and hints about navigating the college bureaucracy. College students also need relationships with peers in which they can share their feelings about the stress, frustration, and anxiety of college life.

Academic support, self-advocacy instruction, and interpersonal relationship strategies must be implemented in high school to encourage future independence instead of fostering dependence. Special educators may inadvertently hinder a student's independence by doing too much for the student, such as editing a paper versus teaching proofreading skills or negotiating accommodations with general education teachers versus teaching the student to self-advocate (Brinckerhoff et al., 1992).

Learn Civil Rights Related to Postsecondary Education

While in high school, students with disabilities receive special education services based on mandates outlined in the IDEA. It is evident that IDEA can have a significant impact on a student's ability to access and succeed in a postsecondary setting through effective transition planning. Unfortunately, IDEA regulations do not apply to postsecondary education settings. A student and his or her family who have not learned what to expect regarding special services at the college level can be overwhelmed and disillusioned to discover a different level of support and guidelines for accessing support than they experienced in the public school system. Students and their parents can literally be caught unaware when special education services drastically decline or cease after high school graduation (Stodden, Conway, & Chang, 2003). While in high school, a student with a disability is guaranteed a free and appropriate public education (FAPE) in the least restrictive environment. Education is a right for students in the public schools, but access to postsecondary education is not a right or a guarantee. Rather, it is a privilege available to those who are qualified to perform postsecondary-level coursework, and no laws require a postsecondary institution to provide FAPE (U.S. Department of Education, 2002b).

Section 504 of the 1973 Rehabilitation Act. **Section 504 of the Rehabilitation Act of 1973** mandates that colleges "may not, on the basis of handicap, exclude any qualified handicapped student from any course, course of study, or other part of its educational program or activity" (34 C.F.R. Sec. 104.43[c]). Postsecondary educational programs use three considerations to determine the qualification of a person with a disability:

1. What are the program or course requirements?
2. What nonessential criteria can be accommodated without changing the essence of the course or program?
3. What are the specific abilities and disabilities of the student within this context (Scott, 1991)?

In addition the law requires that "a recipient [of federal funding] shall operate each program or activity . . . so that the program or activity, when viewed in its entirety is readily accessible to handicapped persons" (34 C.F.R. Sec. 104.22[a]). Although this federal mandate provides for access to full course offerings by students with disabilities, there is no responsibility given to colleges and universities for assisting students in making the transition from high school to postsecondary educational settings. The responsibility for transition lies completely with the public schools under the mandates of IDEA (Frank & Wade, 1993).

Americans with Disabilities Act (1990). As noted in Chapter 1, The 1990 **Americans with Disabilities Act (ADA)** extended civil rights protection set forth in Section 504 for individuals with disabilities in virtually all policies, procedures, and practices within the private arena with specific provisions for the areas of employment, public accommodations, transportation, and telecommunication. Although ADA does not add any additional mandates for postsecondary education institutions, the requirements for the removal of architectural barriers, increased access to societal integration, the reaffirmation of nondiscriminatory practices, and the increased awareness of the civil rights of individuals with disabilities have resulted in colleges and universities' taking a closer look at accessibility issues (Rothstein, 1991). Federal legislation on postsecondary educational institutions impacts multiple areas of operation and prohibits a college or university from:

1. Limiting the number of students with disabilities admitted to the institution.
2. Making preadmission inquiries as to whether or not an applicant has a disability.
3. Using admission tests or criteria to inadequately measure the academic level of applicants with disabilities.
4. Administering tests to students with disabilities at a different frequency rate or an inaccessible location.
5. Giving tests or examinations that do not accurately reflect the student's aptitude and achievement level without the interference of disability-related factors (e.g., providing accommodations and modifications).

6. Limiting access to any student with a disability who is otherwise qualified from any course of study solely on the basis of his or her disability.

7. Counseling students toward more restrictive careers.

8. Instituting prohibitive rules that may adversely affect students with disabilities, such as prohibiting the use of assistive technology or auxiliary aids within the classroom.

9. Refusing to modify academic requirements that would allow students with disabilities opportunities for full participation in all aspects of the institution.

10. Providing less financial assistance to students with disabilities or basing financial decisions on discriminatory information.

11. Providing a different level of housing for students with disabilities than that provided to students without disabilities (e.g., cost, accessibility, quality).

12. Prohibiting full participation in all nonacademic campus programs, resources, and activities (Brinckerhoff, 1985).

All colleges and universities are required to perform ongoing evaluation of their ability to serve students with disabilities and identify potential barriers to the enrollment and participation of this population. Nondiscriminatory policies, procedures, and practices must be in place regarding recruitment, eligibility, testing, admission, academic standards, housing, fees, financial aid, athletic programs, counseling, and any other programs or services offered by the institution. Finally, colleges and universities must also make reasonable modifications and accommodations for individuals with disabilities to assist them in equal access to the opportunities and services available to students without disabilities (Rothstein, 2003).

Identify Possible Accommodations and Modifications at the Postsecondary Education Level

Accommodations and modifications are alterations, adjustments, changes, revisions, or adaptations that provide persons with disabilities equal access to programs they cannot access through traditional or customary means (Fuller & Wehman, 2003) and are necessary only when a person's disability impedes performing a specific academic task. Reasonable accommodations are generally those that will not pose a financial or administrative burden on the institution. For example, if a college provides student housing, then comparable housing that is convenient and accessible must be made available to a student with a physical disability. While discriminatory practices in all aspects of postsecondary programs are prohibited, any requirements essential to a course of study or program (e.g., licensing requirements) cannot be compromised by modifying or lowering curricular standards (Clerc, 1985). Therefore, while a college may approve an alternative manner in which to take a test, there is no expectation that the actual test content will be modified.

Legal Guidelines.   The application of Section 504 and ADA to postsecondary educational settings guides the manner in which services are provided to students with disabilities. Although there are some major differences among postsecondary educational institutions in the intensity of services offered, there are some basic guidelines and procedures generic to all settings. In order to receive the civil rights protections of federal laws in a college setting, students must demonstrate their eligibility. Students with disabilities must provide documentation of their disability to the student disabilities service coordinator to begin the process of obtaining accommodations and modifications. A copy of the IEP or Section 504 plan used during high school is usually not sufficient evidence of eligibility for services. Appropriate evaluations and testing results must be made available to the postsecondary institution, and requirements can be imposed for the documentation to be completed by an appropriate professional (e.g., physician, psychologist, licensed diagnostician).

Information that may be required in documenting a disability includes the diagnosis; dates of the original diagnosis and the most current diagnosis; the prognosis regarding the stability or progression of the disability; the manner in which the diagnosis was determined, including a description of the tests or methods used to make the diagnosis; how the diagnosis affects major life functions and academic performance; treatments, medications, or assistive devices used by the individual; recommendations regarding the types of accommodations, support, and/or modifications that would benefit the individual; and the credentials of the professional making the diagnosis (Lissner, 1999; U.S. Department of Education, 2002b). Since this documentation is similar to what is required for requesting accommodations on college admission tests, as mentioned previously, students should be assisted in gathering the information to avoid extra effort, expense, and frustration.

Funding Needed Assessment.   While public schools are required to pay for evaluations and assessments required under IDEA, postsecondary educational institutions do not have this responsibility. Therefore, students must obtain any needed evaluations required for documentation of eligibility on their own. Since public schools conduct a variety of evaluations at routine intervals, an important part of the transition planning process is to ensure that evaluations meeting postsecondary documentation requirements are conducted during the student's senior year, with results made available to the student and his parents. Other funding sources for documentation of a disability may be Vocational Rehabilitation or private insurance. If a student's future career goal requires completing postsecondary education or training and the student has qualified for Vocational Rehabilitation services, it might be appropriate for this service to be included on his or her individual plan of employment (IPE), which is Vocational Rehabilitation's plan of services for a client.

The Need to Self-Disclose.   A student's responsibility for accessing services at the postsecondary level does not end with obtaining appropriate documentation of his or her disability. In the public school setting, students are often nonpartici-pants, having little or no responsibility for the special assistance they receive. In a college or university setting, the student must self-disclose. **Self-disclosure** means that a student must contact the Office of Disability Services division of the school, provide appropriate documentation of his or her disability, and request accommodations and modifications. As a result, the student must initiate, advo-cate, design, manage, and evaluate his or her own services (Stodden & Jones, 2002). Self-disclosure requires self-advocacy skills, negotiation skills, and knowl-edge of individual strengths and needs (Carroll & Johnson-Brown, 1996; Palmer & Roessler, 2000).

Some students may be hesitant to self-disclose after being accepted into a col-lege or university. Students may perceive that they are free of a label and fear dis-crimination and stigma, which they may have experienced during their years in the public school system (Aune & Friehe, 1996). While this may be a realistic fear in some cases, Hill (1996) reported that, in general, postsecondary faculty have positive attitudes about integrating students with disabilities into the general aca-demic environment. Despite worries about disability disclosure, students must be taught that self-disclosure can alleviate stress, prevent failure, and increase the chances for receiving appropriate services in a coordinated fashion.

Requesting Services.   Usually there are procedures for requesting services that must be followed at the beginning of each semester. Decisions regarding services that will be offered are made based on identified student needs, which means that a student's desire or preference for a specific type of accommodation may not determine the nature or level of services that will actually be provided (Hey-ward, 1996). A student-centered approach is seldom used at the postsecondary level, which results in support being offered from a menu of services instead of being catered directly to student needs. The continuum of services at the postsec-ondary level can range from an office staffed with a single professional who has limited knowledge of disability services, or even just the assignment of disability services as a small part of a staff member's job description, to a comprehensive program with several trained professionals who are competent in assessing stu-dents and assisting them in identifying needs, advocating for accommodations and modifications, and monitoring progress throughout the student's college ex-perience. Institutions of higher learning have wide discretion in interpreting the legal mandates governing the type of assistance that will be provided to students with disabilities. During the transition planning process, as students begin to in-vestigate postsecondary education options they can expect to find a wide vari-ance in the type, range, and availability of many of the services they have come to expect under IDEA (Stodden, Jones, & Chang, 2002).

In general, most postsecondary educational institutions provide access to per-sonal and career counseling, career and vocational assessment, and testing ac-commodations. About half of all colleges and universities offer job placement services and learning labs (NCSPES, 2000a). However, a student with a disability may have a more difficult time locating a college or university that provides disability-specific assessments and evaluations, accessible on-campus transportation, disability-specific scholarships, real-time captioning of educational materials, assistive technology evaluations, advocacy organizations, supports for studying abroad, or assistance in transferring supports to career settings.

Focusing on the development of self-advocacy skills for accessing services and choosing a college that can deliver the special services needed by the student are two very important areas of transition planning since more than 80% of young people with disabilities who pursue postsecondary education require some level of assistance in managing and coordinating the delivery of educational and related services (NCSPES, 2000a). Table 6.1 contains examples of accommodations and modifications that can occur at the postsecondary education level.

Table 6.1
Examples of Accommodations and Modifications at the Postsecondary Level

Instructional Adjustments	Program Accommodations	Access Modifications
Tests read aloud and/or extended test-taking time	Summer or presemester orientation programs	Removal of architectural barriers
Recorded textbooks	Individualized counseling and/or advising	Designated parking spaces
Video- or audiotaped lectures	Part-time schedules	Change of class location
Taped tests	Additional time to complete courses	Transportation assistance
Note-taking modifications or note-takers	Longer time to complete course of study	Barrier guide sheets
Proofreading services	Priority registration	Special seating arrangements
Dictated written reports	Course substitutions	Special lighting
Assistive technology (e.g., calculators, braille readers, computer keyboard modifications, modified word processors)	Waivers for certain coursework with approved substitutions	Special housing arrangements
Readers	Repeating classes	
Instructor-prepared study questions prior to the test	Late class withdrawal without penalty	
Tests taken in locations outside the classrooms	Schedules adjusted for course enrollment at certain times of the day	
Assistance with study and test-taking skills	Alternative admission standards	
Oral tests or projects	Special financial arrangements	

Instructional Adjustments	Program Accommodations	Access Modifications
Use of tape recorders in the classroom	Audit without fee with enrollment in course next semester offered	
Interpreters	Independent study option	
Large-print texts		
Typing services		
Lecture outlines provided by the instructor		
Shorter and/or more frequent tests		
Prehighlighted texts		
Course syllabi provided early to provide time for prereading textbooks and/or assigned readings		
Alternative assignments		
Examples of correctly completed work		

Note: Based on Gajar, 1998; Mull, Sitlington, & Alper, 2001.

Public Versus Private Universities.   The transition planning process should include activities that will ensure that students and their families are aware of the multiple variables affecting delivery of supports at the postsecondary education level. Students must choose between public and private educational settings, 2-year colleges and 4-year universities, colleges with disability-specific support programs and colleges with more generic services, and large schools and smaller schools.

Public institutions are more likely than private institutions to provide programs, services, and accommodations for students with disabilities, and 2-year programs are more likely than 4-year institutions to provide special student services such as learning labs, remedial instruction, disability-specific assessments, interpreters, and assistive technology supports, including equipment and software. In addition, 2-year educational institutions tend to be better connected than 4-year universities through outreach programs with businesses, advocacy groups, and federal programs. However, a 4-year university is more likely to provide a wider range of supports such as class relocation, supports for studying abroad, accessible on-campus transportation, internships, and in-class supports such as note-takers, scribes, and readers. Students with disabilities can also expect larger institutions to offer more educational supports at a higher frequency than smaller institutions (NCES, 1999b). Investigating the range of supports provided is an important step in choosing a college, but the factor that is most important to success in the college setting may be easy access to and a relationship with an academic advisor or learning specialist who can provide advice, support, as-sistance, and encouragement (Vogel, Hruby, & Adelman, 1993).

Explore Technology Options

One area that is important in today's technological society is preparing students to access and use a variety of technology devices. Young people with disabilities will be expected to use technology at the postsecondary level and in the labor force since its use can enhance performance in both arenas. Technology such as computers can be viewed as "electronic curb-cuts" that provide individuals equal access to educational and employment opportunities (Fichten, Barile, & Asun-cion, 1999). However, only 1 in 20 adults with disabilities who could benefit from assistive technology are actually using these devices (Brand, 1997). Even in areas of technology that are more common, such as computers and the Internet, indi-viduals with disabilities lag far behind the general population in ownership and usage (Kaye, 2000). The underutilization of assistive technology is related to many factors, including insufficient training in high schools, lack of assessments, lack of high school faculty awareness and training, limited funding, limited ac-cess to devices, and failure to address assistive technology needs during the tran-sition planning process (Lahm & Nichols, 1999; McGregor & Pachuski, 1996 Raskind & Higgins, 1998).

Selecting Appropriate Technology.   The key to the effective use of technology by students with disabilities is to select technology that accentuates a student's strengths, is based on the student's learning profile, and matches the tasks the student is expected to perform (Taymans & West, 2001). This can be accomplished only if students are active participants in all phases of device selection including assessment, try-outs, identification of funding sources, decision making, training, and upkeep (Scott, 1991). Abandonment of technology by students with disabili-ties occurs about one-third of the time and can be a result of the student's viewing the device as ineffective, unreliable, embarrassing, complicated, nonportable, or expensive to maintain (Todis, 1996). If students have been full partners in making the decisions related to technology and learn to view the use of technology as an accepted practice by all students, not just those with disabilities, many of the

---

DID YOU KNOW?

While students with disabilities who use technology report that acquiring and main-taining technological devices is the single most important issue they face in technol-ogy use, a lack of knowledge regarding funding sources continues to be a common problem (Fichten et al., 1999).

barriers related to the effective use of technology at both the high school level and the postsecondary level can be eliminated.

Technology can also be used to supplement compensatory strategies, support educational needs, maximize independence, gain access to support personnel and services, and increase the chances for students with disabilities to compete academically with their peers without disabilities even in high-tech career fields such as engineering (Burgstahler, 2003). Academic applications for technology at the postsecondary level include calculators, computer-assisted instruction, laser videodiscs, microcomputer-based labs, presentation software, word predication software, text reading software, large-screen monitors, personal digital assistants (PDAs), editing software, and voice activation word processing. Mull and Sitlington (2003) provided a comprehensive review of technology recommendations for spelling, written expression, reading, organization, memory, visual tracking, time management, listening, speech, concentration, and math.

High school personnel must realize that in today's postsecondary education environment technology is no longer an option but a necessity. Today, many colleges require incoming freshmen to have laptops, students routinely use PDAs to keep up with their schedules, and some universities (e.g., Duke University) are even experimenting with the use of iPods as a study tool. Personal digital assistants, which can be adapted for individuals with physical and sensory disabilities, are being used to increase students' organization, foster collaboration, and maximize portability of technology. In May of 2001, the University of South Dakota became the first U.S. postsecondary institution to require the use of hand-held computers by undergraduates (National Center on Accessible Information Technology in Education, 2004).

The future promises many technological advances that will make postsecondary educational institutions even more accessible for individuals with disabilities. Near-eye displays attached to glasses to make screens appear larger, fuel cells to increase the life of handheld devices, virtual keyboards, and handheld printers using random-movement printing are all new inventions that will soon be readily available (Hardy, 2003). Technological devices have become the new pencils and notebooks, and students who have not been sufficiently prepared through training and opportunities for practice and application while in high school will be at a distinct disadvantage in competing with their college-level peers.

Finally, for students with more severe disabilities, assistive technology can enhance the ability to communicate, maintain appropriate body posture, travel, and participate in on-campus social activities (Blackhurst, Lahm, Harrison, & Chandler, 1999). Technology can increase a student's control over his or her life, thereby increasing the students self-determination, independence, and autonomy—all of which are vital to success in postsecondary education.

The transition planning process should be used to ensure that the technology needs of students are adequately assessed (Sitlington, Neubert, Begun, Lombard, & Leconte, 1996); interagency collaboration is utilized to fund and provide equipment; and students, family members, and faculty receive training in the use of devices. Students must be taught to recognize their technological needs and develop the self-advocacy skills to ensure that plans are in place for meeting these needs if they are going to use technology effectively through their high school years, in postsecondary education, and ultimately in adult life (Field & Hoffman, 1994).

SUMMARY

Lifelong learning is an important part of life. Not all students choose to pursue formal training or education past high school, but every student should have a desire for self-improvement. Students with disabilities who do want the opportunity to advance to postsecondary education will face many obstacles and challenges. The combination of the unique characteristics of a student's disability and the complexity of ensuring adequate preparation for admission to higher education, paired with admission procedures, financial aid needs, and parental influences, requires a coordinated and comprehensive transition planning process. As discussed in this chapter, school staff must be committed to the holistic preparation of any student who dreams of one day attending postsecondary education.

CASE STUDY

MALINA

Malina lives with her mother and three sisters in a small rental house. The family moved to the area after emigrating from Mexico. Her father lives in a neighboring state and occasionally visits the family. His financial support is limited due to his seasonal employment. Malina enjoys playing with her pets, listening to music, chatting with her friends on the phone, and watching movies.

Malina attends inclusive classes for all courses but spends one period a day in the resource lab, where she takes an elective curriculum and instruction class. Malina is enrolled in a pathway to prepare her for a 2-year or 4-year college. She has successfully completed all course requirements, but because she has a learning disability in math, she is concerned about being able to complete the math requirements for admission to a postsecondary program.

Malina uses several modifications and accommodations, including extended test-taking time, modified assignments, and more extensive use of a calculator during class assignments. Malina passed the language arts section of the high school exit exam, but she has not passed the math section. She has 3.0 GPA. She receives math tutoring, and she has also participated in review sessions related to the high school exit exam.

Malina is interested in the field of human services, and her career-technical education (CTE) courses have included keyboarding, computer applications I, and child care I. During her sophomore year Malina participated in a child care internship and received excellent evaluations.

During the summer after her freshman year, Malina worked part time in the kitchen at an assisted care facility where she also received good performance evaluations. However, she told the transition coordinator that she enjoyed the interactions with residents but did not enjoy the cooking and cleaning responsibilities. During the summer prior to her junior year, she assisted the recreation therapist 30 hours a week at the same facility. Malina thoroughly enjoyed this position. Malina chose not to work during her junior year because of academic demands.

Malina has been hesitant to enroll in driver education, and her mother noted that she was in a serious car wreck as a child. Malina's mother would like her to get her driver's license.

When Malina was in the seventh grade, her special education teacher talked with her and her mother about Malina's future plans. No one in Malina's immediate or extended family had ever pursued postsecondary education, and Malina had not given much thought to the idea because of her math difficulties.

Also in seventh grade, Malina began attending her IEP/transition team meetings. At first her participation was limited. However, during her freshman year in high school she participated in a self-determination workshop that helped her design a personal action plan to increase her independence.

By ninth grade, Malina was taking a leadership role in meetings. At this point, she was interested in postsecondary education, but she had many questions about financial aid and her ability to perform college-level work. A representative from the local community college, the school guidance counselor, and a vocational rehabilitation counselor were invited to the meeting to provide additional information. Invited school personnel included Malina's special education teacher, her algebra teacher, the transition coordinator, an assistant principal, and the head of the career-technical education department.

Malina began the meeting, sharing with the team her high school experiences, her postsecondary goals, and her questions. She expressed her desire to be more involved in school activities with peers, and her mother shared this desire. During the discussion that followed, Malina and her team targeted the following transition areas and strategies for her 10th-grade year:

♦ Reevaluating accommodations and modifications to determine their effectiveness and potential for continuation in a postsecondary setting.

♦ Participating in weekly career lab sessions with the high school guidance counselor to identify colleges and universities she might attend.

♦ Accessing www.jobshadow.org to learn more about human services careers.

♦ Attending weekly after-school math tutoring sessions to prepare for the math portion of the high school exit exam.

♦ Completing individualized and self-paced study skills, test-taking, and note-taking lessons.

♦ Participating in a training session with the high school guidance counselor on financial assistance for postsecondary education.

◆ Enrolling in driver education and completing the requirements for a learner's permit or a driver's license.

◆ Meeting with teachers to select appropriate school social activities.

◆ Establishing a mentoring relationship with an adult employed in a human services profession to expose her to information about potential careers and to provide additional encouragement.

During the meeting, the high school personnel reviewed Malina's transcript and assured her that she was on track for a high school diploma and higher education. The community college admission representative explained the college's admission policy. Malina's mother asked whether their minister could attend future transition planning meetings to help support Malina's postsecondary education goals, and all team members felt this was an excellent suggestion.

By her 10th-grade meeting, Malina was fully committed to attending college. After working with the guidance counselor, she identified her first college, a 4-year college with a bachelor of arts program in social work. Her primary focus in choosing a career was to help others, preferably the elderly or children. Math remained a big concern for Malina, and she wanted to avoid careers that would require a high level of math skills. Malina had even begun to dream about earning a master's degree in social work.

Malina began the meeting by sharing that she had passed the math section of the high school exit exam—which elicited a round of applause from those assembled—and that she had obtained her driver's license. Malina said that she felt as if two burdens had been lifted from her shoulders, and she felt more confident than ever about her abilities. She shared a portfolio she had prepared outlining the advantages and disadvantages of six postsecondary programs in which she was interested, along with a list of possible sources of financial assistance.

The vocational rehabilitation counselor, the high school guidance counselor, the transition coordinator, Malina's special education teacher, the algebra teacher, the assistant principal, Malina's minister, her mother, and a representative from a state university all attended this meeting. Although Malina was leaning toward a smaller college with a program for students with learning disabilities, she was open to other options and available financial resources.

The high school guidance counselor asked Malina to update the team about her school clubs and activities. She described her involvement in Students Against Drunk Driving (SADD), the Pep Club, and the school newspaper. Malina was particularly proud of an article she had written about SADD that had been published in the school newspaper. Her mother noted that Malina often talked about her new friends. The team again reviewed her transcript and noted that she had passed algebra I. After reviewing the progress made on the previous year's recommendations and listening to Malina's views regarding her needs for the upcoming year, the team developed the following transition activities:

◆ Finalizing a list of financial aid possibilities and complete college applications. Malina's minister volunteered to assist her with this process.

- ♦ Reviewing and studying test preparation materials and registering for the Preliminary Scholastic Aptitude Test (PSAT).
- ♦ Gathering the appropriate documentation and requesting appropriate testing accommodations for the PSAT.
- ♦ Finalizing her choices of postsecondary institutions, scheduling campus tours and meetings with the special student services coordinators, and submitting college applications.
- ♦ Completing an instructional package on civil rights and legislation related to students with disabilities at the postsecondary level.
- ♦ Participating in the Saturday Leadership Academy sponsored by the local United Way agency.
- ♦ Participating in the Rotary Club's mock interviews.
- ♦ Working with the transition coordinator to establish an e-mail mentoring relationship with a student with a disability attending a state university.

By the end of 11th grade, with the assistance of Malina's IEP/transition team members, she had accomplished all of the transition activities set forth at her previous meeting. Malina was very positive about her PSAT testing experience and felt she was much better prepared for the SAT. During the meeting, a review of Malina's transcript confirmed that she remained on track to receive a high school diploma and that her GPA had risen to 3.1. Malina felt that just surviving algebra I and algebra 2 had been major accomplishments. The algebra teacher advised Malina to enroll in geometry to better prepare her for college admission tests and college-level math.

Malina's mother bragged to team members about Malina's commitment to studying and completing her homework, noting that she had even observed Malina turning down social offers so she could stay home and study. With input from Malina and her mother, the following postsecondary education transition activities were designated for Malina's 12th grade year:

- ♦ Completing the paperwork for a Vocational Rehabilitation referral in order to access postsecondary education financial aid.
- ♦ Enrolling in a Rotary-funded SAT preparation class.
- ♦ Completing the necessary paperwork requesting SAT testing accommodations.
- ♦ Attending prospective student weekends at two of the colleges on her list.
- ♦ Investigating the possibility of vocational education credit for completion of an internship at the local Department of Social Services.

Malina did not meet with her full team again until the early spring of her senior year. At this point, she was contacting school staff and the vocational rehabilitation counselor when she needed their assistance. At the meeting, which was attended by all team members, Malina reported that she felt very lucky. After she had visited a nearby private college for a tour, the counselor had "taken Malina under her wing." After discovering that the college had an array of special services for students with learning disabilities, a wide array of social activities, and a variety of financial aid options, Mailina felt this school would be a good choice for her. She was accepted to the college and was offered a financial aid package. The Office of Disability Services also arranged for a work-study job in their department that would provide Malina with clerical and peer counseling experiences to support her plan to pursue a B.A. in human services with a focus on social work. Malina was particularly proud of a scholarship she received from the local Pilot Club. Although it was for only a few hundred dollars, Malina was proud to have been selected from a large number of applicants.

The meeting concluded with the team's agreeing to convene at least once more prior to graduation and acknowledging the team effort led by Malina in taking charge of her course in life.

STUDY GUIDE QUESTIONS

1. How do enrollment and completion rates in postsecondary education of students with disabilities differ from those of students without disabilities?
2. How does participation in postsecondary education affect adjustment to adult life for students with disabilities?
3. What are some of the barriers to postsecondary education for students with disabilities?
4. What strategies should high schools employ to ensure that students with disabilities are adequately prepared for postsecondary education?
5. What are the factors that a transition planning team must consider when assisting a student in getting ready for postsecondary education?
6. How do the legal mandates providing services to high school students with disabilities differ from those covering students with disabilities who are enrolled in higher education institutions?
7. Why is self-determination important to the successful adjustment of students with disabilities to postsecondary education settings?
8. What are some of the factors that a student with a disability should consider when selecting a postsecondary education setting?
9. Why should Vocational Rehabilitation be a major player in the transition planning process for students with disabilities?
10. What postsecondary education options are available to students with significant cognitive disabilities?
11. Which transition activities used in the case study required interagency collaboration? Did any of the transition activities encourage the development of self-determination? If so, how?
12. In the case study, what were the academic supports given to Malina?

13. What are some of the Malina's personal qualities that would lead one to predict that her postsecondary education experience will be successful?

REFERENCES

Algozzine, B., Browder, D., Karvonen, M., Test, D. W., & Wood, W. M. (2001). Effects of interventions to promote self-determination for individuals with disabilities. *Review of Educational Research, 71,* 219–277.

American College Test (ACT). (2001, July 5). *Services for students with disabilities.* Retrieved December 1, 2003, from www.act.org/aap/disab/index.html.

American Council on Education. (2000). *Who took the GED: 1999 GED annual statistical report.* Washington, DC: Author.

Association on Higher Education and Disability (AHEAD). (1996). *Confidentiality and disability issues in higher education.* Columbus, OH: Author.

Astin, A. (1993). *What matters in college: Four critical years revisited.* San Francisco: Jossey-Bass.

Aune, B., & Friehe, M. (1996). Transition to postsecondary education: Institutional and individual issues. *Topics in Language Disorders, 16,* 1–22.

Babbit, B. C., & White, C. M. (2002). Helping students assess their readiness for postsecondary education. *Teaching Exceptional Children, 35,* 62–66.

Baer, R. M., Flexor, R. W., Beck, S., Amstutz, N., Hoffman, L., Brothers, J., et al. (2003). A collaborative follow-up study on transition service utilization and post-school outcomes, *Career Development for Exceptional Individuals, 26,* 7–25.

Barr, V. M., Hartman, R. C., & Spillane, S. A. (1995). *Getting ready for college: High school students with learning disabilities.* Washington, DC: HEATH Resource Center.

Berliner, D., & Biddle, B. (1996). Standards amidst uncertainty and inequality. *The School Administrator, 53,* 42–47.

Blackhurst, A. E., Lahm, E. A., Harrison, E. M., & Chandler, W. G. (1999). A framework for aligning technology with transition competencies. *Career Development for Exceptional Individuals, 22,* 153–183.

Blackorby, J., & Wagner, M. (1996). Longitudinal post-school outcomes of youth with disabilities:

Findings from the National Longitudinal Transition Study. *Exceptional Children, 62,* 399–413.

Blackorby, J., & Wagner, M. (1997). The employment outcomes of youth with learning disabilities: A review of findings from the National Longitudinal Transition Study of Special Education Students. In P. J. Gerber & D. S. Bowen (Eds.), *Learning disabilities and employment* (pp. 57–74). Austin, TX: Pro-Ed.

Brand, C. (1997, July 15). *Meeting the needs of people with disabilities through federal technology transfer.* Testimony before the House Committee on Science, Washington, DC.

Brinckerhoff, L. C. (1985). Accommodations for college students with learning disabilities: The law and its implementations. In J. Garner (Ed.), *Proceedings of the eighth annual AHSSPPE conference* (pp. 89–95). Columbus, OH: Association on Handicapped Student Service Programs in Postsecondary Education.

Brinckerhoff, L., Shaw, S. F., & McGuire, J. M. (1992). Promoting access, accommodations, and independence for college students with learning disabilities. *Journal of Learning Disabilities, 25,* 417–429.

Brinckerhoff, L. C., Shaw, S. F., & McGuire, J. (1993). *Promoting postsecondary education for students with learning disabilities: A handbook for practitioners.* Austin, TX: Pro-Ed.

Burgstahler, S. (2003). The role of technology in preparing youth with disabilities for postsecondary education and employment. *Journal of Special Education Technology, 18,* 7–19.

Carroll, A., & Johnson-Brown, C. (1996). Disability support services in higher education: An extension of the rehabilitation process. *Journal of Applied Rehabilitation Counseling, 27,* 54–59.

Chadsey, J., & Sheldon, D. (1998). Moving toward social inclusion in employment and postsecondary school settings. In F. R. Rusch & J. G. Chadsey (Eds.), *Beyond high school: Transition from school to work* (pp. 383–405). Belmont, CA: Wadsworth.

Clerc, J. (1985). The legal obligation to learning disabled and handicapped allied health students. *Journal of Allied Heath, 14,* 203–211.

Cocchi, W. (1997, April–June). The community college choice. *The Postsecondary LD Report.* Retrieved November 29, 2003, from www.ldonline.org/ld_indepth/postsecondary/block_comcol.html.

Dalke, C., & Schmitt, S. (1987). Meeting the transition needs of college-bound students with learning disabilities. *Journal of Learning Disabilities, 20,* 176–180.

Darling-Hammond, L., Ancess, J., & Falk, B. (1995). *Authentic assessment in action: Studies of schools and students at work.* New York: Teachers College Press.

deFur, S. (2002). Education reform, high stakes assessment and students with disabilities. *Remedial and Special Education, 23,* 203–211.

Durlak, C., Rose, E., & Bursuck, W. (1994). Preparing high school students with learning disabilities for the transition to postsecondary education: Teaching the skills of self-determination. *Journal of Learning Disabilities, 27,* 51–60.

Eisenman, L., & Tascione, L. (2002). How come nobody told me? Fostering self-realization through a high school English curriculum. *Learning Disabilities Research and Practice, 17,* 35–46.

Fichten, C. S., Barile, M., & Asuncion, J. V. (1999). *Learning technologies: Students with disabilities in postsecondary education/Project Adaptech.* (Final report to the Office of Learning Technologies. Ottawa, Canada: Human Resources Development). Retrieved September 1, 2004, from http://adaptech.dawsoncollege.qc.ca/pubs/79160exesum_e.html.

Field, S., & Hoffman, A. (1994). Development of a model for self-determination. *Career Development for Exceptional Individuals, 17,* 159–169.

Field, S., Martin, J., Miller, R., Ward, M., & Wehmeyer, M. (1998). *A practical guide for teaching self-determination.* Arlington, VA: Council for Exceptional Children.

Foster, S. K., Paulk, A., & Dastoor, B. R. (1999). Can we really teach test-taking skills? *New Horizons in Adult Education, 13*(1). Retrieved February 19, 2004, from http://www.nova.edu/~aed/horizons/vol13n1.html.

Frank, K., & Wade, P. (1993). Disabled student services in postsecondary education: Who's responsible for what? *Journal of College Student Development, 34,* 26–34.

Fuller, W. E., & Wehman, P. (2003). College entrance exams for students with disabilities: Accommodations and testing guidelines. *Journal of Vocational Rehabilitation, 18,* 191–197.

Gajar, A. H. (1998). Postsecondary education. In F. R. Rusch & J. G. Chadsey (Eds.), *Beyond high school: Transition from school to work* (pp. 383–405). Belmont, CA: Wadsworth.

Gersten, R. (1998). Recent advances in instructional research for students with learning disabilities: An overview. *Learning Disabilities Research and Practice, 13,* 162–170.

Gray, K. (1996). The baccalaureate game: Is it right for all teens? *Phi Delta Kappan, 77,* 528–534.

Grigal, M., Neubert, D. A., & Moon, M. S. (2002). Postsecondary options for students with significant disabilities. *Teaching Exceptional Children, 35,* 68–73.

Guillory, J. D., Brown, B. B., & Everson, J. M. (2001). *Postsecondary education issues for transition-age adolescents with disabilities and/or special health care needs: A guide for teenagers and their families.* New Orleans: Louisiana State University, Center of Excellence in Developmental Disabilities Education, Research, and Service, LSU Health Sciences Center.

Guy, B., Shin, H., Lee, S. Y., & Thurlow, M. L. (2002). *State graduation requirements for students with and without disabilities.* Minneapolis: University of Minnesota, National Center on Educational Outcomes.

Half the Planet Foundation. (2002). *Disability policy in the 21st century: Moving on up.* Retrieved January 5, 2004, from http://www.halftheplanet.org/departments/think_tank/table_of_contents.html.

Hardy, E. (2003). Six hot technologies that could profoundly change handhelds. Retrieved July 23, 2004, from http://www.brighthand.com/articles/print.php?urlName=Six_Hot_Technologies

Hart, D., Zimbeck, K., & Whelly, T. (2002). *Challenges in coordinating and managing services and supports in postsecondary options.* (Issue Brief 1). Minneapolis: University of Minnesota,

National Center on Secondary Education and Transition.

Hartman, R. C., & Baker, B. (1986, July). *Strategies for advising disabled students for postsecondary education.* Washington, DC: U.S. Department of Education and the American Council on Education.

Hasazi, S. B., Furney, K. S., & DeStefano, L. (1999). Implementing the IDEA transition mandates. *Exceptional Children, 65,* 555–566.

Hatch, T. (1998). How comprehensive can comprehensive reform be? *Phi Delta Kappan, 79,* 518–522.

Henderson, C. (1995). *College freshman with disabilities: A triennial statistical profile.* Washington, DC: American Council on Education/HEATH Resource Center.

Heyward, S. M. (1996). *Frequently asked questions: Postsecondary education and disability.* Cambridge, MA: Heyward, Lawton and Associates.

Higher Education Consortium on Learning Disabilities (HECLD). (1996). *Unlocking the doors: How to enter post-secondary education from high school: A manual for students with learning disabilities.* Minneapolis, MN: Learning Disabilities Association.

Hill, J. (1996). Speaking out: Perceptions of students with disabilities regarding adequacy of services and willingness of faculty to make accommodations. *Journal of Postsecondary Education and Disability, 12,* 22–43.

Hishinuma, E. S. (2000). Summary of test accommodations for the SAT and ACT for students who are learning disabled 1999–2000 school year. *LD Online.* Retrieved January 13, 2004, from http://www.ldonline.org/ld_indepth/transition/hishinuma_actsat.html.

Ignash, J. (1994). How to choose a community college. *LD Online.* Retrieved January 15, 2003, from www.ldonline.org/ld_indepth/postsecondary/eric_comcol.html.

Izzo, M., & Lamb, P. (2002). *Self-determination and career development: Skills for successful transition to postsecondary education and employment.* A White Paper written in collaboration with Ohio State University, the Center on Disability Studies at the University of Hawaii at Manoa, and the National Center on Secondary Education and Transition. Retrieved December 18, 2004, from http://www.ncset.hawaii.edu/Publications/#papers.

Kaye, H.S. (2000). Disability and the digital divide. *Disability Statistics Abstract.* San Francisco: University of California at San Francisco Disability Statistics Center, and Washington, DC: U.S. Department of Education, National Institute on Disability and Rehabilitation Research.

Kezar, A. (1997). At the fork in the path: Some guidance from the research. *The ERIC Review: The Path to College, 5,* 26–29.

Kohler, P., Field, S., Izzo, M., & Johnson, J. (1997). *Transition from school to life.* Arlington, VA: Council for Exceptional Children.

Kurtz, P. D., & Hicks-Coolick, A. (1997). Preparing students with learning disabilities for success in postsecondary education: Needs and services. *Social Work in Education, 19,* 31–42.

Lahm, E., & Nichols, B. (1999). What do you know? Assistive technology competencies for special educators. *Teaching Exceptional Children, 32,* 56–63.

Langenfield, K., Thurlow, M., & Scott, D. (1997). *High stakes testing for students: Unanswered questions and implications for students with disabilities.* Minneapolis: University of Minnesota, National Center for Educational Outcomes.

Lewin, T. (2003, November 8). Change in SAT procedures echoes in disability realm. *The New York Times.* Retrieved April 11, 2004, from http://www.nfbnet.org/pipermail/nobe-1/2003-November/000272.html.

Lissner. L. S. (1999, Winter). Choosing a college. *The Postsecondary LD Report.* Retrieved January 20, 2003, from www.ldonline.org/ld_indepth/postsecondary/lissner_choosing_college.html.

MacArthur, C. A., Schwartz, S., Graham, S., Molloy, D., & Harris, K. (1996). Integration of strategy instruction into a whole language classroom: A case study. *Learning Disabilities Research and Practice, 11,* 168–176.

McGregor, G., & Pachuski, P. (1996). Assistive technology in schools: Are teachers ready, able and supported? *Journal of Special Education Technology, 13,* 4–16.

McGuire, J. M., & Shaw, S. F. (1987). A decision-making process for the college-bound learning disabled student: Matching learner, institution, and support program. *Learning Disability Quarterly, 10,* 106–111.

Mitchell, K. (1997). Making the grade: Help and hope for the first-generation college student. *The ERIC Review: The Path to College, 5(3),* 13–15.

Morningstar, M. E., Turnbull, A. P., & Turnbull, H. R. (1996). What do students with disabilities tell us about the importance of family involvement in the transition from school to adult life? *Exceptional Children, 62,* 249–260.

Mull, C. A., & Sitlington, P. L. (2003). The role of technology in the transition to postsecondary education of students with learning disabilities: A review of the literature. *Journal of Special Education, 37,* 26–32.

Mull, C., Sitlington, P. L., & Alper, S. (2001). Postsecondary education for students with learning disabilities: A synthesis of the literature. *Exceptional Children, 68,* 97–118.

National Center on Accessible Information Technology in Education. (2004). Are personal digital assistants (PDAs) accessible? Retrieved July 27, 2004, from www.washington.edu/accessit.

National Center for Education Statistics (NCES). (1998). *Postsecondary education quick information system: Survey of students with disabilities at postsecondary education institutions.* Washington, DC: U.S. Department of Education.

National Center for Education Statistics. (NCES) (1999a). *Students with disabilities in postsecondary education: A profile of preparation, participation, and outcomes.* (NCES Report No. 1999-187). Washington, DC: U.S. Department of Education.

National Center for Education Statistics. (NCES) (1999b). *An institutional perspective on students with disabilities in postsecondary education* (NCES Report No. 1999-046). Washington, DC: U.S. Department of Education.

National Center for the Study of Postsecondary Education Supports. (2000a, June). *National survey of educational support provision to students with disabilities in postsecondary education* settings. (Tech. Rep.). Honolulu: University of Hawaii at Manoa.

National Center for the Study of Postsecondary Education Supports (NCSPES). (2000b, April). *Secondary curricula issues* (Research Findings Brief). Retrieved September 29, 2003, from http://www.rrtc.hawaii.edu/documents/products/phase1/090-H01.pdf.

National Center for the Study of Postsecondary Education Supports. (2000c, April). *Case reports on students with disabilities in postsecondary education* (Research Findings Brief). Retrieved October 29, 3003, from http://www.rrtc.hawaii.edu/documents/products/phase1/087b-H01.pdf.

National Center for the Study of Postsecondary Education Supports. (2002, July 8). Preparation for and support of youth with disabilities in postsecondary education and employment: Implications for policy, priorities and practice. *Proceedings and briefing book for the National Summit on Postsecondary Education for People with Disabilities.* Retrieved January 7, 2004, from http://www.ncset.hawaii.edu/summits/july2002/briefing/default.htm.

National Council on Disability. (2000, May 15). *National disability policy: A progress report: December 2001–December 2002.* Retrieved October 5, 2003, from http://www.ncd.gov/newsroom/publications/2003/progressreport.final.htm.

NICHCY Transition Summary. (1993, March). *Transition Services in the IEP, 3(1).* Washington, DC: The National Information Center for Children and Youth with Disabilities.

National Organization on Disabilities. (1998). *1998 N.O.D./Harris survey of Americans with disabilities.* Washington, DC: Louis Harris and Associates.

Navicky, J. (1998, Winter). A match made by design, not accident. *The Postsecondary LD Report.* Retrieved October 13, 2004, from www.ldonline.org/ld_indepth/postsecondary/navicky_match.html.

Oakes, J., & Wells, A. (1998). Detracking for high student achievement. *Educational Leadership, 55,* 38–51.

Palmer, C., & Roessler, R. T. (2000). Requesting classroom accommodations: Self-advocacy and conflict resolution training for college students with disabilities. *Journal of Rehabilitation, 66,* 38–43.

Pascarella, E., & Terenzini, P. (1991). *How college affects students: Findings and insights from twenty years of research.* San Francisco: Jossey-Bass.

Phillips, P. (1990). A self-advocacy plan for high school students with learning disabilities: A comparative study case analysis of students', teachers', and parents' perceptions of program effects. *Journal of Learning Disabilities, 28,* 466–171.

Powers, L., Turner, A., Westwood, D., Matuszewski, J., Wilson, R., & Phillips, A. (2001). TAKECHARGE for the future: A controlled field test of a model to promote student involvement in transition planning. *Career Development for Exceptional Individuals, 24,* 89–104.

Raskind, M. H., Goldberg, R. J., Higgins, E. L., & Herman, K. L. (2003). *Life success for children with learning disabilities: A parent guide.* Pasadena, CA: Frostig Center.

Raskind, M., & Higgins, E. (1998). Assistive technology for postsecondary students with learning disabilities: An overview. *Journal of Learning Disabilities, 31,* 27–40.

Rea, P. J., McLaughlin, V. L., & Walther-Thomas, C. (2002). Outcomes for students with learning disabilities in inclusive and pullout programs. *Exceptional Children, 68,* 203–223.

Reamer, A. (1997, Spring). *Transition to college.* National Adult Literacy and Learning Disabilities Center. Retrieved October 30, 2003, from www.ldonline.org/ld_indepth/postsecondary/reamer_trans.html

Reis, S. M., Neu, T. W., & McGuire, J. M. (1997). Case studies of high ability students with learning disabilities who have achieved. *Exceptional Children, 63,* 463–479.

Reisberg, L. (1999, October 15). Average tuition and fees at colleges rose less than 5% this year. *The Chronicle of Higher Education.* Retrieved February 26, 2004, from www.chronicle.com/free/v46/i08/08a05201.htm.

Rojewski, J. W. (1996). Educational and occupational aspirations of high school seniors with learning disabilities, *Exceptional Children, 62,* 463–476.

Roles for youth with disabilities. (2002, July 12). *The Disability Grapevine Online Newspaper, 20.* Retrieved August 1, 2002, from http://www.disabilitygrapevine.com.

Rose, D., & Meyer, A. (2000). Universal design for individual differences. *Educational Leadership, 58*(3), 39–43.

Rothstein, L. (1991, September 4). Campuses and the disabled. *Chronicle of Higher Education,* pp. B3, B10.

Rothstein, L. (2003, March). *Students with disabilities and higher education: A disconnect in expectations and realities.* Washington: DC: George Washington University, HEATH Resource Center, National Clearinghouse on Postsecondary Education for Individuals with Disabilities. Retrieved January 29, 2004, from http://www.heath.gwu.edu/PDFs/Disconnect.pdf.

The SAT: Where it's at: An interview with College Board's Paula Kuebler. (2004, January 16). *The Disability Grapevine Online Newspaper, 1.* Retrieved January 18, 2004, from http://www.disabilitygrapevine.com.

Schuster, J. L., Timmons, J. C., & Moloney, M. (2003). Barriers to successful transition for young adults who receive SSI and their families. *Career Development for Exceptional Individuals, 24,* 47–66.

Scott, S. (1991). A change in legal status: An overlooked dimension in the transition to higher education, *Journal of Learning Disabilities, 24,* 459–466.

Shaw. S., Brinckerhoff, L. C., Kistler, J., & McGuire, J. M. (1991). Preparing students with learning disabilities for postsecondary education issues and future needs. *Learning Disabilities: A Multidisciplinary Journal, 2,* 21–26.

Shaw, S., & Parker, D. (2003, October 23). *Planning for effective transition to post-secondary education.* Presentation at the 2003 CEC-DCDT Conference, Roanoke, VA.

Sitlington, P. L., Neubert, D., Begun, W., Lombard, R., & Leconte, P. (1996). *Assess for success.* Arlington, VA: Council for Exceptional Children.

Stern, D. (2002, Spring). *Building the bridge between the community college and work for students with disabilities.* Retrieved October, 16, 2003, from www.ldonline.org/ld_indepth/postsecondary/building_the_bridge.html.

Stodden, R. A., Conway, M. A., & Chang, K. (2003). *Professional employment for individuals with disabilities.* Retrieved December 19, 2003, from http://www.ncset.hawaii.edu/institutes/feb2003/papers/txt/PROFESSIONAL%20EMPLOYMENT%20.txt.

Stodden, R. A., Galloway, L. M., & Stodden, N. J. (2003). Secondary school curricula issues: Impact on postsecondary students with disabilities, *Exceptional Children, 70,* 9–21.

Stodden, R., & Jones, M. A. (2002). *Supporting youth with disabilities to access and succeed in post-*

secondary education: Essentials for educators in secondary schools (Issue Brief vol. 1, No. 5). Minneapolis: University of Minnesota, National Center on Secondary Education and Transition.

Stodden, R. A., Jones, M. A., & Chang, K. (2002). *Services, supports, and accommodations for individuals with disabilities: An analysis across secondary education, postsecondary education and employment.* Honolulu: University of Hawaii at Manoa. Retrieved November 18, 2003, from http://www.rrtc.hawaii.edu/documents/products/phase3/01.pdf.

Sullivan, C. (1987). *Getting youth with disabilities ready for postsecondary education.* Washington, DC: HEATH Resource Center.

Taymans, J. M., & West, L. L. (2001). *Selecting a college for students with learning disabilities or attention deficit hyperactivity disorder.* Washington, DC: George Washington University/HEATH Resource Center.

Thurlow, M. L., Sinclair, M. F., & Johnson, D. R. (2002). *Students with disabilities who drop out of school: Implications for policy and practice* (Issue Brief, Vol. 1, No. 2). Minneapolis: University of Minnesota, National Center on Secondary Education and Transition.

Tinto, V. (1993). *Leaving college: Rethinking the causes and cures of student attrition.* Chicago: University of Chicago Press.

Todis, B. (1996). Tools for the task? Perspective on assistive technology in educational settings. *Journal of Special Education Technology, 12*(2), 49–61.

Tomlinson, C. (1999). *The differentiated classroom: Responding to the needs of all learners.* Alexandria, VA: Association for Supervision and Curriculum Development.

Turnbull, H., Turnbull, P., Wehmeyer, M., & Park, J. (2003). A quality of life framework for special education outcomes. *Remedial and Special Education. 24,* 67–74.

U.S. Department of Education. (1995). *Seventeenth annual report to Congress on the implementation of the Individuals with Disabilities Education Act.* Washington, DC: Author.

U.S. Department of Education. (2000). *Getting ready: Taking the right courses for college starts in middle school.* Retrieved December 19,
2003, from http://www.ed.gov/pubs/GettingReadyCollegeEarly/step2.html.

U.S. Department of Education. (2002a). *Twenty-fourth annual report to Congress on the implementation of the Individuals with Disabilities with Disabilities Education Act.* Washington, DC: Office of Special Education and Rehabilitative Services.

U.S. Department of Education. (2002b) *Students with disabilities preparing for postsecondary education: Know your rights and responsibilities,* Washington, DC: Office of Civil Rights.

Vaughn, S., Schumm, J., & Brick, J. (1998). Using a rating scale to design and evaluate inclusive programs. *Teaching Exceptional Children, 30,* 41–45.

Vogel, S. A., Hruby, P. J., & Adelman, P. B. (1993). Educational and psychological factors in successful and unsuccessful college students with learning disabilities. *Learning Disabilities Research and Practice, 8,* 35–43.

Wagner, M. (2003, September 18). *National Longitudinal 2 Data.* Presentation at the at the 2003 National Leadership Summit on Improving Results for Youth, Washington, DC. Retrieved February 25, 2004, from http://www.ncset.org/summit03/.

Wagner, M., Blackorby, J., Cameto, R., & Newman, L. (1993). *What makes a difference? Influences on postschool outcomes of youth with disabilities: The third comprehensive report from the National Longitudinal Study of Special Education Students.* Menlo Park, CA.: SRI International.

Wagner, M., D'Amico, R., Marder, C., Newman, L., & Blackorby, J. (1992). *What happens next? Trends in postschool outcomes of youth with disabilities.* Menlo Park, CA.: SRI International.

Wehmeyer, M., & Lawrence, M. (1995) Whose future is it anyway? Promoting student involvement in transition planning. *Career Development for Exceptional Individuals, 18,* 69–83.

Witte, R. H., Phillips, L., & Kakela, M. (1998). Job satisfaction of college students with learning disabilities. *Journal of Learning Disabilities, 31,* 259–265.

Yelin, E., & Katz, P. (1994). Labor force trends of persons with and without disabilities. *Monthly Labor Review, 117,* 36–42.

Zaccarine, D., & Stewart, A. (1991). *Questions to ask when visiting a college.* Cullowhee, NC: Western Carolina University.

Zhang, D., Katsiyannis, A., & Zhang, J. (2002). Teacher and parent practice on fostering self-determination of high school students with mild disabilities. *Career Development of Exceptional Individuals, 25,* 157–169.

Preparing Students for Employment
School-Based Preparation

Chapter 7

Introduction

Chapters 7 and 8 focus on assisting students with disabilities in obtaining their postschool goals in employment. This chapter describes school-based employment preparation opportunities and presents suggestions for designing training. Emphasis is on providing students with an individualized employment preparation program and appropriate curricular options based on assessment results and individual career choices. Case studies illustrate how a wide array of school-based employment preparation opportunities can begin to prepare students for future careers.

Kohler's Taxonomy of Transition Planning includes student development as a program area critical to the delivery of comprehensive transition services. Student development activities include instruction in daily living skills, functional academics, independent and personal living skills, self-determination skills, self-advocacy skills, and employment skills. Instruction in these areas requires the opportunity to generalize to the community, but a variety of school-based activities can establish the instructional foundation needed for skill accomplishment (Kohler, Field, Izzo, & Johnson, 1997).

By the time they reach high school, students should be experiencing the array of transition-related curricular and employment preparation options available through the school system and the adult service provider network. Self-determination skills are needed in accessing and receiving maximum benefit from transition services. A student's use of self-determination skills can increase the quality of the student's placement, curricular, and employment preparation matches and guide service providers in designing a high school experience that matches the student's postschool goals.

A Personal Perspective on School-based Employment Preparation

Holly Godfrey

Transition Teacher, Cleveland County Schools

I teach occupational preparation and self-determination to high-school-aged students with mild to moderate disabilities. All of my students have a common goal to obtain competitive employment after graduation. The curriculum that I use in my instruction not only prepares them for postschool employment but also, I believe, increases their chances of becoming productive employees with a broad sense of the job search process and the ability to understand and advocate employment opportunities.

At the beginning of each school year, it is generally necessary to review and determine what career field a student has interests in. Interest inventories, vocational assessments, informal observations, and parental input have proved to be of value in helping my students think beyond their own cognitive abilities and perhaps limited realizations. Field trips help them see that many jobs are found under one roof. Students hear first hand about the application process, the interview process, a proper work ethic, and other important aspects of working toward and securing employment. Career awareness and exploration are also promoted by inviting guest speakers to our classroom. These people describe the job skills needed in their area of employment, and the students learn that the guest speakers had to complete the job search process just as they are being instructed to do.

Our students are fortunate in that our school has an exceptionally well organized and motivating school-based enterprise. A high-quality school-based enterprise contributes a great deal to creating good employees with a good work ethic. Students practice good work habits and behaviors in the school-based enterprise, and these skills are carried over to future employment. In school-based enterprises, students learn about being on time, gathering necessary materials, reporting to a supervisor, producing quality versus quantity, and, most important, demonstrating ownership and pride in a finished product.

Without a school-based enterprise on campus, many students would not visualize that the key to postschool employment is that having a job makes you feel good about yourself.

My students are eager to learn all about the job search process. They complete many job applications for practice and role-play interview strategies countless times. They learn many job skills and use these skills on various jobs both on campus and off campus. But none of this would be effective for students if they were not capable and unwavering in their efforts to advocate for their rights as individuals. Part of my instruction in self-determination is to foster awareness of the value of making good choices and how self-advocacy can help students in adult life. Many students learn that even making bad choices is okay as long as you learn to make better choices next time. For example, Matthew was a new student to our school. I gave him a classroom chore of washing the chalkboard but explained that I wanted to show him the steps (or task analyze) an easy way to wash the board properly. He chose not to follow these steps one day and instead washed the chalkboard with a mopping solution rather than just plain water. The mopping solution left part of the chalkboard very sticky, and I was unable to write with chalk on this part. Matthew and I had a serious discussion, and he told me that he "made a bad choice" by washing the chalkboard before developing the needed steps to clean it properly. Matthew now says it is "better to wait until my supervisor shows me how," and that is always a good choice.

People demonstrate their desire to be productive in many ways. Many individuals choose to enter the workforce; some pursue volunteer work; and others choose a home-based career such as parenting or telecommuting. In our society it is expected that young people will have choices about the career paths they take after leaving high school. However, this has not been true historically for individuals with disabilities. The mandate for transition services included in the 1990 Individuals with Disabilities Education Act (IDEA) amendments was aimed at narrowing the employment gap for special education graduates.

EMPLOYMENT AND PERSONS WITH DISABILITIES

There has been some progress, but for young people between the ages of 18 and 29 who have disabilities, the employment rate is only 57% compared to a 72% employment rate for individuals without disabilities (National Organization on Disability [NOD], 2004). Three to five years after graduation, only 50% of special education graduates have a competitive job, as compared to 69% of their peers without disabilities, (Fabian, Lent, & Willis, 1998). For individuals with more severe disabilities, the employment rate drops to 25%, and it drops even lower, to only 8%, for individuals with profound disabilities (La Plante, Kennedy, Kaye, & Wenger, 1996). Only 35% of all individuals with disabilities of all working ages report having a full-time or part-time job versus 78% of those without disabilities (NOD, 2004).

Even when students with disabilities do obtain employment, they often find themselves limited to low-paying jobs with limited benefits or in part-time employment (Wagner, Blackorby, Cameto, Hebbeler, & Newman, 1993) earning only about 63% of what their peers without disabilities earn (La Plante et al., 1996). The outlook for employment beyond entry level at above minimum wage holds true even for graduates with learning disabilities. Only about 22% of these individuals are employed in higher-status jobs (Haring, Lovett, & Smith, 1990). Even 10 years past graduation individuals with disabilities earn significantly less ($17,160 annually) than those without disabilities ($27,126 annually; Goldstein, Murray, & Edgar, 1998). Limited employment and the low wages of those who are employed contribute to the fact that three times as many individuals with disabilities live in poverty than those without disabilities (NOD, 2004). Despite federal legislation resulting in nationwide implementation of transition programs, being unemployed or underemployed continues to exemplify most clearly what it means to have a disability (NOD, 1998).

BENEFITS OF EMPLOYMENT

Many of the life activities that characterize independence depend on having an economic base of support. Obtaining and maintaining employment at a competitive wage allows a young person to achieve postschool outcomes such as pursuing postsecondary education, living independently, and participating in recreational activities. But with one in three adults with disabilities having an annual household income of less than $15,000, financial independence and all of its benefits elude many individuals (Butterworth & Gilmore, 2000).

Employment plays a much larger role in a person's life than simply earning a paycheck. The opportunity to work in a satisfying career can provide a sense of accomplishment, increase self-worth, assist in solidifying self-identity, and provide a social network of support and friendship. The National Organization on Disability (NOD, 2004) reported that only 34% of individuals with disabilities were satisfied with life in general. It might be assumed that the high unemployment rate for this population has an impact on life satisfaction. If a school system offers comprehensive transition services, it will include a strong employment preparation component that provides an array of services and activities focused on employment and other activities that foster individual productivity.

IMPORTANCE OF EMPLOYMENT PREPARATION

The definition of transition in the IDEA amendments, as stated in Chapter 1, clearly indicates the expectation for public schools to support students in their attempt to achieve postschool goals in employment by providing an array of activities aimed at increasing employability. Findings from the National Longitudinal Transition Study 2 (NLTS2) indicate that 53% of students with disabilities have a vocational-oriented goal of competitive employment and 40% desire to attend postsecondary employment preparation (Cameto, Levine, and Wagner, 2004). These findings demonstrate the importance of ensuring that schools provide multiple employment preparation experiences paired with appropriate curricular options to assist students in achieving their postgraduation goals.

To be successful, the process of preparing young people for employment must begin long before they reach high school. The high school years are far too late to ensure that students develop the work-related habits, behaviors, and skills needed in today's job market. A longitudinal approach to employment preparation beginning in elementary school and consisting of appropriate curricula interfaced with a wide range of employment preparation experiences is the best approach to ensuring a successful transition from school to the world of work (Brolin, 1995).

SCHOOL-BASED EMPLOYMENT PREPARATION STRATEGIES

Activities associated with preparing students for future employment occur both in school and in the community. Figure 7.1 presents a list of both school-based and community-based employment preparation activities. School-based activities are conducted by a wide variety of school personnel including special education teachers, general education teachers, career-technical education (CTE) teachers, guidance counselors, and special populations coordinators. Activities that occur on the school campus include a career education curriculum, academic coursework, employability skill instruction, career-technical education, on-campus jobs, career counseling, self-determination instruction, school-based enterprises, and vocational assessment. Activities conducted on the school campus must be connected to community-based activities to ensure that a student has opportunities to generalize work skills and ultimately build a work history prior to leaving high school. Employment preparation activities conducted in the community are discussed in Chapter 8.

Base the Curriculum on a Career Education Philosophy

The foundation for preparing students for employment begins with providing an appropriate curriculum. Some students may need a functional curriculum that focuses on life skills, while others will participate in a more traditional academic course of study. Whichever curriculum a student chooses to follow, it is imperative that there be a focus on career development that permeates the student's entire educational career. It is desirable for students to have a combination of classroom instruction and actual work experiences as they enter the high school years. However, some students in an academically focused course of study may

Types of School-Based Employment Preparation Strategies (this chapter).
- ◆ Use a career education philosophy.
- ◆ Integrate employment and academic skills.
- ◆ Consider using a functional curriculum.
- ◆ Conduct ongoing transition assessment.
- ◆ Use career-technical education.
- ◆ Use on-campus training opportunities:
  - ◆ School-based enterprises.
  - ◆ On-campus jobs.
  - ◆ Job clubs or vocational student organizations.

Types of Community-Based Employment Preparation Strategies (described in Chapter 8)

- ◆ Job shadowing
- ◆ Internships
- ◆ Apprenticeships
- ◆ Volunteerism or community service projects
- ◆ Community-based mobile work crews or enclaves
- ◆ Competitive employment

Figure 7.1
Examples of School- and Community-Based Employment Preparation Strategies
and Activities

be consumed with obtaining academic credits and passing graduation exit exams, leaving little time for employment preparation (Stodden, Dowrick, Stodden, & Gilmore, 2001).

Various reform efforts aimed at increased accountability (e.g., high-stakes testing) have exacerbated issues faced by students with disabilities and have made the integration of academic and career technical skills even more difficult. But the alternative of serving students with disabilities in special education classes instead of general education classes so they can access training in adult life skills and employment preparation can result in limited access to the academic classes they need to access postsecondary career training (Gajar, Goodman, & McAfee, 1993; Kohler, 1998).

DID YOU KNOW?

White youths with disabilities are more likely to work than African American youths with disabilities. The earned income of white youths also tends to be higher than that of African American youths even though the types of jobs held and the hours of employment are very similar (Wagner, Cadwallader, et al., 2003).

Career education is one approach that can be used to ensure that all students are prepared for postsecondary employment regardless of the course of study they have chosen or the manner in which special education services are delivered. Many of the elements found within career education are in tandem with past (e.g., School-to-Work Opportunities Act) and present (e.g., Carl D. Perkins Vocational and Applied Technology Act) legislation and can also be seen in reforms aimed at creating career-oriented high schools (e.g., Making High Schools Work; Bottoms, Presson, & Johnson, 1992). Career-oriented secondary schools (e.g., comprehensive high schools, career centers vocational schools) are organized to provide career awareness activities, encourage the development of employability skills, increase the relevance of academics by establishing a connection between classroom instruction and future career goals, and facilitate student involvement in postschool planning (Saunders, Stoney, & Weston, 1997).

The philosophy behind career education, which promotes the infusion of a careers emphasis in all subjects grades K through 12, can be seen in the organization and delivery of services within a career-oriented program. The *career* in career education refers not only to the paid work that an adult might participate in but also to the other roles of adult life, including citizen, family member, and leisure seeker (Brolin, 1995).

Although career education originally was designed for application to all students, special educators have particularly heralded it as a way to overcome the difficulties associated with providing career preparation instruction within general education classes. When career education is infused into existing curricula from kindergarten through high school, employability skills, daily living skills, and personal-social skills experiences can be matched to traditional subject matter, making learning more meaningful. When students are taught curricula that are relevant to their future goals, they are more likely to be motivated to learn the skills needed to live and work in their community after graduation. Also, the skills that students can learn through exposure to career education activities— working independently, following instructions, understanding work routines, being adaptable, responding appropriately to supervision, communicating effectively, and demonstrating good social skills and personal appearance—match the skills that employers rate as being important to job success (McCrea, 1991).

Career education encourages the involvement of educators, community-based professionals, and parents in supporting students in their quest to learn the skills needed for adult life. This team approach matches the expectations of IDEA for transition planning and helps establish a network of support that includes individuals who will play an important role in students' achievement of their postschool goals.

Career education has four stages, beginning in elementary school and extending into high school. Several of these stages overlap, since career education is a developmental process, and some students move more quickly than others through the stages based on their individual abilities and needs. Each stage focuses on the application of skills and expanding the relevance of what is being taught. The Life Centered Career Education (LCCE) curriculum (Brolin, 1995)

Strategies for Family Involvement in School-Based Employment Preparation

◆ Provide family members with information about high school pathways, exit documents, and career pathways so they can assist their young person in choosing courses that best match his or her postschool goals.

◆ Provide family members with suggestions for how work behaviors, work habits, and work skills can be practiced in the home and community.

◆ Ensure that family members understand the CTE course offerings as they relate to various careers and the importance of concentrating in a career pathway.

◆ Provide family members with training in their young person's right to accommodations and modifications so that advocacy can occur when accessing CTE courses.

◆ Enlist family members to volunteer in the school-based enterprise (SBE) as "work buddies" so they can experience first hand employment preparation activities.

◆ Teach family members how to nurture their young person's independence, support risk taking, and strengthen self-advocacy skills through allowing him or her to make choices and decisions.

◆ Establish a system of communication to keep family members informed of their young person's employment preparation experiences so discussions can be initiated concerning matches between interests and abilities and potential careers.

◆ Teach family members the importance of being honest with their young person about the implications of his or her disability in order to facilitate realistic career decision making.

---

provides teaching strategies and lessons plans for grades K through 12 that are designed around the components of career education. The stages of career education as described by Brolin include career awareness, career exploration, career preparation, and career assimilation.

Career Awareness.   The first stage of career education, **career awareness,** begins in elementary school and extends through middle school. The goal of this stage is to provide awareness of the existence of work (paid and unpaid), the role of a worker, and how the student will fit into a work-oriented society as an adult. Students begin by developing initial work-related concepts and values along with the mobility, interpersonal relationship skills, problem-solving skills, and communication skills needed for future careers.

To assist with future career planning and decision making, it is vital that children begin early to develop a strong work ethic along with a high level of self-awareness that includes understanding their own strengths, interests, and limitations. One learning activity related to career awareness is gaining knowledge about various careers by studying community service workers (e.g., police officer, firefighter, doctor, nurse). This activity is common in the early elementary years, but it should be expanded to develop an appreciation of *all* careers, including those in the working class and service occupations, so that students of all ability levels can become familiar with the wide range of available occupations.

Many of the skills associated with future work success should be taught directly to students while they are still in elementary school, with teachers ensuring that students are aware of the skills being taught and the relation of these skills to future careers. In addition to career awareness activities, instruction in skills such as punctuality, perseverance, self-organization, self-control, teamwork, following directions, and task completion can be easily incorporated into elementary education (Garnett, 1984).

Career Exploration.   The **career exploration** stage starts at the middle school level and continues into the high school years. The goal of this stage is to help students explore their interests and abilities in relation to various life-styles and occupations. Students are given the opportunity to explore their own unique abilities and needs through hands-on experiences both on campus and in the community. Activities associated with career exploration include school-based enterprises, on-campus jobs, service learning projects, and community-based job shadowing. These on-campus training options are discussed in more detail later in the chapter. Through these types of activities students can begin to understand how skills learned in the classroom relate to the real world and increase their familiarity with materials and equipment common to various occupations.

Career Preparation.   **Career preparation** begins in elementary school but becomes a priority at the high school level. The focus of the career preparation stage is on facilitating career decision making through the identification of interests, desires, and future life-style choices. Beginning in elementary school, multiple opportunities should be provided for students to develop self-determination, employment preparation skills, and self-knowledge. As they enter high school, students should focus on obtaining job-seeking skills, as well as job-specific skills, through paid and/or nonpaid work experiences.

Career Assimilation.   The final phase of career education, the **career assimilation** stage, occurs during the final years of high school. The focus of this stage is on helping students finalize their plans for transition to various postsecondary environments. Interagency coordination is required during this stage to ensure that students are ready for engagement in their choice of life activities (Flexer, Simmons, Luft, & Baer, 2001).

Integrate Employment and Academic Skills

As mentioned previously, the philosophy of career education can be used within the general education curriculum or as part of a functional course of study. The manner in which students are exposed to employment preparation will vary based on their needs, their chosen course of study, the programs offered by their high school, the manner in which special education services are delivered, and staff expertise. Transition planning can be used to outline how and when employment preparation skills will be taught.

A systematic program using carefully selected materials to assist students in career exploration and the development of job-seeking skills can have a positive impact on career decision making and enhance the development of skills necessary for job obtainment (Farley & Johnson, 1999). The integration of academic and vocational curricula can also make a difference in the achievement and engagement of students with disabilities (Eisenmann, 2000). Methods for ensuring that academics and career preparation activities are integrated for students enrolled in the general education program include the following:

- ♦ Incorporating academic skills into CTE classes.
- ♦ Using specialized curricula that merge academics and career skills to replace standard math, English, or science courses.
- ♦ Modifying vocational and academic courses to encourage both the learning and application of skills.
- ♦ Requiring senior projects in which students participate in a culminating experience related to their chosen career path.
- ♦ Offering classes through occupational clusters, career pathways, or career majors.
- ♦ Giving hands-on assignments that require the application of academic skills to various careers (Grubb, Davis, Lum, Plihal, & Morgaine, 1991; Reid & Tsurzuki, 1994).

Consider Using a Functional Curriculum

Students with severe cognitive disabilities may need an instructional approach that is directed toward the acquisition of basic skills required for daily existence (Snell & Brown, 2000). Since students functioning at this level have difficulty with generalization, functional teaching focuses on using real-life materials and applying skills to the future environments in which the student can be expected to function. Using parts of a functional curriculum is also appropriate to supplement the instruction of a student who is participating in an academically based curriculum in order to ensure that he or she develops independent living skills.

Conduct Ongoing Transition Assessment

As discussed in Chapter 3, regardless of the type of instructional program or curriculum in which a student is enrolled, there should be an ongoing process for helping students determine their employment interests and abilities. This should be obtained through a variety of methods, including interest inventories, aptitude tests, observations, surveys, interviews, and situational assessments. Whatever type of method is used to help students conduct a comprehensive transition assessment, the final result should be a clear vision of the best possible match between the student and the world of work.

Involve Students in Career-Technical Education

Career-technical education (CTE) should be a major component of transition services for the majority of students with disabilities due to the employment training services offered through this discipline, the expertise of CTE staff in preparing young people for future employment, and the important role CTE plays in most high school programs.

The Carl Perkins Vocational and Applied Technology Education Amendments of 1998 (P.L. 105–332) defined career-technical education as:

> *organized activities that offer a sequence of courses that provides individuals with the academic and technical knowledge and skills the individuals need to prepare for further education and for careers (other than careers requiring a baccalaureate, master's or doctoral degree) in current or emerging employment sectors. Vocational technical education includes competency-based applied learning that contributes to the academic knowledge, higher-order reasoning and problem-solving skills, work attitudes, general employability skills, technical skills, and occupational-specific skills or an individual."* (Title III, Section 3: Definitions, 29)

Upon entering high school, students will have to make decisions about the course of study they wish to pursue. The course of study that is chosen should match the student's postschool outcome goals for employment and postsecondary education. A discussion of choosing a course of study related to the pursuit of postsecondary education is discussed in greater detail in Chapter 6. Whether or not a student is going to pursue postsecondary education or employment after graduation, he or she will likely choose to take some CTE courses.

Career-technical education can serve a vital role in preparing students for employment by providing occupation-specific skill training that also contributes to academic knowledge, problem-solving capabilities, and higher-order reasoning skills. All students with disabilities should have access to CTE courses related to their postschool goals in order to develop the occupational awareness and skills needed to pursue a postschool career.

SCANS Competencies.   Career-technical education courses support and contribute to the focus areas established by the Secretary's Commission on Achieving Necessary Skills (SCANS), which was established by the U.S. Secretary of Labor in May 1990 to "advise the secretary on the level of skills required to enter employment" and involved interviewing hundreds of representatives from business and education. The five main SCANS competencies that effective workers can productively use are:

1. Resources: allocating time, money, materials, space, and staff.

2. Interpersonal skills: working on teams, teaching others, serving customers, leading, negotiating, and working well with people from culturally diverse backgrounds.

3. Information: acquiring and evaluating data, organizing and maintaining files, interpreting and communicating, and using computers to process information.

4. Systems: understanding social, organizational, and technological systems, monitoring and correcting performance, and designing or improving systems.

5. Technology: selecting equipment and tools, applying technology to specific tasks, and maintaining and troubleshooting technologies.

The SCANS foundation skills are:

1. Basic skills: reading, writing, arithmetic, and mathematics, as well as speaking and listening.

2. Thinking skills: thinking creatively, making decisions, solving problems, seeing things in the mind's eye, knowing how to learn, and reasoning.

3. Personal qualities: individual responsibility, self-esteem, sociability, self-management, and integrity (Secretary's Commission on Achieving Necessary Skills, 1993).

The results of the research conducted by this commission supported the implementation of many of the transition activities related to the employment domain (e.g., job shadowing, school-based enterprises, internships, apprenticeships) and the teaching of occupationally related skills through participation in CTE, integrated academics, and/or a functional curriculum. Including students with disabilities in CTE courses can provide them with not only direct instruction in vocationally related skills, but also access to a variety of services including vocational assessment, career counseling, career planning, job training, employability skills training, and apprenticeships.

Importance of Career-Technical Education.   Although there has been some decline in the number of students with disabilities taking CTE courses—possibly due to the emphasis on academics during recent years—findings from the NLST2 indicate that more than half of students with disabilities are participating in CTE courses and 34% are enrolled in preemployment preparation courses. Participation is more common among students in their last 2 years of high school (Wagner, Newman, et al., 2003).

There are definite advantages for students with disabilities who have access to CTE courses. Participation in CTE can provide a labor market advantage for students with disabilities as indicated by a higher rate of competitive employment and higher wages (Harvey, 2002). Students can increase their future income by almost 2% for each CTE course completed at the high school level (*Vocational Training News*, 2004). When access is gained to CTE and supports are provided, leading to successful program completion, students with disabilities obtain employment at about the same rate as students without disabilities (Rockwell, Weisenstein, & LaRoque, 1986). Students with disabilities who enroll in CTE classes are also less likely to drop out, and thus complete a program leading to a high school diploma (Colley & Jamison, 1998).

Career-technical education is most effective when students specialize in a career pathway by taking four or more courses related to the same occupational area, since specialization is associated not only with increased employment but also with higher wages. The National Association of Vocational Education (2004) reported that a student's average earnings immediately following graduation could be increased by $1,200 simply by taking four CTE courses. Unfortunately, research has shown that when students with disabilities participate in CTE courses, they typically have non-occupation-specific goals (Wagner et al., 1993). In fact, students with disabilities account for less than 5% of concentrators nationally within CTE (Silverberg, Warner, Goodwin, & Fong, 2002). This means that rather than taking a series of courses designed to prepare for a specific career pathway, students with disabilities typically take a wide variety of CTE courses.

This trend may be changing, though, as the number of occupation-specific vocational credits earned by graduates with disabilities increased by 25% between 1982 and 1994 (Levesque, Lauen, Teitelbaum, Alt, & Librera, 2000). Most recently the NLTS2 found that students usually had at least one occupation-specific course among the CTE courses in which they were enrolled (Wagner, Newman, Cameto, Levine, & Marder, 2003). When advising students on their high school schedules, educators should keep in mind that the most benefit will occur for students who receive the specialized occupational training and hands-on experiences that usually occur only in sequenced series of advanced courses.

Accessing Appropriate CTE Courses.   Special education professionals can help students enroll in occupation-specific courses through the transition planning process by involving CTE personnel, providing appropriate accommodations and modifications, and/or offering CTE courses appropriate to the postschool employment goals of students with more severe disabilities.

During transition planning, special educators and career-technical educators must work in partnership with students and their families to make scheduling decisions based on the students' interests as determined through transition assessment. Once a student's interests and postschool goals have been targeted, the

---

DID YOU KNOW?

According to the 2002 National Assessment of Vocational Education, students with disabilities are overrepresented in the more traditional vocational education areas of agriculture, construction, mechanics and repair, and materials production (Silverberg et al., 2002).

focus should be on providing individualized assistance in accessing, enrolling, and succeeding in the chosen coursework. Accessing higher-level and nontraditional CTE courses designed to maximize marketability in the workforce may be especially difficult for students with disabilities and subgroups within that population such as females (Van Beaver, Kohler, & Chadsey, 2000).

Accessing CTE courses and providing appropriate accommodations and modifications needed to ensure full participation and student achievement requires collaboration and comprehensive planning among IEP team members. The Carl Perkins Act provides legislative guidelines establishing the expectation for the inclusion of students with disabilities in mainstream CTE courses. One aspect of this legislation that affects students with disabilities is the requirement for members of so-called special population groups to have equitable participation in vocational-technical education. (Chapter 1 discusses the special populations groups in greater detail.) The Carl Perkins Act outlines the criteria for services and activities for individuals who are members of these groups. Each student who is a member of a special population is entitled to certain assurances when accessing or participating in CTE services. Figure 7.2 lists these assurances in detail (National Vocational Association, 1998).

Equal Access Assurances

♦ Students with disabilities have equal access to recruitment, enrollment, and placement activities.
♦ Students with disabilities have equal access to the full range of available career-technical education (CTE) programs available to individuals who are not members of special populations.
♦ CTE programs and activities will be provided in the least restrictive environment.
♦ Students with disabilities under Section 504 of the Rehabilitation Act of 1973 are guaranteed rights and protections and will have CTE programs readily accessible with supplementary services, as do students with disabilities under the Individuals with Disabilities Education Act (IDEA).
♦ CTE planning for students with disabilities is coordinated among career technical education, special education, and vocational rehabilitation, when appropriate.
♦ CTE provided for students with disabilities is monitored to determine whether their education is consistent with their individualized education programs developed under (IDEA).

Provision of Information

♦ Members of special populations and their parents shall receive information about CTE offerings at least 1 year prior to the student's entering the ninth grade or at an appropriate age for entering the ninth grade.

Figure 7.2
Summary of Carl Perkins Assurances

Other Assurances

♦ Students who are members of special populations are assisted in entering CTE courses.
♦ Assistance is provided in fulfilling the transition service requirement under IDEA for students with disabilities.
♦ Supplementary services are provided for members of special populations. These services include:
  1. *Curriculum modification* such as analysis of curricular materials to determine academic levels, task analyses, use of lower reading level materials, development of materials that match various learning styles, and use of technology.
  2. *Equipment modification* such as use of auditory/visual signals for students with sensory disabilities, specialized safety devices, note-taking systems, adaptations to regular equipment, and modified furniture.
  3. *Classroom modification* such as modified grading, peer tutoring, oral tests, abbreviated assignments, alternative materials, extended test time, and interpreter.
  4. *Supportive personnel* such as special populations coordinator and CTE assistants.
  5. *Instructional aids and devices* such as taped texts, note-takers, readers, student tutors, enlarged equipment, electronic readers, reaching devices, and augmentative communication devices.
♦ Professionally trained counselors and teachers conduct guidance, counseling, and career development activities.
♦ Counseling and instructional services will be designed to facilitate the transition from school to postschool employment and career opportunities (training, postsecondary education, or military service; American Vocational Association, 1998; North Carolina Department of Public Instruction, 2002).

Figure 7.2
Continued

Setting the instructional stage for students with disabilities to pursue occupation-specific coursework in a chosen career pathway should be a joint priority for both special educators and career-technical educators. Teachers of CTE courses should serve as members of the individualized education program (IEP) team for any student wishing to enroll in career-technical programs. Although joint planning can assist in ensuring that appropriate curricular and instructional strategies are available, success in this area is more likely if schools put measures in place for the delivery of individualized services within CTE courses.

Miller, Lombard, and Hazelkorn (2000) noted that almost two-thirds of secondary teachers had never participated in an IEP team meeting for students enrolled in their classes. The NLTS2 (Wagner, Newman, et al., 2003) found few modifications being made to teacher-driven aspects of courses (e.g., curriculum, materials used, classroom activities, or classroom groupings; Wagner, Newman, et al., 2003).

Without input from educators who are specifically trained to deliver CTE services, it is doubtful that a student's IEP team will have access to the information about CTE courses (e.g., instructional demands, methods of teaching, entry-level skills, grading options, testing options, instructional support practices, feasible modifications, safety issues) they need to ensure a comprehensive plan for obtaining the vocational skills needed to reach career goals.

Working together, teachers from CTE and special education can coordinate and collaborate in scheduling, instructional planning, support services provision, and student assessment. Course blueprints or other documents that outline the instructional objectives of a CTE course can be used to determine priority learning areas, design specialized teaching strategies, target needed support services, and design accountability methods. Because high-stakes testing has entered the CTE arena in many states, testing accommodations or alternate methods of determining achievement (e.g., portfolios) may need to be considered for some students.

Successful inclusion of students in employment preparation activities can be best attained if educators are adequately trained. But often this is not the case. Miller and colleagues (2000) reported that 79% of those involved in delivering employment preparation services received 5 hours or less of training related to inclusion of students with disabilities in school-to-work programs.

The goal of all collaborative planning should be for students to receive the maximum benefit of participating in a rigorous CTE program that ultimately leads to a career in their chosen pathway. For some students, planning will focus on ensuring that they have completed the appropriate combination of academic and CTE coursework to prepare them for postsecondary education and training. The commitment to coordinated planning that is vital to meeting student needs across the spectrum of interests and abilities must be clearly articulated by administrators, ingrained into the expectations for service delivery, reinforced through appropriate inservice training, and supported by organizational beliefs and strategies. Figure 7.3 lists some techniques that can be used by schools embracing a philosophy of collaborative service delivery.

Tech-Prep.   One program outlined in the Carl Perkins Act, tech-prep, is a cooperative secondary and postsecondary program that emphasizes continuity in learning and is designed for students who will participate in a curriculum charted to prepare them for a university, community college, technical school, or the high tech world of work. One aspect of tech-prep includes students taking college credit courses as part of their high school curriculum. The concurrent enrollment in high school and community college results in high school students' participation in college-level educational opportunities, increased equality of educational offerings, increased confidence levels, and enhanced motivation and achievement.

Tech-prep places a strong emphasis on contextual learning, applied academics, integration of vocational education and technology with academics, curriculum

- Ensure that CTE teachers and special educators have the opportunity for staff development aimed at increasing knowledge of each other's instructional areas and the laws directing these areas. Provide joint training opportunities that focus on the goals shared between the two disciplines and encourage the development of positive working relationships.
- Based on staff input, develop a system of formal communication to keep special education staff informed of student progress and provide CTE staff with consultative services for instructional issues and concerns.
- Transition staff and key CTE players (e.g., special populations coordinator, career development coordinator, career counselor) should meet to determine how job responsibilities relate to transition.
- Determine how CTE-initiated plans such as career development plans and career development plus plans can be interfaced with the transition component of the IEP.
- Allow students with moderate to severe cognitive disabilities to take the same CTE course more than one time and receive credit each time. This allows the students adequate time to cover the full range of skills taught in the course at a slower rate. The special education teacher and the CTE teacher should collaboratively identify which competencies will be worked on each year. These competencies should be clearly delineated so that coursework can be modified appropriately. Any end-of-course assessments for students who are taking the same course twice for credit can be designed individually to assess the competencies on which the students have focused.
- Arrange for students to complete CTE internships for credit. The internships should match the students' career pathways and postsecondary career goals. Internships are particularly beneficial for students who learn best through hands-on practice and who have difficulty in generalizing skills. The use of an internship might be a viable option for CTE credit if students are in need of additional hands-on employment preparation and/or the courses available on the school campus do not match the students' postschool outcome goals for employment.
- Special education staff should work closely with CTE staff to determine the types of accommodations students with disabilities will need to be successful in CTE courses.
- Review the school system's Carl Perkins plan to determine what strategies and programs are already in place for students within the special populations categories. Annual meetings should be conducted to discuss future options and develop a long-range plan for improving CTE services to students with disabilities.
- Ensure that CTE is represented on all special education committees and advisory councils (e.g., community-level transition teams, school-level transition teams, IEP teams) and that special education is represented on all CTE committees and advisory councils.
- Ensure that special education staff have access to transition assessment data to assist in registering and placing students with disabilities in appropriate CTE programs.

(continued)

Figure 7.3
Suggested Techniques for Collaborating with Career-Technical Education

---

♦ Ensure that methods are in place to determine whether the CTE services being provided to students with disabilities are consistent with IEPs, and meet with IEP teams if at any point modifications need to be made.

♦ Coordinate CTE recruitment activities (e.g., career day, job fairs) with special education representatives to ensure inclusion of students with disabilities.

♦ Coordinate enrollment of students with disabilities in CTE courses to ensure that all guidelines for class size are met. Coordination should involve special education, CTE, student data personnel, guidance counseling, and school administrators. The goal of the coordination should be to honor students' choices regarding their vocational interests while ensuring that CTE classes are not overloaded with students with special needs to the point that students cannot receive adequate services and job skill training. One of the best practices of exemplary programs is to limit the number of students with disabilities to five per general CTE class (Aspel, 1998).

Figure 7.3
Continued

choices, and preparation for a postsecondary career. These components make tech-prep a good choice for students who are interested in many of today's skilled jobs. The partnership between the school system and the community college system encouraged within tech-prep programs can assist students in making the adult service connections needed for transition from school to adult life (North Carolina Department of Public Instruction, n.d.).

Use On-Campus Training Opportunities

Certainly the chances that a student will achieve his or her postschool employment goals can be enhanced through the provision of an appropriate curriculum that includes the opportunity to enroll in CTE classes. But a student who receives only limited opportunities to apply the skills learned during class instruction may not have the ability to generalize employment preparation skills to actual work environments. It is beneficial to role-play customer service skills during classroom lessons but even better to practice those skills in a variety of situations with real customers.

A comprehensive program designed to prepare a student for employment is based on an appropriate curriculum reinforced with school-based training. Students who possess academic skills in reading, writing, and math as well as employability skills have higher competitive employment rates (Benz, Yovanoff, & Doren, 1997). As discussed earlier, it is a challenge to ensure the inclusion of both academic and vocational skills within a curriculum, but students with disabilities need balanced instruction if they are to avoid reaching graduation without the career awareness and fundamental employability skills needed to obtain and maintain their chosen occupation.

The school campus can provide an excellent environment for creating **on-campus jobs,** work situations similar to those the student will encounter during competitive employment. Of course, the application of classroom skills to simulated and real-life situations on the school campus should always be paired with community-based training. This is discussed further in Chapter 8.

The school environment provides a setting that is typically more tolerant of students who have not yet mastered certain work skills than community-based training sites are. Also, the school campus can provide learning situations in which a variety of variables can be controlled (e.g., level of supervision, pace of work, amount of interaction with others) and can be ideal for the first phase of employment preparation. However, each student's employment preparation needs are different, and transition staff must be flexible in designing individualized plans of training. A training program should never be delivered in a lock-step fashion with students moving through a set continuum of training options. Instead, each student should be evaluated to determine what training approach is most likely to lead to the accomplishment of his or her postschool employment goals.

School-Based Enterprises.   One effective method of simulating a real-life work environment on the school campus is the establishment of a **school-based enterprise (SBE).** An SBE is a work environment created to emulate real working conditions as closely as possible. School-based enterprises allow students to operate small businesses, perform work for area businesses, and/or complete tasks for volunteer organizations. Stern (1994) defined an SBE as "any school-sponsored activity that engages a group of students in producing goods or services for sale or to be used by people, other than the student involved" (p. 3).

An SBE incorporates career-awareness, career-exploration, and career-preparation concepts and provides multiple opportunities for activities associated with these stages of career education. Within the SBE an environment similar to that of an industrial or business setting is replicated, and in that environment students can learn and apply the work habits (e.g., attending regularly, being punctual, organizing work, storing supplies), work behaviors (e.g., staying on task, following directions, working on an assembly line, using tools safely), and social skills (e.g., using social amenities, engaging in social conversations, interacting with coworker) needed to function in a competitive employment setting. Although the ultimate goal is to practice the social and behavioral aspects of working, students may develop specific job-related skills (e.g., use of a copier, use of small hand tools) through the work performed in the SBE. While participating in an SBE, students will be exposed to a variety of job tasks associated with a number of occupational clusters that can assist them in career decision making. Within an SBE students are also typically involved in many of the procedures associated with operating a retail or service-oriented business such as projecting costs, ordering materials, maintaining equipment, marketing products and services, organizing tasks, and taking inventory.

Students can serve in a variety of roles within the SBE, giving them the opportunity to see first hand the value of integrating academic and work-related skills.

Participation in an SBE can also have a positive impact on academic performance, school attendance, and behavior (Tindall, Gugerty, Phelps, Weis, & Dhuey, 1996). It is clear that participation in a well-established SBE, can help students increase their level of self-determination through the choice making, decision making, and teamwork activities associated with its operation.

Space and Funding.   There are many logistical issues to consider when establishing an SBE. An SBE can be implemented in an extra classroom, a large open instructional area, or a mobile unit. The size of the SBE should be based on the number of students to be served and the variety and type of work experiences planned. For example, if projects for finishing and/or painting furniture are planned, a large, well-ventilated area will be needed. If jewelry-making projects are planned, then smaller individual workstations will be appropriate. If an SBE is going to be service oriented—such as a coffee and muffin shop—an area equipped with kitchen equipment will need to be secured. The amount of available space and furniture and equipment will play into the decision-making process regarding SBE work activities and/or services.

Establishing an SBE will require some initial start-up funds for furniture such as work bins, workstations, stools, file cabinets, and work desks as well as equipment and materials. Some supplies are considered basic supplies, while others need to be purchased based on the type of work activities to be conducted. Funding for an SBE can be obtained by using routine instructional supply and equipment funds, grant and foundation funds, donations from civic groups, PTA/PTO funds, contributions from local businesses, profits from work performed through business contracts (after students are paid based on Department of Labor regulations), and fundraising. Often, equipment such as hand tools, paper shredders, woodworking tools, sealers, kitchen appliances, and horticulture items can be obtained from or shared with the CTE department or donated by local businesses. Specific attention should be given to the types of equipment needed to ensure student safety, such as safety glasses, work gloves, and earplugs. If students are going to be involved in activities using materials that might spill or splatter, aprons or smocks should be purchased or made.

The policies guiding student pay need to be considered and appropriate funding sources targeted. As discussed later in this chapter, if students are performing work for area businesses, thereby benefiting the businesses, the Department of Labor guidelines mandate at least minimum wage payment unless a special certificate is obtained. In some cases, Vocational Rehabilitation (VR) work adjustment funds can be used to provide motivational stipends for students in the SBE who are VR clients. Other funds from the school system's special education program or the Workforce Investment Act (WIA) program may also be accessed to pay student wages for specific jobs in the SBE. State rules vary regarding funding sources, and teachers should contact their local adult service provider agency to learn more about options for student pay. Profits from an SBE venture can be used to provide student rewards and/or to maintain the operation of the SBE. It is important to involve the students in the decision-making process regarding how profits will be expended in order to increase their sense of ownership in the entrepreneurial process.

Organization.   An SBE should be organized to closely resemble a real work environment. If a teacher has limited experience with business and industrial settings, it is beneficial to observe various worksites to develop an understanding of issues such as traffic flow, material handling, assembly line set-up, tool usage, and organization of work areas. Local industries can be contacted to request the volunteer services of an industrial engineer who can assist in designing the SBE work areas to increase the authenticity of the work environment.

Consideration must be given to the set-up and arrangement of workstations or work areas. Work products and service delivery must be analyzed along with student abilities and needs to determine whether work should be performed in an assembly line fashion or in a start-to-finish manner. If possible, both options should be provided during training to increase the likelihood of skill generalization. Procedures should be established for general work rules, appropriate dress, breaks, clocking in and out, evaluations, dismissals, lay-offs, suspensions, and promotions. Using storage bins or individual lockers to store students' safety equipment can help them start work in an orderly fashion. The focus during transitional times (e.g., entering and leaving the work area, beginning and ending breaks) should be on reducing downtime. Students should clearly understand the process for clocking in, obtaining their work supplies, reporting to their workstations, and beginning their work assignments in a timely fashion since this is what will be expected in most work situations. Students must also be taught the steps involved in ending work, such as cleaning the work area, storing tools and work supplies, securing equipment, completing any necessary recordkeeping (e.g., production records), and clocking out.

There should be an orientation for all new students to inform them of the policies and procedures involved in participating in the SBE. Just as in a real work situation, students should be provided with written company policies and/or employee handbooks. Opportunities should be made available in the SBE not only to experience different types of work but also to hold various positions such as workstation supervisor, quality control supervisor, material handler, marketing director, inventory controller, accountant, and bookkeeper. Students should obtain these positions through an application and interview process. Promotions within the SBE can be used as a motivational tool for students as they gain more experience.

Ensuring Quality Within the SBE.   The more closely an SBE parallels a real work environment, the more likely it is that students will successfully transfer skills learned in the SBE to future community jobs. Therefore it is essential that priority be given to ensuring a high level of simulation accuracy. Keul (1991) developed criteria that each school-based work experience should meet prior to implementation to ensure realism and increase instructional effectiveness:

1. An accurate task analysis should be developed to fully detail the steps in producing each service or product produced by the SBE.

2. Based on the task analysis, accurate, easy measurements should be developed to measure both quality and speed (production standard) of each product or service.

3. The students should be able to do the vast amount of the tasks in the task analysis once instruction is implemented.

4. School resources and the number of available personnel should be sufficient to deliver a high-quality service and/or product.

5. Conditions closely resembling actual work demands (e.g., stamina, endurance, strength) should be simulated in the SBE.

SBE Work Projects.   In an SBE students receive training by performing work supplied from local businesses, providing a service, or manufacturing items for sale. Performing contract work for area businesses can provide students with the opportunity to improve their quality and quantity of work to accepted production standards and practice generic work behaviors and habits. Doing real work for area businesses has the advantage of allowing students to develop an understanding of business expectations regarding quality standards and timelines for work completion. However, for designing individualized training plans, these expectations result in less flexibility than manufacturing items for sale. In addition, when real work is performed for area businesses the students must be paid for all work completed. More information regarding paid work can be found the Department of Labor section in this chapter and in Chapter 8.

The production of items for sale or the provision of services can be structured to resemble the workings of a small business. This type of structure provides opportunities for the infusion of work-related academic skills based on student needs and the development of marketing skills. For example, students can be involved in choosing the products to manufacture or the service to provide by conducting a local market analysis and computing the costs of materials and equipment. Deciding which items to make or which service to provide can teach students about teamwork and consensus decision making.

Specific guidelines should be considered when determining what items will be manufactured or what services provided by the students in an SBE to keep the focus on the students' employment preparation while at the same time ensuring the smooth operation of the SBE. Students and staff should use the following guidelines when they are making decisions regarding products and services:

1. The service or product should be a relevant, marketable commodity in the community. Care should be taken to find out what the market prices are for services and products, what the quality and quantity demands are, and what consumers desire.

2. Production of the service or product should be feasible within the budgetary and time constraints of the SBE. Considerations include the school schedule,

staff supervision, cost benefits, storage, space, safety issues, and transportation of materials.

3. The service or product should be beneficial to students in both net profit (i.e., after expenses) and actual job skills gained from the experience. Some products may be too teacher directed. Considerations include training value and transference of skills to the community; that is, whether or not similar jobs are available in the community.

4. The service or product should be produced with minimal teacher intervention other than initial training and ongoing supervision.

5. The service or product should be valued and promote inclusion, not exclusion, of students with disabilities. Joint projects with school clubs should be considered.

6. The service or product should permit students to have more vocational choices in the future.

7. The manufacture of the product or the delivery of the service should provide an environment that allows students to practice the work habits and work behaviors associated with job success in competitive employment situations (Keul, 1991).

After the initial planning process is completed, students can learn about ordering materials, planning production, organizing assembly lines or work groups, advertising, handling money, calculating profits, and providing customer service. When the actual work begins, students can practice numerous work behaviors such as staying on task, following instructions, accepting feedback, self-evaluating their work, and assessing the quality and quantity of their work.

Students can also benefit from regularly scheduled performance evaluations. They should receive feedback on their performance in a manner similar to the procedures used in the local labor market. If necessary, performance evaluations can be used to initiate a student performance improvement plan, to suspend a student from a particular job, or even to fire a student if the circumstances warrant that level of intervention. The point is to help students understand the expectations they will face in the competitive world of work. The opportunities to receive initial employment preparation offered in an SBE are almost unlimited. Figure 7.4 provides some ideas for possible SBE projects.

Although SBEs can allow students to practice many skills relevant to future competitive settings, many of the uncontrollable variables related to a real job cannot be experienced through an SBE. Therefore, it is important that students have the opportunity to learn work skills in more realistic work situations. This can be accomplished through the use of on-campus jobs.

On-Campus Jobs. On-campus jobs are paid or nonpaid work experiences in which a student is placed, for a limited time, in a real job within the school under the supervision of a school employee. On-campus jobs introduce students to a work environment that requires many of the same skills and same demands that

Contracts with Local Businesses

♦ Preparing to-go condiment and silverware packages for restaurants
♦ Packaging pens and/or markers
♦ Folding linen napkins for airline first-class service
♦ Labeling test tubes with patient information stickers
♦ Labeling linen for hospitals and/or nursing homes
♦ Labeling file folders
♦ Alphabetizing and preparing invoices for mailing

Service Provision

♦ Laundry service
♦ Sewing and/or mending service
♦ Stripping and refinishing furniture
♦ Silk-screening and printing
♦ Polishing silverware
♦ Errand service
♦ Packaging and wrapping supplies for the Red Cross
♦ Collating and mailing
♦ Cleaning saddles
♦ Recycling
♦ Shredding

Manufacturing Products

♦ Logo/picture/insignia buttons
♦ Potpourri
♦ Gift baskets
♦ Herbs and/or plants
♦ Seasonal crafts
♦ Spirit bracelets
♦ Bead jewelry
♦ Woodcraft items
♦ Cookies in a jar
♦ Soup in a jar
♦ Cloth children's books
♦ Birdfeeders
♦ Flower arrangements
♦ Wreaths
♦ Candles
♦ Picture frames
♦ Keychains
♦ Stationary and cards

Figure 7.4
Examples of School-Based Enterprise Work

they will encounter in community work settings. In some school settings, on-campus jobs are part of a work-study program that may be accessed by both students with and those without disabilities. The NLTS2 found that 11% to 21% of students with disabilities are involved in on-campus work experience in a given school year, with the highest level of involvement occurring in the junior and senior years (Wagner, Newman, et al., 2003).

On-campus jobs allow students to explore their vocational interests and develop job skills. Just as SBEs do, on-campus jobs address the career awareness, career exploration, and career preparation stages of career education. For example, through on-campus jobs students can become aware of the different tasks involved in secretarial, media, custodial, landscaping, and maintenance occupations, and their personal interests and ability levels for these types of careers. Students get first-hand experience in completing job tasks in an acceptable manner, using specialized equipment, interacting with people in a work environment, and following directions—all skills that can be generalized to most jobs.

Potential on-campus job placements can be determined by using staff surveys to assess the school campus. Examples of on-campus jobs include cafeteria worker, office assistant, custodial assistant, teacher assistant, maintenance assistant, groundskeeping assistant, bus maintenance assistant, physical education assistant, biology lab assistant, and art assistant.

Identification, Scheduling, and Student Choice.   Individual student postschool employment goals, as well as individual interests, abilities, and needs should be reviewed to determine appropriate student placements for on-campus jobs. Student schedules and the availability of school personnel have to be considered in deciding when on-campus job placements will be offered. However on-campus job placements should never be based on teacher or administrative convenience. Offering students a variety of on-campus job placements provides ample opportunities for them to further explore and/or confirm their occupational interests. The larger the variety of on-campus jobs a school can offer, the wider the range of student interests that can be addressed. The transition planning process should be used to inform parents and students about the purpose and importance of on-campus job placements to reinforce their role in the decision-making process. Making decisions about on-campus job placements can provide an opportunity for students to practice self-advocacy skills, which they can apply later when seeking a real job or arranging job supports.

The types of job placements and their duration, along with training goals, should be included in the transition component of the IEP as part of the employment domain. It is a good idea to have parents sign a permission form for the student's participation in this component of the employment preparation program to ensure that everyone is fully informed regarding performance expectations, compensation, duration of the placement, and evaluation procedures.

On-Campus Job Placement.   Once on-campus job placements are identified, a job duties form indicating the main duties or tasks of each job should be prepared. When preparing a job duties form, it is best if the teacher can observe the job and interview an employee performing the job.

The job duties form can be used as a guide to assist the student and work supervisor in understanding performance expectations. Task analyses can be prepared for individual tasks listed on the job duties form if a student needs this level of instruction. In some cases, job task modifications or accommodations will need to be made for a student to participate in a particular on-campus job. For example, a student with limited language arts skills who is placed in a clerical assignment may need an alphabetizing guide to help with filing tasks. In a food service assignment, a student using a wheelchair may need to have access to a lower work area to package cookies and brownies for sale in the school cafeteria. Assistive technology (discussed in Chapter 8) should be used if necessary to ensure that students can access all types of work experiences.

All school staff supervising placements should be well informed of behavioral expectations, student evaluation procedures, student goals, methods of communication with special education staff, and methods of instruction related to the job duties. This can be accomplished through training sessions and individual conferences. Students will need an orientation session for each placement to review the job duties form and initiate a contract to document the student's agreement with the training placement, training goals, performance expectations, and rules governing behavior. Evaluation of student performance is an important component of the on-campus job training experience; the actual job supervisor should conduct it to mirror the real world of work. Instructional strategies can be adjusted based on the results of the evaluation, or, if necessary, interventions similar to those that would be found in a real job can be instituted (e.g., performance improvement plan, suspension, termination).

Job Clubs and Vocational Student Organizations. An avenue for school-based employment preparation that should not be overlooked, particularly due to its socialization benefits, is job clubs and vocational student organizations (VSOs). A job club can help students with disabilities develop job-seeking skills while it provides systematic peer support for obtaining and maintaining a job. A job club can be inclusive of students with and without disabilities. Although job clubs lack the national connection and occupational specificity associated with VSOs, they have greater flexibility in being designed to match the local labor market and student needs and interests.

Job clubs typically meet after school hours once a week. A group of students with the common goal of obtaining and maintaining competitive employment meet with a staff sponsor to focus on employment-related activities including the following:

- Using group dynamics to provide peer support for job searches.
- Sharing job leads.
- Developing job-related items such as résumés and references.
- Exploring the local job market.

◆ Visiting local industries and meeting with personnel directors.

◆ Developing job-seeking skills through role playing and peer critiques.

The facilitator of a job club provides instruction, leadership, and encouragement. Job clubs can be separate entities apart from the curriculum or they can be used as a method for reinforcing the skills being taught in career-related classes (Lindstrom, Benz, & Johnson, 1996). Vocational student organizations have similar goals, but they may focus more on assisting students in pursuing the postschool training and education needed for careers in special occupational areas. Examples of VSOs include Future Business Leaders of America, Future Farmers of America, Future Homemakers of America, Health Occupations Student Association, Technology Student Association, and Vocational Industrial Clubs of America.

Department of Labor Considerations.   When scheduling school-based employment preparation activities, care should be taken to ensure that Department of Labor (DOL) guidelines are followed regarding employment preparation for students with disabilities. The Fair Labor Standards Act (FLSA), which is administered by the DOL, outlines rules and regulations governing minimum wage payments, overtime, equal pay, and record-keeping requirements for payment of employees. School-operated employment preparation programs are not exempt from FLSA regulations, and they can be disciplined by DOL if labor regulations are ignored or violated. Abiding by the policies set forth in the FLSA ensures that program participants are treated in a fair and equitable manner. Additional information about DOL guidelines is presented in Chapter 8.

The DOL provides greater latitude in the standards set for employment preparation conducted on a school campus. Basically, the DOL will not enforce FLSA with respect to minimum wages if a student is enrolled in a school-based employment preparation program, as long as compliance with child labor provisions is ensured. However, school personnel must ensure that the purpose of the employment preparation is to benefit the student rather than to meet the school's labor needs. For example, if a student is placed as a cafeteria assistant, the placement should be because the student wants to learn food service and/or cashier skills, not because the cafeteria needs additional help. In general, on-campus training should be limited to one period per day.

Based on DOL policy, on-campus jobs can be viewed as nonpaid employment preparation experiences unless the school district is contracting with a for-profit business for the service area to which the student is assigned. For example, if the school system is contracting with an outside janitorial service to provide custodial services for the school and the school custodians are employees of the outside agency, then a student cannot participate in a custodial on-campus job unless he or she is compensated (Love, 1994). While it would be considered best practice for students to participate in paid, on-campus jobs, they do not have to be paid.

There are some exceptions to the DOL's more lenient policy regarding the application of the FLSA to school campus employment preparation programs. If a school is contracting with private businesses for students to perform work as part of the SBE, the students must be paid at least minimum wage unless the school has applied for and received a subminimum wage certificate from the DOL. Under no circumstances can students benefit private businesses by completing contract work in the SBE unless they are compensated for the work performed.

SUMMARY

A comprehensive employment preparation program provides students with both paid and nonpaid employment preparation experiences prior to graduation. Students should be given opportunities for choice in their training assignments. One variation for delivering on-campus job training is to arrange for a student to begin employment preparation in a training position at his or her home school. After the student has mastered the primary duties of the job, he or she can be reassigned to a similar job at another school in the district. At this point, the student moves from a nonpaid job to a paid work experience. Funding for student wages can come from special education funds, WIA programs, CTE monies, or school district payroll funds. The opportunity to earn wages motivates students to accomplish initial training goals, provides experience in receiving a paycheck and handling money, creates future references, and assists students in building a paid work history.

School-based employment preparation is only one aspect of an employment preparation program. Even the most comprehensive school-based program cannot simulate the real world of work, nor can it provide the generalization experiences students need to make successful transitions into paid competitive employment settings. In some cases, students can learn most effectively through a combination of classroom simulation and community-based instruction (Branham, Collins, Schuster, & Kleinert, 1999). Chapter 8 provides the information needed to establish off-campus employment preparation activities that can complement on-campus training, resulting in a multifaceted program.

The following case study focuses on the aspects of school-based employment preparation. The case study will be continued in Chapter 8.

CASE STUDY

DEBBIE

Debbie has been enrolled in a classroom for students with severe cognitive and physical disabilities since she was 5 years old. She will turn 19 in a few months and will exit the public schools near her 21st birthday with a certificate of graduation. Until about 2 years ago, Debbie missed approximately 30 to 40 days of school each year due to frequent illnesses and hospitalizations resulting from upper-respiratory infections caused by aspirating food. On several occasions the school district placed Debbie on homebound services because she was not medically stable enough to attend school. During these times Debbie struggled with depression. After she received a gastrostomy tube, Debbie's respiratory infections decreased dramatically. However, she continues to experience periods of time when her seizures are not completely controlled, although her seizures are fairly mild.

Debbie has spastic quadraplegic cerebral palsy and uses a motorized wheelchair. The wheelchair requires frequent repairs due to Debbie's tempter tantrums when she becomes frustrated. During the tantrums Debbie thrusts her body forward violently, resulting in damage to the chair's frame and its other special adaptations. A baclafon pump is being considered to decrease the problems associated with Debbie's severe spasticity.

Debbie resides with her grandmother, who is in her early 70s and has experienced some health problems. Debbie obtains services outside of school hours through a special Medicaid waiver program. After-school services are designed to assist Debbie's grandmother with her physical care and to provide Debbie with habilitative activities and additional physical and speech therapy.

Debbie has participated in on-campus employment preparation through the use of job boxes and two class-operated businesses. One of the class businesses involved using an Ellison machine to make and package letters, shapes, and numbers for teachers in the school. Debbie's role in this business was to operate the lever on the Ellison machine and deliver the completed packages of cutouts. In the other classroom business, a paper recycling business, Debbie learned how to operate a paper shredder using a jig, which assisted her in guiding the papers into the machine. For 2 hours each week for the last year, Debbie has performed an on-campus job in the school office. During this vocational experience Debbie shreds confidential papers, staples papers using an electric stapler, sharpens pencils using an electric pencil sharpener, and punches holes in papers using an electric hole-puncher.

Debbie's curriculum has always focused on functional skills supported by physical therapy, speech therapy, and occupational therapy. The priority has been the development of a communication system for Debbie that would be transferrable to a variety of community settings. Using Medicaid waiver funds, the school obtained a laptop computer and communication program with scanning software for Debbie. This device allowed her teachers to program vocabulary related to Debbie's school and community activities. Prior to this, Debbie had successfully used a variety of low-tech devices. The communication system is still functional, but at some point it may need to be updated.

During the on-campus employment preparation experiences, the laptop communication system helped Debbie request assistance and interact socially with coworkers and classmates using preprogrammed social greetings, phrases, and amenities. School staff were provided an orientation to assist them in understanding the importance of allowing Debbie the opportunity to communicate and interact with others using her communication system. Debbie is now 2 years from graduation, and the members of her IEP team feel strongly that she will need to participate in some community-based training experiences to assess her ability for future competitive employment.

STUDY GUIDE QUESTIONS

1. Differentiate between career education and career-technical education.
2. List the four stages of career education and give examples of activities at each stage.
3. How does the Carl Perkins Vocational and Applied Technology Act assist students in accessing CTE education?
4. Define the purpose of a school-based enterprise.
5. What types of work behaviors, work habits, and work skills can be taught through participation in an SBE?
6. List five potential on-campus jobs and the skills that could be learned through these training experiences.
7. What are some of the barriers to collaboration between special education and CTE education? What are some strategies for improving coordination and collaboration between these two areas?
8. How does the Fair Labor Standards Act relate to on-campus occupational training?
9. What types of issues would need to be addressed during joint planning between CTE and special education teachers to ensure access to CTE courses for Debbie? What are some specific strategies that could be used to ensure success for Debbie in CTE classes?
10. In the case study on Debbie, how were her school-based employment preparation activities in alignment with her interests, skills, and future career plans? Describe other school-based employment preparation activities that might have been appropriate for her.
11. What role did Debbie have in planning her school-based employment preparation? How could her role have been expanded?

REFERENCES

American Vocational Association. (1998). *The official guide to the Perkins Act of 1998: The authoritative guide to federal legislation for vocational-technical education.* Alexandria, VA: Author.

Aspel, N. (1998). *North Carolina transition manual.* Raleigh: North Carolina Department of Public Instruction.

Benz, M. R., Yovanoff, P., & Doren, B. (1997). School-to-work components that predict post-school success for students with and without disabilities. *Exceptional Children, 63,* 151–165.

Bottoms, G., Presson, A., & Johnson, M. (1992). *Making high schools work through integration of academic and vocational education.* Atlanta, GA: Southern Regional Educational Board.

Branham, R. S., Collins, B. C., Schuster, J. W., & Kleinert, H. (1999). Teaching community skills to students with moderate disabilities: Comparing combined techniques of classroom simulation, videotape modeling, and community-based instruction. *Education and Training in Mental Retardation and Developmental Disabilities, 34,* 170–181.

Brolin, D. (1995). *Career education: A functional life skills approach.* Upper Saddle River, NJ: Merrill/Prentice Hall.

Butterworth, J., & Gilmore, D. (2000 June/July). Are we there yet? Trends in employment opportunities and supports. *TASH Newsletter, 26,* 5–7.

Cameto, R., Levine, S., & Wagner M. (2004). *Transition planning for students with disabilities: A report from the National Longitudinal Transition Study-2 (NLTS2).* Menlo Park: CA: SRI International.

Carl D. Perkins Vocational and Technical Education Amendments of 1998. (October 31 1998). Title III, §3: Definitions (29).

Colley, D. A., & Jamison, D. (1998). Post school results for youth with disabilities: Key indicators and policy implications. *Career Development for Exceptional Individuals, 21,* 145–160.

Eisenmann, L. T. (2000). Characteristics and effects of integrated academic and occupational curricula for students with disabilities. *Career Development for Exceptional Individuals 23,* 105–119.

Fabian, E., Lent, R., & Willis, S. (1998). Predicting work transition outcomes for students with disabilities: Implications for counselors. *Journal of Counseling and Development, 76,* 311–316.

Farley, R. D., & Johnson, V. A. (1999). Enhancing the career exploration and job-seeking skills of secondary students with disabilities. *Career Development for Exceptional Individuals, 22,* 43–54.

Flexer, R., Simmons, T., Luft, P., & Baer, R. (2001). *Transition planning for secondary students with disabilities.* Upper Saddle River, NJ: Merrill/Prentice Hall.

Gajar, A., Goodman, L., & McAfee, J. (1993). *Secondary schools and beyond: Transition of individuals with mild disabilities.* Upper Saddle River, NJ: Merrill/Prentice Hall.

Garnett, K. (1984). Some of the problems children encounter in learning a school's hidden curriculum. *Journal of Reading, Writing and Learning Disabilities, 1,* 5–10.

Goldstein, D. E., Murray, C., & Edgar, E. (1998). Employment earnings and hours of school graduates with learning disabilities through the first decade after graduation. *Learning Disabilities Research and Practice, 13,* 53–64.

Grubb, W. N., Davis, G., Lum, J., Plihal, J., & Morgaine, C. (1991). *The cunning hand, the cultured mind: Models for integrating vocational and academic education.* Berkeley, CA: National Center for Research in Vocational Education.

Haring, K. A., Lovett, D. L., & Smith, D. D. (1990). A follow-up study of recent special education graduates of learning disabilities programs. *Journal of Learning Disabilities, 23,* 108–113.

Harvey, M. W. (2002). Comparison of post-secondary transitional outcomes between students with and without disabilities by secondary vocational participation: Findings from the National Longitudinal Transition Study. *Career Development for Exceptional Individuals, 25,* 99–122.

Keul, P. (1991) *Consultation to school-based enterprises in Shelby City Schools.* Charlotte, NC: Supported Employment Training.

Kohler, P. (1998). Implementing a transition perspective of education: A comprehensive approach to planning and delivering secondary education and transition services. In F. R. Rusch & J. G. Chadsey (Eds.), *Beyond high school: Transition from school to work* (pp. 159–205). Belmont, CA: Wadsworth.

Kohler, P., Field, S., Izzo, M., & Johnson, J. (1997). *Transition from school to life.* Arlington, VA: Council for Exceptional Children.

La Plante, M. P., Kennedy, J., Kaye, S. H., & Wenger, B. (1996) *Disability statistics abstract* (No. 11). Washington, DC: U.S. Department of Education, National Institute on Disability and Rehabilitation Research.

Levesque, K., Lauen, D., Teitelbaum, P., Alt, M., & Librera, S. (2000). *Vocational education in the United States: Toward the year 2000.* Washington,

DC: U.S. Department of Education, National Center for Education Statistics.

Lindstrom, L. E., Benz, M. R., & Johnson, M. O. (1996). Developing job clubs for students in transition. *Teaching Exceptional Children, 29*(2), 18–21.

Love, L. (1994). *Applying the FSLA when placing students into community-based vocational education.* Phoenix: Arizona Department of Education.

McCrea, L. D. (1991). A comparison between the perceptions of special educators and employers: What factors are critical to job success? *Career Development for Exceptional Individuals, 14*, 121–130.

Miller, R. J., Lombard, R. C., & Hazelkorn, M. N. (2000). Teacher attitudes and practices regarding the inclusion of students with disabilities in school-to-work and technical preparation programs: Strategies for inclusion and policy implications. In D. Johnson & E. Emanual (Eds.), *Issues influencing the future of transition programs and services in the United States* (pp. 127–136). Minneapolis: University of Minnesota, National Transition Network, Institute on Community Integration.

National Association of Vocational Education. (2004, June). *Earning, learning, and choice: Career and technical education works for students and employers.* Washington, DC: NAVE Independent Advisory Panel.

National Organization on Disability (NOD). (1998). *Harris survey on employment of people with disabilities.* New York: Author.

National Organization on Disability (NOD). (2004). *Louis Harris survey of Americans with disabilities.* Washington: DC: Author.

National Vocational Association. (1998). *The official guide to the Perkins Act of 1998: The authoritative guide to federal legislation for vocational-technical education.* Alexandria, VA: Author.

North Carolina Department of Public Instruction. (2002). *Special populations challenge handbook.* Raleigh: North Carolina Department of Public Instruction, Division of Career-Technical Education.

North Carolina Department of Public Instruction. (n.d.). *Tech-prep education.* Raleigh: North Carolina Department of Public Instruction, Division of Career-Technical Education.

Reid, M. E., & Tsurzuki, M. (1994). *National roster of local practices in the integration of vocational and academic education.* Berkeley, CA: National Center for Research in Vocational Education.

Rockwell, G., Weisenstein, G., & LaRoque, I. (1986). *Cooperative education: A transition option for high school youth with disabilities: A literature review and empirical study of cooperative education programs in Washington state.* Seattle: University of Washington.

Saunders, L., Stoney, S., & Weston, P. (1997). The impact of work-related curriculum on 14- to 16-year-olds. *Journal of Education and Work, 10*, 151–167.

Secretary's Commission on Achieving Necessary Skills. (1993). *Teaching the SCANS competencies.* Washington, DC: U.S. Department of Labor.

Silverberg, M, Warner, E., Goodwin, D, & Fong, M. (2002). *National assessment of vocational education: Interim report to Congress.* Washington, DC: U.S. Office of Education.

Snell, M., & Brown, F. (Eds.). (2000). *Instruction of students with severe disabilities* (5th ed.) New York: Merrill.

Stern, D. (1994). *School-based enterprise: Productive learning in American schools.* San Francisco: Jossey-Bass.

Stodden, R., Dowrick, P., Stodden, N., & Gilmore, S. (2001). *A review of secondary school factors influencing post-school outcomes for youth with disabilities.* Honolulu: University of Hawaii at Manoa, National Center for the Study of Postsecondary Education Supports.

Tindall, L. W., Gugerty, J. J., Phelps, B. R., Weis, C. L., & Dhuey, S. (1996). *Integrating vocational and academic education: A handbook featuring four demonstration sites including students from special populations.* Madison: University of Wisconsin, Center on Education and Work.

Wagner, M., Blackorby, J., Cameto, R., Hebbeler, K., & Newman, L. (1993). *The transition experiences of young people with disabilities: A summary of findings from the National Longitudinal Transition Study of Special Education Students.* Menlo Park: CA: SRI International.

Wagner, M., Cadwallader, T., Newman, L. Marder, C., Levine, P., Garza, N., et al. (2003). *Life outside the classroom for youth with disabilities. A report from the National Longitudinal Tran-*

sition Study-2 (NLTS2). Menlo Park, CA: SRI International.

Wagner, M., Newman, L., Cameto, R., Levine, P., & Marder, C. (2003). *Going to school: Instructional contexts, programs, and participation of secondary school students with disabilities. A report from the National Longitudinal Transition Study-2 (NLTS-2).* Menlo Park, CA: SRI International.

Van Beaver, S. M., Kohler, P. D., & Chadsey, J. G. (2000). Vocational education enrollment patterns of females with disabilities. *Career Development for Exceptional Individuals, 23,* 87–104.

Vocational Training News. (2004, August). *NAVE shows mixed results for vocational education.* Horsham, PA: LRP Publications.

Preparing Students for Employment
Community-Based Preparation

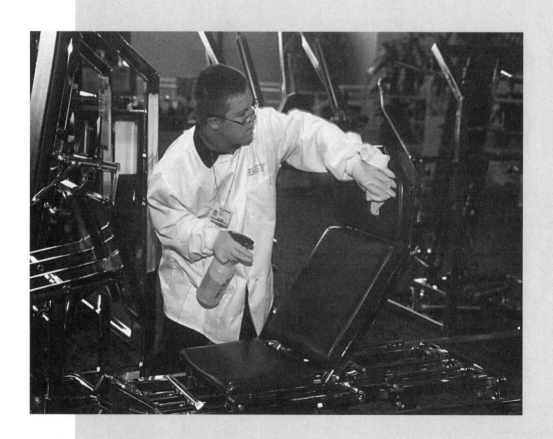

Chapter 8

Introduction

This chapter focuses on providing a variety of community-based instructional experiences to assist students with disabilities in attaining postschool employment goals. Community-based employment preparation opportunities are presented with specific how-to instructions for designing appropriate experiences that lead to competitive employment. The roles of school and business personnel are described as well as ideas for encouraging school–business partnerships. The chapter describes proven practices for addressing common barriers to employment preparation and employment for individuals with disabilities, including transportation, health and medical conditions, behavioral challenges, and lack of family support. A case study demonstrates the importance of community-based employment preparation to students' achievement of competitive employment that matches their interests and desires for postschool life.

Kohler's taxonomy for transition programming recognized the importance of teaching employment skills. As a subcategory of student development, employment skills encompass a wide range of school-based and work-based experiences. Teaching employment skills requires interagency collaboration, a vital component of transition programming. To obtain competitive employment placements for students with disabilities, there must be a cooperative effort between all key players both on the school campus and in the community (Kohler, 1998).

Comprehensive employment preparation while in high school and the development of a work history can enhance a student's ability to obtain competitive employment after graduation. However, to obtain and maintain employment that matches their interests and life-style preferences, young people with disabilities must also possess the self-determination skills needed to exercise power, control, and influence over their lives.

Developing self-determination skills is vital to postschool success, and community-based employment preparation provides realistic environments and situations in which these skills can be applied and practiced.

Key Terms

community-based training
job shadowing
internships
volunteerism
job task analysis
self-instruction
Fair Labor Standards Act (FLSA)
self-employment
job market screening
natural supports
Impairment-related work expenses (IRWE)
job carving
Plan for Achieving Self-Support (PASS)

A Personal Perspective on Preparing Students for Employment

Dale McKillop

Plant Manager, Mayflower Vehicle Systems

I am the plant manager of Mayflower Vehicle Systems in Kings Mountain, North Carolina. Mayflower is a company that assembles heavy-duty truck cabs using spot welds controlled by robotics and manpower. We employ approximately 200 people from a 30-mile radius. All perspective employees must be high school graduates and pass an entry-level test on general manufacturing skills. We believe that education is fundamental and encourage our employees to further their education by providing tuition reimbursement at the community college and university levels.

Mayflower has been fortunate in having a wonderful working relationship with our local school system. I have worked with a transition coordinator from one of the local high schools in securing employment for several students. I am especially proud to tell you about Robert, who has been employed with Mayflower for nearly 1 year. From the beginning I knew that we had discovered a hard-working individual.

Robert works 5 hours a day as a custodial assistant. Using a forklift, he removes all excess cardboard from the manufacturing area—approximately 180,000 square feet. After removing the cardboard, he disposes of it in a large trash compactor. His job may not sound very important; at best, it may sound repetitive. Robert, however, provides a valuable service to the individual work cells in the manufacturing area. Each work cell can now run more efficiently without having to stop the production line to dispose of the accumulated cardboard. Because of Robert, the work areas are free of materials that can be a safety and fire hazard. Robert does his job with a smile, an eagerness to please, and a true dedication to the work ethic that is disappearing in many workplaces.

I believe Robert would not be such an exceptional employee were it not for the preparation he received in career education at his high school. He conducted himself well during all phases of the application and interview processes. He strives to make every effort to complete his job tasks in a timely manner. When his job performance elicits some minor criticism, he listens intently and asks appropriate questions to correct his mistakes. He is always on time, treats others courteously, and is proud of the work he accomplishes. We are proud to call him an employee of Mayflower Vehicle Systems and hope he remains with us for many years.

Relying solely on school-based employment preparation denies students the opportunity to generalize skills to future work sites and limits their opportunity to interact with the variety of coworkers usually present at a real job site. Although school-based training can lay a sound foundation for more job-specific training, even under the best circumstances it is impossible for a school environment to simulate real-world expectations and job tasks. What a teacher expects of a student in the area of job performance may greatly differ from the expectations that will exist in a real job. Educators who have worked with students with disabilities recognize that to adequately prepare a student for a career after graduation, they must provide community employment preparation (Agran, Snow, & Swaner, 1999). When students expand their employment preparation activities into the community, the process must be infused with a high level of student involvement and choice to ensure good matches between student interests and training experiences and, ultimately, competitive job placements.

COMMUNITY-BASED TRAINING

Community-based training is instruction conducted in the community with the ultimate goal of securing competitive employment, independent living, and community adjustment. Community-based training can have a positive impact on

DID YOU KNOW?

Research has shown that students who participate in community-based instruction receive higher wages and achieve better community integration outcomes (Helms, Moore, & McSweyn, 1991).

students' achievement of skills in a variety of life domains; the amount of community-based instruction to which a student is exposed to can be a more powerful predictor of skill achievement than I.Q, presence of challenging behaviors, or mobility skills (McDonnell, Hardman, Hightower, Keifer-O'Donnell, & Drew, 1993). When work experience corresponds with emerging career interests, students demonstrate improved postschool outcomes (Benz, Lindstrom, & Yovanoff, 2000).

Community-based training promotes skill generalization and allows students to practice skills in the appropriate contextual setting. When students are given the opportunity to apply skills to real-life situations, there is a higher likelihood that they will understand the purpose and proper use of the skills learned in a classroom setting. In fact, in some cases, the impact of community-based employment preparation can be powerful enough to eliminate the need for prior instruction in simulated settings (Bates, Cuvo, Miner, & Korabek, 2001).

Community-based training sites that are successful in preparing students for future employment offer a high level of interaction with individuals without disabilities. A high level of integration provides students with the opportunity to practice the social skills needed to interact with coworkers. Successful sites are supported by employers who understand the purpose of the community-based training program and realize that student participation is based on the training needs of the student, not the needs of the business. This understanding assists in creating an environment that is conducive to student learning. Community-based training should result in students' having multiple opportunities to perform a variety of tasks (Beakley, Yoder, & West, 2003).

Offering students a wide range of occupational areas within a community-based training program can increase their chances of being exposed to a wide range of job tasks. This can result in their attainment of job-specific skills and assist them in making future career choices based on experience. The types of community-based training sites offered vary from community to community. The employment preparation sites should reflect local labor market needs to increase students' potential for employment. This community-referenced approach to designing employment training options increases the likelihood that graduates will develop job skills that are economically viable (McDonnell, Wilcox, & Hardman, 1991).

Types of Community-Based Training

Community-based training can consist of paid and nonpaid experiences ranging from short-term job shadowing or job sampling assignments to long-term internships. The goal is to design a training program consisting of multiple options that will meet the needs of all students. As students move closer to graduation, training needs change from exploring careers to developing actual career-related skills.

The menu of community-based training options should provide for a variety of supervision levels and instructional intensity. Employees of the business, school personnel, or adult service provider staff may supervise at community-based training sites. Specially trained teacher assistants (who may be called job coaches) or job coaches funded through vocational rehabilitation (VR) or outside funding sources often oversee community-based training sites. Job coaches assist with job development, orientation to training sites, skill training, supervision, and performance evaluation. Some of the more common types of community-based training include job shadowing, internships, apprenticeships, volunteerism, work crews, and competitive employment.

Job shadowing.   **Job shadowing,** sometimes called *job sampling,* provides opportunities for students to try out a job by working alongside employees of area businesses and agencies. This allows students to develop a comprehensive understanding of the job duties associated with a particular position. Usually a student spends a few hours at a single work site before being moved to another business or agency. Through job shadowing, students can develop a better understanding of their personal interests and capabilities.

Internships.   **Internships** allow students to spend an extended amount of time on a single job site to develop specific skills and knowledge needed for that occupational area. Internships typically last for several weeks or months. Internships may be paid or nonpaid, and they may or may not be attached to earning high school credits.

Apprenticeships.   Apprenticeships offer the opportunity to learn an occupation while under the supervision of an experienced worker. Usually an apprenticeship lasts 3 to 4 years, allowing the student to work part time while in high school. Over time, the student assumes increasing amounts of responsibility on the job as he or she learns more advanced skills. Apprenticeships are paid work experiences, and students often earn high school credits for participation in the program. After graduation, the student continues to work with the company and pursues additional postsecondary education or training related to the occupation. Apprenticeships can be sponsored by unions, public agencies, or businesses. Examples of apprenticeships include furniture craftsman, loom builders, and other highly skilled professions that require on-the-job training and experience.

Volunteerism or Community Service Projects.   Individual or group volunteer projects can provide students with the opportunity to practice employability skills. All volunteer work should be recognized as legitimate **volunteerism** and should meet Department of Labor guidelines for students with disabilities placed in volunteer settings. Students may never volunteer at a for-profit business (Love, 1994).

Mobile Work Crews or Enclaves.   Mobile work crews or enclaves offer a format for providing community-based employment preparation to students who require more intensive supervision. Enclaves and mobile work crews involve a group of students who train for or perform work for area businesses or agencies while under continuous supervision. A mobile work crew moves from site to site performing similar job tasks (e.g., landscaping, custodial) at each location. An enclave is stationed at one location with students working cooperatively to perform a set of job tasks. These employment preparation experiences may be paid or nonpaid, but if a student performs real work for a business, then he or she must be paid.

Competitive Employment.   The opportunity to participate in paid employment experiences prior to graduation is a good predictor of a student's future success in the real world of work. For example, Colley and Jamison (1998) found that 52% of former special education graduates who had paid work experience while in high school obtained full-time employment, compared to a rate of only 30% for those who graduated without a paid work history. The positive impact of working for pay while in high school has been shown to hold true for a variety of disability groups, including those with learning disabilities (Sitlington, Frank, & Carson, 1992), mental retardation (Hasazi, Gordon, Roe, Hull, et al., 1985), and behavioral and/or emotional disabilities (Sample, 1998). Therefore, including paid work experience as part of an employment preparation program is considered to be best practice (Kohler, 1993).

As discussed in Chapters 3, 4, and 5, the type of community-based training experience that best matches a student's training needs can be determined through transition assessment and student interviews. Decisions regarding community-based training should be part of the transition planning process involving the student, the student's family, and adult service providers.

Factors in Successful Community-Based Employment Preparation

Delivering comprehensive and meaningful community-based employment preparation requires a programmatic framework, student buy-in, family support, and interagency collaboration. The value of community-based employment preparation also depends on the quality of the instruction a student receives at a job site. Many of the same instructional strategies used on campus, such as verbal instructions, gestures, physical assists, modeling, time delay, response cues, and various reinforcement procedures, are appropriate when delivering off-campus training (Moon, Inge, Wehman, Brooke, & Barcus, 1990). However, unlike a school-based site, where opportunities for generalization must be planned and simulated materials and situations provided, instructors at community-based training sites have immediate access to real-world materials and equipment with built-in opportunities for generalization.

However, there are occasions when specific employment or employment-related skills need to be taught prior to community placement to maintain the student's dignity, to ensure safety, or to increase the likelihood of a successful placement. When a student lacks a skill needed for success in a community-based site, on-campus training can be designed to program for generalization. To accomplish this, teachers train across stimuli (e.g., different cues, materials, trainers, environments), across responses (e.g., adding additional behaviors similar to the one initially taught, such as learning to use a drink machine and also applying this skill to using a candy vending machine), and across time (e.g., continuing to practice the skill after it has been learned; Test & Spooner, 1996). The ultimate usefulness of the skill should always be a priority with successful generalization of the skill being the ultimate indication of skill attainment.

ESTABLISHING COMMUNITY-BASED TRAINING SITES

When establishing and implementing community-based training, it is helpful to have a sound philosophical understanding of the need for this component to be included as an employment preparation activity. Educators and administrators should view community-based training as a credible option for delivering career awareness, exploration, and training. Implementation strategies should be designed to ensure that all students with disabilities, regardless of their educational placement (e.g., general education, self-contained), have access to community-based training if their transition planning process indicates a need.

Logistically, many things must be considered when planning community-based training, including training site location(s), funding, staffing, transportation, liability, safety, insurance, Fair Labor Standards Act regulations, and accommodating students in inclusive educational placements. A successful community-based training program has in place approved policies that ensure the ongoing, safe, affordable, and effective delivery of off-campus instruction for all students.

Locating Training Sites

Winning the cooperation of area businesses and developing business partnerships requires initiating contacts with local employers and conducting ongoing public relations activities. But before talking with representatives from local businesses and industry, school staff must do some preliminary research to learn about the local business community and identify potential job sites. Conducting a **job market screening** by analyzing the local job market to identify available jobs and possible job leads through a variety of sources (e.g., Chamber of Commerce, classified ads, civic groups) can be a first step toward locating training sites. Figure 8.1 lists some strategies for locating possible community-based vocational training opportunities and/or job placements for students.

It is necessary to contact employers individually to negotiate the type of partnership that is desired. Whether program personnel are approaching an employer regarding obtaining a community-based training opportunity (e.g., job shadowing, internship) or seeking an individual paid position for a student, some basic guidelines should be followed. These guidelines are summarized in Figure 8.2.

♦ Conduct a **job market screening** to identify the types of occupations available, location of jobs, and disability-friendly businesses by contacting the Chamber of Commerce, meeting with Employment Security Commission representatives, monitoring local want ads, checking job listing information boards, looking for help-wanted signs, reviewing the Yellow Pages, performing Internet searches, and simply knocking on doors (Ludlow, Turnbull, & Luckasson, 1988).

♦ Obtain information about available jobs from the school vocational rehabilitation counselor and ensure that the counselor is involved in all aspects of job development and placement.

♦ Make a list of businesses that have problems that could possibly be solved through paid community-based training contracts or by individual employment of persons with disabilities. Such problems include
  ♦ Underutilization of workers on routine tasks.
  ♦ High turnover or absenteeism.
  ♦ Low productivity due to boredom.
  ♦ Setting work aside that is not cost effective or would be too labor intensive.
  ♦ Routine overtime pay.
  ♦ Employees taking work home.
  ♦ Use of expensive manpower service contracts.
  ♦ Lack of compliance (or wishing to show good intent) with affirmative action programs or the Americans with Disabilities Act.
  ♦ Expanding or opening a new facility (Pane, 1992).

♦ When establishing vocational training sites and seeking individual jobs, make every attempt to obtain placements in occupations that pay good wages and provide benefits.

♦ Meet with others who are approaching businesses for potential placements to coordinate business contacts. Local employers will quickly become frustrated if too many people are knocking on the door.

♦ Conduct natural supports surveys or interviews with students to determine potential job leads that may already be available to them.

♦ Get involved in activities that allow networking with local employers. Offer to host a Chamber of Commerce gathering, join business-related groups, and do presentations for business-related organizations (e.g., Rotary, Kiwanis, Jaycees, Business Leader clubs).

♦ Have each student register with the local Employment Security Commission through the One-Stop Career Center.

Figure 8.1
Strategies for Locating Community-Based Vocational Training Sites and/or Individual Competitive Employment Placements

Funding Community-Based Training

Ongoing adequate financial support is vital to the success of a community-based employment preparation program. The costs of implementing community-based training may differ from those encountered in on-campus training or school-based enterprises, but they are not necessarily greater. In fact, considering that

---

- ◆ Prepare an attractive brochure and/or information package about the school's employment preparation program that describes the opportunities for hiring and training young people with disabilities. Include pictures of students working and recommendations from satisfied business partners.
- ◆ Make appointments to visit the employer at a convenient time (Moon et al., 1990). Initial appointments should not last more than 10 to 15 minutes.
- ◆ Approach employers in a friendly, positive manner. Show an interest in helping the employer as well as meeting the needs of the students.
- ◆ Try to talk to the person in the business who has the authority to approve a school–business partnership or at least has the clout needed to convince the boss. In larger companies this may be the human resources manager, but in smaller companies you may need to talk directly with the owner.
- ◆ Dress professionally and handle the contact with the employer as if it were a job interview.
- ◆ Use terms that the employer can understand. Refrain from special education jargon (Moon et. al., 1990).
- ◆ When meeting with a business representative, be prepared to explain the role of school personnel and the role of the business in participating in various types of vocational training.

Figure 8.2
Guidelines for Approaching Employers

community-based training does not require setting up an artificial environment (e.g., school-based enterprise) and that equipment and materials needed for instruction are readily available, community-based training may be less costly. However, if enclaves or mobile work crews are being used to deliver community-based training, there are often costs associated with purchasing equipment and materials needed to perform work assignments (e.g., landscaping or custodial equipment and supplies).

The best method for funding community-based training is to assess the total instructional program and reprioritize the use of basic instructional supplies money to match the focus on community-based training. This will make it clear that materials needed for traditional classroom instruction (e.g., textbooks) can be replaced with real-life materials. Many of these real-life materials can be obtained at no cost (e.g., applications, employee handbooks, newspapers). If additional funds are needed after redirecting money for instructional supplies, school staff can investigate funding sources such as grants, donations, foundation awards, and fundraising projects. Business partnerships are an excellent source of donations, particularly for materials, supplies, and equipment.

Staffing Considerations

Community-based employment preparation requires schools to rethink traditional methods of assigning staff and designing student schedules. School personnel must be available to provide instruction and supervise student performance during community-based training activities. The level and intensity of supervision required is based on the type of training model being used and the needs of the students. For example, during job shadowing or job sampling, actual employees at each business site can be used to train and supervise students since this type of employment preparation is typically used with students who have at least a minimum level of independence. Also, job shadowing sites are usually established for individual students rather than groups of students, although multiple training options might be provided within a single location, in which case a school supervisor might be needed. For mobile work crews and enclaves, school staff are needed continuously to provide focused training and ongoing supervision.

Several resources can be tapped to ensure adequate staffing patterns for community-based training. Various configurations of school personnel can be explored, including team teaching, using teacher assistants as job coaches, and integrating therapeutic support personnel into the program (Baumgart & VanWalleghem, 1986). Team teaching allows greater flexibility in scheduling classroom instruction and community-based training by ensuring coverage in both areas by licensed staff. When paraprofessionals (e.g., teacher assistants) are trained in safety issues, instructional strategies, transportation guidelines, and business relationships, they can assume a greater level of responsibility in the community.

Therapeutic support staff in physical therapy, speech therapy, and occupational therapy can provide valuable hands-on therapy in the environments in which the students will ultimately need these skills. Providing therapeutic support at a training site will result not only in additional staff for community-based training but also in increased skill generalization. In some cases it is absolutely necessary to practice communication skills or mobility skills in real-life situations since the school environment does not emulate the conditions found in the community (Baumgart, Johnson, & Helmstetter, 1990). For example, if a student is receiving mobility training or is learning to use a communication system, where better to learn and practice these skills than in the work settings in which the student will ultimately be expected to perform?

Initial implementation of a community-based training program may require reassigning responsibilities, rewriting job descriptions, adjusting performance expectations, and changing roles. If all staff can learn to view the community as an extension of the classroom and recognize the benefits of community-based training, the changes in their roles and job expectations will be accepted more easily.

It may also be necessary to look outside of the school for additional staff resources. When given proper orientation and training, volunteers (e.g., work buddies), college interns, and parents can assist with community-based training. Also, if adequate staffing is a concern, the manner in which students are grouped and scheduled for community-based training can be adjusted to allow for greater flexibility. Using a single site for multiple skill training, along with assistance from business employees, can reduce the number of school staff needed. For example, a large retail store can provide training sites for customer service, food service, stocking, clerical work, plant or animal care, and custodial work all in one location. In this type of setting a number of students can be assigned throughout the business with designated employee supervisors. A single school staff person can then "float" at the site, supervising and instructing as needed. Hospitals, nursing centers, day care centers, malls, and manufacturing plants are also good settings for multiple training options. Heterogeneous grouping can also be used to reduce the number of staff members needed by allowing cooperative learning and peer tutoring opportunities between students of varying abilities as well as with students without disabilities (Baumgart & VanWalleghem, 1986).

Transportation Considerations

Without reliable and easily accessible transportation, a community-based training program will come to a standstill, both literally and figuratively. Therefore, educators must consider the type of transportation that will be used, when transportation can be accessed, and the funding sources available to cover transportation costs. Transportation for community-based training requires additional funds, but the actual cost will vary based on the geographical characteristics of the school system and the type of transportation chosen. Transition staff should work closely with the school system's director of transportation to ensure that staff are licensed to operate school-owned vehicles and that vehicles are readily accessible when needed.

Prior to establishing community-based training sites, school personnel must know when and what form of transportation will be available to students so that they can develop job sites and schedule training times. The most logical mode of transportation is school buses and activity buses, which usually are available on a school campus. Other types of school-owned vehicles such as cars or vans might be appropriate depending on state and local guidelines for transporting students during school hours. In a more urban school system, public transportation can be used or students might even be able to walk to job sites. Some students may be able to drive themselves to job sites if they have a personal vehicle. Parents can even be solicited to provide transportation, particularly if the student is involved in competitive employment, which ends after school hours. Transition staff should inform parents of the manner in which their young person will be transported to community-based training sites, and the parents should sign appropriate permissions. As with all phases of a student's education, parental involvement in employment preparation can have a significant impact on the success of a training program.

Liability Considerations

Educators and parents alike are concerned about student safety. While classrooms located in a school building are perceived as safe environments, they are not the most effective environment for delivering employment preparation to students with disabilities. If students are expected to live, learn, work, and play in their community after graduation, then training in community settings must be provided prior to graduation. The community must be viewed as an extension of the classroom for students with disabilities.

If community-based training is viewed as a legitimate and necessary teaching environment, then establishing procedures to ensure student safety and provide liability protection for educators should be a priority. Having reasonable policies and procedures in place that have been approved by the school board (Falvey, 1989), along with providing adequate supervision at training sites, can eliminate many potential negligence issues. The ultimate goal is to prevent physical injury to students while ensuring that they are not exposed to any situation that would be detrimental or cause harm. All involved staff should take care to ensure that a student's specific disability does not pose an increased chance of injury at a specific job or training site. If good matches are made between training sites and student interests and needs, this should not be a concern. However, businesses are liable for all injuries that occur to anyone on their property, and therefore businesses that host community-based sites will be held responsible for making their work sites safe for use by employees, customers, and student trainees (Wehman, Wood, Everson, Goodwyn, & Conley, 1988).

Safety Considerations

There are many methods for ensuring student safety and simultaneously protecting school staff from liability issues. It should be standard operating procedure to fully inform all parents and students regarding the various training components of a program, types of community-based settings offered, and expectations for behavior during the training experiences. This can be accomplished during transition planning meetings when the training goals and objectives are established for the individualized education program (IEP). It is imperative that each student's IEP reflect the need for participation in various community-based training options by stating exactly what the student is to learn and where this learning will occur. Parents should sign written permission forms for all community-based training activities. A sample parent permission form is shown in Figure 8.3. Even if the student is 18 years old or older, it is still a good idea to involve the parents in decisions surrounding community-based training. Parents should also be asked to provide medical information (e.g., medical conditions, allergies, medications, special care considerations, primary physician, health insurance) for their son or daughter and sign permission to obtain medical care if needed in an emergency. These forms, along with basic contact information for each student, should be readily available to all community-based training staff. Students should be required to sign contracts indicating their understanding and willingness to abide by all behavioral and safety expectations related to the training experience.

Transition staff should provide adequate work safety training to students prior to their participation in community-based training sites. Martella and Marchand-Martella (1995) stated that work safety skills in certain occupations must be a top priority for training. It cannot be assumed that students will know how to perform skills needed to ensure their safety on a job site, and training in

Dear Parent,

Your child will have the unique opportunity to participate in the community-based training through the Transition Program at _____ High School, in order to prepare for employment after graduation. This training program should not be considered a "job." This is not employment. In order for your child to participate in the program, we must have your permission and agreement to certain conditions. Please complete this form and return it to the school immediately so that your child can begin his or her vocational training. Attached is a description of the vocational training arrangements that have been made for your child. You may detach this sheet and retain it for your information.

I give permission for my child to participate in the community-based training program.

_____ Yes _____ No

In case of an emergency, I give permission for employees of the community-based training site or school personnel to obtain medical care for my child.
_____ Yes _____ No

I understand that my child must have school insurance before participating in the community-based training program. _____ Yes _____ No

Attached is a school insurance form. If you have problems affording the cost of school insurance, please contact your child's teacher and a payment plan will be worked out for you.

I understand that my child's performance in the community-based training program will count as part of his or her grade. _____ Yes _____ No

I understand that my child **will not** be entitled to a job at the community-based training site at the conclusion of the training period. _____ Yes _____ No

I understand that my child **will not** be entitled to wages or workers' compensation benefits during the vocational training period. _____ Yes _____ No

I give permission for my child to be transported to community-based training sites by school personnel. _____ Yes _____ No

Student Name _____   Teacher _____

Parent Signature _____   Date _____

Figure 8.3
Sample Parent Permission Form for Community-Based Training
Note. Reprinted with permission from Cleveland County Schools (2000).

work-related safety skills should be included in the employment preparation curriculum (Pelland & Falvey, 1986). Work safety training should include identifying
unsafe work conditions, practicing safe work behaviors, and responding appropriately to an accident. Since students with disabilities may have medical conditions
(e.g., seizures), sensory deficits, or motor impairments that can increase the likelihood of an accident, it is imperative that work safety instruction be considered a
survival skill for employment. Although businesses are responsible for ensuring
safe work environments, school personnel are also responsible for adequately
training students in safety awareness skills. Otherwise, in the event of a work site
accident, liability issues might arise (Agran, Swaner, & Snow, 1998).

Staff Safety Training Considerations.   Community-based training staff must be
trained in appropriate instructional strategies, student evaluation, behavioral interventions, work site safety evaluation, first aid, safety rules, safety equipment,
CPR and first aid, and child labor regulations. First aid kits should be available
on all vehicles used for transporting students to community-based training sites,
and the location of first aid equipment at training sites should be determined in
advance (Hamre-Nietupski, Dander, Houselog, & Anderson, 1988). Another
proactive measure involves notifying local emergency medical personnel that
students with disabilities will be training in the community so that these professionals will be prepared in case of an emergency (Falvey, 1989). A crisis plan
should be in place for handling any medical emergency that might occur. All staff
with community-based training responsibilities should be well versed in following the crisis plan. It is a good idea to conduct practice emergency drills several
times a year to keep staff and students up to date on emergency procedures.

Evaluating Training Sites for Safety.   Prior to placing students in community-
based training sites, staff should evaluate each site for safety to ensure that placing students there will not violate child labor laws. (Child labor laws are
discussed in more detail later in this chapter.) Preplacement safety assessments
of training sites will assist in preparing comprehensive safety awareness training
for students.

If a site requires the use of machinery, the staff can develop a safety skill checklist and students can be required to pass a test prior to operating the machinery.
Staff should consult with employees at the business sites to obtain training materials used with employees and use these same materials with students. Best practice would allow students to participate in the safety training alongside actual
employees of the business.

Insurance Coverage

Another factor that must be considered when planning a community-based training program is insurance coverage. Students should have some type of medical
insurance coverage in case of an accident at the community-based training site.
Some students may have Medicaid and others may have private health coverage.
One option is to have students covered through the school system's student

insurance policy, which is usually available for a small annual fee. This ensures that students who are not covered by insurance will have at least a minimum policy in place while students covered by private insurance will have additional coverage in the case of deductibles and copayments.

Liability insurance should also be provided for staff. The school system liability policy should be amended to provide coverage for employees who are conducting community-based training activities as part of a student's educational program. Liability coverage should also be pursued for local businesses that sponsor training sites. In some cases, this type of insurance may already be in place for work-based training programs operated by the career-technical education department (e.g., cooperative education, apprenticeships) and can be extended for use by the special education program. Being able to offer liability insurance for businesses may assist in encouraging larger businesses and industries to host a training site.

Fair Labor Standards Act Considerations

As mentioned earlier, staff must adhere to child labor laws when delivering community-based instruction. Child labor laws fall under the **Fair Labor Standards Act (FLSA),** which governs several factors related to vocational training and competitive employment. Staff responsible for arranging and coordinating community-based training at local businesses and organizations should be well versed in the federal regulations governing the establishment of an employment relationship to prevent violations that could result in serious financial repercussions for the school system and its business partners. It is important to ensure that students are participating in training that clearly is for their benefit and that matches their postschool goals. In any case in which a student is benefiting a company or an employer–employee relationship is established, the student must be compensated for his or her work.

In a memorandum of understanding (also referred to as the "Dear Colleague" letter) issued jointly by the U.S. Department of Labor (DOL) and the U.S. Department of Education (DOE) in 1992, guidelines were set forth for providing community-based training for students with disabilities. Figure 8.4 summarizes the DOL/DOE memorandum of understanding.

These guidelines were designed to guarantee that school systems implementing training programs specifically aimed at student instruction are in compliance with federal guidelines in employment-related areas covered by the FLSA. The FLSA is administered and enforced by the Wage-Hour Division of the Department of Labor and establishes minimum wage, overtime pay, equal pay, employment-related recordkeeping requirements, and child labor regulations.

If *all* of the trainee criteria stated in the DOL/DOE memorandum of understanding are met for every student at every community-based vocational training site, the school system should meet the requirements set forth in FLSA. School staff must be very careful to ensure that students' needs are met first (over the needs of the business), with the employer deriving no advantage, and that

- Participants will be youths with physical and/or mental disabilities for whom competitive employment at or above minimum wage is not immediately obtainable and who, because of their disability, will need intensive ongoing support to perform in a work setting.
- Participation will be for vocational exploration, assessment, or training in a community-based placement work site under the general supervision of public school personnel.
- Community-based placements will be clearly defined components of individualized education programs (IEPs) developed and designed for the benefit of each student. A statement of needed transition services established for the exploration, assessment, training, or cooperative vocational education components will be included in the student's IEP.
- Information contained in a student's IEP will not have to be made available; however, documentation as to the student's enrollment in the community-based placement program will be made available to the Departments of Labor and Education if requested. The student and the parent or guardian of each student must be fully informed of the IEP and the community-based placement component and have indicated voluntary participation with the understanding that participation in such components does not entitle the student participant to wages.
- The activities of the students at the community-based placement site do not result in an immediate advantage to the business. The Department of Labor will look at several factors:
  - There has been no displacement of employees, vacant positions have not been filled, employees have not been relieved of assigned duties, and the students are not performing services that, although not ordinarily performed by employees, clearly are of benefit to the business.
  - The students are under continued and direct supervision either by representatives of the school or by employees of the business.
  - Such placements are made according to the requirements of the students' IEPs and not to meet the labor needs of the business.
  - The periods of time spent by the students at any one site or in any clearly distinguishable job classification are specifically limited by their IEPs.
- While the existence of an employment relationship will not be determined exclusively on the basis of the number of hours, as a general rule, each component will not exceed the following limitations during any one school year:

Vocational Exploration	5 hours per job experienced
Vocational Assessment	90 hours per job experienced
Vocational Training	120 hours per job experienced

- Students are not entitled to employment by the business at the conclusion of their IEP. However, once a student has become an employee, the student cannot be considered a trainee at that particular community-based placement unless in a clearly distinguishable occupation.

Figure 8.4
Summary of the 1992 Department of Education/Department of Labor Memorandum of Understanding

students are not being used to displace employees, fill positions, provide additional services, or relieve employees from regularly assigned duties. This means that a business cannot avoid hiring needed employees, use present employees to perform additional duties, or terminate employees due to the presence of community-based student trainees.

Pumpian, Fisher, Certo, Engel, and Mautz (1998) reviewed and analyzed litigation related to conducting nonpaid community-based training. They discovered that the courts have looked at four factors when determining employer benefit and the educational relevance of training. Based on rulings in relevant cases, each training placement should be evaluated by asking the following four questions:

1. Does the employer derive first and primary benefit?
2. Does the employer derive substantial benefit?
3. Does the trainee replace regular workers?
4. Is the experience educationally valid?

In previous rulings some of the reasons associated with failing to meet the FLSA criteria for establishing training situations include:

♦ Trainees working at the convenience of the employer.
♦ Training so poorly organized that the trainees receive no advantage.
♦ Trainees being counted as staff members and responsible for their own training.
♦ Employers being allowed to review training performance prior to actually hiring the trainee for a paid position.
♦ Profit structure of the business being significantly improved by the presence of trainees.
♦ Number of paid employees being reduced due to the work of trainees.
♦ Trainees being responsible for learning skills through their own initiative.

Figure 8.5 offers suggestions based on the FLSA for school systems to follow when designing and implementing vocational training programs. These guidelines can help ensure that the primary focus of the community-based training experience is on the needs of the student, not the participating businesses.

Child Labor Laws. Although child labor laws are not addressed in the DOL/DOE memorandum of understanding, restrictions for youths regarding hours worked and allowable occupational areas are covered by the FLSA. These laws, which relate to students under the age of 18, must be strictly adhered to in all aspects of paid and nonpaid employment preparation. Child labor laws are designed to prevent work from interfering with a child's education or endangering a child's health or well-being.

The minimum age for employment is 14 years, with some exceptions such as newspaper delivery, radio and TV performance, or working in some approved

- The transition component of the IEP for each student involved in nonpaid community-based vocational training should clearly state goals and objectives for the training. The training should be relevant to the student's postsecondary employment outcomes. Ideally, students should be given the opportunity to choose among a variety of training sites.
- Prior to placement on a training site, student trainees should receive adequate orientation. Once students are at the work site, comprehensive training involving demonstration, verbal directions, modeling, student observation, and ongoing performance evaluation should be provided (Certo, Pumpian, Fisher, Storey, & Smalley, 1997). Staff should conduct assessment of student abilities and skill attainment during the training period. Teacher checklists, anecdotal records, portfolios, rubrics, and performance graphs are all methods of evaluation appropriate for community-based training sites. Employees of the business should be involved in trainee performance evaluations to determine how the student's performance compares to that of the average worker (Beakley et al., 2003).
- The training conducted at the work site should directly relate to preestablished goals on the student's IEP. The IEP goals and objectives serve as the justification for the student's placement at a particular site and confirm that the placement is to meet the student's needs.
- Although the time limits set forth in the DOL/DOE memorandum of understanding for vocational exploration, vocational training, and vocational assessment will not be the sole basis upon which an employment relationship will be determined, these time frames should be followed as closely as possible. However, flexibility should be allowed since trainees will learn at different rates and some will acquire the desired level of independence sooner than their peers.
- All nonpaid community-based vocational training should be conducted within normal school hours and should be based on documented student needs.
- Parental permission must be obtained for a student's participation in the community-based vocational training program. Parents must also be kept informed of changes in the program and of the student's progress. The parental permission form should contain (a) a statement concerning student insurance; (b) an indication as to how the student's performance on the training sites will be used to determine grades or credits; (c) a clear statement indicating that the student will not be entitled to wages or to a job after the completion of training; (d) a statement concerning transportation arrangements; and (e) a statement granting permission for school staff to obtain medical care in the event of an emergency at the training site.
- A release-of-information form should be signed for each student so that relevant information about the student can be shared with appropriate representatives of the business at the training site.
- Students should sign a written agreement concerning their participation in the community-based vocational training program. The student agreement should contain the following information: (a) how performance at the training site will

Figure 8.5
Summary of Suggestions for Designing Community-Based Vocational Training Programs That Meet Fair Labor Standards Act Guidelines

affect grades or credits; (b) a clear statement indicating that there is no entitlement to wages or a job after completion of the training; (c) behavioral expectations; and (d) consequences for behavior problems related to the training site.

♦ Signed written agreements should be in place between the school system and
the local businesses and industries providing the training sites. These agreements should include the responsibilities of the local business, FLSA compliance
issues, the responsibilities of the school, the schedule for community-based vocational training, and any other special conditions relevant to the training site.

♦ There should be clearly designated supervisors for all students on community-
based vocational training sites. If a member of the school staff is not going to be
present at all times on the training site, an employee of the business should be
designated as the students' supervisor. Also, a member of the school staff
should be designated as the indirect supervisor and school contact for the training site.

♦ Records (e.g., timesheets) should be maintained indicating the dates and times
a student is involved in various community-based training experiences. Students
should be given responsibility for maintaining these records and adult assistance
should be provided if needed.

Figure 8.5
Continued

parent-owned businesses. Until a child reaches his or her 16th birthday, work for
pay during school hours is not allowed. Any child under the age of 18 must obtain a work permit (also referred to as an *employment certificate*) to be hired as an
employee of a business or industry. Outside of school hours, child labor laws provide restrictions for students under the age of 18 on the time of day or night work
can occur and the total number of hours that can be worked. These regulations
become less restrictive as a child moves toward his or her 18th birthday, but until
the child reaches age 18 a business must adhere to child labor guidelines (Child
Labor Coalition, 2004).

Child labor laws identify 17 occupational areas in which children under the
age of 18 may not participate for purposes of vocational training or competitive
employment. The restrictions on the types of work performed are even stricter for
students under 16 years of age. Among the types of work 14- and 15-year-olds
are not allowed to perform include any manufacturing occupation, mining, processing, public messenger services, operation of various types of machinery,
warehousing, public utilities, construction, cooking, and baking (with some exceptions). More in-depth information about child labor laws can be found at the
U.S. Department of Labor's Youth and Labor site at http://www.dol.gov/
dol/topic/youthlabor/.

Volunteerism and FLSA.   Performing volunteer work or participating in community service projects can provide access to training for a variety of potential

careers for students. But assisting students in accessing volunteer training experiences does not alleviate a school system's responsibility to comply with the FLSA. In fact, when students are involved in volunteer experiences as part of the school's training program, the school should take special care to ensure that the experiences are truly voluntary and meet the accepted definition of volunteerism. In general, all individuals have the right to volunteer their time and/or services for humanitarian purposes without any expectation of employment or compensation. Due to the potential vulnerability of students with disabilities, precautions should be taken to ensure that the student chooses to volunteer at a particular nonprofit site and is not being pressured to do so as a result of teacher expectations or program requirements. Before a student with a disability is allowed to volunteer as part of a vocational training program, Love (1994) suggested asking the following questions for each situation:

1. Is the individual choosing to volunteer even after the offer of other paid and nonpaid vocational training opportunities has been made?

2. Is the volunteer placement an accepted and bona fide volunteer position in the community and not just a position created specifically for this student?

3. Are there other individuals without disabilities volunteering at this organization in a similar capacity?

4. Is the student competent to volunteer his or her services? If not, has the parent or guardian approved of the volunteer work? In other words, have all involved parties agreed to the volunteer placement?

5. Is the volunteer work being performed significantly different from work for which the student is paid at other times or would be paid for in another situation?

6. Have all parties agreed that pay will not be expected in return for the volunteer work?

Providing Employment Preparation to Students in Inclusive Educational Placements

Many students with disabilities are served in inclusive settings, which may create a challenge to providing community-based employment preparation outside of the typical career-technical education classes. If general education is focused on obtaining a certain level of academic competency for all students with regular assessments to monitor accountability, employment preparation may be neglected. However, inclusion in general education classes can result in students' obtaining the reading, writing, math, and social skills that have been associated with higher rates of competitive employment (Benz, Yovanoff, & Doren, 1997). In these situations, special educators must serve as facilitators to ensure that skill training in the critical areas needed for employment success is infused into the general education program.

Students who receive special education services in inclusive settings are more likely than students served in self-contained settings to obtain competitive employment (Luecking & Fabian, 2000), so it is important to consider meaningful inclusion as part of the package when preparing students with disabilities for a productive future. However some teachers who are key players in providing employment preparation to students with disabilities, such as career-technical education teachers, report that they are not prepared to meet the educational needs of students with disabilities who are enrolled in school-to-work programs (Miller, Lombard, & Hazelkorn, 2000). Even in elementary school, where the foundation for many of the work behaviors, habits, and skills is laid, career education activities might be overlooked due to high-stakes testing, lack of career-oriented teaching materials, lack of training, and the belief that preparing for a future career can wait until the young person is older (Clark, Carlson, Fisher, Cook, & D'Alonzo, 1991).

Curriculum differentiation and employment preparation activities do not have to be associated with segregated, self-contained programs. Parents and students should not have to sacrifice instruction in functional life skills, vocational training, and self-determination skills because of participation in inclusive academic classes. These activities can be provided in inclusive settings if all educators understand the importance of meeting the needs of all students.

Some students with disabilities enrolled in the general education curriculum will choose to continue their career training at a postsecondary educational institution such as a 4-year university, community college, or technical school. Unfortunately, the option of continuing postsecondary education to gain the skills needed to pursue a chosen career is not accessed by a large portion of special education graduates (Fairweather & Shaver, 1991). Students should be involved in career awareness activities to assist them in understanding the education and training requirements for various careers. In addition to the inclusion of employment preparation activities within the general education curriculum, students should also be provided with the encouragement and support needed to make informed decisions about postsecondary educational options. Postsecondary education was discussed in more in more detail in Chapter 6.

Students who access community-based training will need proven, individualized instructional strategies. The manner in which instruction is to be delivered should be planned prior to placing students in training environments. Ideally, instructional strategies will be determined through a team approach that includes the student.

INSTRUCTIONAL STRATEGIES

Specific instructional strategies will vary according to a student's abilities, targeted training goals and objectives, the work environment, and the amount of time available at a site. Prior to placing students in job sites, it is important that school staff clearly understand the job environment and work expectations in order to develop instructional and evaluation plans for each student. The following paragraphs describe strategies that school staff can implement to prepare students for participation in community-based training and to ensure the effective delivery of instruction.

Conduct an Environmental Analysis

As a first step, school personnel should visit each training site to conduct an environmental analysis prior to assigning students. An environmental analysis provides educators with information regarding the environmental characteristics of the work site (e.g., traffic flow, parking, lighting, noise level, temperature, smells), safety issues, the frequency and types of employee interactions, critical skills needed to perform the job tasks, and the actual job tasks being performed. An environmental analysis can assist educators in establishing appropriate training goals and instructional strategies for students that are matched to the characteristics of the training site (Moon et al., 1990).

A careful analysis of a work site can also assist in identifying potential natural supports. A **natural support** is any type of support that is typically found in a work environment and that would routinely be available to any employee of the business (e.g., orientation by a coworker). It is important during employment preparation activities not to overlook the assistance that can be provided by coworkers. The support provided by a job coach or school staff and the support given by coworkers should be complementary, not mutually exclusive. The use of natural supports makes sense since no one knows the particular demands and nuances of a job better than those who are already employed in that position (i.e., coworkers). In all jobs, employees depend on each other for assistance with job tasks, advocacy support, advice on job performance, informal communication, social networks, emotional support, and assistance with problem solving. If students are to be successful in future careers, they must learn the social and self-determination skills needed to access and if needed, develop their own natural supports (McNair, 1991).

Conduct a Job Analysis

It is also important to know the types of employment preparation activities a student will be involved in at each site. This can be accomplished by performing a job analysis for each job at each training site. A job analysis identifies all the tasks associated with a job, the order in which they are performed, the equipment used in performing the tasks, and other social or nonvocational tasks and skills that are needed to perform a job successfully. From a job analysis a list of job duties can be developed and shared with students to assist them in making decisions about the training opportunities they would like to experience.

Often, obtaining job descriptions used by the company can help in completing a job analysis. Employees of the business should review the job analysis to check for accuracy and identify acceptable shortcuts for completing various jobs (Moon et al., 1990).

Develop Job Task Analyses

To best assist with instructional planning, larger job tasks should be divided into a series of smaller steps. A **job task analysis** is a written description of a particular task or job divided into individual components, actions, or steps necessary to successfully complete the task or job. A job task analysis can be very detailed if a student's skill level or the complexity of the job task requires a more detailed breakdown (Snell, 1987). For example, for work in a florist shop, one of the daily tasks required is "plant care"; one of the tasks included under "plant care" is "watering plants." A task analysis can further break down the task of "watering plants," providing the specific information needed to perform this job task up to industry standards. The steps for "watering plants" could include such detailed steps as indicating directionality (e.g. which hand to use or which side of the watering can to hold) and how to turn on the water to fill up the water can. Or the job task analysis could be much less specific, simply listing the general steps for watering plants. In some cases, the job task analysis can be used as a to-do list to assist students with a higher level of skills in ensuring completion of an entire task.

Using a job task analysis during employment preparation assists in providing comprehensive instruction so that critical skills and tasks are not overlooked that would result in failure on the job. As noted in Chapter 3, a job task analysis can also be used as a pretest and posttest or to collect ongoing data for evaluating student progress. In addition, when a shortened written format is used or pictures or symbols are added, a task analysis can be used by students as a self-monitoring checklist to help decrease dependence on instructors and/or supervisors. Figure 8.6 is an example of a self-monitoring checklist that includes picture prompts.

Choosing Appropriate Instructional Strategies

Once an instructor has a thorough understanding of the training environment, work expectations, and required job tasks, nonintrusive instructional strategies that encourage independence should be initiated. The types of instructional strategies chosen will depend largely on the individual student, including the student's primary learning mode, the barriers posed by the disability, the level of motivation, expressive and receptive communication skills, and fine and gross motor skills.

School staff should use the student's educational history, including previous instructional strategies that have been effective, to make instructional decisions for the training site. If outside agency personnel (e.g., job coach) are providing training, it is imperative that the educator share information needed about what instructional strategies work best with the student to avoid wasted time and effort. Although there are numerous community-based instructional methods, self-instruction has been chosen for discussion due to its emphasis on the student's acting as his or her own change agent.

Picture/Symbol Form for Housekeeping

Task Sheet

Student: _____ Week of: _____ Observer: _____

		M	T	W	Th	Comments
🚌	1. Job needs (e.g., name tag, lunch).					
	2. Get work assignment.					
	3. Get cart.					
	4. Find and enter room.					
	5. Check drapes.					
	6. Check TV.					
	7. Make bed.					
	8. Dust.					
	9. Stock amenities.					
	10. Empty wastebaskets.					
	11. Clean bathroom.					
	12. Vacuum.					
	13. Fill out hotel checklist.					

Figure 8.6

Picture/Symbol Form for Housekeeping.

Note. From "Using a picture/symbol form for self-monitoring within a community-based training program" by Carol P. Allen, June White, and David W. Test, *Teaching Exceptional Children,* Vol. 24, No. 2, 1992, pp. 54–56. Copyright 1992 by The Council for Exceptional Children. Reprinted with permission.

Self-Instruction

The work performance of students with disabilities greatly improves when they can assume responsibility for remembering job tasks and problem-solve job-related issues. Since there is so much inconsistency in real-life work environments, if students can learn to provide their own prompts and cues their chances of surviving changes in the routines of the job site are enhanced. **Self-instruction** is appropriate for students who have some language skills, can attend to auditory and visual stimuli, and can initiate communication (traditional or nontraditional). Prior to initiating self-instruction training, students should be provided with a clear explanation of the strategy and its benefits (Agran & Moore, 1994).

Training sessions should use a model–practice–feedback–reinforcement format. All of the methods of self-instruction can be modified through the use of verbal labels, self-reinforcement, picture cues, self-monitoring, peer tutors, and group instruction to meet a wide variety of student needs. Before self-instruction begins, a task analysis should be prepared and training sequences developed from the task analysis. Agran and Moore (1994) described four types of self-instruction strategies, discussed in the following section.

Types of Self-Instruction

Problem Solving. This method of self-instruction helps students identify and resolve problems in a work situation. The students (a) state the problem, (b) come up with a solution, and (c) direct themselves to perform the planned response. Examples of when this approach is helpful include running out of supplies or other materials, misplacing a tool or other item, and needing to ask a question.

Did–Next–Now. This method of self-instruction is applicable to sequenced tasks. The verbalizations, which match the Did–Next–Now sequence, allow students to identify what task was just completed (Did) and what task needs to be done next (Next) and direct themselves to perform that task (Now). This method can be modified to a shorter version for students with communication difficulties. The method is useful to students who are performing sequenced job tasks such as cleaning a house, bulk mailing, packaging materials, and/or collating projects.

What–Where. This method of self-instruction is appropriate for students who can already perform the task(s) but are exhibiting inconsistent performance or difficulties in generalization. Students remind themselves of what needs to be done (What) and where the task is to be performed (Where). This method can be used in jobs in which students are assigned to more than one area of a business (e.g., cleaning offices or motel rooms).

Interactive Did–Next–Ask. This method of self-instruction is interactive in nature and appropriate for tasks requiring social interactions, particularly in the area of customer service. Repeating the self-instruction aloud reminds the student what to do while performing the task and interacting with another person without making a negative impression on others. The first verbalization (Did) reminds the student of the task just completed. The second step (Next) directs the student to do the next step of the process. The third step (Ask) involves the student's addressing a question to the person with whom the student is interacting. For example, a student can use this form of self-instruction when preparing a sandwich, taking a food order, checking in drycleaning, assisting a customer in picking up a pre-ordered item, or gift-wrapping.

Self-instruction can be paired with self-evaluation when students are on community-based training sites to provide a training package that will ultimately allow them to self-monitor their performance and make adjustments as needed to maintain a high level of productivity. Students should also be trained in setting performance goals and should be taught the skills necessary to assist them in reaching these goals (Grossi & Heward, 1998).

All community-based instruction should be delivered with the understanding that ultimately the student must be able to perform the job skills independently unless a long-term job coach is going to be available. In that case, a student should still be taught to perform work tasks as independently as possible. During the training phase, adequate support must be provided; however, trainers must teach students to continuously assess their own performance and seek out the natural job supports that will eventually lead to a level of independence comparable to that of coworkers without disabilities.

INCLUDING PARENTS AND FAMILIES IN COMMUNITY-BASED EMPLOYMENT PREPARATION

Parent Involvement

Often the determining factor for whether a student succeeds or fails in obtaining and maintaining competitive employment is parental support. Parents have a significant impact on numerous factors related to future productivity such as school attendance, academic achievement, and self-esteem (Morningstar, Turnbull, & Turnbull, 1995).

Unfortunately, active and appropriate parental participation and support does not always occur. It is the educator's job to initiate strategies to teach, encourage, and support parent efforts to assist their children in reaching their postschool employment goals. Even with early preparation and ongoing parental involvement, occasionally parents or guardians will disagree with their child's postschool employment goals. When this occurs every attempt must be made to resolve the disagreement and elicit parental support. Conflicts can involve minor issues such as the type of job the student is pursuing or the work schedule chosen by the student or major issues such as a desire for the student to be served in a sheltered vocational setting versus a competitive employment setting.

The first key to the removal of barriers resulting from a lack of parental support is to determine the factors that are influencing the parents' concerns, fears, or beliefs. This information can assist educators in negotiating and compromising between the student and the parents or guardians. Some questions that are helpful to consider in these situations include the following:

1.   Have the parents or guardian been truly informed about best practices regarding employment issues for persons with disabilities? If not, might the parents simply not understand the possibilities for their young person in today's society?

2.   Have the parents or guardian been well informed regarding the variety of adult agency support services available to their young person after graduation? If not, might the parents fear that their young person will not have the support needed to be successful in the real world of work?

3.   Have the parents or guardian been well informed of the young person's abilities, needs, and vocational interests? If not, might the parents have unreasonable expectations regarding the type of employment most appropriate for their young person?

4.   Have the parents or guardian been well informed regarding the student's legal status upon reaching the age of majority? If not, could the parents be making decisions for their young adult under the assumption that they will always be the young person's guardian because the young person has a disability?

5.   Have the family been provided with the resources needed to support their young adult in obtaining and maintaining employment? If not, might the parents' apparent lack of involvement and/or support be due to a lack of knowledge and/or access to resources (e.g., transportation, child care)?

6.   Have the parents or guardian been well informed regarding financial planning issues—particularly those related to Social Security and Medicaid? If not, might the parents fear the loss of guaranteed income (e.g., SSI check) and not understand that work incentives combined with the young person's earned wages could result in a higher level of economic independence?

Social Security and Work Incentives

An issue that is often of great concern to students and their families is the loss of benefits. When a student is receiving Supplemental Security Income (SSI) or will be receiving SSI at age 18, it is important to ensure that education is provided about SSI work incentives. Most parents and students are simply unaware of existing SSI work incentives and therefore fail to pursue them (Dreilinger & Timmons, 2001).

Supplemental Security Income is a federal needs-based income support program provided through the Social Security Administration (SSA), which provides a monthly stipend and medical benefits for individuals with disabilities who have limited income and resources (National Transition Network, 2000). Recipients must show evidence of a physical or mental impairment that results in severe functional limitations. There are definite advantages to the benefits of monthly cash assistance, but the receipt of SSI may impede the transition from school to work if families have become dependent on government assistance and fear its loss. The National Health Interview Survey on Disability Supplement (NHIS-D; National Center for Health Statistics, 1994–1995) reported that the percentage of young adult SSI participants (aged 18–29) who reported having worked was substantially lower than for individuals with disabilities who did not receive SSI. More information about SSI can be found at www.socialsecurity.gov. The SSA provides several work incentive programs to encourage individuals to move from government dependence to economic independence.

Plan for Achieving Self-Support.   The **Plan for Achieving Self-Support (PASS)** is a work incentive program designed to allow individuals to set long-term goals for achieving employment. Individuals receiving SSI have set limits regarding the amount of money they are allowed to save before these saved funds are considered in calculating benefits. The use of a PASS can provide a student with the opportunity to set up an account specifically for an employment-related goal and have these savings excluded from consideration in determining monthly benefit amounts. PASS plans must be pre-approved by the SSA, and each plan must include a realistic work goal, a clear savings and spending plan, and a date for achieving the employment goal. Since a PASS is time limited, students will need assistance in establishing a PASS that they can realistically accomplish (The Study Group, Inc., 1998).

Impairment-Related Work Expenses.   **Impairment-related work expenses (IRWE)** are the costs for services and equipment that a person needs to be able to work due to a disability. Examples of IRWEs include wheelchairs, braces, prosthetics, job coach services, assistive technology, and personal assistants. There is no need for prior approval of IRWEs by SSA; the costs of these services and equipment are deducted from a person's earnings, resulting in a larger SSI benefit. Benefit recipients simply present receipts during the SSI review process for the items or services purchased for as long as the support is needed ("Primer," 2004).

There are several other work incentives that allow individuals to try out work for a period of time, keep their Medicaid coverage while employed, reinstate benefits quickly if needed, and work as student trainees without losing benefits. More information about SSI work incentives is available at http://www.ssa.gov/work/ResourcesToolkit/workincentives.html. Technical assistance on work incentives can also be accessed through each state's benefit planning and outreach network, established through the Ticket to Work legislation. More information about Ticket to Work can be found at http://www.ssa.gov/work/Ticket/ticket_info.html.

Parental Support

Although the optimal situation is one in which a student is assisted by his or her family in accomplishing postschool dreams, there may be some situations in which students will have to be supported, upon reaching the age of majority, in exerting their right to make decisions without the approval of their parents or guardians. In these cases, it is likely that students will need additional supports and resources since they may be unable to count on their families to support post-graduation plans with which the families do not agree.

There may also be situations involving students whose parents or guardians prefer that they not pursue a postschool employment goal. In these cases, professionals must do all they can to reach a compromise that will meet the students' needs. Interagency involvement is often helpful in these situations, since multiple professionals may be able to resolve parental issues and concerns. At some point, educators must consider the following issues:

1. If the student ultimately is able to pursue an optimal level of involvement in productive activities after graduation, whether that be full-time competitive employment, part-time competitive employment, or volunteer work in a chosen field, will there still be the family support needed to ensure success?

2. If the parents ultimately obtain their wishes regarding productive activities after graduation for their young person, will the young person still possess the motivation and interest level needed for success and happiness in adult life?

It is apparent that beginning discussions with parents regarding their child's future as early as elementary school, providing comprehensive, ongoing parent education, and ensuring that parents understand their young person's potential are essential to preventing misunderstandings when planning postschool employment activities.

PROMISING PRACTICES FOR ADDRESSING COMMON EMPLOYMENT PREPARATION CHALLENGES

After a community-based program has been established and logistical and instructional issues resolved, there will still be challenges to delivering employment preparation services to students. A community-based employment preparation program should have the flexibility to serve students from diverse backgrounds with a variety of unique characteristics. In other words, rather than having students "fit the program" the program should "fit the student." This requires that educators be prepared and willing to use innovative and promising practices to address student needs. If a community-based program is going to ultimately serve all students, then plans must be made to address issues such as assistive technology, medical needs, and challenging behavior.

Use Assistive Technology

As technology advances, so do the possibilities for individuals with severe disabilities to live and work independently within the community. Mobility, communication, and environmental control devices are now available that open doors

Strategies for Family Involvement

◆ Provide training to elementary teachers in the area of transition and employment for young people with disabilities. Encourage early discussions with parents about their young person's future to expose parents to concepts such as self-determination, normalization, and person-centered planning. Set the expectation that students will graduate from high school and have a career. Assist parents in preparing their young person for employment by giving them specific strategies that can be used at home and in the community (e.g., home chores, talking about what type of work is done at various community businesses, budgeting allowance, reading aloud stories about various occupations).

◆ Provide training to equip parents with the skills needed to assist their young person in making good career choices and obtaining the supports needed in getting a job. Parents can play an important role in providing assistance in job-search and job-obtainment tasks (Technical Assistance on Transition and the Rehabilitation Act [TATRA] Project, 1996). Training can be conducted through small-group sessions, written materials, videos, tapes, Web sites, or informal individual sessions. Adult service agencies that assist students in the area of employment should be involved in providing training. Suggested training topics include advocacy, adult service agency terminology and acronyms, services, legislation related to employment of persons with disabilities, SSI work incentives, and transition planning. An excellent resource for obtaining parent-friendly training materials is the federally funded Parent Training and Information Centers (PTIs) located in each state. These centers have training packages, a lending library, and consultation and advocacy services. More information about the services provided by each state's center can be found at http://www.dssc.org/frc/TAGuide/pti.htm.

◆ Establish both informal and formal methods of communicating with parents to make sure they are in the communication loop. Convey to parents the importance of the information they hold regarding their young person's likes, dislikes, abilities, and needs and how this information can assist in making successful job matches.

◆ Analyze the transition planning process to determine whether the routine nature of the meeting, emphasis on documents and forms, and use of jargon create the impression that parents are not key members of the team (deFur, Todd-Allen, & Getzel, 2001). Make changes to ensure that meetings are parent friendly and that team members demonstrate through their actions the belief that parents are capable of understanding the system, making informed and objective decisions, and serving as partners in the employment preparation of their young person (Cutler, 1993).

◆ Ensure that all educators involved with the family are sensitive to cultural diversity and respectful of cultural issues that need to be considered when making plans for a young person's future career pathway (Harry, Allen, & McLaughlin 1995).

◆ Recognize that the parents' perception of the quality of their relationship with the professionals involved in their young person's transition is the key factor influencing the level of family involvement (deFur et al., 2001). Build a relationship with the parents. Become involved with the student and the family. Demonstrate an interest in the vocational success of the young person by interacting with family members in a personal, caring, and concerned manner. Join parents in dreaming about the possibilities for their young person's future success on the job, and provide opportunities for celebrating successes.

♦ Establish a parent network or parent support group encouraging parents to discuss their fears and concerns about employment for their young person. Parents can learn the importance of risk taking and the benefits of supporting vocational independence through conversations with other parents.

♦ Encourage parents to involve their young person in their own career or the career pathways of other relatives and friends through job shadowing, internships, or simply talking about jobs. Ensure that parents understand the value of modeling and communicating a solid work ethic (Penick & Jepsen, 1992).

♦ Assist parents in setting reasonable but high expectations for their young adult. Few parents of students with severe disabilities expect their child to have part-time or full-time employment following graduation (Kraemer & Blacher, 2001). Although parents of students with mild disabilities express greater hopes for competitive employment placements for their young adults, most expect employment in entry-level and low-paying jobs in the clerical or food service fields (Tilson & Neubert, 1989).

♦ Parents should be kept informed about their young person's vocational evaluation results, interests, and performance during employment preparation activities. Involve parents in focused discussions that include the young person about the type of employment that has the highest likelihood of long-term success. Share the success stories of former graduates so that parents can see the possibilities for their young person's employment future. Ensure that transition planning is focused on the young person's strengths instead of weaknesses to send a clear message to parents regarding their young person's ability to work. Interview parents to assist them in identifying natural supports in the young person's life that might assist with job development, job training, transportation, and mentoring.

♦ Remember that sometimes the school must *first* assist in meeting the needs of the family to better equip family members in supporting the young person's attempts to enter the world of work. For example, some families may need help in obtaining a vehicle to provide transportation to work for the young person. Other families may need help with financial planning if the young person's SSI check has been part of the household budget. Other parents may need counseling to assist them in overcoming fears related to their young person's adult status.

that were previously closed to them in the business world. In many cases, the only limits placed on accessing career possibilities through assistive technology are those of funding and staff expertise.

The Assistive Technology Act of 1998 defines an assistive technology device as "any item, piece of equipment, or product system, whether acquired commercially off the shelf, modified, or customized that is used to increase, maintain, or improve functional capabilities of a child with a disability". Assistive technology can be high tech or low tech. Low-tech devices are simple and low cost, including things such as nonskid matting, Velcro attachments, reachers, and pencil grips. Many low-tech devices can be purchased in the community or can be designed from commonly available materials. High-tech devices are commercially manufactured by specialized vendors, are expensive, and involve a high level of electronics or computerized components.

A major function of the transition process for students with physical, communication, and/or sensory disabilities should be to ensure that proper technological devices are accessible to students for use in all life domains. Although assistive technology is not going to eliminate all barriers to employment or ensure vocational success for all individuals, it should not be considered a luxury. For some individuals assistive technology is a necessity; lack of access to it will likely eliminate the possibility of competitive employment (Scherer & Galvin, 1996).

There are several categories of assistive devices to be considered when planning for employment of students with disabilities. There should be at least one person in the school system associated with the employment preparation program who is responsible for keeping up with the rapidly changing field of assistive technology. Since the use of assistive technology is highly individualized and can cover a number of functional areas, it is necessary to specifically match a student's vocational need with the appropriate device. Figure 8.7 summarizes a report prepared by the Electronic Industries Association (1994) describing several areas to consider when making assistive technology matches.

Assistive technology devices used on a school campus to enhance instructional effectiveness or to aid in vocational training may or may not be appropriate for use in the community. In a school environment, trained educators and therapists are available to facilitate the use of fairly complicated devices, make adjustments and repairs to devices, and modify the environment to maximize the effectiveness of the devices. However, in the community students will encounter situations in which there is no assistive technology available. Therefore it is imperative that students receive a comprehensive assessment by a team of qualified professionals to determine the type of assistive device(s) needed for the various work environments they will encounter during training and competitive employment. Figure 8.8 offers suggestions for ensuring that a student's success in the work site is enhanced through the use of technology.

Consider Medical and Health Needs

Some students participating in employment preparation activities have medical or health considerations that require advance planning and accommodations at the work site. These may include conditions such as seizure disorders, metabolic disorders, bowel or urinary conditions, asthma, diabetes, and heart conditions. From an early age the goal for students with medical or other health needs

Mobility Aids

Mobility devices include wheelchairs (manual and motorized), walkers, braces, crutches, or any other piece of equipment that aids in movement.

Augmentative Communication Devices

Augmentative communication devices include nonelectronic aids such as communication boards (using letters, pictures, and symbols) and electronic aids such as speech synthesizers, voice recognition systems, switches, computers, and/or any other device that allows an individual to communicate needs, wants, and desires and/or to converse with others.

Activities of Daily Living Devices

Devices that allow individuals to exert control over the environment and perform routine tasks independently include light-pointing devices, intercoms, voice-activated environmental control devices, dual switches, head pointers, page turners, cerebral palsy feeders, robotics, mouth sticks, and animal assistants.

Employment Devices

Persons with physical disabilities can use a variety of switches and specially designed "jigs" to modify a job to accommodate the disability. For example, a switch can assist with quality control (e.g., stopping a conveyer belt when a substandard item is observed), obtaining dry cleaning, stapling, punching holes, binding, and using power tools and appliances. Other low-tech devices include clamps, folders, high-friction surfaces, reachers, lazy susans, larger keyboards, and key guards.

Devices for Persons with Hearing Impairments

Devices in this category include closed-caption decoders, compact personal amplifiers, computer-assisted note-taking, group listening systems, telecommunication devices for the deaf (TDDs), telephone relay systems (TRSs), and a wide variety of signaling devices using vibration and lights.

Devices for Persons with Visual Impairments

Computers are capable of writing braille and taking notes in braille. Talking calculators, talking clocks, and electronic reading devices allow the presentation of information in an audible format. Telephones can be equipped to allow voice-activated dialing. Other devices in this category include buzzers, magnifiers, and tactile markings.

Figure 8.7
Employment-Related Assistive Technology Devices
Note. Adapted from Electronic Industries Association, Consumer Electronics Group. (1994). *Extend their reach.* Arlington, VA: Author.

♦ Consider all aspects of a typical workday, including getting ready for work, getting to and from work, breaktime and meals at work, bathroom use, work endurance, eating and drinking, communication, mobility, hand use, medical needs, and transportation (Sowers & Powers, 1991).

♦ Consider issues such as portability (i.e., the ease with which the device can be transported), expansion (i.e., the potential of the device to be expanded as the student's vocational needs change), maintenance (i.e., the ease with which the device can be maintained and repaired), adaptability (i.e., the ability of the device to be used in a wide range of environments and situations), and preference (i.e., what type of device the student is most at ease in using).

♦ Get specialists (e.g., physical therapist, speech therapist, occupational therapist) involved in planning sessions.

♦ Access the services of a rehabilitation engineer through Vocational Rehabilitation. Rehabilitation engineers can provide evaluation and assessment of the client, environment, and equipment; information about technology; recommendations for modifications, adaptations, and prototype development; and follow-up services to the individual to determine the ongoing effectiveness of the technology (Wehman et al., 1988).

♦ Identify possible funding sources, including traditional Medicaid, Medicaid waiver programs, Vocational Rehabilitation, the public schools, private insurance, supplemental security income work incentives, and private pay.

♦ Provide an orientation period in the work environment to evaluate the effectiveness of a device.

♦ Ensure that the employer and key employees of the business understand the importance of the assistive device to the student's success and have been given strategies for supporting the student in the use of the device.

♦ If school personnel have been primarily responsible for coordinating the purchase, upgrading, and maintenance of assistive devices for the student, measures must be taken prior to graduation to provide the student and his or her family with the knowledge needed to conduct these activities in the future.

Figure 8.8
Suggestions for Using Technology to Ensure Student Work Site Success

should be focused on educating students about their conditions and teaching them to independently implement healthcare procedures (e.g., glucose monitoring, medication administration, colostomies/ileostomies, cauterization).

The first priority for a student with a medical problem is maintaining and improving health. Preparing for future employment can actually enhance the health of an individual due to the emotional and psychological benefits associated with independence and community inclusion. Figure 8.9 lists practices and strategies to consider when planning community-based training and job placements for students with specialized medical or other health conditions.

- Gather all information about a student's medical condition by obtaining signed releases from the student and/or parent to obtain medical records. Ensure that records include the names and contact information for all physicians and/or specialists, the student's medical history, prescribed medications, specialized medical procedures, physical restrictions, prognosis, and any other health-related information.
- Help parents obtain physician opinions regarding the types of work environments and tasks in which the student might encounter difficulty.
- Develop a package for each student that contains parental permission for participation in community-based vocational training, specific instructions for performing all medical or health procedures, basic medical information (e.g., allergies, medication administration schedule, medication side effects, medical emergency information, physician contact information), parental permission for medical emergency care, and any work restrictions. Ensure that all work supervisors (school and/or business) are aware of the information and its location on the job site.
- Use transition planning sessions to help parents and students use physician recommendations, situational assessment results, and student interests and desires to design employment preparation experiences that will ultimately lead to a successful job match.
- Begin in elementary school to provide training to enable the student to independently perform medical care procedures and self-administration of medication.
- Prior to a student's going into the community to train or work, determine the types and amount of medical equipment and supplies that will be needed and a method for ensuring their accessibility to the student while on the job site.
- Begin early to equip students with self-advocacy skills to prepare them to coordinate their healthcare. Students should learn to negotiate and problem-solve with medical care professionals regarding changes in medical care that can facilitate employment, with adult service providers regarding services needed for employment, and with employers regarding job accommodations and modifications. As early as possible, students should be involved in decision making regarding their health and medical care.
- Involve therapeutic support staff and school health professionals in planning for employment preparation activities and job placement.
- Provide training to parents and students on Section 504 of the Rehabilitation Act and the Americans with Disabilities Act to increase their awareness regarding civil rights issues in the employment process.

Figure 8.9
Strategies to Use When Planning Community-Based Training Opportunities for Students with Specialized Medical and Health Needs

Respond to Challenging Behaviors

Students with challenging behaviors present a complex array of transition issues related to employment. In addition to behavioral and emotional disorders, many of these students may also be dealing with issues related to a history of physical or sexual abuse, prior court system involvement, past or present probation, substance abuse problems, previous institutionalizations, frequent changes in residential arrangements, poor interpersonal relationships, poor school attendance, and poor academic achievement. The challenges these students face are reasons for ensuring that comprehensive employment preparation becomes an early priority. Many students with behavioral and emotional problems drop out of school before they have the opportunity to obtain the training needed to adjust to adult life (Butler-Nalin & Padilla, 1989). As a result, it is not surprising that this population of students has one of the highest rates of unemployment (Hasazi, Gordon, & Roe, 1985).

Students who face challenging behavioral and emotional issues typically need a number of services during and after high school. Thus, students with behavioral and emotional disorders should not be left out when planning and establishing employment preparation activities. Sometimes the presence of behavioral and emotional issues limits a student to employment preparation in simulated environments and controlled settings because educators are fearful of problems that might occur in the community. If students with behavioral and/or emotional concerns are required to meet an inflexible list of prerequisites prior to entering community-based training, they may never get off campus to experience the real world of work. To avoid this, it is important to remember that often students who exhibit severe behavior problems on campus exhibit much less challenging behaviors in a community-based environment. By using strategies such as comprehensive and proactive planning, additional supervision at the job site, environmental accommodations and/or modifications, positive behavior support, and placement in group training situations, failure on the job site and potential public relations problems can be prevented.

One of the most important aspects of community-based training for students with behavioral problems is creating positive behavior support plans that can be implemented successfully at a community-based training site. Although employers at community-based training sites usually understand that student trainees may impede the normal activities of the business to a small degree, they do not tolerate severe disruptions to their businesses. Therefore, developing behavior support strategies focused on self-management paired with adequate supervision and advance preparation of the business employees is often required.

While students should be prepared with a basic repertoire of strategies aimed at anger management, impulse control, and self-reward, it is not always possible to predict the variety of job site situations that might result in behavioral issues. Therefore, it is important that educators provide ample opportunities for students to practice their responses and actions through on-campus training, instructional activities, role playing, counseling, and job clubs prior to community placement.

DID YOU KNOW?

"The last group of people in this country who can keep the economy going for all of us, with low inflation, are Americans with disabilities—who want to work, who can work, and who are not in the workforce. Every American citizen should have a selfish interest in the pursuit of this goal in the most aggressive possible way." (President Clinton, June 4, 1999).

BARRIERS TO EMPLOYMENT OF INDIVIDUALS WITH DISABILITIES

Many of the potential difficulties facing students with disabilities as they enter the world of work, such as a lack of experience, low expectations, limited inter-agency coordination, poor transition planning, and lack of long-term follow-up, can be overcome through participation in an employment preparation program that incorporates interagency collaboration and emphasizes student involvement and parental support. However, advance preparation will not eliminate all the barriers to employment for individuals with disabilities. Following are some possible solutions to some of the more common barriers facing students with disabilities as they make the transition from school to work. The barriers addressed include employer perceptions and attitudes, unrealistic career goals, a lack of early planning and training, limited adult service options, high unemployment rates, and limited employment options. All of these must be taken into consideration when seeking to ensure postschool employment.

Overcoming Employer Perceptions and Attitudes

In some cases employers have not had the opportunity to hire someone with a disability, and they base their attitudes toward hiring young people with disabilities on this limited experience base. Conversely, Levy, Jessop, Rimmerman, and Levy (1992) found that employers who had previously hired individuals with disabilities were supportive and open to the benefits that having a diverse workforce can provide.

It is important that those conducting job development activities have the knowledge needed to counteract misconceptions held by many employers. For example, some employers may fear the need for expensive accommodations and modifications to the work site if they hire someone with a disability. However, studies have shown that most accommodations cost $500 or less and that 73% of employees with disabilities require no accommodations at all (Dixon, Kruse, & Van Horn, 2003). Employers fearing safety issues must be taught that employees with disabilities have fewer disabling work-related injuries than the average worker when exposed to the same job tasks and about the same number of minor injuries (E.I. Dupont de Nemours and Company, 1990). Since about 22% of individuals with disabilities report encountering job discrimination (National Organization on Disability, 2004), students must be fully aware of civil rights protections offered to them under the law and educators must be prepared to intervene with advocacy assistance if needed during the job search and job placement process.

Employers in general believe that some of the main benefits of hiring individuals with disabilities include community image, dedication of the employees, and personal satisfaction in helping others. But employers who have actually hired individuals with disabilities report that the overall quality of work is one of the top three benefits (Nietupski, Hamre-Nietupski, Vanderhort, & Fishback, 1996). Hiring individuals with disabilities is not about charity; it is about hiring people who want to work and who can benefit the employer with their skills and commitment. When conducting job development it is important to be armed with facts and help employers realize that this population of potential employees are:

♦ Experienced in finding creative and unique ways to perform routine tasks, resulting in valuable problem-solving skills.

♦ Dependable, dedicated, hardworking, and productive.

♦ An asset to employee morale, motivation, and productivity.

♦ Reflective of the population in general and can assist the employer in maintaining a diverse workforce (U.S. Department of Education and the U.S. Chamber of Commerce, 2003).

Responding to Unrealistic Career Coals

Students may be focused on career goals that are viewed as unattainable by their family and teachers. Although it is important to never underestimate a student's abilities, it is also important to ensure that students understand the limitations posed by their disabilities and the job market. In these situations it is important to determine the essence of each student's dream and provide career planning that highlights what interests the student about his or her dream job. Is it the environment in which the job is performed, the job tasks associated with that career, the "trappings" of the job, or the social status given to individuals in that type of work? It is also important to determine how the student developed this dream job and to pinpoint the essence and help the student explore similar or related jobs

DID YOU KNOW?

In a study conducted in North Carolina in 1999 involving over 10,000 employers, it was discovered that 67% of the employers reported they had never hired a person with a disability simply because they had never been asked (Positive Influence, 1999).

that are more appropriate (Hagner & Dileo, 1993). For example, if a student wants to play basketball for the NBA and this is an unrealistic goal, look for sports-related jobs such as working at the Recreation Department or at a sporting goods store. It is also possible that a dream job can be changed to an active avocation. For example, a student who dreams of being a movie star may be happy working at or managing a video store and becoming a member of a local theater group.

Overcoming Limited Early Training and Planning

Unfortunately some students arrive at high school with limited exposure to employment preparation activities. Due to a lack of teacher training and appropriate curriculum materials and/or a lack of emphasis on school-to-work issues in the early grades, a student's educational history may not include any formal opportunities until middle school or early high school for being prepared for a career. In these situations the transition assessment process is vital to establishing instructional priorities for the student. A student who has been unsuccessful in academically oriented classes and has not been exposed to career counseling or career training may be at high risk for dropping out due to frustration arising from a poor curriculum match. Comprehensive transition planning upon entering high school can assist students and their parents in making good choices related to a high school course of study and future employment goals, eliminating problems that can occur from a lack of early discussion about the future.

Overcoming a Lack of Adult Service Options

The adult service world is one of eligibility rather than entitlement. There are no federal mandates guaranteeing services to adults with disabilities in the manner in which IDEA assures services for school-aged students with disabilities. Consequently, successful employment outcomes may be affected by the quality and quantity of service agencies available to the student after graduation. In rural areas there may be a limited number of supported employment providers with few options for creative planning (e.g., enclaves, mobile work crews, self-employment). In these situations strong collaboration among agencies that are available, coupled with a base of community support, must be developed. To increase the availability of services, a community needs assessment should be organized followed by grassroots advocacy aimed at convincing local officials and policymakers of the need for additional support services. There are no easy solutions to limited service options and eliminating this barrier to employment may take months or years. However, without an array of appropriate employment-related service options, student employment outcomes can be limited.

Surviving High Unemployment Rates

While the economic well-being of people without disabilities is severely impacted by a depressed economy, the impact on people with disabilities is greater. In a community that has experienced large layoffs and local factory closings, finding jobs for students with disabilities can become a daunting task. Job development activities have to be increased and expanded along with creative attempts to design unique employment options. Self-employment, home employment, and telemarketing might provide employment opportunities for some students. National companies (e.g., Marriott, IBM, Hewlett Packard, Dupont, KOA Campgrounds, Pizza Hut) who have corporate policies aimed at hiring employees with disabilities should be approached for assistance in job placement if they are located in or near the community. Students may need to consider postsecondary training or education instead of entering the world of work immediately after graduation. In a tight job market, those with marketable skills will certainly have more choices.

Self-Employment.   Over the last few years, **self-employment** has grown from a seldom used employment option to one that is increasingly more accepted, to the point that people with disabilities report being self-employed at a higher rate than people in the general population (Arnold, Seekins, & Ravesloot, 1995).

Self-employment can often involve work opportunities that are not available through existing job placements in the community. The 1998 Rehabilitation Act amendments under the Workforce Investment Act (WIA) of 1998 recognized self-employment as a viable type of employment, thereby paving the way for funding assistance to individuals with disabilities who desire this option. As individuals with disabilities gain more rights in the adult service arena in the areas of consumer choice and management of personal budgets, professionals have had to rethink past views regarding the abilities and preferences of those desiring to start their own businesses (Callahan, Shumpert, & Mast, 2002). Although self-employment can require some complex business skills and possibly lower wages, this employment option can also provide the flexibility, autonomy, and life-style preference match needed for some individuals (Doyel, 2002). In situations in which students will ultimately need a variety of accommodations and modifications (e.g., work schedule, work hours) and desire a work situation that uniquely matches their talents and interests, self-employment might be a good option (Hagner & Davies, 2002).

Self-employment can be varied, including businesses such as rare book finding services, clowning services, kosher foods caterers, second-hand clothing stores, authors, assistive technology consultants, advocacy speakers, sandwich deliverers, computer or word processing services, auto detailers, photography services, and laundry services (Callahan et al., 2002). Although self-employment can be labor intensive and require time to generate income, it has the advantage of being uniquely individualized to a person's skills, interests, and talents.

During employment preparation activities, students with disabilities should be provided with information regarding self-employment to ensure awareness of this employment option. Transition planning teams should also be prepared to provide support if a student chooses self-employment as a career option. Support can include business classes while in high school, admission to postsecondary training, development of natural supports, adult service follow-up, and funding assistance (Rizzo, 2002).

Overcoming Limited Employment Options

A high-quality transition program will strive to ensure that students have access to career pathways matched to their interests. However, studies show that a significant percentage of students with disabilities obtain jobs in fields that have high turnover and a high proportion of entry-level positions (e.g., food and beverage, building and related services, sales, production and stock clerks, domestic service), with the highest percentage locating jobs in the food and beverage industry (Morgan, Ellerd, Jensen, & Taylor, 2000). Ensuring that each student's interests drive job development may increase job diversity. Those responsible for job development and job placement can increase employment possibilities though the use of **job carving,** which involves reassigning job tasks to one or more workers to increase the company's efficiency and productivity. After a work environment has been analyzed, job carving can be used to match an individual's unique talents and skills to a specific need within the business (Griffin, 1996). Job developers should also explore hidden job markets and investigate employer needs and job market trends to make inroads into occupational areas not typically pursued by special education graduates (Bissonnette, 1994).

SUMMARY

Preparing students for employment through community-based training should be an accepted component of a school's transition service delivery system. The positive impact that community-based training can have on a student's ability to obtain and maintain future employment is more than worth the time and effort it takes to plan, implement, and coordinate this transition activity. Generalizing skills to the community environments in which they will ultimately be used is important not only for the employment domain of transition but for all domains, including community living, postsecondary education and training, and community participation.

Students who are given the opportunity to apply skills learned on the school campus to the community will be more likely to not only remember those skills but also to understand their importance and relevance to their postschool goals. The walls of the school have expanded to include all aspects of community life for students with disabilities. Preparing students with disabilities for employment through community-based training is helpful in ensuring student achievement and also can serve as an accountability measure for the effectiveness of the educational services being delivered within the classroom. With careful planning that cultivates partnerships between the school and local business, policies that ensure student safety, compliance with state and federal labor laws, and effective community-based instructional strategies, students can ultimately move from training in the community to successfully working and living in the community.

CASE STUDY

DEBBIE

This case study began in Chapter 7 with background information on Debbie and a description of the school-based employment preparation in which she was involved. This portion of Debbie's case study focuses on her community-based employment preparation experiences.

Due to Debbie's medical history and severe physical disabilities, opportunities for community-based employment preparation were limited to three sites. A personal assistant (paid with Medicaid funds) accompanied Debbie to each of the community-based training sites. Debbie's first job-shadowing experience was in a local bakery, where she used a switch-activated sealer to assist in packaging baked goods. This community-based training assignment lasted 8 weeks, during which time Debbie was at the site each Tuesday and Thursday for 2 hours each day. Debbie's second job-shadowing experience was at an assisted living center, where her primary job duties consisted of assisting the recreation director in planning and implementing in-house activities for the residents. Debbie's final job-shadowing experience was the most successful. It was conducted at a mailing center. Debbie prepared mailings using an electric letter folder, put labels on envelopes, and sealed envelopes. Her personal assistant provided help in completing tasks when needed and checked Debbie's quality of work.

During her community-based training experiences, Debbie's augmentative communication device was not used as effectively as it could have been. Debbie appeared to rely on the school staff member or personal assistant who accompanied her to the site as a communication intermediary.

During the past year Debbie was exposed to a variety of occupations through visits to a wide range of businesses, industries, volunteer agencies, and community agencies. Each of these visits lasted approximately 2 hours, during which time Debbie was given an opportunity to watch employees performing various tasks and to try a few work tasks herself, assisted by a school staff member. During these visits observational information was collected regarding Debbie's response to the environment, her ability to navigate using her motorized wheelchair, her ability to initiate interactions using her communication device, and her ability to perform various work tasks. In addition, following each visit Debbie was interviewed to determine her level of interest in the occupational area.

Debbie also completed a nonpaid internship with the local mental health center, in which she shredded confidential documents, handed out visitor badges, and put labels on new client folders. For the last 3 months, Debbie has held a part-time job with a local pizza restaurant; she hands out discount coupons at the local mall on weekends and encourages people to patronize the business. Debbie has used her communication device effectively during this work experience.

Based on the information gathered from Debbie's on-campus and off-campus vocational training experiences, situational assessments, and part-time job, the transition team concluded that Debbie was definitely interested in pursuing a job after leaving high school. With Debbie's input, her potential future career options were narrowed down to one with the following characteristics:

♦ An environment that would accommodate Debbie's use of a motorized wheelchair and a communication device, as well as her need for assistance with physical care.

♦ A high to moderate level of interaction with coworkers.

♦ Job tasks that use mechanical or electronic devices that can be modified for use with a switch or one-handed controls.

♦ A work environment that values quality over quantity and that is not dead-line driven.

♦ An environment that is conducive to job sharing, job carving, part-time hours, and flexible scheduling.

At a school-level transition team meeting attended by Debbie, her grand-mother, the special education teacher, the transition coordinator, a case manager from the Mental Health/Developmental Disabilities Division, a VR counselor, a community college representative, a job coach, Debbie's uncle, and her one-on-one worker (a medicaid-funded habilitation assistant), Debbie's future employment was discussed. Everyone was in agreement that Debbie would require a one-on-one job coach in order to work at a competitive job. Funding for this service would come from a combination of sources, including Medicaid waiver funds and VR. Transportation was another barrier to employment. Possible solutions included having Debbie's grandmother provide transportation using a wheelchair-equipped van, allowing the one-one-one worker to use the van to provide transportation to work, or using a specialized transportation service. Debbie's grandmother was open to using her van or allowing it to be used for transportation, but she wanted to obtain information from the local specialized transportation service about schedules and fees.

Debbie's grandmother also voiced her fear that Debbie's employment might result in a loss of social security and Medicaid benefits. The transition coordinator reminded Debbie's grandmother of the training she had attended the previous year on social security work incentives. A brief review was provided and a recommendation made that an individual meeting be arranged between some of the team members, Debbie's grandmother, Debbie, and a work incentive consultant from the regional Ticket to Work program.

Another potential problem associated with future employment was locating a supported employment provider familiar with developing jobs for individuals with severe physical disabilities. The team recommended contacting an agency operated by United Cerebral Palsy in a neighboring town and making a recommendation to VR for an assessment by a rehabilitation engineer. Team members also noted that Debbie's therapists, both school-based and community-based, should be involved in future transition planning meetings. They suggested that additional therapeutic support evaluations be obtained that focus on Debbie's communication and motor skills in employment sites.

School staff discussed the need for coordinated situational assessment activities between school staff and a job coach, as well as additional community-based vocational training opportunities. The team decided that Debbie would participate in a minimum of six experiences during the next 8 months with placement in a long-term internship in the occupational area deemed most conducive to success during the last 3 months of school.

Based on Debbie's medical and health history, her severe cognitive and physical disabilities, and the high rate of local unemployment, team members felt a need to discuss the possibility that placement in full-time competitive employment might not be feasible by the time of graduation. All team members agreed that despite any obstacles Debbie faced, a commitment to obtaining a job for her had to be a high priority. They recommended that the school nurse and Debbie's special education teacher contact Debbie's primary physician and medical specialists for information related to medical and health issues that might affect Debbie's long-term employment success.

Due to the complex issues facing Debbie as she moved toward future employment, the team members determined that she would be placed on the agenda for review at least every other month. The meeting was adjourned after the team unanimously approved the resolution that various team members would conduct the following transition activities:

- ◆ Follow up on obtaining a baclafon pump to decrease Debbie's spasticity.
- ◆ Refer Debbie to the local assistive technology center for an evaluation of her present communication system and recommendations for possible modifications to the system or a new system.
- ◆ Provide communication training in the community at various sites to ensure that Debbie effectively uses her communication system.
- ◆ Coordinate between Debbie's mental health case manager and the VR counselor to ensure funding for a supported employment job coach and long-term follow-up.
- ◆ Investigate the possibility of using specialized transportation for Debbie's transportation to and from work.
- ◆ Refer Debbie's grandmother and Debbie to a social security work incentive consultant through the Ticket to Work program.
- ◆ Contact the United Cerebral Palsy supported employment agency to determine the referral process for obtaining services.
- ◆ Refer to VR for an evaluation by a rehabilitation engineer.
- ◆ Establish six community-based training experiences for Debbie based on her interests and abilities. Coordinate the planning of these experiences with the job coach in order to conduct some joint situational assessment.

 ♦ Invite Debbie's therapists to future transition planning meetings and request supplemental therapy evaluations focusing on employment-related issues.

 ♦ Make a referral to the local WIA program to obtain a paid employment internship for Debbie during her senior year.

 ♦ Register Debbie at the Employment Security Commission One-Stop Center for employment referrals.

 ♦ Contact Debbie's physicians to obtain up-to-date medical information that may be helpful in making a good job match for her.

STUDY GUIDE QUESTIONS

1. Describe each type of community-based vocational training option and give an example of each.
2. What are some characteristics of effective community-based training?
3. What issues should be considered when locating community-based training sites?
4. Describe strategies for handling issues associated with the implementation of community-based training such as staffing, transportation, and liability.
5. What are some of the things transition staff must remember when placing students in nonpaid community-based vocational training sites? (Pay careful attention to the information in the "Dear Colleague" letter; see Figure 8.4.)
6. What are some strategies for ensuring that students included in the general curriculum have access to the occupational preparation activities needed to pursue a career after graduation?
7. Describe strategies that can be used to teach self-instruction and provide examples of when these strategies might be helpful to a student in a community-based training site or competitive employment placement.
8. What things must be considered when students with disabilities use volunteerism as a way to prepare for future employment?
9. How can family involvement have a positive impact on a student's community-based training experiences?
10. In your opinion, are there any challenging behaviors that could not be managed in a community-based training site? If so, what are these behaviors and why do you believe that they are incompatible with skill-training within the community?
11. After reading the case study in this chapter and Chapter 7, identify the community-based vocational training strategies used and make suggestions for future employment-related activities that would be appropriate based on Debbie's skills, interests, desires, and needs.

REFERENCES

Agran, M., & Moore, S. (1994). *How to teach self-instruction of job skills*. Washington, DC: American Association on Mental Retardation.

Agran, M., Snow, K., & Swaner, J. (1999). A survey of secondary level teachers' opinions on community-based instruction and inclusive education. *Journal of the Association for Persons with Severe Handicaps, 24,* 58–62.

Agran, M., Swaner, J., & Snow, K. (1998). Work safety skills: A neglected curricular area. *Career Development for Exceptional Individuals, 21,* 33–44.

Allen, C. P., White, J., & Test, D. W. (1992). Using a picture/symbol form for self-monitoring within a community-based training program. *Teaching Exceptional Children, 24*(2), 54–56.

Arnold, N., Seekins, T., & Ravesloot, C. (1995). Self-employment as a vocational rehabilitation employment outcome in rural and urban areas. *Rehabilitation Counseling Bulletin, 39,* 94–106.

Assistive Technology Act of 1998, 105–394, 5. 2432, 3(A)(3) (1998).

Bates, P.E., Cuvo, T., Miner, C. A., & Korabek, C. A. (2001). Simulated and community-based instruction involving persons with mild and moderate mental retardation. *Research in Developmental Disabilities, 22,* 95–115.

Baumgart, D., Johnson, J., & Helmstetter, E. (1990). *Augmentative and alternative communication systems for persons with moderate and severe disabilities*. Baltimore: Brookes.

Baumgart, D., & VanWalleghem, J. (1986). Staffing strategies for implementing community-based instruction. *The Journal of the Association of the Severely Handicapped, 11,* 92–102.

Beakley, B. A., Yoder, S. L., & West, L. L. (2003). *Community-based instruction: A guidebook for teachers*. Arlington, VA: Council for Exceptional Children.

Benz, M. R., Lindstrom, L., & Yovanoff, P. (2000). Improving graduation and employment outcomes of students with disabilities: Predictive factors and student perspectives. *Exceptional Children, 66,* 509–524.

Benz, M. R., Yovanoff, P., & Doren, B. (1997). School-to-work components that predict post-school success for students with and without disabilities. *Exceptional Children, 63,* 151–165.

Bissonnette, D. (1994). *Beyond traditional job development: The art of creating opportunity*. Chatsworth, CA: Milt Wright and Associates.

Butler-Nalin, P., & Padilla, C. (1989). *Dropouts: The relationship of student characteristics, behaviors, and performance for special education students*. Menlo Park, CA: SRI International.

Callahan, M., Shumpert, N., & Mast, M. (2002). Self-employment, choice, and self-determination. *Journal of Vocational Rehabilitation, 17,* 74–85.

Certo, N., Pumpian, I., Fisher, D., Storey, K., & Smalley, K. (1997). Focusing on the point of transition. *Education and Treatment of Children, 20,* 68–84.

Child Labor Coalition. (2004). *Child labor in the United States*. Retrieved May 26, 2004, from http://www.stopchildlabor.org/Uschildlabor/fact1.htm

Clark, G. M., Carlson, B. C., Fisher, S., Cook, I. D., & D'Alonzo, B. J. (1991). Career development for students with disabilities in elementary schools: A position statement of the Division on Career Development. *Career Development for Exceptional Individuals, 14,* 109–120.

Clinton, W. J. (1999, June 4). Speech at presentation of the President's Award for Furthering Employment and Empowerment of People with Disabilities at a White House ceremony, Washington, DC.

Colley, D. A., & Jamison, D. (1998). Post school results for youth with disabilities: Key indicators and policy implications. *Career Development for Exceptional Individuals, 21,* 145–160.

Cutler, B. C. (1993). *You, your child, and special education: A guide to making the system work*. Baltimore: Brookes.

deFur, S. H., Todd-Allen, M., & Getzel, E. E. (2001). Parent participation in the transition planning process. *Career Development for Exceptional Individuals, 24,* 19–36.

Dixon, K. A., Kruse, D., & Van Horn, C. E. (2003). *Restricted Access: A survey of employers about people with disabilities and lowering barriers to work*. Rutgers, NJ: The State University of New

Jersey, John J. Heldrich Center for Workforce Development.

Doyel, A. W. (2002). A realistic perspective of risk in self-employment for people with disabilities. *Journal of Vocational Rehabilitation, 17,* 115–124.

Dreilinger. D., & Timmons, J. (2001). *From stress to success: Making Social Security work for your young adult: Tools for inclusion.* Boston: Children's Hospital, Institute for Community Inclusion.

E. I. DuPont de Nemours and Company. (1990). *Equal to the task II.* Wilmington, DE: Author.

Electronic Industries Association, Consumer Electronics Group. (1994). *Extend their reach.* Arlington, VA: Author.

Fairweather, J. S., & Shaver, D. M. (1991). Making the transition to post-secondary education and training. *Exceptional Children, 5,* 264–270.

Falvey, M. A. (1989). *Community-based curriculum: Instructional strategies for students with severe handicaps.* Baltimore: Brookes.

Griffin, C. (1996). Job carving as a job development strategy. In D. DiLeo & D. Langton (Eds.), *Facing the future: Best practices in supported employment* (p. 36). St. Augustine, FL: TRN Publishing.

Grossi, T. A., & Heward, W. L. (1998). Using self-evaluation to improve the work productivity of trainees in a community-based restaurant training program. *Education and Training in Mental Retardation and Developmental Disabilities, 33,* 248–263.

Hagner, D., & Davies, T. (2002). "Doing my own thing": Supported self-employment for individuals with cognitive disabilities. *Journal of Vocational Rehabilitation, 17,* 65–74.

Hagner, D., & Dileo, D. (1993). *Working together: Workplace culture, supported employment, and persons with disabilities.* Cambridge, MA: Brookline Books.

Hamre-Nietupski, S., Dander, D. J., Houselog, M., & Anderson, R. J. (1988). Proactive administrative strategies for implementing community-based programs for students with moderate/severe handicaps. *Education and Training in Mental Retardation, 23,* 138–146.

Harry, B., Allen, N., & McLaughlin, M. (1995). Communication versus compliance: African-American parents' involvement in special education. *Exceptional Children, 61,* 364–377.

Hasazi, S., Gordon, L., & Roe, C. (1985). Factors associated with the employment status of handicapped youth exiting high school from 1979–1983. *Exceptional Children, 51,* 455–469.

Hasazi, S., Gordon, L., Roe, C., Hull, M., Finck, K., & Salembier, G. (1985). A statewide follow-up on post high school employment and residential status of students labeled mentally retarded. *Education and Training of the Mentally Retarded, 20,* 222–234.

Helms, B., Moore, S., & McSweyn, C. A. (1991). Supported employment in Connecticut: An examination of integration and wage outcome. *Career Development for Exceptional Individuals, 14,* 159–166.

Kohler, P. D. (1993). Best practices in transition: Substantiated or implied. *Career Development for Exceptional Individuals, 16,* 107–121.

Kohler, P. D. (1998). Implementing a transition perspective of education: A comprehensive approach to planning and delivering secondary education and transition services. In F. R. Rusch & J. G. Chadsey (Eds.), *Beyond high school: Transition from school to work* (pp. 159–205). Belmont, CA: Wadsworth.

Kraemer, B. R., & Blacher, J. (2001). Transition for young adults with mental retardation: School preparation, parent expectations, and family involvement. *Mental Retardation, 39,* 423–435.

Levy, J., Jessop, D., Rimmerman, A., & Levy, P. (1992). Attitudes of Fortune 500 corporate executives toward the employability of persons with severe disabilities: A national study. *Mental Retardation, 30,* 67–75.

Love, L. (1994). *Applying the FSLA when placing students into community-based vocational education.* Phoenix: Arizona Department of Education.

Ludlow, B., Turnbull, A., & Luckasson, R. (1988). *Transitions to adult life for people with mental retardation: Principles and practices.* Baltimore: Brookes.

Luecking, R., & Fabian, E. S. (2000). Paid internships and employment success for youth in transition. *Career Development for Exceptional Individuals, 23,* 205–221.

Martella, R. C., & Marchand-Martella, N. E. (1995). Safety skills in vocational rehabilitation: A qualitative analysis. *Journal of Vocational Rehabilitation, 5,* 31–435.

McDonnell, J., Hardman, M. L., Hightower, J., Keifer-O'Donnell, R., & Drew, C. (1993). Impact of community-based instruction on the development of adaptive behavior of secondary level students with mental retardation. *American Journal of Mental Retardation, 97,* 575–584.

McDonnell, J., Wilcox, B., & Hardman, M. L. (1991). *Secondary programs for students with developmental disabilities.* Boston: Allyn & Bacon.

McNair, J. (1991). *Co-worker involvement in employment programs for persons with mental retardation.* San Bernardino, CA: California State University.

Miller, R. J., Lombard, R. C., & Hazelkorn, M. N. (2000). Teacher attitudes and practices regarding the inclusion of students with disabilities in school-to-work and technical preparation programs: Strategies for inclusion and policy implications. In D. R. Johnson & E. J. Emanuel (Eds.), *Issues influencing the future of transition programs and services in the United States.* Minneapolis: University of Minnesota National Transition Network.

Morningstar, M. E., Turnbull, A. P., & Turnbull, H. R. (1995). What do students with disabilities tell us about the importance of family involvement in the transition from school to adult life? *Exceptional Children, 62,* 249–260.

Moon, S., Inge, K., Wehman, P., Brooke, V., & Barcus, M. (1990). *Helping persons with severe mental retardation get and keep employment.* Baltimore: Brookes.

Morgan, R. L., Ellerd, D. A., Jensen, K., & Taylor, M. J. (2000). Survey of community employment placements. *Career Development for Exceptional Individuals, 23,* 73–86.

National Center for Health Statistics. (1994–1995). *National Health Interview Survey on Disability.* Hyattsville, MD: U.S. Department of Health and Human Services, Centers for Disease Control and Prevention.

National Organization on Disability. (2004). *Louis Harris survey of Americans with disabilities.* Washington, DC: Author.

National Transition Network. (2000). *Supplemental security income: So you have decided to apply* (Parent Brief). Minneapolis: University of Minnesota, Institute on Community Integration.

Nietupski, J., Hamre-Nietupski, S., Vanderhort, N. S., & Fishback, K. (1996). Employer perceptions of the benefits and concerns of supported employment. *Education and Training in Mental Retardation and Development Disabilities, 31,* 310–323.

Pane, R. (1992). *Handbook for developing community-based employment.* Tuscon, AZ: RPM Press.

Pelland, M., & Falvey, M. A. (1986). Domestic skills. In M. A. Falvey (Ed.), *Community-based curriculum: Instructional strategies for students with severe handicaps.* Baltimore: Brookes.

Penick, N., & Jepsen, D. (1992). Family functioning and adolescent career development. *The Career Development Quarterly, 49,* 208–222.

Positive Influence. (1999). *Business survey on supported employment in North Carolina.* Raleigh: North Carolina Developmental Disabilities Council.

Primer: Using work incentives for social security recipients and beneficiaries, (2004, July/August). *InfoLines, 15*(6), 4–5.

Pumpian, I., Fisher, D., Certo, N. J., Engel, T., & Mautz, D. (1998). To pay or not to pay: Differentiating employment and training relationships through regulation and litigation. *Career Development for Exceptional Individuals, 21,* 187–202.

Rizzo, D. (2002). With a little help from my friends: Supported self-employment for people with severe disabilities. *Journal of Vocational Rehabilitation, 17,* 97–105.

Sample, P. L. (1998). Postschool outcomes for students with significant emotional disturbance following best practice transition services. *Behavioral Disorders, 23,* 231–242.

Scherer, M. J., & Galvin, J. C. (1996). An outcomes perspective of quality pathways to the most appropriate technology. In J. C. Galvin & M. J. Scherer (Eds.), *Evaluating, selecting, and using appropriate assistive technology* (pp. 1–26). Gaithersburg, MD: Aspen.

Sitlington, P. L. (1996). Transition to living: The neglected component of transition programming for individuals with learning disabilities. *Journal of Learning Disabilities, 29,* 31–41.

Snell, M. E. (1987). *Systematic instruction of the moderately to severely handicapped* (3rd ed.). Upper Saddle River, NJ: Merrill/Prentice Hall.

Sowers, J. A., & Powers, L. (1991). *Vocational preparation and employment of students with physical and multiple disabilities.* Baltimore: Brookes.

The Study Group, Inc. (1998). *Meeting the needs of youth with disabilities: Handbook on supplemental security income work incentives and transition students.* Minneapolis: University of Minnesota, National Transition Network, Institute on Community Integration.

Technical Assistance on Transition and the Rehabilitation Act (TATRA) Project. (1996). Family network is important in job success of people with disabilities. *Point of Departure, 2*(2), 5.

Test, D., & Spooner, F. (1996). *Innovations: Community-based instructional support.* Washington, DC: American Association on Mental Retardation.

Tilson, G. P., & Neubert, D. A. (1989). School-to-work transition of mildly disabled young adults: Parental perceptions of vocational needs. *The Journal of Vocational Rehabilitation, 11,* 33–37.

U.S. Department of Education and U.S. Chamber of Commerce. (2003). *Disability employment 101: Learn to tap your "hire" potential.* Washington, DC: Author.

U.S. Department of Labor and U.S. Department of Education. (1992). *Agreement regarding community-based vocational training programs for students with disabilities and the FLSA.* Washington, DC: U.S. Government Printing Office.

Wehman, P., Wood, W., Everson, J., Goodwyn, R., & Conley, S. (1988). *Vocational education for multi-handicapped youth with cerebral palsy.* Baltimore: Brookes.

Preparing Students for Community Living Opportunities

Chapter 9

Introduction

Why is the spectrum of community living options still limited for so many teenagers and young adults with disabilities? There are numerous reasons. However, living opportunities are impacted more by limited professional knowledge, diminished professional expectations, prevailing service delivery models, uncertain community attitudes, and the limited financial resources of this largely unemployed group of people than they are by disability characteristics (Klein & Nelson, 2000; Racino, Walker, O'Connor, & Taylor, 1993; Wilson & Everson, 2000).

To improve community living outcomes for these young adults, planning and instruction for community living outcomes must be infused into all aspects of the taxonomy for transition planning (Kohler, 1996). Educators and other individualized education program (IEP) team members charged with developing and overseeing transition goals and activities play an important role in preparing students for community living. They must help students acquire knowledge about community housing options and develop the skills and experiences to make informed, appropriate housing decisions that best meet their wants and needs.

Limited self-determination abilities and access to community living opportunities also are closely linked. Studies indicate that young adults must be able to "leave home" physically and emotionally to complete the transition process from adolescence to adulthood (Graber & Dubas, 1996). Leaving home is the culmination of self-determination knowledge, skills, and opportunities. To improve community living outcomes, self-determination instruction and opportunities must also be infused into transition planning activities.

This chapter was authored with the assistance of Ms. Nancy Robertson, Project Director and Associate Professor with the Human Development Center, Louisiana State University Health Sciences Center, New Orleans.

This chapter provides educators and families with the information and resources they need to open the full spectrum of community living opportunities to young adults with disabilities. The chapter examines issues critical to preparing students to live more independently. It begins with a brief overview of the living options and services historically available to adults with disabilities and continues with a description of emerging supported living models and services. The next section provides an overview of community living resources potentially available to transition-age young adults and their families. The chapter also examines the competencies needed by education professionals to teach transition-age students how to make choices and live successfully in the community. It concludes with a section summarizing teaching methods and activities for educators to consider in developing students' self-determination abilities and community living competencies. Throughout, the chapter provides case studies illustrating individuals with disabilities who transitioned from their family's homes into a variety of community living options.

Key Terms

affordable housing
asset building
centers for independent living (CILs)
community participation
community presence
independent living movement
individual development accounts (IDAs)
intermediate care facilities for the mentally retarded (ICF-MRs)
Medicaid home and community-based waivers
normalization
Olmstead decision
supported living

A Personal Perspective on Community Housing

from a Community Lending Representative

Sharon Mee

Vice-President, Community Lending, Whitney National Bank

When the bank was first approached about developing a loan product that would assist persons with disabilities in becoming homeowners, I was a little hesitant. "How could someone with a cognitive disability be a successful homeowner?" several bank employees and I asked. However, with an open mind and some trepidation, the bank decided to proceed. Now, almost 8 years later, we have provided mortgages to more than 60 individuals with disabilities to become homeowners.

What we learned during the process is that the barriers these individuals faced were related to low incomes and a lack of adequate personal supports. The low-income barriers were overcome by relaxing underwriting criteria and partnering with other programs to provide financial assistance for the required down payment and closing costs. The individuals who become successful homeowners had a strong circle of support of people (e.g., family members, friends, employers) who worked closely with the individual and bank staff to navigate the homeownership process.

Some individuals were able to overcome the barriers to homeownership in as little as 9 months; for others, it took as long as 3 years. To date we have had no individuals default on their mortgages. Each year, my loan officers receive an increasing number of applications from persons who identify themselves as having a disability, and I am happy to say that each loan officer is now comfortable with assisting them and their support teams through the process.

To become a homeowner, the most important skill a person can acquire in high school is budgeting and managing credit. The road to becoming a homeowner was the longest for those individuals who had gotten themselves into credit problems.

Section 8 Home Choice Voucher Administrator

The Section 8 Home Choice Voucher program was designed to provide rental assistance to persons with low incomes, including those with disabilities. In fact, Section 504 of the Rehabilitation Act requires public housing authorities (PHAs) to make reasonable accommodations and modifications to ensure that individuals with disabilities can benefit from the program. In addition, the United States Department of Housing and Urban Development provides funding for Mainstream Vouchers that are designated for use only by persons with disabilities. Unfortunately, the need for the vouchers often exceeds their availability, and many PHAs have long waiting lists. That is why it is important for students with disabilities to consider possible needs for vouchers in advance and put their names on the waiting list.

The process for obtaining a voucher at times can be complex and cumbersome. Understanding the process and how to complete the necessary paperwork will help make the experience less difficult. The recent change by the Department of Housing and Urban Development to allow Section 8 voucher holders to use the voucher for homeownership has opened up an opportunity that previously had been denied to many people. Over the past year my program has assisted five Section 8 voucher holders with disabilities to become homeowners. It is a great feeling when one of my long-term Section 8 renters is able to become a homeowner.

Moving away from home for the first time is a milestone looked forward to with great anticipation by most teenagers and young adults (Chang, 1992; Fedman & Elliott, 1990). Parents, too, look forward to this milestone, often with fear as well as anticipation (Kastner & Wyatt, 1997). For some teenagers and young adults, reaching this milestone means moving into a college dormitory or into a rented apartment or home. For some, it means purchasing a home or a condominium of their own. For others, it means moving into a supervised living option such as a group home or apartment program or participating in an education and training program such as a center for independent living. Whatever the option chosen, these teenagers and young adults face new opportunities to exercise their self-determination abilities, as well as new challenges in developing community living skills and receiving personal assistance and other community support services.

Until recently, the full spectrum of community living options open to most Americans was severely limited for those with disabilities (O'Hara & Miller, 2000). However, as more Americans with disabilities enter the workforce and exercise their self-determination abilities, and as more educators learn about locally available options, the spectrum is beginning to open up for those with disabilities. As a result, in some parts of the United States participation in independent living centers (DeJong, 1979), access to personal assistance services (Dautel & Frieden, 1999), access to supported living services (Racino et al., 1993), and even homeownership options (Klein & Nelson, 2000) have become attainable transition goals for many young adults with disabilities.

Nevertheless, nationally, adults with disabilities still are more likely than their nondisabled peers to live with parents or other family members (Braddock, Hemp, Parish, & Westrich, 1998). They are more likely to live in homes with several other nonrelated people (Braddock et al., 1998). They are more likely to live in homes that are owned by, or even rented in the name of, someone else (McNeil, 1997). They are more likely to live in substandard housing (O'Hara & Miller, 2001). They are more likely to dedicate a greater percentage of their monthly income to housing costs (O'Hara & Miller, 2001). Given these findings, it should not be surprising that many adults with disabilities are dissatisfied with their current living opportunities and with the self-determination opportunities provided by these arrangements (Duvdevany, Ben-Zur, & Ambar, 2002; United States Department of Health and Human Services, 1990).

HISTORY OF HOUSING AND DISABILITIES

The history of living options and services for Americans with disabilities is largely a story of segregation, isolation, and, far too often, abuse and neglect. It is a story about programs, placements, and policies—not about people and their preferences.

The Charity and Benign Neglect Period

Until the mid-20th century, most individuals with disabilities and their families were offered limited housing and support services from their communities and local social service agencies. Many individuals with disabilities lived their entire lives with their parents or with other relatives in their communities. Those who were considered able to do so might live alone in their communities with informal supports provided by family, neighbors, and faith-based organizations. The vast majority of parents who gave birth to children with severe developmental or multiple disabilities were advised to institutionalize their children shortly after birth in state-run facilities and to forget about them. At the peak of the institutionalization period in the United States, more than 200,000 people lived in state-run facilities (Meyer, Peck, & Brown, 1991).

The Institutional Reform Period

Beginning in the 1960s, media attention began to focus on the often horrific living conditions in these facilities (e.g., Blatt & Kaplan, 1966). In response, the first President's Panel on Mental Retardation (1962) articulated the need for a comprehensive national approach to addressing the educational, residential, medical, professional development, and research-based needs of Americans with disabilities. The concept of "normalization," first articulated by Wolfensberger (1972) became the cornerstone of a progressive effort to reform these facilities, and professionals, parents, and policymakers largely shaped the movement. **Normalization** is a framework for professionals and policymakers to use when planning, implementing, and evaluating high-quality services and environments for individuals with disabilities. Normalization defines appropriate environments and services as those that make patterns and activities of everyday life available for people with disabilities as close as possible to those that are available to those of same-age peers without disabilities.

The reform movement led to developing better medical and educational services in these facilities, as well as to establishing smaller residential facilities known as **intermediate care facilities for the mentally retarded (ICF-MRs).** These are highly regulated residential facilities that require provision of a highly structured teaching and support plan known as active treatment. The supplemental security income (SSI) program and the Medicaid health care programs were also established during this time period to support ICF-MRs and other residential reforms. Gradually, the preferred housing model, especially for those with developmental disabilities, changed from large institutions to smaller ICF-MRs of between 3 and 16 residents. National chains of for-profit organizations began to contract with social service agencies in many states to operate these ICF-MR options.

The Independent Living Movement

The premise of the earlier period was reform. But even as these reforms began to reshape residential services, new voices—those of people with disabilities—began to be heard. The **independent living movement** may be defined as a grassroots, consumer-driven approach to building the self-determination abilities of individuals with disabilities around access to and control of community housing, education, employment, and other resources. The independent living movement was led by Americans with disabilities. It grew out of the Kennedy-era commitment to disability issues and the driving principles of the African-American civil rights movement. Initially, the independent living movement was limited to a small group of students, primarily those with physical disabilities, on the campus of the University of California in Berkeley. Their goal was to challenge the university to makes its programs and facilities accessible to students with physical disabilities. Ultimately, the movement spread to other college campuses, to services and facilities other than postsecondary education, and to other disability self-advocacy groups.

By the late 1970s, the independent living movement was fully articulated both as a civil rights movement led by self-advocates and as an alternative to the institutional and medical housing model (DeJong, 1979). The movement was strengthened by the Rehabilitation Act of 1973, which established and funded a national network of **centers for independent living (CILs),** consumer-controlled, nonresidential organizations operated as nonprofits. They provide cross-disability services to individuals, such as personal assistance services, peer counseling, mobility, rehabilitation technology, supported living, and transportation. By the opening of the 21st century, the independent living movement had resulted in fundamental shifts in thinking about people with disabilities managing and controlling their services and supports along with fundamental shifts in funding and policies for Medicaid services.

The Supported Living Movement

Today, much has changed in residential services and supports for Americans with disabilities. Although large, state-run institutions do still exist in a few states and far too many individuals still live in nursing facilities, the vast majority of Americans with disabilities now live in the community (Lakin, Hill, White, & Write, 1988). They may live in group homes (including small ICF-MRs) with several other individuals with similar disabilities. They may live in homes with unrelated adults who provide foster care. These homes may be typical single-family dwellings in communities or specially built and designed homes with multiple accessibility features. Individuals with disabilities may live in apartments, either alone or with others who have disabilities. Like group homes, these apartments might be units in typical community complexes or specially designed and built complexes of apartments for people with disabilities.

Most adults with disabilities live in group homes, ICF-MRs, and nursing facilities that are owned and operated by public or private disability service organizations or in homes or apartments that are owned or leased not in the renter's name, but in the disability service organization's name. All too often, the same agency or organization that provides residents with services and supports also owns the homes. As a result, homes often become transitional places for residents. They may move from home to home, through a continuum of support services according to their disability label, behavioral characteristics, or medical needs. They may also be terminated from the program and thus forced out of their homes if they do not conform to the program's skill or behavioral requirements.

In many communities, adults with disabilities and their families are still encouraged to choose community living options based on disability labels and support needs. As a result, adults with the most severe and low-incidence disabilities are more likely to reside in group homes than in apartments leased in their own names or in homes that they own.

The problems inherent in this intermarriage of housing ownership and support provision (Racino et al., 1993) led to the current residential service paradigm, the supported living movement. **Supported living** is defined as a movement to provide individuals with disabilities access to community housing options that are (a) typical residences that might be considered homes by adults without disabilities, (b) not owned by the same agency that provides support services to residents of the home, and (c) chosen by the resident with a disability and shared with other people at the person's discretion.

Recipients of supported living services may lease or own homes or apartments in their own names, or the homes may be leased or owned by parents, other family members, or housing organizations or trusts. If residents need support services, a separate municipal or for-profit organization provides them with Medicaid-funded support services.

For example, Rodney, a high school student with autism and behavioral support needs, and his family chose a supported apartment program as a transition planning outcome. His team agreed that he would benefit from having his own one-bedroom apartment in a complex with a swimming pool and a health club. They also agreed that Rodney would benefit from activities during his final 2 years of high school that would develop his personal care, housekeeping, and laundry skills and that he would need one-on-one support for the foreseeable future to enable him to use the swimming pool and health club with other apartment complex residents.

Supported living plans ensure the provision of traditional Medicaid-funded support services such as skill training and medical service: They also provide supports to connect the person to his or her community using community, civic, family, and faith-based environments and activities.

In supported living, if an individual needs new or different support services, instead of moving to a different home, the person remains in his or her home and the supports change to meet the individual's needs and preferences. Thus, in Rodney's example, after he moves into his apartment his team might agree that the apartment's features remain a good fit for his needs, but that he needs additional behavioral supports to redirect his vocalizations and body movements when he is in public. Rodney would receive these supports instead of moving into a group home for residents with behavioral disability labels.

Supported living opportunities have grown tremendously over the past two decades (Racino et al., 1993). Unfortunately, far too few adults with disabilities know about these options and thus continue to live at home with their families or on their own without supports. Other adults remain on waiting lists as their municipalities struggle to fund the burgeoning need for affordable housing and the skyrocketing costs of Medicaid services. Still other adults, especially those with less severe disabilities and without the need for extensive Medicaid-funded support services, find themselves unable to find affordable housing because of their low incomes and poor employment prospects.

HOUSING CHALLENGES FOR THE NEW MILLENNIUM

Three challenges face educators, adults with disabilities, and their families today. The first is to obtain affordable housing and community presence for those who wish to live in the community. The second is to build assets and to ensure community participation for those who are living in the community. The final challenge is to provide comprehensive and flexible support services, delivered in community housing options, to the people who need them. This final challenge includes individuals with the most severe and intensive support needs—those who may need 24/7 medical, behavioral, and skill supports—as well as those with less intensive support needs who may need daily, weekly, or even monthly assistance with medical appointments and treatments, financial planning, transportation, personal care, and housekeeping supports.

Affordable Housing

Affordable housing in the United States began with the passage of the Housing Act of 1937. This legislation created the first federal framework for affordable housing by establishing and funding public housing authorities. In 1974, the act was amended to include Section 8 subsidies to landlord owners of private housing to promote rental opportunities for low-income individuals and families. The Housing and Community Development Act of 1992 amended Section 8 to extend homeownership opportunities for individuals and families with low incomes. Today, nearly every state has a vast network of state and local housing authorities that build, own, and operate affordable housing for individuals with low incomes.

More recently, Fannie Mae[1] chartered by the U.S. government to make housing more affordable and now the nation's leading mortgage lender, developed HomeChoice, a mortgage product designed to enhance both rental and home ownership opportunities for individuals with disabilities and for families who have a child with a disability. The HomeChoice initiative is available in several states. More information on this product can be obtained from Fannie Mae.

---

[1]For more information on Fannie Mae's HomeChoice as well as other Fannie Mae programs, visit http://www.efanniemae.com/hcd/single_family/mortgage_products/comm_homechoice.html

> ## DID YOU KNOW?
>
> According to The United States Census Bureau (2001):
>
> ◆ The median monthly mortgage for American homeowners is $669.
>
> ◆ 27,629,000 homeowners spend less than $499 in total monthly housing costs (i.e., mortgage plus maintenance).
>
> ◆ 9,579,000 homeowners report an annual income of $14,999 or less.
>
> ◆ 1,894,000 homeowners receive SSI or other forms of public assistance.
>
> ◆ 9,012,000 owner-occupied homes are valued at less than $49,999.
>
> ◆ 26,079,000 owner-occupied homes are valued between $50,000 and $99,999.

Community Presence

Community presence is a concept promoted by O'Brien (1987) and his colleagues to support opportunities for individuals with disabilities to live, work, recreate, be educated, and in other ways be present in typical communities of their choosing. Proponents suggest that people must be physically present in typical community settings, programs, and environments before other quality-of-life issues can be addressed. Thus, community presence is a prerequisite to supporting additional desired opportunities such as community participation. Community presence is an important value inherent in the supported living movement because it seeks opportunities for people to live in typical homes in typical communities.

In 1999, the U.S. Supreme Court rendered an historic decision with implications for community presence and housing. The **Olmstead decision** addressed the case of two women from Georgia who resided in state institutions. The women were obligated to remain living in the state institutions, even though human service professionals and advocates all agreed that they could live in the community, because no programs or funding were available to support their needs. In its decision, the Court ruled that states are required to provide community-based treatment when the state's treatment professionals determine that such a placement is appropriate. To fully support the Olmstead decision's intent, the federal government has encouraged states to develop reform plans to fully integrate people with disabilities into the least restrictive setting (Fox-Grage, Folkemer, & Lewis, 2003).

Asset Building

In 1996, President Clinton signed into law the Personal Responsibility and Work Opportunities Act. In 1998, he signed the Assets for Independence Act (AFIA). These two pieces of legislation introduced and expanded a concept known as

individual development accounts (IDAs)[2]. IDAs are essentially dedicated savings accounts that may be used by individuals with low incomes for **asset building**—saving money to purchase a first home, pay for postsecondary education or job training, or establish a business. Local communities can establish IDA funders who match the IDA savings of participants. More recently, the Social Security Protection Act of 2003 removed many of the social security savings barriers that had previously excluded many individuals with disabilities from participating in this program.

IDAs offer individuals with disabilities a wonderful but too often underutilized resource for saving money for housing down payment and closing costs (Klein, 2000). For example, as a high school student, Keisha expressed interest in becoming a homeowner after she completed high school and secured a job. While she was still in high school, Keisha's transition plan included community living goals and activities about personal budgeting, managing credit, home care and maintenance skills, and advantages and disadvantages of home ownership. As a result, 1 year after leaving high school, Keisha was able to establish an IDA by contributing $100 a month from her paycheck, which was matched by $100 a month from a local nonprofit organization that managed IDAs in Keisha's community. After 12 months, Keisha had saved $1,200 of her own income and had received an additional $1,200 in matching funds to begin exploring home ownership options.

Community Participation

Community participation (O'Brien, 1987) is a complex construct that promotes full and equal inclusion of people with disabilities in all aspects of typical living, working, recreation, education, and other community programs and services. Similar to community presence, community participation is an important value in the supported living movement because it seeks opportunities for people with disabilities to participate in typical settings, routines, and situations with typical peers. When people live in supported living settings, service providers face daily challenges in ensuring that those who are physically present in their communities are not isolated from their communities. Person-centered planning offers many tools for encouraging community participation. For example, circles of support (Mount & Zwernik, 1988; O'Brien & O'Brien, 2002) are frequently used to identify key people in an individual's life and then use these people to strengthen the individual's connections to the community.

Comprehensive and Flexible Supported Living Services

The supported living model requires comprehensive, flexible, and individualized support services. For many individuals with disabilities, especially those with severe developmental or multiple disabilities, these services will be necessary re-

---

[2]For more information on how IDAs may affect eligibility for federal programs, visit http://www.cbpp.org

gardless of the option chosen. Supported living services are generally funded using **Medicaid home and community-based waivers.** These waivers enable people to live in community living options and still receive services and supports.

Case managers or service coordinators from the adult services agency responsible for providing Medicaid waiver services and other disability services typically coordinate and provide supported living services. These personnel are typically employed by a local public disability agency or by a private agency with which a state or local agency brokers services. Increasingly, but still too rarely, people with disabilities or their families control the funds for these services and use these funds to purchase or broker services from the people and agencies of their choice (Blumberg & Ferguson, 2000).

No matter who provides them or how they are funded, high-quality supported living services must be comprehensive. They must include both skill training and the supports necessary to enable individuals to be present, participative, competent, and satisfied in their homes and communities.

Comprehensive supported living services should, as needed, provide services in the following areas:

- ◆ Budgeting and managing finances.
- ◆ Homemaking activities.
- ◆ Home maintenance and repairs.
- ◆ Self-care activities.
- ◆ Communication and social skills.
- ◆ Health, safety, and medical issues, including personal assistance services.
- ◆ Use of community resources.
- ◆ Community travel and mobility.
- ◆ Leisure activities.

Educators who use the methods and activities suggested later in this chapter to assess students' skills and preferences and provide skill training will enhance the likelihood that young adults will attain community living outcomes that are most appropriate to their needs and preferences.

High-quality supported living services must also be flexible and individualized. This means that funding mechanisms and policy and procedural guidelines, which originally were intended for ICF-MRs and large congregate group care facilities, must be reconceptualized to support separation of housing services and support services. They must enable individuals and their families to request, design, and receive the supports they need to live in homes of their choosing, homes that are typical of those in which people without disabilities reside. The relatively recent development of Medicaid waivers has been a positive move toward making supported living services more flexible and individualized. Likewise, the 1999 U.S. Supreme Court Olmstead decision has increased the visibility of supported living services.

Nevertheless, much work remains to be done. In many states, large numbers of individuals with disabilities remain on lengthy waiting lists for waivers. Many others require and wait for assistive and therapeutic equipment, attendant care or personal assistance services, transportation services, and/or home modification supports.

COMMUNITY HOUSING RESOURCES

The continually evolving supported living model requires educators and other transition planning team members to begin addressing housing and community living as part of comprehensive high school transition planning. The next section of this chapter provides educators with the information and resources they need to prepare transition-age students with disabilities and their families for choosing and designing the living options of their choice. Using the supported living model's criterion of separating housing and supports as a framework, this section of the chapter provides an overview of resources potentially available to transition-age young adults and their families.

Individuals with disabilities face several obstacles in their quest for community living options. The three most pressing are (a) a lack of affordable housing in safe, preferred communities; (b) physical inaccessibility of affordable homes; and (c) the need for provision of comprehensive and flexible support services within the home. Of these, the primary obstacle, and the one least addressed by education and rehabilitation professionals, is affordability (O'Hara & Miller, 2000, 2001).

Housing affordability is inextricably linked with the poor employment outcomes faced by so many Americans with disabilities. No income or low income, lack of credit or poor credit, lack of money for security deposits on rental units and utility deposits, lack of money for renovations and modifications, and lack of money for down payment and closing costs all limit housing options available to adults with disabilities. In many instances, however, these obstacles can be significantly reduced when education and other transition planning professionals partner with community housing professionals. Thus, young adults with disabilities, their families, and the professionals who help them plan for their transition from high school all need to be aware of these potential resources. Even young adults who lack the cognitive abilities to assume total independence in managing their finances and navigating their way through the rental and home ownership systems, can benefit from these options when their IEP team prepares all team members with the knowledge and skills to support young adults in accessing these options.

The amount and type, as well as availability of, affordable housing resources varies tremendously according to a community's demographics and commitment to affordable housing. Tables 9.1 and 9.2 summarize the potential rental and homeownership resources, along with suggested resources for learning more about the specific resources available in your community.

Rental Assistance Programs

As summarized in Table 9.1, federal and local rental assistance programs usually provide an individual or a household with a financial subsidy to reduce monthly

DID YOU KNOW?

Nearly every municipality in the United States has a vast array of affordable housing resources available to citizens with low incomes. These resources may be categorized as one of two types: rental subsidies and homeownership subsidies and incentives. These resources can make supported living realistic transition outcomes for young adults, even in some of the nation's most expensive municipalities.

Table 9.1
Potential Community Housing Rental Resources

Rental Resource	Type of Assistance	Suggested Resources
Section 8 Housing Choice voucher program	• Tenant based	• Local Public Housing Authority • State housing agency • Local housing agency • U.S. Department of Housing and Urban Development (HUD)
HOME Investments Partnerships Program (HOME) rental assistance	• Tenant based	• State or local Department of Community Affairs • State or local Department of Community Development • State or local Housing Finance Agency • State or local Department of Economic Development
Bridge rent subsidy program	• Tenant based	• Local Public Housing Authority • State or local housing agency
Section 8 housing	• Project based	• Local Public Housing Authority
Section 811 Supportive Housing for Persons with Disabilities Program	• Sponsor based	• HUD • State Department of Health
Section 521 Rural Rental Assistance Program	• Project based	• Housing Assistance Council • U.S. Department of Agriculture (USDA) • Local Rural Development Office
Low-income housing tax credit units	• Project based	• HUD • State housing agency

housing expenses. The amount of subsidy provided is based on the number of people in the household, monthly income, and the cost of rental housing in the community. Rental assistance is provided in one of three ways: tenant-based, project-based, or sponsor-based.

Tenant-based subsidies are attached to an individual or a household. That is, the individual or household receives the subsidy and applies it to the rent for an approved housing unit. The option allows tenants to choose a home from a variety of eligible units that meet their unique needs. An important feature is that, because tenant-based subsidies are attached to people, tenants may take their subsidy with them if they choose to move, as long as they move to an approved unit.

Project-based subsidies are attached to a specific unit that is owned by a local public housing authority. As long as individuals or households live in an approved unit, they receive a financial subsidy toward the monthly rent. If they move to another unit that is not an approved project-based unit, they lose the subsidy.

Sponsor-based subsidies are attached to programs that provide housing assistance to target populations. For example, many programs that provide housing to persons who are homeless use sponsor-based subsidies. Programs using this option lease units from private landlords and then sublet the units to eligible tenants. Tenants pay a reduced monthly rental rate based on their income, and the sponsoring program pays the remaining costs.

Advantages and Disadvantages of Renting. Many public and private providers of housing services for individuals with disabilities already take advantage of these resources for recipients of supported living services. For example, they may secure a number of rent-subsidized apartments in a typical apartment complex and lease the apartments in the name of the agency on behalf of the resident with a disability. Or the agency may lease typical single-family homes, townhomes, condominiums, or duplexes. In these instances, the agency typically pays the rental unit deposit and utility deposits, again in the name of the agency. The agency chooses residents from its client pool to live in the housing. Typically, two or three individuals are selected to share each housing option. Residents are usually chosen by the agency, according to disability characteristics, support needs, and their position on a waiting list. The agency also provides the residents with support services, either from a live-in person who shares the home with them or from a person who lives elsewhere but provides regular daily or less frequent support services to the residents in their homes and in the community.

Many individuals with disabilities and their families choose this supported living model. It has several advantages. First, the option allows individuals with disabilities to move into typical community housing options without incurring move-in costs (i.e., rental unit security deposits, utility security deposits). Second, because the homes have been certified as Section 8 units and because the residents have documented low incomes, this option allows renters to pay significantly lower monthly rents than they would if they attempted to rent from the apartment complex, owner, or real estate company. Finally, the option provides a package deal—a place to live along with support services.

This model also has several disadvantages that should be considered by individuals with disabilities and their families. First, in most instances, individuals do not get to choose where they live or with whom. Instead, choices are dictated by the availability of housing units, clustering of residents' support needs to ease staff assignments, and residents' positions on waiting lists. Second, because leases and deposits are in the agency's name, the agency—not the resident—builds a credit history. Lack of a credit history will become a concern if the resident desires to purchase a home later on.

Finally, as noted earlier, when leases and services are provided by one agency, residents are more vulnerable to losing both their homes and their supports if medical, behavioral, accessibility, or staffing issues arise. This concern can be alleviated when housing is provided by one agency and support services are provided by another agency. In this scenario, if the home becomes inaccessible to a resident because of the resident's aging or declining mobility, he may move to another home, with the help of the housing agency, but would keep the same support staff and services with the help of the second agency. Or if a resident is comfortable and satisfied in her home but is dissatisfied with the quality of support services provided, she might remain in her home but change service providers. For an example, see Deidre's case study at the end of this chapter.

Home Ownership Assistance Programs

For individuals—including those with disabilities—to become homeowners, they must be able to save money and budget for two types of expenses: (a) upfront expenses, which include the costs of purchasing a home, and (b) ongoing expenses, which include the costs of paying a mortgage and maintaining and repairing a home. As illustrated in Table 9.2, federal and local home ownership assistance programs can provide a variety of assistance to potential homeowners. Typically, these programs provide one or more of the following options: (a) assistance with down payment expenses; (b) low-interest rate mortgages; (c) assistance with closing costs; (d) forgivable loans; or (e) assistance with renovations, accommodations, and maintenance.

Advantages and Disadvantages of Home Ownership. The largest growth in homeowners over the next decade is predicted to be from culturally and linguistically diverse groups and from those with low incomes (Homeownership Alliance, February 12, 2002). Although opportunities have expanded tremendously over the past decade, home ownership still remains an elusive dream for most Americans with disabilities (Klein & Nelson, 2000). In a national report prepared for the Washington, DC, based Homeownership Alliance, economist and author Todd Buchholz indicated that 68% of Americans own their own homes (Homeownership Alliance, February 12, 2002). However, this percentage is in sharp contrast to the estimate that less than 5% of Americans with disabilities own their own homes (Technical Assistance Collaborative, Inc. & Consortium for Citizens with Disabilities Task Force, 2000). Thus, it is probable that today's transition-age students with disabilities will become a part of this predicted

Table 9.2
Potential Community Housing Ownership Resources

Home Ownership Resources	Type of Assistance	Suggested Resources
HOME Investments Partnerships Program (HOME)	• Down payment assistance • Low interest rates for mortgages	• State or local Department of Community Affairs • State or local Department of Community Development • State or local housing finance agency • State or local Department of Economic Development
Community Development Block Grant (CDBG)	• Down payment assistance • Closing costs assistance • Interest rate subsidies • Mortgage principal subsidies	• State or local Department of Community Affairs • State or local Department of Community Development • State or local housing finance agency • State or local Department of Economic Development
Local Banks	• Specialized portfolio mortgage loans	• State or local housing finance agency
Mortgage revenue bonds	• Below-market interest rates for mortgages	• State housing agency
HomeChoice mortgage program	• Single-family mortgage loans specifically for persons with disabilities	• Fannie Mae (Federal National Mortgage Association)
Community development housing organizations (CHDOs)	• Home ownership counseling • Down payment assistance • Closing costs assistance	• State or local Department of Community Affairs • State or local Department of Community Development • State or local housing finance agency • State or local Department of Economic Development
Individual development account (IDA) programs	• Down payment assistance • Closing costs assistance • Maintenance and repairs assistance	• State or local Department of Community Affairs • State or local Department of Community Development • State or local housing finance agency • State or local Department of Economic Development

growth. Increasingly, many individuals with disabilities and their families are choosing home ownership opportunities when this supported living model is made available to them. As is the case with renting, there are both advantages and disadvantages to choosing this model.

First, home ownership provides housing stability. Homeowners with or without disabilities cannot be evicted from homes that they own unless they cannot or do not pay their mortgages. Perhaps because of their frequent history of moving from one home to another, this sense of permanence and stability may be more important to potential homeowners with disabilities than previously has been recognized (Everson & Wilson, 2000). In the Everson and Wilson qualitative study of new homeowners with developmental disabilities, for example, homeowners commented on the sense of control, self-determination, and pride that home ownership provided them as contrasted with renting.

Second, home ownership may provide financial stability and enable homeowners to accumulate equity (Wilson & Everson, 2000). Fixed rate mortgages provide homeowners with relatively fixed monthly housing expenses, whereas rental units generally increase their rental rates annually. Thus, home ownership provides a degree of budget stability and a safety net against inflation and increased housing costs. In addition, historically, home ownership has provided Americans with an opportunity to accumulate equity. Over time, homeowners who make regular monthly mortgage payments build equity in their homes that may be borrowed against or used as leverage to purchase newer, larger, or otherwise more desirable homes[3]. For an example, see Glen's case study at the end of this chapter.

As any homeowner will tell you, there are also disadvantages to home ownership. Not surprisingly, the only dissatisfaction expressed by new homeowners in the Everson and Wilson (2000) study was the responsibility and costs associated with property maintenance and repairs. Homeowners with disabilities and their case managers may require training in preventive maintenance to be responsive to maintenance and repair needs (Robertson & Dufresne, 2000).

One of the advantages of home ownership may also be a disadvantage. That is, while home ownership provides housing stability, it also decreases housing flexibility. When an individual enters into a lease arrangement for an apartment or a home, there is an agreed-upon timeframe—usually between 6 months and a year—during which the tenant is required to maintain the lease. When the lease expires, the individual is free to move to another apartment or home or renew the lease. Although it is not impossible, moving from a home one owns, especially during the initial years of home ownership, can be both costly and time consuming. If an individual enjoys moving frequently or is unsure of where he or she wants to live, purchasing a home may not be the best option.

---

[3]The U.S. Congress has mandated that every state implement a policy for recovery of benefits from individuals, upon their death, who have received Medicaid benefits. This law was enacted to assist in recovering assets of people who are elderly and are spending down their resources in order to qualify for Medicaid benefits. While this legislation does not specifically target homeowners with disabilities, it is important that homeowners who receive Medicaid benefits investigate how their state implements this policy and then engage in careful estate planning with their families and attorneys.

For many individuals with disabilities, especially for those who have low incomes, a final disadvantage to home ownership is the need to save some amount of money before purchasing a home to use for down payment and closing costs. Although some of the resources summarized in Table 9.2 may provide potential homeowners with some assistance, in most cases, homeowners will have to also set aside some money of their own.

TEACHING COMPETENCIES AND METHODS NEEDED BY EDUCATORS TO PREPARE STUDENTS FOR COMMUNITY LIVING OPPORTUNITIES

Supported living is no longer an unrealistic, long-term transition goal for interested students with disabilities or their families. To help young adults achieve this goal, however, educators must be able to infuse student-focused planning, skill development in community housing, and family involvement into all aspects of Kohler's (1996) taxonomy. Educators must become more knowledgeable about community housing options, including interagency collaboration (see Chapter 5). They must be more knowledgeable about employment options (see Chapter 8). They must be willing and able to structure community living information and skills within high school curricula.

Specifically, to teach students to make the best use of community housing opportunities, educators must be competent in (a) assessing students' dreams and preferences; (b) guiding students, their families, and other IEP team members in acquiring knowledge about housing opportunities and financial considerations; (c) helping students develop individualized housing and financial profiles; and (d) teaching independent living skills. The concluding section of this chapter describes some suggested methods and activities that educators and families can use to prepare students for choosing and succeeding in various community housing options.

DID YOU KNOW?

Studies of individualized transition planning indicate that transition teams dedicate few resources to goals and activities associated with community and independent living options (Everson, Zhang, & Guillory, 2001; Grigal, Test, Beattie, & Wood, 1997).

Assessing Students' Housing Dreams and Preferences

Person-centered planning approaches (O'Brien & O'Brien, 2002) offer some useful teaching methods for educators to use to help individuals with disabilities think about their dreams and preferences for housing options. Figure 9.1, for example, provides educators with some examples of probing questions to help adolescents develop housing assessment and planning "maps." Maps are visual and graphic depictions of a person's unique dreams, preferences, and experiences that are developed with support from family and educators. They may consist of drawings, words, photographs, magazine clippings, or other visual depictions of the individual's aspirations. As a housing self-assessment and planning tool, they provide educators with a roadmap, a source of data upon which to plan a student's community living IEP goals.

Adolescents, along with their families, should be encouraged to begin thinking about their dreams and preferences during early adolescence and to continue exploring and refining them as they approach adulthood. By developing maps such as those in Figure 9.1, students and their families can begin thinking about their housing preferences and dreams and explore the relative advantages and disadvantages of renting versus home ownership. They can begin thinking about needs and preferences for support services and about the community living skills and experiences they want to include in their IEPs. As they progress through adolescence, students should be encouraged to refine and update their maps and use them as a tool to accompany their vocational planning, postsecondary education planning, and financial planning.

Educators may guide adolescents by infusing these activities into a number of curricular areas, including language arts and social studies. Once their maps are developed, students should be encouraged to share them during their IEP meetings. These maps can provide students, families, and IEP teams alike with a self-determined guide to independent living goals and plans.

Acquiring Knowledge About Housing Opportunities and Financial Considerations

Encouraging students and their families to think about housing dreams and preferences is just the beginning. Providing them with knowledge about locally available housing opportunities and guiding them in developing financial planning skills is the next step. It is only when they are provided with knowledge about the full spectrum of housing options open to them that they can truly dream and express their preferences. To help them acquire this knowledge, there are a number of methods and activities that educators should consider incorporating within various curricular areas. Figure 9.2 provides some examples of these educational programming activities.

The methods and activities illustrated in Figure 9.2 can be infused into language arts, mathematics, and social studies. They can also be included in high school transition fairs and job fairs. Collectively, they will help students, their families, and educators learn more about affordable housing opportunities and programs.

Students, their families, and IEP teams can and should consider the broad array of housing opportunities available to them in their local communities. This means ensuring that students have exposure to various housing options,

Questions to Think About:

Using Person-Centered Planning to Explore Community Housing Opportunities

DEVELOPING A PLACES MAP

1. Where do you spend most of your time? (For example, where do you work or plan to work? Where do you spend your free time? Where do your family and friends live?)

2. Where would you like to live? Would you like to live in a city, suburb, or in the country? Are you thinking about a specific neighborhood or street?

3. What places would you like to live near? (For example, work, a family member's home, a friend's home, shopping, church, a particular doctor or clinic, a favorite park or restaurant, etc.)

4. How important to you is living in a safe place? What make a place safe to you? (For example, having a deadbolt or alarm, well-lit front door, neighborhood patrols, etc.) What places do you feel are safe?

5. Do you need to live near public transit? If you work, how do you get there? How do you get to church, shopping, restaurants, and the homes of friends and/or family?

DEVELOPING A RELATIONSHIPS MAP

1. Would you consider living with a housemate? If so, do you have a person in mind?

2. Who are the important family members in your life?

3. Who are the important service providers in your life?

4. Are there other important people in your life? (For example, friends, co-workers, church members, etc.)

5. How might these people help you move into and live in your dream home?

Figure 9.1
Questions to Help Adolescents Develop Housing Assessment and Planning Maps.

DEVELOPING A PREFERENCES MAP

1. What features would you like in your home? What features would you not like? (For example, a duplex, a fenced-in yard, one-story, a walk-in closet, an accessible bathroom and kitchen, a front porch, wall-to-wall carpet, a shower stall instead of a bathtub, etc.)

2. What characteristics would you like in a housemate? What characteristics would you not like? (For example, someone your age, a male or female, a non-smoker, someone who is quiet, someone who works with you, someone who can help with yardwork, etc.)

3. What characteristics would you like in a neighborhood? What characteristics would you not like? (For example, sidewalks, big yards, lots of houses on a street, lots of activity and people, near businesses and work, near parks, near public transit, etc.)

DEVELOPING A DREAM MAP

1. Think about all of the questions you have answered so far.
    What would your ideal home look like? Draw a picture or find examples in magazines and real estate sections of the local newspaper.
    Write down a description of the home. Please be as specific as possible.
    (For example, number of rooms, number of bedrooms, one floor or two floors, old or new, brick or frame, town home or condo, garage or carport, carpet or bare floors, accessible entrances, bathrooms, and kitchen, etc.)

2. When would you like to move into your home? (For example, when I finish high school or college, when I have worked for a year or two, when I have saved enough money, when my current lease ends, etc.)

3. What steps do you need to take to make your housing dream a reality? What additional information do you need to have? What additional skills do you need to learn? What can you do now to begin taking action? How can the people in your life support you?

◆ Invite guest speakers from housing authorities, banks and lending institutions, credit counseling companies, housing nonprofit organizations, and real estate companies to speak to students and families during transition and career events.

◆ Invite staff and residents from local supported living organizations to speak to students and families during transition and career events.

◆ Assign students to conduct interviews with professionals from housing authorities, banks and lending institutions, credit counseling companies, housing nonprofit organizations, and real estate companies and to write term papers or make class presentations about their experiences.

◆ Have students interview their families or other adults about the advantages and disadvantages of renting and home ownership.

◆ Have students research local housing opportunities and home ownership and rental data on the Internet by visiting Web sites for state and local housing authorities, municipalities, real estate agencies, and the local Chamber of Commerce.

◆ Have students review the real estate section of the local newspaper and discuss geography, affordability, and availability.

◆ Have students explore volunteer opportunities such as Habitat for Humanity.

◆ Tour a local center for independent living (CIL) or have a self-advocate from a CIL speak to the class about housing and self-determination.

Figure 9.2
Suggested Methods and Activities to Guide Acquisition of Community Housing Knowledge

knowledge about available options so that they may make the choice that best matches their wants and needs, knowledge and skills in financial planning, and knowledge and skills to seek out desired programs and professionals when their wants and needs change.

Developing Individualized Housing and Financial Profiles

As students continue exploring their housing preferences and dreams and acquire more information about housing opportunities and financial considerations, they are ready to create their own unique housing and financial profiles. The self-determination experiences students acquire as they explore housing dreams and preferences provides educators with unique opportunities to infuse additional housing knowledge into language arts, social studies, mathematics, and science classes. Figure 9.3 provides some examples of educational programming activities that educators should consider. The activities suggested in this figure can help students begin to explore the relationship between employment, housing, and financial responsibility.

Teaching Independent Living Skills

Young adults with and without disabilities need certain skills in order to move away from home and live more independently. Many transition-age young adults will continue to live at home for a period of time after leaving high school or will

---

+ Have students look up definitions of housing terms (e.g., *credit report, deed, lease, down payment, equity, escrow, mortgage, foreclosure, title search, private mortgage insurance, purchase agreement, property taxes*). Incorporate the terms in word search games, crossword puzzles, and word math problems.
+ Provide students with case study worksheets describing adults with varying employment and supplemental security income, and have them develop monthly budgets.
+ Provide students with instructions on opening and using checking accounts and savings accounts and establishing credit. Engage students in discussions about the advantages and disadvantages of establishing credit and using credit cards.
+ Develop worksheets and case studies for students to complete that require them to use math skills to determine how much money they could spend on various rental and ownership options. Or give them worksheets with various home sale prices and have them determine monthly mortgage expenses using varying interest rates.
+ Obtain sample HUD settlement statements from mortgage companies and have students identify various down payment and closing expenses.
+ Invite guest speakers from banks and lending institutions, credit counseling companies, housing nonprofit organizations, and real estate companies to discuss financial planning and considerations with students.
+ Invite guest speakers from local hardware and home maintenance stores to speak to students about strategies for and costs of basic home maintenance and repairs.

Figure 9.3
Suggested Methods and Activities to Guide Acquisition of Financial Planning Knowledge

Educators should review some of the commercially available educational resource catalogs that have recently begun to offer curricula focusing on independent living and financial planning. In addition, the Home of My Own project has developed a comprehensive package of lesson plans and a board game appropriate for high school students with developmental disabilities. For more information on this package, contact Nancy Robertson at www.hdc.lsuhsc.edu.

live in somewhat sheltered settings such as college dormitories or transitional living programs. The high school years and those that follow afford young adults rich opportunities to develop and practice personal budgeting, housekeeping, and home maintenance skills while still receiving support. Numerous commercially available assessments and curricula provide educators and families with teaching tools that address independent living skills. In addition, CILs often provide valuable independent living resources specifically for individuals with disabilities. Finally, many community colleges offer continuing education programs on personal budgeting and home ownership and maintenance.

Independent living skills, like most curricular areas, are best taught in a combination of school-based and community-based settings with ample opportunities to teach and test using natural environments, natural materials, and natural cues. The competencies suggested in Figure 9.4, infused into traditional curricular areas, will help students develop the skills necessary to live more independently in any of the available community living options.

Transition-age students should be able to do the following independently or with support:

1. Perform routine household cleaning chores (e.g., dishwashing, vacuuming, laundry).
2. Plan and shop for nutritious meals.
3. Store perishable food appropriately.
4. Prepare meals and follow a nutritious diet.
5. Recognize household hazards.
6. Use assistive devices appropriately and efficiently (e.g., flashing fire alarms, vibrating kitchen timers, bathroom rails, ramps).
7. Know and practice basic first aid and emergency procedures.
8. Know where and whom to call for basic and emergency health and medical services.
9. Maintain household records and pay bills (e.g., use checking account, file bills and warranty/repair records, address and mail bills).
10. Maintain acceptable personal and dental hygiene.
11. Use transportation (e.g., drive and maintain an automobile, read a bus schedule, ride a public bus, contact transit providers to make arrangements).
12. Move around the community safely and efficiently (e.g., follow pedestrian and traffic signs, use mobility canes and service animals, communicate with others to find locations or to give and receive directions).
13. Interact with others in the home and community (e.g., avoid victimization, manage sexual relations, engage in reciprocal conversations, cope with feedback, follow rules, respect the privacy of others).

Figure 9.4
Suggested Independent Living Skills for Transition-Age Students

SUMMARY

Community living is an important and all too frequently underexplored area of transition planning. The supported living model offers students and their families opportunities for expressing self-determination skills and behaviors, building community presence and participation, and building financial assets. Educators and other transition team members must become aware of the current supported living movement, challenges, and resources and share this information with students and their families. The goal of this chapter was to open the full spectrum of housing options to individuals with disabilities by making educators aware of housing possibilities and the potential advantages and disadvantages of various options, and by suggesting educational strategies to use with transition-age students.

Strategies for Family Involvement

♦ Assign household chores to young adults and discuss how these chores help the household function. Increase the number and complexity of tasks as students enter and complete high school.

♦ Assign young adults an allowance and help them budget for various expenses. Encourage short-term and long-term financial goals.

♦ Involve young adults in family discussions about the family's housing situation, choices, finances, and long-term plans.

♦ Involve young adults in neighborhood and community functions such as Habitat for Humanity, Neighborhood Watch, and other community housing events.

♦ Encourage young adults to think about and discuss their housing preferences and dreams.

♦ Discuss with young adults the relationship between housing and employment.

♦ Encourage young adults to attend residential camps and other events away from home, and discuss independent living responsibilities.

CASE STUDIES

DEIDRE

Deidre is an energetic and outgoing young woman who is seldom shy about expressing her preferences and dreams. She attended special education classes and graduated from high school. The high school program provided her with some opportunities to explore community housing. For example, she completed a home economics class, and for her humanities class she volunteered at a local homeless shelter. She also received assistance from a vision teacher to help explore the use of assistive low-vision devices for meal preparation and other independent living needs. However, when asked about her independent living goals during her annual IEP meeting, Deidre just shrugged and said, "I don't know. I guess I will live in an apartment one day, after I get a job." As a result, Deidre's IEP goals and educational programming addressed the development of independent living skills, but no attention was given to identifying her desired community housing outcomes and ensuring that she had the skills and abilities to pursue these long-term dreams once she left high school.

During her final year of high school, Deidre began working part time at a local fast food restaurant. She was a productive and well-liked employee who received regular, positive evaluations from her employer. With help from her teacher, she established checking and savings accounts.

Like many of her peers, after her high school graduation Deidre continued to work part time and, soon after, began thinking about moving away from her

Deidre and her mom celebrate her new home.

parents' home and into a home of her own. She began talking to her family and friends about getting her own apartment. While her family and friends were supportive of Deidre's dreams, they couldn't imagine how she would ever be able to afford an apartment based on her monthly income and wondered whether she could live on her own with her visual impairment and cognitive disabilities. As her mother summarized, "I just don't know how Deidre could afford to rent an apartment, pay utilities and phone bills, buy food, and have any money left over for fun on a monthly income of $700 [i.e., $500 from a monthly SSI check and $200 from her employment income]. A small one-bedroom apartment in our community rents for almost $400!"

Because Deidre and her family had received limited information about community living options during Deidre's high school years, they spent several years trying to locate an affordable apartment for Deidre. Everyone became more frustrated. While her SSI income remained steady, her income from her part-time job was often inconsistent and unreliable. "If the economy slows down, her hours at work are cut way back," said her mother. "It is very frustrating for Deidre because she never knows from week to week how many hours she will be able to work and how much money she will make. However, she likes her job, her employer likes her, and even if we found her a full-time job, I am not sure that Deidre has the physical stamina to work full time." Because Deidre and her family had almost no information about affordable housing, they believed that her limited employment hindered her ability to move into an apartment.

Eventually, Deidre's case manager told the family about the Section 8 Home-Choice voucher program available through the local public housing agency (PHA), which assists persons with low incomes to obtain affordable housing. They quickly realized that this program could help Deidre afford an apartment of her own. If she received a voucher, Deidre would be required to spend only approximately 30% of her income on monthly rent. She would receive a monthly subsidy to pay her remaining rent. Unfortunately, there was a long waiting list for this program, and it might be years before Deidre received a voucher. Deidre's mother was frustrated. "Why didn't someone tell us about this program when Deidre was in high school?"

Finally, Deidre became eligible for a Section 8 voucher that was designed specifically to assist individuals with disabilities and low incomes to obtain affordable housing. Deidre was elated; she couldn't stop talking about all the features she wanted in her new apartment!

Because she has a disability, she requested several reasonable accommodations that would make it easier for her to obtain and use her voucher. For example, the PHA made the application available in large print to accommodate Deidre's vision impairment. Because of her limited reading abilities, they allowed her sister to be designated as a secondary contact person to receive copies of all correspondence sent to Deidre. Deidre began her apartment search that very day and soon located a small one-bedroom apartment, close, but as Deidre noted, "not too close" to her family. The apartment was also close to her job, allowing her to travel easily between the apartment and the job site.

Deidre chose an apartment that rented for $485 a month. With her Section 8 voucher, she is responsible for paying $110 of the monthly rent, and the landlord receives the remaining $375 from the PHA. Deidre has been living in her apartment for almost 3 years. She receives supported living services from her case manager, who visits her weekly to help her with grocery shopping, housekeeping, and travel to and from medical appointments and to ensure that any other disability support needs are being met. She also receives informal supports from her mother and sister, who visit her frequently to provide additional transportation and housekeeping assistance and encourage her to spend leisure time in the community.

Like many renters, Deidre has times when her budget is tight and she has to make spending choices. However, she enjoys having a place of her own that she can decorate the way she wants and where she can entertain her friends. "Since I don't have to pay so much rent, I can even save some money sometimes," she comments.

Recently, Deidre learned that her Section 8 voucher could also be used to help pay a monthly mortgage if she chooses to buy a house. As a result, she has decided to deposit $25 each month in her savings account. Her mother laughs, "Now she is reading the Homes for Sale section in the newspaper and bugging us about buying a house!"

GLEN

Glen is a self-determined young man who is quiet and thoughtful. He likes to listen to others before sharing his own ideas and dreams. Although he uses a motorized wheelchair for mobility, he is very independent and, according to his family, "always on the go." Glen has seven siblings, and even as adults they remain close to each other and to their mother.

Although he has lived in the same community his entire life, Glen remembers moving around a lot during his childhood years. He summarized, "Sometimes we moved because the house wasn't accessible for me, other times we moved because our rent was too high." He continued, "Sometimes we found ourselves living in a two-story apartment where the living area and some of the bedrooms were upstairs. When this happened, my brothers and I had to share a bedroom downstairs." This arrangement offered Glen little opportunity for privacy, and at times it isolated him from other members of his family.

As a student, Glen attended both general education and special education classes. While attending math and business classes in high school, he listened to other students discuss their employment, college, and housing dreams. Fearful of being ridiculed, Glen did not willingly share his dreams with his classmates or teachers. However, he remembers that he held many of the same dreams as his peers and that his teacher encouraged him to share his dreams during his IEP meetings.

As part of his transition planning, Glen's teachers provided him with opportunities to visit local affordable housing programs and to write a class term paper on his experiences. He completed several community-based vocational training experiences, opened a checking account, and studied budgeting in his mathematics classes. His family also helped him enroll in a summer program at the local community college that provided him with skills in independent living. He also volunteered one summer with his church youth group for Habitat for Humanity.

After graduating from high school, Glen wanted to get a job and move out on his own. His mother noted, "All his life, Glen wanted to be as independent as possible." Glen soon obtained employment as a part-time clerk at a nonprofit organization, but he found that he was financially unable to move away from home.

After several years of successful employment and saving money, Glen decided to share his dream of living on his own. Because of the number of times his family moved while he was growing up and the inability of many apartments to meet his accessibility needs, living in an apartment did not appeal to Glen. He dreamed of the stability offered by home ownership and the ability to make permanent accessibility modifications to accommodate his unique physical disabilities. Glen knew that his low income and his need for an accessible house would present some challenges to becoming a homeowner. However, he remembered some of the community housing activities that he experienced in high school and decided to investigate housing possibilities with his case manager.

With help from his case manager, he first learned of a local individual development account (IDA) program that would allow him to save up to $1,000 and receive matching funds of $4,000 toward the down payment on a house. As his savings grew, he became more confident about sharing his dream with his family and service providers. Some family members were supportive of his goal, but others were not. Because of everyone's limited knowledge of local housing resources, his family and case manager were not always certain how to help him.

Finally, Glen, his case manager, and some of his family members began meeting monthly to develop a plan to help him achieve his goal of becoming a homeowner. Soon, Glen's case manager learned about a local nonprofit program that helped people with low incomes become homeowners. Glen was selected to participate in the program. Program staff, knowledgeable about affordable housing, joined Glen's team.

During the year it took him to achieve his savings goal, Glen attended a homebuyer education class and a financial literacy class. Once he achieved his savings goal, his team assisted him in selecting a real estate agent, obtaining a loan pre-qualification amount, obtaining needed financial assistance for down payment and closing costs, and locating a house.

Finding a house that could be modified and was affordable took many more months. Glen sometimes became discouraged, but his team helped him persevere. Finally, a real estate agent located a one-story, three-bedroom, two-bath house in a neighborhood served by Glen's special transit program and on a route that would allow him to travel back and forth to work.

With support from his team, Glen submitted an offer to purchase the house. His offer was accepted, and 18 months after beginning the process, Glen moved into his own home. At the closing, Glen's case manager hugged him and exclaimed, "I am so happy for you! I can't wait to help someone else become a homeowner!" Glen's response was "I can't believe *we* did it." Glen is quick to tell anyone who asks that he could not have achieved his goal if he hadn't had the support of his family, teachers, and service providers.

Glen purchased his home for $59,000. He obtained a 30-year 6% fixed-rate portfolio loan mortgage of $49,000 from a local bank. He received approximately $5,000 in down payment and closing cost assistance from a local community development HOME fund program and $5,000 from the local IDA program ($1,000 from Glen's savings account and $4,000 in matching funds). Glen also needed to contribute an additional $500 of his own funds to help cover the cost of homeowner's insurance. His monthly mortgage payment is $350, which includes insurance and taxes. After residing in the house for 1 year, Glen received more than $3,000 from a local community development program and $2,500 from the Medicaid Waiver Program to complete the needed accessibility modifications. These modifications included a wheelchair ramp, a roll-in shower, lever door handles, widening two doors, and replacing the carpeted floors with linoleum.

Two years after Glen bought his house, his brother became his roommate. Glen enjoys sharing his home and, more important, appreciates the financial assistance provided by having a roommate. Glen admits that being a homeowner is a big challenge for him. "There is always something that needs to be done around the house, from cleaning the kitchen to mowing the lawn." However, Glen, his family, and service providers have developed a plan to help him maintain his house and address emergency repair issues. Glen has developed a budget and puts $50 a month into a savings account for house maintenance. His support team continues to meet monthly to discuss maintenance and financial issues. Glen periodically attends minor home repair workshops at a local home building and hardware store, where he has learned how to check and maintain his water heater, air conditioner, and plumbing; repair small holes in sheetrock; and shut off water in an emergency.

Glen is proud of his new role as a homeowner. He often shares words of wisdom with others. "Don't assume you can't be a homeowner, because you have a disability and are not rich. Be patient. Work with the people who support your goal, and take one step at a time."

STUDY GUIDE QUESTIONS

1. What are the major barriers to expanding community housing options for young adults with disabilities? What can educators do to increase these options?
2. What are the defining characteristics of supported living programs and services? According to the authors, why is the separation of housing and supports so important?
3. What are the major affordable housing resources? Why are they important to expanding community housing options for young adults with disabilities? Find out which of these options are available in your community.
4. Discuss the Olmstead decision's impact on community housing programs, policies, and funding. How is it being implemented in your state?
5. Discuss the relationship between housing and employment among adults with disabilities. How might an individual's interest in community housing outcomes support his or her pursuit of employment goals?
6. How were Deidre and Glen's self-determination knowledge, skills, and opportunities addressed by their high school programs in the two case studies? What else could have been done by educators to expand their abilities?

REFERENCES

Blatt, B., & Kaplan, F. (1966). *Christmas in Purgatory: A photographic essay on mental retardation.* New York: Allyn and Bacon.

Blumberg, E. R., & Ferguson, P. M. (2000). *The community support brokerage: Information and tools for support brokerages.* Eugene: University of Oregon, Specialized Training Program.

Braddock, D., Hemp, R., Parish, S., & Westrich, J. (1998). *The state of the states in developmental disabilities* (5th ed.). Washington, DC: American Association on Mental Retardation.

Chang, H. (1992). *Adolescent life and ethos: Ethnography of a U.S. high school.* London: Falmer Press.

Dautel, P. J., & Frieden, L. (1999). *Consumer choice and control: Personal attendant services and supports in America* (Report of the Blue Ribbon Panel on Personal Assistance Services). Houston, TX: Independent Living Research Utilization.

DeJong, G. (1979). Independent living: From social movement to analytical paradigm. *Archives of Physical Medicine and Rehabilitation, 60,* 435–446.

Duvdevany, I., Ben-Zur, H., & Ambar, A. (2002) Self-determination and mental retardation: Is there an

association with living arrangement and lifestyle satisfaction? *Mental Retardation, 40,* 379–389.

Everson, J. M., & Wilson, P. G. (2000). What do homeowners with disabilities tell us about being homeowners? A qualitative report. *Journal of Vocational Rehabilitation, 15,* 121–129.

Everson, J. M., Zhang, D., & Guillory, J. D. (2001). A statewide investigation of individualized transition plans in Louisiana. *Career Development for Exceptional Individuals, 24*(1), 37–49.

Fedman, S. S., & Elliott, G. R. (Eds.). (1990). *At the threshold: The developing adolescent.* Cambridge, MA: Harvard University Press.

Fox-Grage, W., Folkemer, D., & Lewis, J. (2003, February). *The states' response to the Olmstead decision: How are states complying?* Washington, DC: Forum for State Health Policy Leadership, National Conference of State Legislators.

Graber, J. A., & Dubas, J. S. (1996). *Leaving home: Understanding the transition to adulthood.* San Francisco: Jossey-Bass.

Grigal, M., Test, D. W., Beattie, J., & Wood, W. M. (1997). An evaluation of transition components of individualized education programs. *Exceptional Children, 63*, 357–372.

Homeownership Alliance. (2002, February 12). *Opening doors. A housing publication for the disability community.* Available: http://www.homeownershipalliance.com

Kastner, L. S., & Wyatt, J. F. (1997). *The seven-year stretch: How families work together to grow through adolescence.* Boston: Houghton Mifflin.

Klein, J. (2000). The history and development of a national homeownership initiative. *Journal of Vocational Rehabilitation, 15*, 59–66.

Klein, J., & Nelson, S. (2000). Homeownership for people with disabilities: The state of the states in 1999. *Journal of Vocational Rehabilitation, 15*, 67–77.

Kohler, P. D. (1996). *A taxonomy for transition programming linking research and practice.* Champaign: University of Illinois, Transition Research Institute.

Lakin, C., Hill, B., White, C., & Write, B. (1988). *Longitudinal change and interstate variability in the size of residential facilities for persons with mental retardation.* Minneapolis: University of Minnesota, Center on Residential and Community Services.

McNeil, J. (1997). *Americans with disabilities 1994–1995. Current population reports: Household economic studies.* Washington, DC: United States Census Bureau.

Meyer, L. H., Peck, C. A., & Brown, L. (1991). *Critical issues in the lives of people with severe disabilities.* Baltimore: Brookes.

Mount, B., & Zwernik, K. (1988). *It's never too early, it's never too late: A booklet about personal futures planning* (Publication No. 421-88-109). St Paul, MN: Metropolitan Council.

O'Brien, J. (1987). A guide to lifestyle planning: Using the Activities Catalog to integrate services and natural supports systems. In B. Wilcox & G. T. Bellamy (Eds.), *A comprehensive guide to the Activities Catalog: An alternative curriculum for youth and adults with severe disabilities* (pp. 175–189). Baltimore: Brookes.

O'Brien, C. L., & O'Brien, J. (2002). The origins of person-centered planning. A community of practice perspective. In S. Holburn & P. M. Vietze (Eds.), *Person-centered planning: Research, practice, and future directions* (pp. 3–27). Baltimore: Brookes.

O'Hara, A., & Miller, E. (2000). *Going it alone: The struggle to expand housing opportunities for people with disabilities.* Boston: Technical Assistance Collaborative, Inc., and Washington, DC: Consortium for Citizens with Disabilities Housing Task Force.

O'Hara, A., & Miller, E. (2001). *Priced out in 2000. The crisis continues.* Boston: Technical Assistance Collaborative, Inc., and Washington, DC: Consortium for Citizens with Disabilities Housing Task Force.

President's Panel on Mental Retardation. (1962). *A proposed program for national action to combat mental retardation.* Washington, DC: U.S. Government Printing office.

Racino, J., Walker, P., O'Connor, S., & Taylor, S. (1993). *Housing, support, and community: Choices and strategies for adults with disabilities.* Baltimore: Brookes.

Robertson, N., & Dufresne, D. (2000). Homeownership for individuals with disabilities: Defining professional knowledge, roles, and responsibilities. *Journal of Vocational Rehabilitation, 15*, 91–100.

Technical Assistance Collaborative, Inc., and the Consortium for Citizens with Disabilities (CCD) Housing Task Force. (2000). *Opening doors. A housing publication for the disability community.* Available from: http://www.c-c-d.org/od-dec00.htm

United States Census Bureau, American Housing Survey Branch. (2001). *American housing survey for the United States: 2001.* Washington, DC: Author.

United States Department of Health and Human Services. (1990). *Independence, productivity, and integration for people with developmental disabilities: A summary of reports prepared by state developmental disabilities planning councils.* Washington, DC: Author.

Wilson, P. G., & Everson, J. M. (2000). Social validation of outcomes achieved by the Louisiana Home of My Own (LA-HMO) initiative. *Journal of Vocational Rehabilitation, 15*, 131–145.

Wolfensberger, W. (1972). *The principle of normalization in human services.* Toronto: National Institute on Mental Retardation.

Preparing Students
for Community Participation

Chapter 10

Introduction

Adolescence, *the period between childhood and adulthood, is generally defined as the years roughly between ages 12 and 21 (Elliott & Fieldman, 1990). It is a period characterized by many complex transitions. During this period, adolescents may make physical transitions, such as moving from a high school campus to a college or university campus and from living in a home with parents, siblings, or extended family members to living in a dorm, apartment, or home with a spouse, roommates, or even alone. They may make role transitions, such as changing from a student to an employee and from a passenger to a driver. They may make service transitions, such as moving from educational services to employment services and from pediatric health care services to adult health care services. Adolescents also become legal adults with all the rights and responsibilities that come with this role.*

Making these transitions successfully requires adolescents, often for the first time in their lives, to demonstrate self-determination abilities in multiple settings and situations. Self-determined adolescents, independently or with support from others, must be able to make decisions and set attainable goals in many sensitive areas, such as sexual and reproductive health, relationships with friends and families, nutrition, fitness, leisure, financial planning, transportation, community and civic involvement, and legal competence and responsibilities. Determination of individual goals in each of these areas during the transition planning process and attainment of goals as they exit high school and enter adulthood will enhance their community participation in a variety of ways.

Community participation is a broad construct, one that does not always lend itself easily to transition goal-setting and the measurement of tangible outcomes. Broadly defined in the Individuals with Disabilities Education Improvement Act of 2004 (IDEA) and in current transition literature, community participation encompasses life-style outcomes, services, and supports in areas as diverse but as interrelated as leisure and recreation, relationships, health and medical, transportation, civic and community, financial, and legal matters. As such, it is a construct that is deeply embedded within quality indicator measures of successful transition planning and postschool employment, postsecondary education, adult services and/or independent living outcomes. Community participation outcomes should also be considered a measure of self-determination aptitude. For all these reasons, community participation is embedded within all components of Kohler's (1996) taxonomy for transition programming.

This chapter encourages educators and families to address individualized community participation goals, activities, and accomplishments within all student-focused planning, student development, and postschool goal-setting aspects of transition planning. The chapter begins with an overview of important concepts, including community participation and related concepts such as person-centered planning, and self-determination, all of which are designed to address IDEA mandates and improve community participation outcomes. It continues with specific methods and activities for educators to use to build students' skills and self-determination abilities in multiple community participation areas, including partnering with families and coordinating with adult service providers. Throughout, the chapter provides case studies illustrating individuals with disabilities who have achieved successful community participation outcomes as a result of individualized transition planning activities.

Key Terms

adolescence
community participation
friendship
healthy
leisure
nondrivers education
person-centered planning
recreation
self-determination
social capital

Personal Perspective on Recreation and Transition

from a Transition Coordinator

Joyce Godshall Ivester

Secondary Transition Specialist, South Carolina State Department of Education

Recreation is a critical component of a comprehensive IEP and transition plan and a measurable outcome of successful community participation. Like other adolescents, teenagers with disabilities need opportunities and resources for recreation and leisure to lead well-balanced, healthy lives. Recreation activities offer teenagers occasions to spend time with their peers. They also offer them opportunities to develop new skills that can be generalized to employment, postsecondary education, and community living outcomes. Unfortunately, too few teenagers with disabilities take advantage of the community recreation activities available to them, and in turn, too few communities design and market their activities to include teens with disabilities.

Often, communities already have interagency teams in place to address specific community service needs such as recreation. If there is not such a team, one can easily be established. It is important however that teams include representatives from community recreation centers and services along with school personnel, families, youth with disabilities, and other local leaders. In one community in South Carolina where we established an interagency team to address recreation needs for teenagers, including those with disabilities, we found that one of the biggest obstacles was that teenagers were simply not aware of the recreation activities already available. Putting together a cross-agency calendar and getting it in the hands of teens and their families was the team's initial task. It was a relatively simply task, and one that increased participation among teens, but one that could not have been completed without the resources of an interagency team.

Transition-age youth must, themselves, be asked what they currently do in their free time and what they would like to do if opportunities and resources were available. In addition, they—not professionals—need to identify the barriers. In the South Carolina community where we addressed recreation, this was our second task. Once we identified specific activities of interest to teenagers and some of the barriers that kept them from participating, we were able to offer them some new and additional recreation activities. Families and young adults must help in identifying both the needs and the possible solutions, as well as partner with others to get the solutions in place and evaluate the results.

As mandated by IDEA 2004, the process of individualized transition planning must encourage students and their families to make many results-oriented decisions as students prepare to leave high school. Furthermore, the transition planning team must consider four specific outcome areas: (a) postschool employment; (b) postsecondary education; (c) adult services; and/or (d) independent living areas. In addition to these four areas, there is a fifth and less specific outcome area mandated by IDEA 1997. This fifth area is community participation.

BUILDING A FOUNDATION FOR COMMUNITY PARTICIPATION

Community participation was articulated first by O'Brien (1987) as one of five accomplishments that human service systems should use to design and evaluate service frameworks for people with disabilities. Briefly, community participation accomplishments are achieved when people with disabilities have the same community opportunities available as their peers. It is defined as full and active participation in the communities of their choice, to whatever extent these individuals desire. It includes the provision of whatever supports individuals need to build and sustain this participation. Community participation is also related to and depends on the concept of social capital (Putnam, 2000). **Social capital** refers to the social connections and networks that people form among themselves and use to improve their individual lives and communities. Social capital is the "glue" that holds communities together; it is one of the frequently untapped assets that communities offer to young adults with disabilities and their IEP teams as they seek to improve community participation outcomes.

Expanded upon later by other professionals (e.g., Holburn & Vietze, 2002), community participation has broadened into a construct that does not always lend itself easily to transition goal-setting and the measurement of tangible outcomes. However, it is generally agreed that community participation outcomes include a broad array of adult life-style opportunities in specific outcome areas such as leisure and recreation; relationships with friends, family, and community; health and medical services; and access to transportation. Thus, individualized transition planning should consider community participation outcomes, services, and supports in all of these areas as students make the transition from adolescence to adulthood. Person-centered assessment and planning and attention to self-determination abilities are two strategies that educators, families, and other transition team members can use to help pave the way toward comprehensive community participation outcomes.

Person-Centered Planning

Person-centered planning (see Chapter 4 for more detail) encompasses a set of specific models and approaches, all designed to enhance community participation outcomes for individuals with disabilities by increasing their control of the assessment process, the planning process, and available resources. O'Brien and O'Brien (2002) summarized the common characteristics of person-centered planning models as those models that (a) describe individuals as people rather than as diagnostic labels; (b) use ordinary language and images rather than professional jargon; (c) actively search for a person's gifts and capacities in the context of community life; and (d) strengthen the voices of people who know the individuals best. All person-centered planning models seek community participation outcomes for individuals with disabilities and thus are closely aligned with individualized transition planning.

Self-Determination

Self-determination (see Chapter 2 for more detail) is a set of attributes that enables individuals to make choices and then use these choices to determine future behaviors, opportunities, and consequences. Wehmeyer (1996) defined a self-determined individual as someone who acts as the "primary causal agent in ones' life, making choices and decisions regarding one's quality of life free from undue external influence or interference" (p. 24).

Self-determined individuals possess a number of characteristics that are linked to successful postschool community participation outcomes. These abilities include:

♦ Choice-making skills.
♦ Decision-making skills.
♦ Problem-solving skills.
♦ Goal-setting skills.
♦ Independence, risk-taking, and safety skills.
♦ Self-evaluation skills.
♦ Self-instruction skills.
♦ Self-advocacy and leadership skills.
♦ Internal locus of control.
♦ Positive attributions of efficacy and outcome expectancy.
♦ Self-awareness.
♦ Self-knowledge (e.g., Field, Martin, Miller, Ward, & Wehmeyer, 1998; Price, Wolensky, & Mulligan, 2002; Wehmeyer, Agran, & Hughes, 1998).

Educators and families must provide students with ample opportunities to develop and practice these attributes. Teaching methods designed to enhance self-determination attributes and community participation outcomes are an important component of transition planning.

Putting It All Together: Preparing Students for Community Participation Outcomes

How might an educator begin to prepare students for outcomes as broad those encompassed by the term *community participation*? As we have learned, community participation encompasses a broad array of life-style outcomes in areas as diverse but as interrelated as leisure and recreation; relationships with friends, family, and community; health and medical; and transportation planning. Each year, as part of the transition planning component of the IEP meeting, it is essential to offer all of these areas for discussion.

One strategy widely used by IEP teams in many local school districts is a preprinted and comprehensive menu of all transition areas that invites students, families, and other IEP team members to choose the areas of interest and concern to them. This menu should include all mandated transition planning areas (i.e., postschool employment, postsecondary education, adult services, community living, community participation). Furthermore, to encourage and guide discussion, the menu should break down transition areas—especially community participation—into more discrete and behavioral options such as "life demands" (Cronin & Patton, 1993). For example, the relationships subdomain of the community participation domain might include such life demands as (a) developing new friendships with peers; (b) maintaining relationships with peers; (c) developing intimate relationships; (d) managing sexuality and intimate relationships; (e) managing marital relationships; (f) parenting; and (g) becoming more involved in one's community.

A student's interests, and those of the family and other team members, will ebb and flow during the adolescent years as the student gains new skills and experiences and begins thinking seriously of life beyond high school. For example, when a student is age 14, community housing may not be a concern at all if the family envisions the young adult living at home forever or is unaware of other community housing options. At age 15, vocational training and employment may be a primary concern as peers begin to secure part-time and summer jobs and discuss postschool career goals. At age 16, transportation may be a pressing but frequently unaddressed concern as peers begin to acquire drivers' licenses and the independence that comes with this new role. At age 17, postsecondary education may become a concern (and one that has not been addressed early enough for students with support needs), as peers begin to apply to colleges and universities. And at age 18 and beyond, as the student becomes a legal adult, health and medical responsibilities and financial responsibilities may become a primary focus of discussion. Providing a pre-printed and comprehensive menu of all transition outcome areas to prompt discussion allows teams opportunities to address issues of immediate concern while also encouraging growth and supplying information and resources for areas of minimal concern.

Most adolescents, including those without disabilities, need varying levels of services and supports from family, peers, professionals, and other adults as they navigate the road to adulthood. Some need specific goals and skill-building activities in multiple areas over a number of years whereas others need extensive services in one or two areas, but only written resources in other areas.

Person-centered planning and self-determination concepts can be infused easily into many general high school curricular and extracurricular activities. They lend themselves well to inclusive educational settings, where they can benefit all students in transition from adolescence to adulthood. As appropriate, these concepts can also be applied to curricula and classroom settings specifically designed for students with disabilities. Table 10.1 suggests teaching methods and activities for educators to use to enhance students' self-determination abilities and achievement of community participation outcomes. Supplemental methods and activities in specific community participation curricular areas can be found in many of the

Table 10.1

Suggested Teaching Methods and Activities to Guide Acquisition of Self-Determination Abilities and Pursuit of Community Participation Outcomes

Self-Determination Abilities	Suggested Teaching Methods and Activities
1. Choice making	♦ Have students develop preferences maps of their likes and dislikes using person-centered planning tools. Encourage students to use these maps to open discussion during their individualized education program (IEP) meetings.
	♦ Encourage students to identify new potential activities and resources. Use these newly identified activities to expand IEP goals and activities.
	♦ Reward students when they pursue new experiences.
	♦ Teach students to make choices by providing contingent and natural consequences for their choices.
	♦ Present students with multiple predetermined opportunities from which to choose. Include options from their preferences maps and include new, unfamiliar options from which they may make choices.
	♦ Facilitate discussions among students about the choices they make, the consequences, and the limits within which some choices can be made.
	♦ Provide assistive communication supports to students who need them (e.g., photographs of activities, preprinted written instruction cards).
	♦ Invite guest speakers from recreation centers, transportation providers, volunteer and service organizations, and social and professional groups to discuss opportunities available in the community. Encourage student projects that promote community participation.
	♦ Invite adults with disabilities to discuss the leisure, relationship, health and medical, civic, and transportation choices they have made.
2. Decision making	♦ Teach students to prioritize preferences, list choices and possible consequences, and make decisions accordingly.
	♦ Facilitate discussions, role plays, mock elections, and other activities that require students to practice making decisions and discuss their actions and the outcomes.
3. Problem solving	♦ Teach students to respond to problem-solving questions such as "What is the problem?" "How can I solve it?" "If my planned solution doesn't work, how can I change it?"
	♦ Facilitate discussions, role plays, and other activities that provide students with opportunities to identify problems, propose solutions, ask questions, listen, and summarize events. Incorporate adult driving and nondriving decisions, health decisions, leisure decisions, and relationship decisions within these activities.
4. Goal setting	♦ Have students define concepts such as *goals, future,* and *vision.* Incorporate the words into word search games, crossword puzzles, and math word problems.
	♦ Facilitate discussions, role plays, and other activities that provide students with opportunities to think about the future and discuss potential personal goals.

(continued)

Table 10.1
Continued

Self-Determination Abilities	Suggested Teaching Methods and Activities
	◆ Have students set goals, set time frames, determine the benefits of reaching goals, and prioritize among goals.
	◆ Have students identify potential supports and match them to their needs.
	◆ Facilitate discussions, role plays, and other activities that require students to determine specific plans to reach their goals. Identify examples of adults engaging in these skills in literature and current events.
	◆ Invite adults with disabilities to share their goals and the experiences they had as they transitioned from high school to adult life.
5. Independence, risk taking, and safety	◆ Advocate for students to have opportunities to engage in age-appropriate behaviors and activities that promote independence (e.g., school-sponsored driver's education programs, student government, senior class trips and projects, school recreation and social clubs and events).
	◆ Have students identify potential supports and match them to their needs (e.g., assistive technology).
	◆ Teach students to identify cues and prompts that might alert them to risky or unsafe situations.
	◆ Facilitate reading assignments, videos, discussions, role plays, and other activities that allow students to identify and respond to novel, safe, unsafe, or risky situations. Identify examples of adults using these skills in literature and current events.
	◆ Whenever possible, teach and test students in community environments to provide natural cues, prompts, and consequences.
6. Self-evaluation	◆ Teach students to self-assess and self-manage the actions they follow in pursuit of their personal goals.
	◆ Provide students with opportunities to self-assess and self-manage their goals, timeframes, and actions.
	◆ Facilitate discussions, role plays, and other activities that enable students to self-assess and self-manage their goals. Identify examples of adults using these skills in literature and current events.
	◆ Invite adults with disabilities to share their goals and the experiences they had as they transitioned from high school to adult life.
7. Self-instruction	◆ Use multiple teaching methods to teach students to perform tasks (e.g., model the task, provide verbal and written instruction, provide redundancy cues).
	◆ Promote maintenance and generalization of newly learned skills by teaching and testing in multiple environments and with multiple instructors.
8. Self-advocacy and leadership	◆ Teach students about the legal rights and responsibilities of adults. Invite speakers from centers for independent living, the League of Women Voters, and advocacy groups to speak to students.
	◆ Teach students the meaning of concepts such as *assertiveness, self-advocacy,* and *leadership*. Identify examples of adults using these skills in literature and current events.

Self-Determination Abilities	Suggested Teaching Methods and Activities
	◆ Teach students effective social, communication, and conflict-management skills.
	◆ Facilitate discussions, role plays, mock elections, and other activities that allow students to practice self-advocacy and leadership skills.
	◆ Invite adults with disabilities to share their goals and the experiences they had as they transitioned from high school to adult life.
9. Internal locus of control	◆ Teach students about and provide opportunities to learn about the relationship between their behavior and performance.
	◆ Clearly define behavior and performance expectations.
	◆ Provide students with rich opportunities for positive reinforcement.
	◆ Model and provide opportunities to work cooperatively with peers and adults on group projects that promote teamwork. Ensure that students with disabilities have opportunities to engage in community and volunteer events in which they give back to the community.
10. Positive attributes of efficacy and outcome expectancy	◆ Have students develop preferences and future maps of their attributes, gifts, and capacities using person-centered planning tools.
	◆ Encourage students to try new activities and pursue new experiences.
	◆ Have students identify potential supports and match them to their needs.
	◆ Have students explore and encourage use of assistive technology to increase transportation opportunities, voter participation, recreation experiences, and health and medical independence, for example.
	◆ Provide students with rich opportunities for positive reinforcement.
	◆ Invite adults with disabilities to share their goals and the experiences they had as they transitioned from high school to adult life.
11. Self-awareness	◆ Have students develop preferences and future maps of their attributes, gifts, and capacities using person-centered planning tools.
	◆ Provide students with factual education about their disabilities and the functional impact of their disabilities on, for example, driving, health and medical independence, and legal rights.
	◆ Provide students with opportunities to interact with peers and adults with similar disabilities to explore their characteristics and experiences.
	◆ Teach students compensatory strategies to address their disabilities.
	◆ Explore and encourage use of assistive technology.
12. Self-knowledge	◆ Have students develop preferences and vision maps of their attributes, gifts, and capacities using person-centered planning tools.
	◆ Provide students with factual education about their disabilities.
	◆ Provide students with opportunities to interact with peers and adults with similar disabilities to explore their characteristics and experiences.

commercially available curricula, Web sites, and other resources referenced throughout this chapter and the rest of this book.

The remaining sections of this chapter describe current practices and teaching methods to help educators and IEP teams structure programming across the various community participation areas: (a) leisure and recreation; (b) relationships with friends, family, and community; (c) health and medical planning; and (d) transportation planning. A case study of a transition-age student illustrates each outcome area.

LEISURE AND RECREATION

Leisure and *recreation* are terms that are often used synonymously, so they will be used interchangeably in this chapter. A **leisure** program or activity may be defined as any pursuit that an individual engages in during free time strictly for relaxation, enjoyment, or diversion from work (Moon, 1994; Schleien, Ray, & Green, 1997). Plainly stated, **recreation** may be anything that an individual indicates is fun!

Leisure pursuits are critical to adolescents' and adults' physical and mental health. Physically and emotionally healthy adolescents and adults engage in a variety of indoor, outdoor, individual, and group leisure pursuits alone and with family, friends, community members, and even coworkers. Recreation activities enable children and adolescents to develop motor skills, communication skills, social skills, and even academic skills. Recreation activities enable adolescents and adults to build relationships with neighbors, friends, and coworkers. Finally, leisure activities and skills are a vital link to community participation outcomes in other areas such as relationships and transportation and to other transition planning areas such as postsecondary education, employment, and community housing. Nevertheless, leisure has never emerged as a transition planning priority in special education programming or transition planning models.

Historically, leisure and recreation opportunities have been available to students and adults with disabilities primarily through segregated programs and from therapeutic recreation professionals or others with specialized training in recreation for individuals with disabilities. More recently, however, community recreation facilities and programs have become more accessible to people with disabilities, and specialized programs for individuals with disabilities have become more aware of the need for community presence and inclusive practices.

This section focuses on methods for increasing the participation of students in two leisure areas: (a) participation in structured community recreation programs and settings that are designed for all residents of a community and (b) participation in less structured leisure pursuits that are typically pursued by individuals in their homes and communities. By encouraging educators and families to address leisure within student-focused planning, student development, and the post-school goal-setting aspects of transition planning, professionals can make

DID YOU KNOW?

Younger adolescents are more likely to engage in organized events such as team sports and other group events such as scouts and church youth groups, whereas older adolescents are more likely to engage in less structured activities such as shopping, talking on the telephone, watching movies, playing video games, or simply "hanging out" with only one or two other people (Moon, 1994).

recreation a planning priority and improve leisure community participation outcomes among transition-age students. The goal of transition planning that targets leisure pursuits is twofold: (a) to individualize outcomes and activities to the unique preferences of individual students and (b) to assist high school students in making the transition from school-based and school-sponsored leisure pursuits to adult pursuits.

Assessing Leisure Interests and Skills

The first step in developing the leisure skills of high school students with disabilities is to find out what general-curriculum and same-age students do for fun during their free time. This step is important because research indicates that adolescents engage in different leisure activities than do children and adults, and young adolescents engage in different pursuits than do older adolescents (Moon, 1994). In addition, high school students engage in different pursuits than do adults (Moon, 1994). Finally, research indicates that students with disabilities may have fewer leisure interests than their peers without disabilities simply because they are not aware of and/or invited to participate in and explore an array of leisure activities open to typical children and adolescents (Moon, 1994).

To determine students' interests, educators might develop simple checklists or questionnaires to distribute to middle or high school students and members of church or other youth groups, or they might hold short focus groups with organized groups of teenagers. Questionnaires should be distributed to students with disabilities as well as their typical peers. Questionnaires should also be distributed to postsecondary education students and adults who have made the transition from high school to work and to living in homes of their own. The questionnaires should include open-ended questions such as the following: *What are your three favorite things to do during your free time? What did you do last weekend for fun? How did you spend last evening? What would you do if you had a few extra hours of free time? Who do you spend your free time with? Do you spend your free time alone, with family, with friends, or with coworkers?*

Figure 10.1 is an example of a recreation needs assessment that an interagency community-level team in Abbeville, South Carolina, developed to find out what

Hi! Would you mind answering a few quick questions about recreation in _____ County?

1. Do you live in _____ county? YES NO (If response is no, end the survey.)
2. How old are you? _____
3. Circle one: MALE FEMALE
4. What things do you enjoy doing most in your free time?

1. _____   4. _____
2. _____   5. _____
3. _____   6. _____

5. Do you ever participate in activities sponsored by _____ department of recreation?
   YES   NO (If response is no, go to question 6.)

   What activities have you participated in during the past 2 years?
   _____

6. Would you be interested in any of these activities? (Record yes or no.)
_____ Art classes (such as drawing, painting, pottery, jewelry making)
_____ Baseball
_____ Basketball
_____ Cheerleading
_____ Dance
_____ Drama or theatre
_____ Football
_____ Karaoke contest
_____ Martial arts (such as karate)
_____ Movie nights
_____ Soccer
_____ Swimming
_____ Tennis
7. Are there any other activities you would be interested in?
   _____
8. What do you like most about recreation and fun in _____ County?
   _____
9. What do you like least?
   _____

Figure 10.1
Community Recreation Survey for Transition-Age Students

transition-age youth in their community did for fun. Team members, including the high school transition coordinator and representatives from the county recreation department, used this needs assessment to learn more about the recreation interests of middle and high school students, both general curriculum and special education curriculum students, and young adults living and working in Abbeville. They gathered information by asking teachers to distribute the survey to their students, interviewing people who attended various recreation department-sponsored events, and canvassing adolescents and young adults at various community sites (e.g., movie theaters, shopping malls).

The Abbeville team found that there were numerous community recreation activities available, but that many of them were poorly attended by teenagers with and without disabilities. They also identified a number of potential leisure events that teenagers indicated they would participate in if they were locally available. With the needs data they collected, the Abbeville team members were better prepared to set community recreation goals for the team and participating organizations to pursue. The Abbeville team agreed on two initial goals: (a) to increase coordination and marketing of currently available recreation opportunities so that more students, including those with disabilities, would participate and (b) to offer additional, alternative recreation opportunities identified by teenagers with disabilities as desirable.

Results from needs assessment activities like these provide educators and families with a snapshot of how typical teenagers in a specific community spend their leisure time. This snapshot is important because it enables transition team members to assess popular activities among specific age groups in specific communities and to assess the extent to which teenagers with and without disabilities share interests, experiences, barriers, and opportunities.

Once this snapshot is obtained, the next step is to assess the specific and personal interests, preferences, experiences, and skills of individual students with disabilities. This task can be as simple as asking them and/or their families questions about what they currently like to do for fun, what novel activities they would like to experience, and what additional skills they would like to learn. This can be accomplished through written checklists or questionnaires, personal interviews, or small focus groups. For example, educators might consider compiling a list of typical leisure activities enjoyed by citizens in the community and asking individual students or their family representatives to check all activities of potential interest. They might want to assist students and their families in developing "preferences" maps. For students with more significant disabilities and/or fewer leisure experiences to choose from, educators might wish to supplement these methods with direct observations of students engaging in activities during free time and conduct systematic preference assessments (Reid, Parsons, & Green, 1991).

Figure 10.2 offers a framework of leisure and recreation activities typically pursued by high school students and young adults. This list is intended only to serve as a broad guide. It should be modified to reflect leisure activities of specific local interest. For example, in some communities ice hockey might be a very popular leisure activity, whereas in other communities it might be relatively unheard of, but "frogging" might be a popular local activity.

Using the community leisure snapshot as a framework will give educators a more focused picture of typical leisure activities among teenagers and adults in general and the specific leisure activities of individual students with disabilities, as well as untapped leisure opportunities. These interests and opportunities must now be transformed into IEP goals and recreation activities.

Athletic and Sports Events

Baseball	Basketball
Bowling	Canoeing
Camping	Cheerleading
Equestrian events	Football
Golf	Gymnastics
Hiking	Karate
NASCAR	Pool
Sailing and water sports	Skiing and other snow sports
Soccer	Softball
Summer camp	Swimming
Tennis	Track and field events
Walking	Yoga

Drama and Theatre

Band	Choir
Dance groups	Drama club
Neighborhood/summer theatre	Public speaking
Puppetry	

Socializing with peers

Eating at restaurants	Going to mall
Going to movies	Going to spas
Watching videos	Talking on the telephone
Working	

Hobbies and Clubs

Animals and pet care	Arcades and video games
Arts and crafts	Baseball card collecting
Church groups	Computer games
Cooking	Crochet and needlework
Puzzles and games	Reading
Scouts, 4-H clubs, Interact, etc.	Stamp collecting
Volunteer groups	Woodworking

Figure 10.2
Suggested Framework for Leisure and Recreation Activities for High School Students

CASE STUDY

VONG

Vong is a 15-year-old sophomore of Hmong descent who attends his local high school. He is enrolled in a self-contained study skills class for students with attention deficit with hyperactivity disorder (ADHD), but he is included in most academic classes with his peers. He is a quiet teenager who prefers to spend time alone or with no more than one or two classmates at a time. Although he takes medication to help him control his impulsive behaviors and his temper, he has difficulty participating in team sports and completing fast-paced leisure activities such as video games. He is inquisitive and enjoys science and math courses, especially lab assignments.

Vong can be easily distracted and sometimes paces obsessively back and forth in the classroom when he is frustrated by his studies. From a questionnaire that he and his family completed with the help of an interpreter, Vong's IEP team learned that he enjoys attending NASCAR events with his older brother and building model race cars. He has expressed interest in enrolling in a summer Motorsports program at the local community college. His mother thought that he might be interested in joining the high school's cross-country team.

At his most recent IEP meeting, Vong and his team set three goals related to leisure:

1. Vong will participate in a sophomore physical fitness class with his classmates Mondays, Wednesdays, and Fridays for 50 minutes. By the end of the semester, he will be able to run or walk a mile independently on the track in 20 minutes or less with only verbal prompts.

2. Vong will attend junior varsity cross-country team practice 3 days a week during the upcoming fall season.

3. With help from his family, Vong will enroll in and complete the 6-week Motorsports summer program at the community college this summer.

4. While participating in track practice and in the Motorsports program, he will complete a self-monitoring behavioral checklist at the end of each day. If he engages in no more than three target behaviors each week, he and his brother will attend or watch on TV a weekend NASCAR event of his choice.

Teaching Leisure and Recreation Pursuits

Once goals and activities have been agreed upon, the next step is to provide students with opportunities and instruction in an array of leisure activities that are of individual interest. Teaching leisure pursuits encompasses much more than skill development. Teaching self-determination is a fundamental component of leisure education. Leisure is about fun, and this means teenagers must develop the self-knowledge to determine what is and is not fun and the choice-making skills to choose fun activities to pursue. Leisure is also about setting goals, solving problems, developing independence, taking risks, practicing safety, self-evaluation, self-advocacy, and self-knowledge. Vong, for example, is learning to express and self-advocate for his leisure preferences, set and self-manage skill and behavioral goals, become more independent, and practice safety behaviors. Leisure and recreation instruction enables teachers to address nearly all of the self-determination attributes and teaching methods summarized earlier in Table 10.1.

Transition-age students should receive recreation instruction in a variety of age-appropriate and community-based settings. Inclusive high school physical education classes (Huettig & Roth, 2002), community recreation centers, high school organizations and events (Moon, 1994; Schleien et al., 1997), and broader community organizations and events such as Interact Clubs, scouts, and church groups all provide excellent teaching opportunities.

Leisure and recreation instruction for transition-age students should be characterized by

♦ Providing multiple opportunities for choice-making among both preferred and novel activities.

♦ Using community and natural environments and materials.

♦ Making participation success-oriented.

♦ Promoting age-appropriate activities and materials.

♦ Building on peer and inclusive relationships.

♦ Providing skill instruction.

♦ Offering disability awareness to students, staff, and other participants.

♦ Matching supports to students' needs.

♦ Providing opportunities for self-assessment and evaluation of experiences and skills (Moon, 1994; Schleien et al., 1997; Strand & Kreiner, 2001).

Figure 10.3 summarizes suggested leisure and recreation skills needed by transition-age students and young adults.

Transition-age students should, independently or with support, be able to:

♦ Identify an array of preferred leisure interests and activities (e.g., group, solitary, community based, home based, spectator, participant).
♦ Recognize free time.
♦ Describe their disability or health condition and the functional implications of their leisure and recreation pursuits.
♦ Suggest and use adaptations to activities or modifications to equipment, materials, and rules as appropriate.
♦ Suggest and use assistive technology as appropriate.
♦ Identify opportunities and resources to access preferences.
♦ Request information from community recreation resources about schedules, costs, eligibility, rules, equipment, and materials.
♦ Use community resources appropriately (e.g., follow rules for facility usage, participate in groups, share materials and equipment with others).
♦ Contact friends and other individuals to suggest and schedule leisure events.
♦ Engage in solitary leisure pursuits.
♦ Demonstrate the appropriate skills necessary to participate in identified activities (e.g., Is the activity a class in which skills will be learned or a competitive activity in which skills need to be evidenced?).

Figure 10.3
Suggested Leisure and Recreation Skills for Transition-Age Students

RELATIONSHIPS WITH FRIENDS, FAMILY, AND COMMUNITY

Developing and sustaining relationships with other people is a basic human need. Adults typically develop and maintain a variety of social relationships with friends and family, intimate relationships with spouses and partners, and civic and community relationships with neighbors, coworkers, church members, and others. Opportunities for and quality of relationships may be impacted dramatically by other transition outcomes such as employment status, workplace culture and job characteristics, postsecondary education settings, community housing options, health and medical needs, and transportation availability. Regardless of whether other transition outcomes are attained or not attained, however, community presence and participation are essential aspects of friendships and other relationships for people with disabilities (O'Brien & O'Brien, 1993). Community presence and participation are necessary for both the development and sustenance of adult relationships.

Perske (1993) proposed a list of functions that friendships and other relationships can and cannot perform. Among the functions he noted, families provide things that friends cannot. However, families can be limiting, and friends can stretch people beyond their limits. Specifically, friends can help people move beyond human services goals, rehearse adult roles, and serve as role models. Friends can teach reciprocity and serve as havens from stress.

Hunt (1991) suggested four defining dimensions to the concept of **friendship:** (a) attraction, the frequently unexplained something that draws people together; (b) embodiment, the unique ways in which people interact together and engage in their friendships; (c) power, the balance and accommodations that people make choices about within their friendships; and (d) community, the situation of relationships within a civic and social body.

For students in transition from adolescence to adulthood, developing new relationships with family members as well as relationships with other adults and same-age peers is an essential task. Forging new relationships with parents and other family members while simultaneously forging new relationships with friends, spouses, coworkers, neighbors, college roommates, and other significant peers is one of the most complex and least understood tasks of adolescence (Graber & Dubas, 1996). In recent studies, parents of adolescents with disabilities appeared to understand the complexity of and need for new family and peer relationships and welcomed the inclusion of these tasks within transition planning (e.g., Kolb & Hanley-Maxwell, 2003; Morningstar, Turnbull, & Turnbull, 1995; Whitney-Thomas & Hanley-Maxwell, 1996).

Assessing Relationship Interests and Skills

As Perske (1993) noted, professionals cannot program friendships. Nevertheless, educators can assist and support relationship development by teaching relationship skills and providing opportunities and supports to develop and maintain relationships.

IEP and transition planning should enable teams to identify the relationship skills needed by high school students and to teach them the skills necessary to develop healthy relationships. It should also enable teams to provide students with opportunities to initiate and nurture friendships and other relationships. One effective method to get started is to help students identify their current relationships by developing a "relationships map" using person-centered planning tools. A relationships map may be developed by individual students or with support from families, educators, and other IEP team members. A relationships map may be developed as a school assignment in a social studies or health class or as a club, church, or scouts project.

A relationships map (see Figure 10.4 for an example) is a pictorial listing of the people identified as significant in a person's life. A relationships map may be used to identify relationship preferences and patterns, strengthen existing relationships, identify opportunities for new relationships, and even identify relationships that may no longer be working for the student.

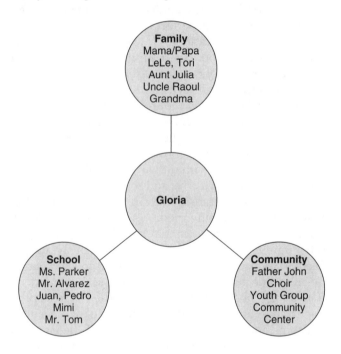

Themes:
1. Gloria has strong family ties; multigenerational family lives in household or within 10 miles.
2. School acquaintances Juan, Pedro, and Mimi will transition to high school with Gloria, but in middle school they had few opportunities to socialize outside of the classroom.
3. Mr. Tom, the itinerant vision teacher, has been a favorite teacher and will continue working with Gloria.
4. Gloria's family is involved in church and the community center. Are there untapped possibilities for Gloria?

Figure 10.4
Gloria's Relationships Map

High school students may have limited relationships simply because they are in transition from one setting to another. They may have lost contact with high school friends but not yet developed relationships with new coworkers, neighbors, or other adults. Thus, families and other IEP team members should be encouraged to expand students' relationships by identifying their social networks—that is, the social capital they can bring to the transition planning table. For example, team members may provide vital contacts for job leads and volunteer positions. They may provide resources for carpools. They may provide resources for rental units or contacts for real estate agents or mortgage brokers. They may be able to identify tutors for postsecondary education courses, workout buddies for YMCA facilities, and peer buddies for church youth groups.

Hughes and Carter (2000) offered some additional relationship assessment methods to consider, including (a) observing students interacting with general curriculum peers outside of the classroom; (b) interviewing parents, employers, and fellow educators to learn how well they think students fit in; and (c) preparing checklists for peers, educators, and/or employers to complete that identify the social skills needed in specific environments and activities.

In addition, Benson, Galbraith, and Espeland (1998) suggested some self-assessment group discussion questions that educators might consider using with adolescents to help them think about their current circle of friends: (a) *Which of your friends do you most want to be like?* (b) *What do you like most about your friends?* (c) *What bothers you about your friends? and* (d) *How do you feel when you are with your friends?* Benson and colleagues further suggested that parents and family discuss their teenagers' friends with them, asking what they think of their current circle of friends, and using their comments to open doors of communication about healthy relationships during the transition years.

Each of these and many other tools offer educators resources for assessing the quality and quantity of students' relationships. These assessments serve as a foundation for the next step, increasing opportunities for building new relationships, sustaining important relationships over time, and teaching relationship skills and self-determination attributes. Like leisure education, relationship education should be addressed within the broader construct of building community participation experiences and outcomes.

DID YOU KNOW?

Research shows that friendships generally differ in males and females (Pogrebin, 1987). Although there are always exceptions, girls and women gravitate toward one-to-one relationships that may evolve into more intimate and personally intense relationships than do those of boys and men. Boys and men gravitate toward groups of males with whom they share common interests. Girls and women most value friends with whom they may share secrets, and men most value friends who they perceive as being loyal.

CASE STUDY

GLORIA

Figure 10.4 is an example of a relationships map developed by Gloria along with her family and her IEP team. They created this map as part of Gloria's IEP meeting as she prepared to make the transition from her middle school into her much larger community high school.

Gloria is a 16-year-old who is described by her teacher as "inquisitive and outgoing." She is physically active and "moves confidently around familiar environments" in spite of being legally blind. Gloria is also hard of hearing and wears hearing aids in both ears. Her teacher and speech therapist agree that Gloria "uses a rich and personal system of gestures along with many ASL [American Sign Language] signs to communicate fairly competently with others."

When frustrated by the inability of others to understand what she is attempting to communicate, Gloria attempts to physically lead people to representative places, people, and objects. This method of communication can be frightening to people who do not know her well and frustrating to Gloria when people do not respond the way she desires. Her close and extended family communicate only in Spanish, but they use and understand most of Gloria's communications. Gloria's teacher and her classmates communicate only in English. It is uncertain how much auditory information Gloria understands, but she clearly prefers ASL and gestures, smiling and nodding broadly when she understands something.

Gloria and her family are active members of their church and the Latino Community Center. Recently, like many other teenagers, Gloria has expressed through her behaviors a desire to spend more time with her same-age peers and less time with her parents by "hanging out near other girls during church and community events." Her parents have observed these behaviors, but at her IEP meeting they expressed reluctance to let Gloria spend time away from them and with same-age peers, fearing that her peers would misunderstand her communication behaviors and, as a result, make fun of her and cause her to become angry.

The IEP team and Gloria's family developed a relationships map and used it to identify some of Gloria's current relationships that should be continued as well as to prioritize some potential resources for new and expanded relationships as she entered high school. The team helped Gloria's family identify environments, situations, and supports that would increase their comfort with Gloria's increased independence. Subsequently, her IEP was written to provide her with a richer schedule of inclusive activities with general education high school classmates that included participation in a Spanish youth leadership club, a fitness and stretching class, and an art class. Gloria's teachers agreed to teach some of Gloria's basic ASL signs and communication behaviors to the peer students who would be interacting most with her. Her family began to provide Gloria with more independence and choices in her church and community youth group activities.

Within 2 years of transitioning to her high school, Gloria was spending time with three new general curriculum friends who helped her with skill development as well as transportation, communication, and a sighted guide. At last year's IEP, Gloria's teachers and parents agreed that Gloria had become more self-confident, more communicative, and more open to the needs of others and that her family and other team members were more aware of possible vocational and leisure interests and preferences.

Expanding and Teaching Relationship Skills

One of the most effective ways to increase a person's relationships is to increase his or her community presence and participation in school and community activities. As students with disabilities become more visibly present in academic, extracurricular, and community environments and activities, educators can begin to teach relationship skills in a variety of naturally occurring ways. For example, disability awareness and simulation days can be a component of school-sponsored diversity events. Care can be taken, for example, when career events are planned, to ensure that adults with disabilities are invited along with other adults to share their career experiences. When students are included in general curriculum classes, care can be taken to arrange desks, group tables, and assign projects to student teams so that all students are comfortable seeing, hearing, moving, communicating about, understanding, and completing assignments. School-sponsored clubs and athletic teams can be encouraged to set goals to make their memberships more inclusive.

An important and frequently overlooked aspect of relationships and community participation is volunteerism and civic activities for teenagers with disabilities. Encouraging teenagers to volunteer their time for service groups such as Habitat for Humanity and Interact, voter registration drives, community fundraising events for the Humane Society or local schools, church yard sales, and other groups gives them valuable community presence, opportunities to build relationships, and, in many cases, transferable vocational skills.

Nearly all teenagers will benefit from the structured skill development and educational experiences that can be taught using the numerous commercially available curricula and teaching methods for expanding and building relationships.

DID YOU KNOW?

The Bubel Aiken Foundation offers grants to students with disabilities to develop and engage in service learning opportunities. For more information go to www.thebubelaikenfoundation.org.

The Council for Exceptional Children and the Disney Channel offer a *Learning to Serve* Web site that has step-by-step guidelines for starting a service-learning project that connects to academic standards. For more information, visit www.disney.go.com/disneychannel/learningtoserve/index.html.

Most of them have the following characteristics in common: (a) they use natural, community environments, activities, and materials; (b) they identify one-on-one "peer buddies" to model appropriate behaviors and skills; and (c) they use social networks or "circles of friends" to expand and enhance social networks and community connections.

What skills should be taught to encourage healthy relationships with friends, family, and community members? Figure 10.5 offers educators a framework of relationship skills that adults may need. This list is intended only to serve as a broad guide. It should be modified to reflect the goals and objectives of individual students.

For example, attention to civic and voting skills may be of interest to many transition-age adolescents as they approach adulthood, yet this area is often given minimal attention during transition planning. The National Organization on Disability (NOD, 2004) found that 21% of surveyed Americans with disabilities wanted to vote but were unable to do so for a variety of reasons. Survey

---

Transition-age students should, independently or with support, be able to:

- Identify the people with whom they have significant relationships and the roles they play in their daily lives and activities.
- Describe the characteristics of friends and list their own personal attributes that make them good friends.
- Greet people appropriately in school, places of employment, church, recreation sites, and other social settings.
- Identify appropriate boundaries, settings, and behaviors for intimate relationships and behave accordingly.
- Identify and respond appropriately to peer pressure.
- Be a good sport.
- Ask other people questions and listen to their responses.
- Respond to other people's body language.
- Appropriately describe personal experiences and events to others.
- Respect other people's rights, feelings, and property.
- Deal with personal anger and with the anger of others.
- Know when and how to apologize.
- Ask for help when needed and express gratitude for help when it is provided.
- Be assertive about their wants and needs.
- Be able to negotiate and compromise their wants.
- Be a good parent.
- Be a good spouse or partner.
- Be a good coworker.
- Be a good citizen.
- Be a good neighbor.

Figure 10.5
Suggested Relationship Skills for Transition-Age Students

respondents cited lack of accessible transportation, eligibility challenges, lack of accessible polling places, inability to understand how the voting machines operated, fear of embarrassment, lack of alternative voting formats such as large print, and lack of services such as ASL interpreters (NOD, 2004). Voting is an excellent example of skills that may be infused into general curriculum high school social studies, government, and civics coursework as well as in high school student government organizations and civic events such as Interact Clubs, scouts, and church groups. Voting and other relationship instruction enables educators to address all of the self-determination attributes and teaching methods summarized earlier in Table 10.1. It is especially appropriate for instruction in inclusive high school settings, as well as curriculum and programs designed specifically for students with disabilities.

HEALTH AND MEDICAL ISSUES

Thinking and talking about health and medical issues are important but frequently overlooked aspects of transition planning. This may be because health and medical issues are considered very personal, something to be discussed only at home or with medical professionals instead of at school. Or perhaps educators and other IEP team members are unaware of students' and families' health and medical concerns during the transition process, assuming that if they have questions they will ask them during IEP meetings.

Whatever the reasons for this lack of communication and planning, all adolescents, with or without disabilities, are expected to transition from the pediatric health care system to the adult health care system around age 21. In addition, when adolescents reach the age of majority as determined by a specific state, they become legally responsible for all of their health care decisions unless legal actions are taken to limit some or all of these decisions. This important transition will occur more easily and efficiently if it is planned. Ideally, planning will take place across multiple years and will be coordinated with a student's IEP and transition planning as well as with the experienced health and medical professionals. The goal of transition planning targeting health and medical needs is twofold: (a) to transition teenagers systematically and seamlessly from the pediatric health care system to the adult health care system and (b) to provide students with the skills and experiences necessary to enable them to assume as much independence as possible regarding their health and medical needs and services.

Assessing Health and Medical Needs

Healthy adolescents may be defined as those who engage in self-determined behaviors about their disability, their health and medical needs, and their adult choices and options. Determining individual students' health and medical needs and skills is an important initial step for educators and IEP teams to address.

Specifically for students with special health care needs, a good foundation for this assessment is the school nurse and the transition planning that he or she has been doing with the student to ensure educational success. Educators and IEP teams should also consult students and their families along with the questions and medical records they have accumulated as a foundation for planning.

To assess students' health and medical skills and needs further, educators might consider developing a simple checklist or questionnaire to distribute to students and their families. Assessment questions to consider might include the following:

- ◆ What does "healthy" mean to you? What, if anything, would you like to discuss and know more about during your transition planning activities?
- ◆ What are some of the things that you do to keep yourself healthy?
- ◆ Do you take any medications or treatments? If so, do you need assistance with any of these?
- ◆ Do you have a doctor? A dentist?
- ◆ Do you have insurance? Do you understand how insurance works?
- ◆ How do you keep up with your medical records?
- ◆ Do you need assistance in scheduling or completing appointments?

Teaching Health and Medical Skills

Once educators have a more focused picture of health and medical skills for specific students, the next step is to begin providing skill instruction and opportunities to practice and refine theses skills. School-sponsored and commercially available health and sex education classes and curricula are available in most high schools and are an excellent place to include students with disabilities. Pomeroy, Everson, Guillory, and Fass (2001) have offered a specific health and medical curriculum guide designed for transition-age students with disabilities and special health care needs. In addition, Blanchett and Wolfe (2002) have provided sex education curriculum adoption guidelines specifically for students with moderate and severe disabilities.

These resources, and many others, may be used to (a) stimulate discussion and role playing about health and risk-taking choices and behaviors, (b) assist in gathering information regarding health plans and support, and (c) develop IEPs and transition goals that gradually support adolescents in taking more responsibility for their health and medical needs.

Figure 10.6 summarizes suggested health and medical skills needed by transition-age students and young adults. Like leisure and relationships education, health and medical instruction should be addressed within the broader construct of building community participation experiences and outcomes. In addition, health and medical instruction should build self-determination abilities such as self-knowledge, choice-making, goal-setting, decision-making, and self-monitoring.

Transition-age students should, independently or with support, be able to:

♦ Describe their disability and/or their health condition and the implications for their daily lives and activities.
♦ Access and understand their health and medical records.
♦ Take responsibility for administering prescribed medications and medical treatments.
♦ Know when and how to use nonprescription medications.
♦ Know when to use and how to read a thermometer.
♦ Take responsibility for scheduling medical and dental appointments and treatments.
♦ Take responsibility for getting to and from appointments.
♦ Share medical insurance coverage information; their height, weight, birthdate, blood type, and allergies; and/or carry the information in a wallet.
♦ Share an emergency contact name and telephone number and/or carry the information in a wallet.
♦ Describe the various roles of the medical professionals involved in their treatment.
♦ Know and practice basic first aid and emergency procedures.
♦ Know where and whom to call for basic and emergency health and medical services.
♦ Take responsibility for basic hygiene and self-care needs.
♦ Discuss concerns with a primary health care provider.
♦ Hire and supervise a personal care attendant (PCA).
♦ Make simple maintenance and repairs on wheelchairs and other assistive equipment and know where and whom to contact for more complex maintenance and repair needs.
♦ Understand the employment-related mandates of the Americans with Disabilities Act (ADA) as they concern their disability and/or health and medical conditions.
♦ Appropriately discuss disability and/or health and medical needs with future employers and/or postsecondary education professionals.

Figure 10.6
Suggested Health and Medical Skills for Transition-Age Students

Note. For more detailed information on teaching these health skills to adolescents, please see *Health and Medical Issues for Transition-Age Adolescents with Disabilities and/or Health Care Needs and Their Families: A Guide for Teenagers and Their Families,* Second Edition, by M. Pomeroy, J. M. Everson, J. D. Guillory, and A. L. Fass, 2001, New Orleans: Louisiana State University Health Sciences Center, Human Development Center.

CASE STUDY

PHILIP

Philip was an 18-year-old high school junior when he first began to think seriously about enrolling in the state's largest public university when he graduated from high school. During an IEP meeting, with prompting from his mother,

Philip shared his goal of becoming a child psychologist so that he could help other children with physical disabilities understand and live with their abilities and disabilities. Philip was described by his teacher as "quiet, persistent, and intelligent—not someone you easily say 'no' to!"

Diagnosed with a rare degenerative muscular syndrome as an infant, Philip has gradually transitioned from walking to using an electric wheelchair and from talking to using a computer-driven communication device. Philip is also dependent on a ventilator for breathing. His mother, a single parent, has dedicated much of her time to providing Philip with personal care and educational support services. Philip is enrolled in his community high school, where a classroom aide and student peers provide him with assistance such as note-taking, page-turning, and after-school tutorials. Although he tires easily and frequently misses school for medical appointments and treatments, Philip has maintained a rigorous academic schedule and has so far passed all academic courses and tests required by his state for graduation.

Although his IEP team was supportive of Philip's goal to attend the state university, his mother and the team were surprised when he also expressed a goal of living in a dorm on campus with other students. Philip's goal generated a great deal of discussion, and many potential barriers and challenges were raised. Several subsequent meetings and additional discussions ensued, including appointments with Philip's pediatrician, vocational rehabilitation counselor, high school nurse, university officials, staff from a regional CIL, and outreach staff from a regional children's hospital.

During Philip's senior year of high school, his IEP and transition plan included two new goals. First, Philip would enroll in one college transfer course, 2 days a week, at the local community college. Second, Philip would assume responsibility for interviewing, hiring, and supervising his newly authorized Medicaid-funded personal care attendant (PCA).

Philip and members of his team met with community college officials and agreed on a plan to provide transportation, educational supports, and medical supports. Philip and his vocational rehabilitation counselor met with the course instructor, and they agreed on a plan to ensure Philip's successful completion of the course and its requirements. When the professor described Phillip's needs and asked for volunteers, two students in his class volunteered to provide supports such as note-taking, setting up his books, and meeting at his home for a study group when needed. One of the assistive devices provided to Philip by his vocational rehabilitation counselor was a cellular phone with an adapted switch for Philip to use in emergencies. The counselor also provided a written medical emergency plan for Philip to carry around in his backpack. Philip assumed almost total responsibility for overseeing the hiring and supervising of a male PCA who accompanied him to class.

Philip successfully completed his first community college course, but as a result of his experiences and medical needs, he decided to modify his postschool goals slightly. When Philip graduated from high school, he enrolled in the community college part time. Within a year, he moved away from home into a specially equipped and accessible apartment near the campus, accessible transportation, and medical providers. He shares the apartment with another young man who also has a physical disability, and they receive PCA services. As Philip's mother summarized, "Philip is reaching his goals, he is safe—and he is not too far away from home either!"

TRANSPORTATION

Perhaps the greatest barrier to community participation among students and adults with disabilities is a lack of public, accessible, and and/or affordable transportation. In fact, it may be the single greatest barrier to community participation for all nondriving citizens in many communities, such as the elderly and residents of rural communities (Everson, Guillory, & Ivester, 2005).

Obtaining a driver's license is a traditional right of passage among adolescents, and it is related to a number of self-determination attributes (Corn & Rosenblum, 2000; McGill & Vogtle, 2001), including choice-making, goal-setting, independence, risk-taking, and self-evaluation. Nevertheless, few students with disabilities participate in driver's education programs, and few educational alternatives are offered to nondriving transition-age students (Corn & Rosenblum, 2000; McGill & Vogtle, 2001).

Transportation is a critical aspect of community participation. Students with transportation skills and opportunities have vastly increased opportunities to pursue leisure and relationship opportunities. Adolescents who miss out on this rite of passage may find their opportunities drastically reduced when their peers begin to drive. For these reasons, high schools that offer driver's education programs to general curriculum students must begin to make these programs more accessible and welcoming to students with disabilities who can and will be drivers in the future. In addition, educators and IEP teams must begin to teach students with disabilities who may never be drivers the nondriver skills and self-determination abilities needed to gain control over their transportation wants and needs.

Nondrivers are defined as high school students who have been unable to obtain driver's licenses, are considered unable to obtain driver's licenses, and/or choose to use other transportation resources because of their disabilities. This section of the chapter describes teaching methods and activities for providing **nondriver's education** to transition-age students. As with the other areas discussed in this chapter, nondriver's education should be provided in the context of achieving richer community participation outcomes. The goal is to provide students with the self-determination abilities and knowledge of transportation options to enable them to be as independent as possible in their transportation arrangements.

Assessing Transportation Interests and Skills

Every state has specific requirements that may impact a student's ability to obtain a driver's license. These include: (a) visual requirements; (b) physical requirements; (c) health and medical requirements; (d) knowledge of driving mechanics and state laws; and (e) demonstration of driving abilities and experiences. Therefore, the first task for educators and IEP teams is to become familiar with these requirements, provide access to this information to students and their families, and assist them in assessing students' potential driving abilities. This assessment should take into consideration access to (a) school-sponsored driver's education, including teaching and testing supports for nonreaders, low-level readers, and students whose primary language is not English, and (b) assistive devices, such as hand controls for students with physical disabilities and optical devices for students with low vision. Many educators and family members will find that this assessment process is best facilitated by a team of educators, health and medical providers, rehabilitation professionals (including low vision, rehabilitation engineering, and orientation and mobility specialists), and community or state representatives from the department of transportation or motor vehicles.

Including adolescents in self-assessing their driving abilities is critical. Although research on driving and students with disabilities is minimal, there is some evidence that adolescents with visual impairments and those with physical disabilities who are part of the assessment and decision-making process may be more willing to pursue nondriving options (Corn & Rosenblum, 2000; McGill & Vogtle, 2001) than those who are told by their parents or professionals that they cannot or should not consider becoming drivers.

Teaching Transportation Skills

Driver's education curricula for high school education students exist in nearly every community and are tailored to the driving requirements of each state. McGill and Votgle (2001) emphasized the need for high school students with driving potential to be included in these programs and for these curricula to be expanded to expose all students to information on assistive devices and modifications for drivers with disabilities.

More difficult is the need to provide curricula for students who are nondrivers. One of the best of these curricula is Corn and Rosenblum's (2000) curriculum, which, although designed for nondrivers with visual impairments, can be used as a framework for nondrivers with other disabilities. The goal of this curriculum is to provide students with the knowledge, skills, and abilities they need to gain control over their transportation needs. Figure 10.7 summarizes suggested nondriver skills, emphasizing the need for students to acquire and practice self-determination abilities to gain control over their transportation needs.

CASE STUDY

JANICE

Janice is a 15-year-old teenager who has learned to navigate her way through her crowded high school using landmarks and tactual cues. Janice has been legally

Transition-age students should, independently or with support, be able to:

- ◆ Describe the functional implications of their disabilities for driving and non-driving transportation options.
- ◆ Describe their experiences and feelings about not obtaining a driver's license and not being able to drive, and be able to share these feelings with friends, family and coworkers.
- ◆ Identify destinations, days of week, times of day, and reasons that they anticipate needing transportation currently and in the future.
- ◆ Identify how current and future transportation needs might influence their lifestyle choices (e.g., where they choose to live, where they choose to work).
- ◆ Identify public and private transportation resources in their communities.
- ◆ Request information from these resources about schedules, routes, fares, and eligibility.
- ◆ Use these resources appropriately (e.g., make reservations, calculate schedules, communicate with drivers and other personnel, socialize appropriately with other riders, use resource safely, transact fare, follow route to destination).
- ◆ Identify other potential options (e.g., asking family members to drive, carpooling with coworkers, hiring a driver, exchanging tasks for rides with friends and neighbors).
- ◆ Demonstrate skills in asking for rides, declining rides, negotiating payment for carpools or ride sharing, exchanging tasks for rides.
- ◆ Hire and supervise a driver.
- ◆ Establish a weekly and monthly transportation budget.
- ◆ Establish a weekly and monthly transportation schedule.
- ◆ Self-evaluate personal transportation options and revise plans as needed.

Figure 10.7
Suggested Nondriver Skills for Transition-Age Students
Note. For more detailed information on teaching these nondriver skills to adolescents, please see *Finding Wheels: A Curriculum for Nondrivers with Visual Impairments for Gaining Control of Transportation Needs* by A. L. Corn and L. P. Rosenblum, 2000, Baltimore: Paul H. Brookes Publishing Co.

blind since birth and has learned to tell people what she can and cannot see and to ask for help when needed. She has a sense of humor about her vision, and her friends quickly feel comfortable when she jokes about the hazards of "blindly" applying makeup and cooking. She is fiercely independent, using a guide dog around her community and shunning the use of a cane.

When first asked during her IEP meeting about her postschool plans for transportation, Janice seemed surprised. She responded, "I'll learn to drive, I guess." Her grandmother and IEP team were not sure how to respond; everyone seemed to have assumed that Janice knew that she would not be able to drive because of her vision impairment. Janice's vision teacher quickly suggested that Janice be enrolled in the high school's driver's education class along with her same-age peers, and the team readily agreed. Two new IEP goals were written: (a) *Janice will enroll in and successfully complete the high school sponsored classroom driver's education class;* and (b) *Janice will complete a comprehensive low-vision assessment to determine her future driving possibilities through the local department of vocational rehabilitation and center for independent living.*

During the classroom component of the class, Janice's vision teacher gave a lecture to all of the students on vision requirements for driving and demonstrated potential assistive devices for drivers with low vision. Janice learned that even with assistive devices she would not be able to secure a driver's license. Initially, she was embarrassed and angry. However, the driver's education teacher encouraged her and her classmates to discuss their feelings about driving and non-driving. By the end of the course, Janice was still disappointed, but she felt that her closest friends who were learning to drive were sensitive to her needs and fears. As a result, she felt comfortable identifying options that enabled her to plan leisure and social activities for which she could use the city bus, ask her friends for shared rides, and budget and pay for gas from her allowance. "Sometimes, I still feel like a burden when I have to ask for help, but I also know that I have a lot of transportation options. I have even realized that someday I may be able to buy a car and pay someone to drive me around—how cool would that be!"

Strategies for Family Involvement

♦ Include the teenager in planning family and individual activities during evening and weekend free time. Include activities of interest to the teenager as well as activities that are of interest to the entire family.

♦ Encourage the teenager to make plans with friends and consider schedules, transportation, and expenses associated with the activities.

♦ Assign the teenager an allowance and financial responsibility for budgeting and paying for leisure and transportation activities.

♦ Encourage the teenager to introduce you to friends and discuss relationships.

♦ Encourage the teenager to set goals and think through the actions needed to accomplish the goals. Recognize and discuss failures as well as successes.

♦ Discuss responsibilities and costs associated with driving, and identify and use public transportation opportunities.

♦ Discuss the teenager's disability factually. Provide the teenager with opportunities to spend time with other teenagers who have similar disabilities.

♦ Discuss healthy behaviors and family life-style expectations.

♦ Provide opportunities for the teenager to assume gradual responsibility for making some health choices more independently and for assuming more control over medical treatments.

♦ Provide the teenager with opportunities to meet privately with his or her physician(s).

SUMMARY

Adolescence is a period characterized by many complex transitions for teenagers and their families. Anticipating, discussing, planning for, and supporting these transitions are essential if they are to make successful transitions and achieve desired community participation outcomes. Self-determined adolescents have many of the attributes they need to gain control over these transition discussions and plans. Therefore, educators and families are encouraged to incorporate person-centered planning tools and self-determination curricula into high school transition planning in order to maximize community participation outcomes for all high school students.

STUDY GUIDE QUESTIONS

1. Identify and describe the major tasks and transitions of adolescence. Are these tasks and transitions comparable for adolescents with disabilities and those without disabilities?
2. What is the role of educators and transition planning teams in supporting these tasks and transitions?
3. What is community participation? How does the construct apply to your own life?
4. Why have the areas discussed in this chapter—recreation, relationships, heath and medical issues, and transportation—received so little attention in transition planning models and the literature? What can educators do to increase attention to these areas and foster successful outcomes?
5. Why are self-determination skills such an important foundation to the attainment of community participation outcomes?
6. Select one of the areas discussed in this chapter and identify specific educational activities that you could incorporate into your curriculum and classroom immediately.
7. Select one of your students and identify strategies for addressing one of more of the content areas discussed in this chapter into his or her IEP and transition planning activities.

REFERENCES

Benson, P. L., Galbraith, J., & Espeland, P. (1998). *What teens need to succeed. Proven, practical ways to shape your own future.* Minneapolis: Free Spirit.

Blanchett, W. J., & Wolfe, P. S. (2002) A review of sexuality education curricula: Meeting the sex-uality needs of individuals with moderate and severe disabilities. *Research and Practice for Persons with Severe Disabilities, 27,* 43–57.

Corn, A. L., & Rosenblum L. P. (2000). *Finding wheels: A curriculum for nondrivers with visual impairments for gaining control of transportation needs.* Baltimore: Brookes.

Cronin, M. S., & Patton, J. R. (1993). *Life skills instruction for all students with special needs: A practical guide for integrating real-life content into the curriculum.* Austin, TX: Pro-Ed.

Elliott, G., & Fieldman, S. (1990). Capturing the adolescent experience. In S. Fieldman & G. Elliott (Eds.), *At the threshold: The developing adolescent* (pp. 1–13). Cambridge, MA: Harvard University Press.

Everson, J. M., Guillory, J. D., & Ivester, J. (2005). *Community development in action: Illustrations from communities in South Carolina and Louisiana.* Columbia: University of South Carolina School of Medicine, Center for Disability Resources. (Grant # 90DN1029 funded by the Department of Health and Human Services).

Field, S., Martin, J., Miller, R., Ward, M., & Wehmeyer, M. (1998). *A practical guide for teaching self-determination.* Arlington, VA: Council for Exceptional Children.

Graber, J. A., & Dubas, J. S. (1996). *Leaving home: Understanding the transition to adulthood.* San Francisco: Jossey-Bass.

Holburn, S., & Vietze, P. M. (2002). *Person-centered planning: Research, practice, and future directions.* Baltimore: Brookes.

Huettig, C., & Roth, K. (2002). Maximizing the use of APE consultants: What the general physical educator has the right to expect. *Journal of Physical Education, Recreation & Dance, 73*(1), 32–35.

Hughes, C., & Carter, E. (2000). *The transition handbook. Strategies high school teachers use that work!* Baltimore: Brookes.

Hunt, M. E. (1991). *A fierce tenderness: A feminist theology of friendship.* New York: Crossroad.

Kohler, P. D. (1996). *A taxonomy for transition programming linking research and practice.* Champaign: University of Illinois, Transition Research Institute.

Kolb, S. M., & Hanley-Maxwell, C. (2003). Critical social skills for adolescents with high incidence disabilities: Parental perspectives. *Exceptional Children, 69,* 163–179.

McGill, T., & Vogtle, L. K. (2001). Driver's education for students with physical disabilities. *Exceptional Children, 67,* 455–466.

Morningstar, M. E., Turnbull, A. P., & Turnbull, H. R. (1995). What do students with disabilities tell us about the importance of family involvement in the transition from school to adult life? *Exceptional Children, 62,* 249–260.

Moon, M. S. (1994). *Making school and community recreation fun for everyone. Places and ways to integrate.* Baltimore: Brookes.

National Organization on Disability. (2004, October 19). *Barriers restrict voting by people with disabilities.* Retrieved October 21, 2004, from www.nod.org.

O'Brien, C. L., & O'Brien, J. (2002). The origins of person-centered planning: A community of practice perspective. In S. Holburn, & P. M Vietze, (Eds.), *Person-centered planning: Research, practice, and future directions* (pp. 3–27). Baltimore: Brookes.

O'Brien, J. (1987). A guide to lifestyle planning. In B. Wilcox & G. T. Bellamy (Eds.), *A comprehensive guide to the activities catalog* (pp. 175–189). Baltimore: Brookes.

O'Brien, J., & O'Brien, C. L. (1993). Unlikely alliances. Friendships and people with developmental disabilities. In A. Amado (Ed.), *Friendships and connections between people with and without developmental disabilities* (pp. 9–39). Baltimore: Brookes.

Perske, R. (1993). Introduction. In A. Amado (Ed.), *Friendships and community connections between people with and without developmental disabilities* (pp.1–6). Baltimore: Brookes.

Pogrebin, L. C. (1987). *Among friends. What we like and what we do with them.* New York: McGraw-Hill.

Pomeroy, M., Everson, J. M., Guillory, J. D., & Fass, A. L. (2001, October). *Health and medical issues for transition-age adolescents with disabilities and/or health care needs and their families: A guide for teenagers and their families* (2nd ed.). New Orleans: Louisiana State University Health Sciences Center, Human Development Center.

Price, L. A., Wolensky, D., & Mulligan, R. (2002). Self-determination in action in the classroom. *Remedial and Special Education, 23,* 109–115.

Putnam, R. D. (2000). *Bowling alone: The collapse and revival of American community.* New York: Simon & Schuster.

Reid, S. H., Parsons, M. B. & Green, C. W. (1991). *Providing choices and preferences of persons who have severe handicaps.* Morganton, NC: Habilitative Management Consultants.

Schleien, S. J., Ray, M. T., & Green, F. P. (1997). *Community recreation and people with disabilities: Strategies for inclusion.* Baltimore: Brookes.

Strand, J., & Kreiner, J. (2001). Recreation and leisure in the community. In R. W. Flexer, T. J. Simmons, P. Luft, & R. M Baer (Eds.), *Transition planning for secondary students with disabilities* (pp. 475–498). Upper Saddle River, NJ: Merrill/Prentice Hall.

Wehmeyer, M. L. (1996). Self-determination as an educational outcome: Why is it important to children, youth, and adults with disabilities? In D. J. Sands & M. L. Wehmeyer (Eds.), *Self-determination across the lifespan: Independence and choice for people with disabilities* (pp. 17–36). Baltimore; Brookes.

Wehmeyer, M. L., Agran, M., & Hughes, C. (1998). *Teaching self-determination to students with disabilities: Basic skills for successful transition.* Baltimore: Brookes.

Whitney-Thomas, J., & Hanley-Maxwell, C. (1996). Packing the parachute: Parents' experiences as their children prepare to leave high school. *Exceptional Children, 63,* 75–97.

Transition Program Evaluation

Chapter 11

Introduction

Transition services have always been defined within an outcome-oriented process. Because the Individuals with Disabilities Education Act (IDEA; 1997) dramatically shifted the focus of assessing educational programs from measuring processes to measuring outcomes, it is natural that we would support a more systematic approach to collecting data to evaluate the effectiveness of transition programs. Program evaluation is also incorporated within the Taxonomy for Transition Programming *(Kohler, 1996) as a key component under "Program Structures and Attributes." The taxonomy reminds us that an effective process for collecting transition program evaluation data is needed to ensure continuous program improvement and students' achievement of their dreams. In addition, a thorough program evaluation process must include opportunities for students to practice their emerging skills in self-determination and self-advocacy by participating in focus groups, being involved with evaluation teams, and participating in consumer satisfaction surveys.*

This chapter introduces the reasons for collecting program evaluation data, as well as the types of data that can be collected and strategies for collecting it. With the current focus on student accountability, conducting a program evaluation is one method of determining the success of a school's or school system's transition services.

Key Terms

formative evaluation
summative evaluations

postschool outcome data
consumer satisfaction data
interagency collaboration
IEP team processes
student performance data

A Personal Perspective on Transition Program Evaluation

Dr. Patricia E. Austin

Director of Special Education, Scottsboro City Schools

The provision of high-quality transition services and supports has been a priority of the Scottsboro City Schools during the 1990s and the beginning of the 21st century. The special education leadership of our school system began to develop a framework of how to address the transition needs of students with disabilities. Our first steps were to review the professional literature regarding transition services to identify best practices in the field. Second, we examined the needs and barriers students were encountering in the local community.

In 1994 we formed our own Scottsboro Community Transition Team and assessed our community resources relating to transition using the community transition team model (CTTM) (Halpern, Benz, & Lindstrom, 1992). A community transition team's member-ship is comprised of stakeholders of the transition process—school personnel, community agency representatives, business leaders, students, parents, and others who express an interest in our mission. It was through the CTTM needs assessment that our community transition team identified strengths and barriers for students with disabilities as they move from school to postsecondary employment, education, and services. Once our com-munity transition team identified barriers or areas of need, we prioritized the needs and selected four areas as targeted goals. We then developed an action plan, and the commu-nity transition team divided into committees to focus attention on specific need or bar-rier areas.

In the years following, many identified barriers had been removed or resolved. Link-ages among stakeholders were made with student transition needs in mind. Our team still functions, but we have merged with another community team that focused on stu-dent skill development and employment opportunities within our community.

The transition program of services and supports presently in place in Scottsboro has evolved over the years. To help us continue to improve, we conduct an annual school sys-tem evaluation regarding the transition program of services and supports. This School System Self-Assessment is a checklist of transition quality indicators that solicits infor-mation in the following areas:

♦ *School-based activities*

♦ *Connecting activities*

- ♦ *Community/work training activities*
- ♦ *Student involvement*
- ♦ *Parent and family involvement*
- ♦ *Transdisciplinary school involvement*
- ♦ *Transition and the IEP*
- ♦ *Workplace readiness*
- ♦ *Adult living curriculum.*

Information gathered from this annual assessment is reviewed by the school's transition team to identify areas that need further attention or development.

This annual review process helps us keep focused on the needs of our students and continue to strive for program improvement. Our mission is to help all students with disabilities prepare for and move into adulthood with a planned direction leading to successful lives in the community.

Determining the success of a school's or school system's transition services requires conducting a program evaluation. While there are many different approaches to program evaluation (e.g., objective oriented, management oriented, expertise oriented), all involve collecting and providing information to enhance decision making (Worthen, Sanders, & Fitzpatrick, 1997). Program evaluations can be either formative or summative. A **formative evaluation** is conducted to provide program staff with information that can be used to improve a program. Formative evaluations are usually conducted when a program is developed. The audience for formative evaluation data is often the personnel involved in developing the program.

Summative evaluations are typically conducted and made public to provide decision-makers and consumers with information to judge a program's worth or merit relative to important criteria. Summative evaluation data are often used to help make decisions such as whether to terminate, continue, or expand a program. The audiences for summative program evaluations typically include program personnel and consumers.

Developing methods for evaluating transition programs involves both formative and summative systems since the data produced provides audiences with information that can be used to (a) make programmatic changes and (b) allow judgments of the merit or worth of programs in terms of improving student postschool outcomes.

REASONS FOR COLLECTING PROGRAM EVALUATION DATA

The bottom-line in any evaluation of transition services provided by a school or a school system is to ensure that the program is improving the postschool outcomes of students with disabilities. As both Darrow and Clark (1992) and Sample

(1998) noted, school programs and services benefit from improved program evaluation that tracks students over time in relation to the programs and services they receive while in high school. In fact, Halpern (1990) made the argument that collecting postschool outcome data is actually cost-effective:

> While costliness and unmanageability have been cited as reasons why follow-along is not commonly used, it should be pointed out that it is not cost-efficient to use scarce resources to gather imprecise information that may inaccurately guide program development. (p. 84)

A second reason for collecting program evaluation data is to harness the power of consumer support for a transition program. By collecting consumer satisfaction and student outcome data, a transition program can use consumer feedback to expand and improve its services and better prepare students to become successful adults. Consumer satisfaction data can also be used to demonstrate public support for services. Supporters (e.g., parents, students, teachers, human resource personnel, business owners) can be extremely helpful in helping transition efforts gain the necessary attention to move forward. With support often comes protection (Aspel, Bettis, Test, & Wood, 1998).

Finally, because transition has been defined by IDEA 2004 as "a coordinated set of activities" that are "focused on improving the academic and functional achievement" that are designed to "facilitate movement to/from post-school activities" [Section 602(34)(A)], it seems logical that evaluation of transition programs must address at least three questions:

1. Did transition services provide high-quality postschool outcomes?
2. Did transition services meet student needs and preferences?
3. Are transition services coordinated among the various agencies concerned with students?

To gather data needed to answer these three questions, school systems must collect four types of data: (a) postschool outcome data; (b) consumer satisfaction data; (c) interagency collaboration and IEP team processes data; and (d) data on student performance in the transition program. Each of these types of transition program evaluation data is described in the next section.

DID YOU KNOW?

Better data can help schools make better decisions about serving students with disabilities (American Youth Policy Forum and Center on Education Policy, 2002).

TYPES OF TRANSITION PROGRAM EVALUATION DATA

Postschool Outcome Data

Postschool outcome data are collected to gather information about students who have left school in terms of their current employment, educational, residential, and leisure and recreation status. These data are typically collected on an annual basis for up to 3 to 5 years after a student graduates from high school. Postschool outcome data serve at least three purposes:

1. Obtaining a measure of the current status of former special education students.
2. Improving policies and practices.
3. Program planning when improving secondary curricula and transition practices.

    Examples of systems for collecting postschool outcome data are available at the national level for both students receiving special education services (Blackorby & Wagner, 1996; Fairweather & Shaver, 1990) and students enrolled in vocational education (Harvey, 2002). At the state level, examples are available for both students in special education (Austin, 2001; Rabren, Dunn, & Chambers, 2002; Storms, 2003) and all students (Repetto, Webb, Garvan, & Washington, 2002). At the local school system level, examples are available for students in special education (Aspel et al., 1998; Benz, Lindstrom, & Yovanoff, 2000; Hoisch, Karen, & Fanzini, 1992; Malmgrem, Edgar, & Neel, 1998).

    IDEA (2004) now requires school systems to collect postschool outcome data as part of the Part B State Performance Plan and Annual Performance Report. Data must be collected on "Percent of youth who had IEPs, are no longer in secondary school and who are completely employed, enrolled in some type of postsecondary school, or both, within two years of leaving high school as compared to nondisabled youth no longer in secondary school" [20 U.S.C. 1416(a)(4) and 1416(a)(2)(A)]. For more information on collecting postschool outcome data, visit the Web site of the National Post-School Outcomes Center at http://psocenter.org.

Consumer Satisfaction

Consumer satisfaction data can be collected from a variety of stakeholders, including students, educational personnel, business community representatives, parents and families, and adult service agency personnel. Consumer satisfaction data can be collected as part of a comprehensive postschool outcome data-collection system or while students are currently enrolled in high school (e.g., at the end of each IEP meeting). Consumer satisfaction data have been collected at the state level (Indiana Department of Education, 2000–2001) and at the local level (Aspel et al., 1998; Hoisch et al., 1992; Roessler, Brolin, & Johnson, 1990).

Interagency Collaboration and IEP Team Processes

Interagency collaboration can be measured using a variety of methods, including evaluating formal written agreements, collecting consumer satisfaction data, reviewing minutes of local transition team meetings, and tracking policy and procedural changes made by cooperating agencies. Evaluation of **IEP team processes** and student participation should address several factors to determine the effectiveness of the program in helping students make short-term and long-range decisions that align with their long-term postschool goals. These factors include representation of appropriate professionals and external agencies on the team, direct participation of the student in the process, the degree to which the IEP addresses both participation in the general secondary curriculum and transition support services, review of the student's long-range postschool goals, and preparation of the student for the age of majority. Interagency collaboration information has been collected at both the state level (Agran, Cain, & Cavin, 2002; Johnson, Zorn, Tam, Lamontagne, & Johnson, 2003) and the local level (Aspel et al., 1998; Roessler et al., 1990; Sample, 1998).

Student Performance in Program

Evaluation of students' performance in their transition program or high school course of study can take many forms, including the use of standardized educational and vocational tests, on-the-job performance measurements, and grades (Cross, Darby, & D'Alonzo, 1990; Kohler & Hood, 2000). Performance should be evaluated in the context of content standards and benchmarks, particularly, in this case, career readiness standards.

Thus, it is apparent that a comprehensive transition program evaluation involves collecting a variety of data from many different sources. The next four sections provide information on how to collect each type of data.

COLLECTING POSTSCHOOL OUTCOME DATA

Student postschool outcome data can be collected to determine students' outcomes and satisfaction in the areas of employment, postsecondary education, community participation, community housing, and satisfaction with their high school program. Darrow and Clark (1992) differentiated between "follow-up" and "follow-along" data. Follow-up data are collected at a single point in time, while follow-along data assess student progress at multiple points. As a result, follow-along data can provide school personnel with more complete information.

Student postschool outcome data are typically collected in two phases. The first set of data, sometimes called an *in-school survey* or an *exit survey,* is gathered at the end of the senior year, before students leave school. Figure 11.1 shows an example of this type of survey. For an exit survey, only Part I, General

EXIT/FOLLOW-UP ASSESSMENT

I. General Information

   A. <u>Personal Identifiers:</u>

      1. Name: Last _____ First _____
      2. Sex: M F
      3. DOB: _____
      4. ID# _____
      5. Classification Category (Check one) AU ☐ BEH ☐ EMH ☐ HI ☐ MU ☐ OI ☐ HI ☐ LD ☐ S/LI ☐ TBI ☐ TMH ☐ VI ☐
         Other: _____
      6. Ethnic Code (Check one): White ☐ African American ☐ Hispanic ☐ Asian ☐ Indian ☐
      7. Parent or Guardian: _____ Secondary Reference: _____
         Address: _____ Address: _____

         Phone: _____ Phone: _____

   B. <u>Exit Information:</u>

      1. Date of Public School Exit: Month _____ Year _____
      2. Reason for Exit: (a) Graduation (Diploma) _____
                 (b) Graduation (Alternative Diploma) _____
                 (c) Graduation (Certificate) _____
                 (d) Drop-out
                 (e) Completion of Eligibility _____
                 (f) Other: _____

   C. <u>Interview Information</u>:

      1. Date of Interview: Month _____ Day _____ Year _____
      2. Interviewer: _____
      3. Interviewee(s): _____

   D. <u>Marital/Family Status of Former Students</u>

      1. Marital/Status: (a) Single _____ (b) Married _____ (c) Divorced _____ (d) Engaged _____
      2. Number of Children: _____

II. Follow-Up Assessment

   A. <u>Employment:</u>

      1. Has person been employed at any time since school exit? Yes _____ No _____ (If no, go to A10)
      2. Does person currently have a job? Yes _____ No _____ (If no, go to A10; if yes describe): _____

(continued)

Figure 11.1
Sample Exit Survey and Postschool Outcome Survey

Note. From *Touch the Future: Light the Way. North Carolina Transition Manual* by the Public Schools of North Carolina, 1998, Raleigh: Public Schools of North Carolina, Exceptional Children Division. Reprinted with permission.

3. How did person get current job? (a) Self _____ (b) School _____ (c) Rehabilitation agency _____ (d) Family/friend network _____ (e) Other (Describe) _____

4. What is the classification of person's current job? (a) Competitive _____ (b) Supported _____ (c) Sheltered _____ (d) Other: _____

5. How long has person had this job? Months _____

6. How many hours per week does this person work? _____

7. What is person's pay per hour for this work? _____ per hour

8. How satisfied is person with this job? (a) Very _____ (b) Somewhat _____ (c) Not very _____ (d) Not at all _____

9. If person is employed, is any agency or service involved at this time? _____ Yes _____ No (If yes, describe) _____
_____
_____

10. Is person in need of additional employment assistance from an adult agency or service? Yes _____ No _____ (if yes describe) _____

11. Amount of time unemployed since school exit? _____ Months

12. Reason for unemployment? _____

13. Is person receiving government benefits? _____ SSI _____ SSDI _____ Medicaid Other (describe): _____

14. Has working affected benefits? _____ Yes _____ No (if yes, how?) _____
_____

B. Post-Secondary Education

1. Is person receiving any post-high-school educational services? _____ Yes _____ No (if no go to B5)

2. Where is person receiving these educational services? (a) University _____ (b) Community college _____ (c) Sheltered workshop _____ (d) Other (Describe)
_____

3. If person is involved in postsecondary educational services, does person receive assistance from any agency or support services? _____ Yes _____ No (If yes, describe)
_____

4. How satisfied is person with these educational services? (a) Very _____ (b) Somewhat _____ (c) Not very _____ (d) Not at all _____

5. Is person in need of additional educational services? _____ Yes _____ No (If yes, describe) _____
_____

C. Residential

1. Where does person live now? (a) With parent or guardian _____ (b) Alone _____ (c) With spouse or roommate _____ (d) Group home _____ (e) Other:
_____

2. If a person lives at home, how likely will person eventually live away from home? (a) Definitely will _____ (b) Probably will _____ (c) Probably won't _____ (d) Don't know _____

Figure 11.1
Continued

3. Do you see this person's residential status changing in the next five years? _____ Yes _____ No

4. Describe the residential arrangement that you anticipate for this individual in the future.

_____

_____

5. How satisfied is the person with current residential situation? (a) _____ Very (b) _____ Somewhat (c) _____ Not very (d) _____ Not at all

6. Is any agency or service involved with person's residential situation at this time? _____ Yes _____ No (If yes, describe) _____

_____

7. Is person in need of additional residential assistance from any agency or service? _____ Yes _____ No (If yes, describe) _____

_____

D. Social-Interpersonal and Recreation/Leisure

1. How frequently does person get together with friends? (a) _____ Less than once a week (b) _____ Once a week (c) _____ 2–3 times a week (d) _____ 4–5 times a week (e) _____ More than 5 times a week

2. Does person belong to any community groups like a sports or church group? _____ Yes _____ No (If yes, describe) _____

_____

3. How many good friends does person have? (a) _____ None (b) _____ 1(c) _____ 2–3 (d) _____ 4–5

4. How often does person attend community social events? (a) _____ Daily (b) _____ Weekly (c) _____ 6 or more per month

5. Does person have a recreation/leisure hobby? _____ Yes _____ No (If yes, describe)

_____

_____

6. How often does person make purchases in the community? (a) Daily _____ (b) Weekly _____ (c) _____ Monthly (d) _____ Yearly (e) _____ Never

7. Is any agency or service involved with person's social-interpersonal and recreation/leisure life? _____ Yes _____ No (If yes describe) _____

_____

8. Is person in need of any additional assistance from an agency or service to assist with his/her social-interpersonal and recreation/leisure life? _____ Yes _____ No (If yes, describe) _____

_____

9. How does the person travel to and from community activities? _____

_____

10. Does person need assistance to travel in the community? _____ Yes _____ No (If yes, describe) _____

_____

11. How satisfied is the person with present social-interpersonal and recreational/leisure life? (a) _____ Very (b) _____ Somewhat (c) _____ Not very (d) _____ Not at all

E. Previous High School Experience

1. How satisfied were you with the high school program? (a) _____ Very (b) _____
   Somewhat (c) _____ Not very (d) _____ Not at all
2. How satisfied were you with transition planning? (a) _____ Very (b) _____ Somewhat
   (c) _____ Not very (d) _____ Not at all
3. What are the strengths and weaknesses of the high school program?

   _____
   _____
   _____

4. What concerns you most about the future? _____

   _____
   _____

Please note additional comments on the back.

Interviewer: _____

Date: _____

Figure 11.1
Continued

Information, would be completed. Exit surveys are given to students in either 11th grade (Statewide Systems for Collecting Post-school Follow-up Data, 2002) or their final year of school (Aspel et al., 1998). Surveys can be administered at student IEP meetings or as part of a class. Students who cannot complete the exit survey independently will need help from parents or school personnel. In either case, it is important that someone in the school system check each student's survey for accuracy.

Exit surveys typically include questions about students' course of study, level of participation in the IEP and transition planning process, future plans in each postschool outcome area, satisfaction with their high school preparation, and information (e.g., phone number, address, e-mail) on how to contact them once they have left school.

The second set of data collected are postschool outcome data. Figure 11.1 also gives an example of one school system's postschool outcome survey. While these data could be gathered using a mailed questionnaire, Aspel and colleagues (1998) and Baer and colleagues (2003) have both suggested having either a transition coordinator or classroom teachers gather these data by telephone. Because of the questions that are asked in this phase, it is important that the caller be someone who is both familiar with and familiar to the student and family. In addition, having program personnel collect these data helps to increase their investment in making program improvements (Baer et al., 2003).

Calls should be made on a set schedule. While many schools collect data every 12 months for up to 5 years, data could be collected every 6 months or every other year. The point is to collect data over time that will allow program personnel and other consumers to judge the impact of the transition program and to make changes that will improve the program services provided to students. Telephone calls typically last from 15 to 45 minutes depending on the level of co-operation and information provided. Finally, every effort should be made to talk directly to the student and use the student's responses in filling out the survey form. However, if a student's verbal skills are limited, the interviewer may choose to interview a family member who knows the student's situation well enough to provide accurate information.

COLLECTING CONSUMER SATISFACTION DATA

Transition programs cannot operate effectively without the support of many partners. These include parents, adult service providers, other school personnel, the business community, and students. Because transition programs have such varied partners and consumers, it is important to get at least annual input from each group about their views of the current transition program. This is done by collecting consumer satisfaction data. By collecting all consumer satisfaction data annually during the last month of school, personnel can compile the results and review them in time to make any programmatic changes needed for the next school year.

Student Satisfaction Data

Student satisfaction data can be gathered either in a one-to-one situation with the questions read to the student or in small groups with a teacher (or other school personnel) available to help with vocabulary. To increase the chances that students will answer the questions honestly, every effort should be made to ensure that the student's teacher is not involved in collecting the data. Also, to increase comprehension, the questions should be worded so that students can give a yes or no response. While a Likert scale could be used, if students have not had prior experience with this type of scale it can be confusing to them. Student satisfaction data can be gathered from all students, or they can be collected from a random sample of students or classes as long as the entire range of student ages, disabilities, and services received is sampled. The following are examples of student satisfaction questions that can be used:

1. Do you feel that the transition program is preparing you to get a job?
2. Do you feel that the coursework is relevant to your future goals?
3. Do you feel that the transition program is preparing you to live in the community?
4. Do you feel that the program is preparing you to use services in the community?

5. Do you feel that the program is preparing you to access postsecondary education opportunities?

6. Do you feel that the program matches your abilities and interests?

7. Do you feel that you have an active role in planning your future?

Parent Satisfaction Data

Parent satisfaction data are collected annually either by mailing a survey to each family or by having parents complete the survey during their young person's IEP meeting. We suggest using a 4-point Likert scale (1 = strongly disagree, 2 = disagree, 3 = agree, 4 = strongly agree), but questions could also be asked to elicit a yes or no response. The following are examples of questions that could be used in a Likert-type parent satisfaction questionnaire:

1. My young adult enjoys going to the vocational training site.

2. Since becoming involved in the program, my young adult has shown positive changes.

3. Since becoming involved in the program, my young adult has shown negative changes.

4. I have been kept informed about my young adult's progress at the training site.

5. I have been kept informed about any problems.

6. I think the amount of time my young adult spends in the program is adequate.

7. My young adult communicates with me regularly about the program.

8. I am familiar with the tasks my young adult does in the program.

9. I think the curriculum is appropriate for my young adult.

10. I think my young adult feels good about the program.

Adult Service Provider Satisfaction Data

Adult service provider satisfaction data are typically collected annually by mailing a questionnaire to each person. If your school system has an interagency team meeting near the end of the school year, questionnaires could be distributed and collected at that meeting. We suggest using a 4-point Likert scale, but the questions could also be worded to collect yes or no answers. The following are examples of some questions that could be used in an adult service provider questionnaire:

1. I have had an active role in the transition process.
2. I have a good understanding of my role in the transition process.
3. I have had the opportunity to communicate on a regular basis with school personnel about transition issues.
4. I feel that school personnel have a good understanding of my agency's/organization's procedures/policies.
5. I believe the transition program is adequately preparing students for postschool employment.

6. I believe the transition program is adequately preparing students to live in the community.

School Personnel Satisfaction Data

School personnel satisfaction data should be collected from all school system employees involved in providing transition services. These could include job coaches, transition specialists, school counselors, administrators, vocational education teachers, general education teachers, special education teachers, and paraeducators, to name just a few. Questionnaires should be distributed and collected annually via the school system's mail system. We suggest using a 4-point Likert scale, but questions could also be worded to elicit a yes or no response. The following are some examples of school personnel questions:

1. I have had an active role in the transition process.
2. I have a good understanding of my role in the transition process.
3. I have had the opportunity to communicate on a regular basis with school system personnel about transition issues.
4. I believe the transition program is adequately preparing students for postschool employment.
5. I believe the transition program is adequately preparing students to live in the community.

Business Community Satisfaction Data

Business community satisfaction data should be collected at least annually from individuals at each of the community-based instructional sites used by the transition program. In some cases this might be the owner (if it is a small business) or in other cases it might be a manager, supervisor, or coworker (for larger companies). The purpose is to gather satisfaction data from the person who has the most contact with the student and your transition program.

We suggest that questionnaires be distributed near the end of each school year if the instructional site is used all year. If the work site is only used for a single semester, the questionnaire should be distributed at the end of that semester. One way to make sure that the questionnaire gets to the appropriate person at each business is to have the school system site coordinator hand deliver each questionnaire. Including a stamped, self-addressed envelope will increase the chances that the questionnaire will be completed. The following are some examples of questions on a questionnaire based on a 4-point Likert scale:

1. The student consistently arrives and leaves work on time.
2. Attendance is acceptable.
3. Tasks are performed to the agreed-upon criteria.
4. The student displays behavior appropriate to the workplace.

5. The student interacts appropriately with others at the work site.

6. The trainer interacts appropriately with others at work site.

7. The student doesn't interfere with normal operations.

8. Coworkers and customers are comfortable interacting with the student.

9. The trainer provides adequate training and supervision.

10. The trainer's interactions with the student do not interrupt business.

11. The student appears to enjoy the experience.

12. The student's appearance is satisfactory.

13. The trainer is available and cooperative.

14. The student's performance has improved.

15. I would consider having my business serve as a site again.

COLLECTING INTERAGENCY COLLABORATION AND IEP TEAM PROCESS DATA

The third type of data that can be collected as part of a program evaluation of transition services are data that evaluate both interagency collaboration and the IEP team process used. Possible data include evaluating the level of interagency collaboration (see Chapter 5), the quality of the transition component of the IEP, and consumer satisfaction data.

Evaluating Interagency Collaboration

Kochhar-Bryant (2003) suggested that interagency collaboration can be evaluated based on six possible outcomes by:

1. Studying formal written agreements to determine the level of collaboration and implementation. In other words, did each agency carryout its responsibilities as written in the interagency agreement?

2. Documenting interagency training and staff development activities. In addition, evaluations could be conducted to determine the usefulness of training activities.

3. Cataloging parent and community outreach and dissemination activities and collecting consumer satisfaction data.

4. Studying the databases that are shared among agencies, as well as how any postschool outcome data and consumer satisfaction data are shared across agencies.

5. Documenting local, state, and/or national policy advocacy efforts to improve transition services, as well as any outcomes that may have occurred. In addition, data could be collected on the percentage of students who were

identified as needing the support of specific adult service agencies as stated on the students' IEPs relative to those who actually received the stated services (Roessler et al., 1990; Sample, 1998).

6. Tracking any organizational and/or interagency changes that were made based on program evaluation data collected.

Evaluating the Transition Component of IEPs

As described in Chapter 4, the transition component of the IEP should drive each student's course of study and all related school- and community-based instruction. As such, it makes sense to systematically evaluate the quality of student IEPs as a measure of transition program evaluation.

There are two ways in which transition-related IEPs have been evaluated. First, Storms, O'Leary, and Williams (2000) have developed a Transition Requirements Checklist that corresponds to specific sections of IDEA 1997 and the final transition regulations published in the *Federal Register* of March 12, 1999. Their assumption is that student transition services will be improved if school systems align their transition planning practices with the transition requirements of IDEA 1997. The Transition Requirements Checklist consists of 22 yes or no questions divided into six categories: Transition Services Participants (34 CFR § 300.344), Parent Notice (34 CFR § 300.345), Exception to FAPE and Prior Written Notice (34 CFR § 300.122 (a) (3) (i,ii,iii) & § 300.503), Content of the Individualized Education Program (IEP) (34 CFR § 300.347), Transfer of Rights (34 CFR § 300.517, § 300.347 (c)), and Agency Responsibilities for Transition Services (34 CFR § 300.348).

The Transition Requirements Checklist was developed for a variety of audiences, including state, district, and school personnel; families; and institutions of higher education. State agency personnel, local education agency administrators, and teachers use it for evaluating and improving the transition requirements in IEPs. Students and families may find it useful to understand transition requirements and their ability to actively plan for a student's future. Institutions of higher education could use it as a teaching tool and resource. However, before using the checklist, be sure to check with your local or state special education agency for rules and forms particular to your state or school. Figure 11.2 provides a sample from the Transition Requirements Checklist. The entire guide can be found online at http://interact.uoregon.edu/WRRC/trnfiles/trncontents.htm.

The second strategy, suggested by Grigal, Test, Beattie, and Wood (1997) involves evaluating the transition-component format of the IEP for compliance with IDEA's mandate and use of best practices. To do this, the transition component of each student's IEP is evaluated using a modified version of the Transition Services Review Protocol (Lawson & Everson, 1993). This protocol was originally designed to evaluate the transition services of students who are deaf-blind and was used in a study that reviewed 52 student plans from 22 states. In its original form, it was reviewed by seven external reviewers from a variety of service backgrounds, including state department of education personnel, local educational agencies (LEAs), and staff from institutions of higher education, who made

IDEA '97 Transition Requirements: A Guide

Section IV: **Transition Requirements Checklist**

Contents | Section III | Section V

The following checklist corresponds to specific sections of the Individuals with Disabilities Education Act Amendments of 1997 (IDEA '97) and the final regulations related to the transition requirements that were issued in the *Federal Register* on March 12, 1999. The checklist may be used by public agencies to help align their practices with the transition requirements of the IDEA '97.

Transition Services Participants (34 CFR § 300.344)

When a purpose of the IEP meeting is the consideration of transition services:
1. Yes No Did the public agency invite the student?
2. Yes No If the student did not attend the IEP meeting, did the public agency take steps to ensure that the student's preferences and interests were considered in the
   N/A development of the IEP? (If the student attended the meeting, indicate N/A [Not Applicable.])

3. Yes No Did the public agency invite a representative of any other agency that is likely to be responsible for providing or paying for transition services?
4. Yes No If an agency was invited to send a representative to a meeting and did not do so, did the public agency take other steps to obtain his or her participation in the
   N/A planning of transition services? (If the agency attended the meeting, indicate N/A [Not Applicable].)

Parent notice (34 CFR § 300.345)

Does the parent (and student, if rights have been transferred) notice:
1. Yes No Indicate, for a student beginning at age 14 (or younger, if appropriate), that a purpose of the meeting will be the development of a statement of transition service needs?
2. Yes No Indicate, for a student beginning at age 16 (or younger, if appropriate), that a purpose of the meeting is the consideration of needed transition services?
3. Yes No Indicate that the public agency will invite the student beginning at age 14 (or younger, if appropriate)?
4. Yes No Identify any other agency that will be invited to send a representative?
5. Yes No Indicate the time and location of the meeting and who will be in attendance?

Figure 11.2

Transition Requirements Checklist

Note. From *The Individuals with Disabilities Education Act of 1997 Transition Requirements: A Guide for States, Districts, Schools, Universities and Families* by Jane Storms, Ed O'Leary, and Jane Williams, 2000, a collaborative effort of the Western Regional Resource Center, Mountain Plain Regional Resource Center, Arizona State University West, and the National Transition Network. Retrieved November 30, 2004, from http://interact.uoregon.edu/wrrc/trnfiles/Checklist.htm.

6.   Yes   No   Inform the parents that they may invite other individuals who have knowledge or special expertise regarding their child, including related services personnel, as appropriate?

Exception to FAPE and Prior Written Notice (34 CFR § 300.122(a)(3)(i, ii,iii) & § 300.503)

If the student will graduate with a regular* high school diploma, does the IEP team provide the parent (s) (and student, if rights have been transferred) with:

1.   Yes   No   Prior written notice (in accordance with 34 CFR § 300.503) that graduation from high school with a regular diploma constitutes a change in placement and that the high school student is no longer entitled to provide a free appropriate public education (FAPE)? (NOTE: A state may choose to continue to provide FAPE. Check with your state for requirements that may go beyond Federal requirements.)

* does not apply to students who have graduated but have not been awarded a *regular* high school diploma.

Content of the Individualized Education Program (IEP) (34 CFR § 300.347)

If the student is 14 (or younger, if appropriate), does the IEP include:

1.   Yes   No   A statement of current performance related to transition service needs?
2.   Yes   No   A statement of transition service needs that specifies courses of study that will be meaningful to the student's future and motivate the student to complete his or her education?

If the student is 16 (or younger, if appropriate), does the IEP include:

1.   Yes   No   A statement of needed transition services that is a coordinated set of activities and considers:

        Yes   No   a. Instruction?
        Yes   No   b. Related services?
        Yes   No   c. Community experiences?
        Yes   No   d. Development of employment and other post-school adult living objectives?
        Yes   No   e. If appropriate, acquisition of daily living skills?
        Yes   No   f. If appropriate, a functional vocational evaluation?

2.   Yes   No   The activities in the statement of needed transition services are presented as a coordinated set of activities that promotes movement from school to desired post-school activities?

3.   Yes   No   A statement of needed transition services that addresses one or more of the following post-school activities:

        [ ] Post-secondary education?
        [ ] Vocational training?
        [ ] Integrated employment (including supported employment)?
        [ ] Continuing and adult education?
        [ ] Adult services?
        [ ] Independent living?
        [ ] Community participation?

(continued)

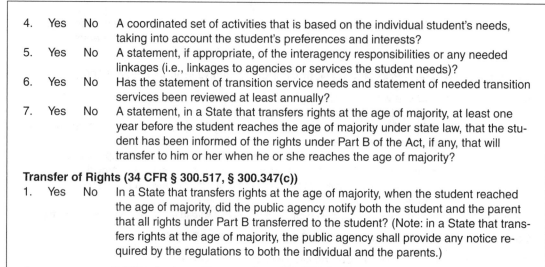

4. Yes No   A coordinated set of activities that is based on the individual student's needs, taking into account the student's preferences and interests?

5. Yes No   A statement, if appropriate, of the interagency responsibilities or any needed linkages (i.e., linkages to agencies or services the student needs)?

6. Yes No   Has the statement of transition service needs and statement of needed transition services been reviewed at least annually?

7. Yes No   A statement, in a State that transfers rights at the age of majority, at least one year before the student reaches the age of majority under state law, that the student has been informed of the rights under Part B of the Act, if any, that will transfer to him or her when he or she reaches the age of majority?

Transfer of Rights (34 CFR § 300.517, § 300.347(c))

1. Yes No   In a State that transfers rights at the age of majority, when the student reached the age of majority, did the public agency notify both the student and the parent that all rights under Part B transferred to the student? (Note: in a State that transfers rights at the age of majority, the public agency shall provide any notice required by the regulations to both the individual and the parents.)

Agency responsibilities for transition services (34 CFR § 300.348)

1. Yes No   If a participating agency failed to provide agreed-upon transition services contained in the IEP, did the public agency responsible for the student's education reconvene the IEP team to identify alternative strategies to meet the transition
    N/A   objectives for the student set out in the IEP? (If the agency provided services, indicate N/A [Not Applicable].)

Contents | Section III | Section V

Figure 11.2
Continued

suggestions about comprehensiveness and clarity (Lawson & Everson, 1993). We modified the original protocol to change its focus from deaf-blind services to use with all disability categories. In addition, we modified the protocol to extend the evaluation of compliance with IDEA mandates, evaluate the quality of written goals, and examine how personnel and timelines were designated. The modified review protocol allowed the protocol to be used in a variety of settings and in evaluations of any transition component format.

The revised instrument consists of 25 questions organized into four sections: demographics, transition component format, compliance with IDEA's mandate, and reflection of best practices. Demographic information includes gender, category of disability, number of years the transition component has been in place, and graduation document to be earned. The second section, on the transition component format, focuses on information such as family input, expansion of goals, timelines, and follow-up. The third section addresses compliance with IDEA outcome areas in which goals were written, such as postsecondary education, independent living, and the people involved in developing the transition component. The final section focuses on special education best practices, such as opportunities for integration with people without disabilities and evaluation procedures.

Figure 11.3 provides a sample from the modified Transition Services Review Protocol. While sometimes it may be possible to review all students' IEPs in a given school or school system, we suggest collecting a sample of IEPs, making sure to collect a proportional sample across ages 14 to 21 and across disabilities based on each school system's demographics.

EVALUATION OF TRANSITION SERVICES

1. DEMOGRAPHICS
   1.1 Student's age _____
   1.2 Student's gender _____
   1.3 Number of years projected to graduation _____
   1.4 Disability classification _____
   1.5 Number of years IEP has been in place _____
   1.6 What graduation document will be received? _____
   1.7 Other pertinent factors _____
2. TRANSITION COMPONENT FORMAT
   2.1 The student's transition component of IEP is:
      _____ Present
      _____ Not present
   2.2 The transition component of the IEP is:
      _____ Individualized to address each student's wants/needs
      _____ Individualized to the community
      _____ Not individualized
   2.3 The transition component of the IEP reflects the student/family's dreams for the student by:
      _____ Including a statement or attached documents of student/family dreams for the future.
      _____ Including IEP goals and/or transition action steps that extend beyond a one-year plan:
      _____ Not present
   2.4 The transition component of the IEP includes space for the team to write/expand information on individualized adult outcomes:
      _____ Yes
      _____ No
   2.5 The transition meeting took place:
      _____ As a separate meeting from the IEP annual review meeting
      _____ During the annual IEP annual review meeting
      _____ Did not occur
   2.6 The transition component of the IEP includes space specifically identifying individual(s) designated responsible for action steps:
      _____ Yes
      _____ No

(continued)

Figure 11.3
Transition IEP Protocol

If "Yes":
    Adult service action steps are organized to identify Steps for each target adult service agency (i.e., rehabilitation, MR, DD, etc.)
    _____ Yes
    _____ No

2.7 The transition component of the IEP includes specific timelines for completion of action steps:
    _____ Yes
    _____ No

If Yes, has the space been used?
    _____ Yes
    _____ No

2.8 The transition component includes space to document follow-up on completed action steps:
    _____ Yes
    _____ No

2.9 Were the planning documents present?
    _____ Yes
    _____ No

If Yes, were they updated yearly?
    _____ Yes
    _____ No

3. COMPLIANCE WITH IDEA'S MANDATES

3.1 Goals/activities are included on the IEP/transition component transition services that reflect the following outcome areas as identified by IDEA: (check all that apply)
    _____ Postsecondary education
    _____ Vocational training
    _____ Integrated employment
    _____ Continuing adult education
    _____ Adult services
    _____ Independent living
    _____ Community participation

3.2 Goals/activities are included on the IEP/transition component transition services that reflect the following outcome areas. In addition to those identified by IDEA: (check all that apply)
    _____ Living arrangements
    _____ Homemaking needs
    _____ Transportation
    _____ Medical
    _____ Relationships
    _____ Financial
    _____ Leisure/recreation
    _____ Advocacy/legal
    _____ Other

Figure 11.3
Continued

For the next question, check the appropriate column as described below:

3 = Detailed   (i.e., specific instructions are provided for school personnel regarding all activities listed on the student's plan)

2 = Adequate   (i.e., specific instructions are provided for some of the activities listed on the student's plan; the remainder of the activities contain non-specific instructions)

1 = Minimal   (i.e., non-specific instructions are provided for school personnel on some of the activities listed on the student's plan; some activities contain no action steps)

0 = Non-existent

3.3 Action step goals in the following areas are:
(state goal as written on plan)

Goals	Rating of goals	Rating of no-goal Explain	Personnel designated responsible	Timeline
Employment				
Residential				
Recreation				
Education/Training				

3.4 Which goals and objectives were not designated to personnel?

Employment	Residential	Recreation	Education/training
_____	_____	_____	_____
_____	_____	_____	_____
_____	_____	_____	_____

3.5 Evidence exists of transdiciplinary team involvement in the development and implementation of the IEP/transition componenttransition services: (check all that apply)
_____ School administrator
_____ Special education teacher
_____ Regular education teacher
_____ Orientation and mobility specialist

(continued)

_____ Speech/language/communication specialist
_____ Family/advocate
_____ Student
_____ Transition Specialist
_____ Vocational education teacher
_____ Community-based instruction coordinator
_____ Guidance counselor
_____ School psychologist
_____ Other _____
_____ Signatures not delineated (no titles)

3.6 Evidence exists of adult services involvement in the development and implementation of the IEP/transition component transition services: (check all that apply)
_____ Rehabilitation counselor
_____ Adult services case manager (MR/DD, etc.)
_____ Employment trainer (job coach)
_____ Community college personnel
_____ Four-year college personnel
_____ Residential personnel
_____ Other _____
_____ Signatures not delineated (no titles)

3.7 Did plan have to be revised?
_____ Yes
_____ No
If "yes", why?

_____

4. REFLECTIVE OF BEST PRACTICES

4.1 The IEP transition services component identifies regularly-scheduled activities which support student participation in environments in which adults without disabilities engage on a daily basis:
_____ Yes   _____ No
If "yes" above, check all environments in which activities are identified:
_____ The student's home
_____ The student's workplace
_____ Recreational settings
_____ School
_____ Other community settings

4.2 The IEP/transition component of IEP contains descriptions of adaptations to activities and/or materials to support the student's individual needs:
_____ Yes   _____ No
If "yes" above, check all that apply:

	Where found: ITP	IEP
_____ Modified tests	_____	_____
_____ Augmentative/computer assistance	_____	_____
_____ Transportation/mobility	_____	_____

Figure 11.3
Continued

390

_____ Visual/hearing adaptations   _____   _____
_____ Aide/personal assistant   _____   _____
4.3 Descriptions of evaluation procedures for classroom and community activities are contained
    in ITP/IEP?
    _____ Yes   _____ No
    If "yes", type of evaluation are:
                                                        Where found: ITP   IEP
                                                        _____   _____

    _____ Case notes   _____   _____
    _____ Tests   _____   _____
    _____ Skills checklist   _____   _____
    _____ Task analysis   _____   _____
    _____ Rating sheets   _____   _____
    _____ Observations   _____   _____
    _____ Other _____

Figure 11.3
Continued

Interagency Collaboration Consumer Satisfaction Data

As with the earlier description on collecting consumer satisfaction data from adult service providers, similar data can be collected from all interagency teams. We recommend collecting these data annually using a 4-point Likert scale. The following are examples of interagency collaboration questions:

1. Interagency collaboration agreements are implemented as written.
2. I understand the roles of each member of our team.
3. I understand my role on the team.
4. Our team has an impact on improving transition services provided to students.
5. Our team makes decisions based on evaluation data.
6. Students get needed postschool supports.

COLLECTING STUDENT PERFORMANCE DATA

The final set of data that we recommend collecting as a part of a comprehensive transition program evaluation is **student performance data.** Such data could include student academic performance as measured by course grades and/or any local or state end-of-grade tests and GPA, as well as student performance at

---

DID YOU KNOW?

Students with disabilities are less likely to take a full academic high school curriculum than students without disabilities (American Youth Policy Forum and Center on Education Policy, 2002).

---

community-based instructional sites. While student academic data could be interesting for all students, they are particularly important for students who are exiting into postsecondary educational settings. For students who wish to attend 2- or 4-year colleges or technical schools, their success clearly depends on achieving passing grades and test scores. Therefore, it is important to know what percentage of students pass courses and tests, their overall GPAs, and even their SAT scores.

For information on student performance in community-based instructional sites, we refer you to Chapters 3, 8, 9, and 10. Each of these chapters includes information about collecting student performance data at community instructional sites. Finally, the box entitled "Questions Families can ask to Evaluate Transition Programs" provides a summary of the highlights of this text.

Questions Families Can Ask to Evaluate Transition Programs

1. What types of transition assessments are conducted?
2. How are community participation and community living skills assessed?
3. How are students involved in their IEP process?
4. When and how do you teach self-determination and self-advocacy skills?
5. Who is typically invited to transition planning meetings? What agencies have been involved?
6. How do you involve families in the transition process?
7. What school- and community-based training is provided for employment, community living, and community participation?
8. What percentage of students become employed upon graduation? What do you do to ensure that students are prepared?
9. What percentage of students enroll in postsecondary education after graduation? What do you do to ensure that students are prepared?
10. How satisfied are parents, students, school personnel, adult service providers, and the business community with your current transition program?

CASE STUDIES

TRANSITION PROGRAM EVALUATION

Transition program evaluation can take place at the national, state, and/or local level. Examples of collecting transition program evaluation data at the national level include the National Longitudinal Transition Study-2 (Wagner, Cameto, & Newman, 2003) and the National Education Longitudinal Study (Harvey, 2002). Each of these was described in Chapter 1. In this chapter we provide case studies of state and local transition program evaluation.

State-Level Transition Program Evaluation: New York

In April 2003, the Western Regional Resource Center, the National Center on Secondary Education and Transition, and the Transition Coalition co-sponsored a 2-day workshop called "Northwest Passages" (Storms, 2003). The purpose of the workshop was to learn how various states collected and used postschool outcome data to improve secondary programs for students with disabilities. While Northwest Passages highlighted the efforts from 14 states (see Table 11.1 for a summary of the data collected, methods for collecting data, and how data were used), this case study describes the efforts of one state: New York.

What data are collected?

New York collects data in six areas: student characteristics, career development activities, employment planning and outcomes, postsecondary education planning and outcomes, community living preparation and participation, and involvement with services (Shepard, 2003).

How are data collected?

Data are collected from students in special education and students in general education. Students are selected using stratified cluster sampling to ensure a representative statewide sample. Data are collected through a contract with the State University of New York at Potsdam.

Data are collected initially via a search of student folders conducted by school system personnel. Next, the Senior Exit Survey is completed by each student in May or June of his or her final year. Finally postschool outcome data are collected through telephone interviews with students (parents or other family members are interviewed if former students are not available). Table 11.2 summarizes what, when, and how student data are collected.

The following are some sample Senior Exit Survey questions:

1. The type of diploma the student expected to receive in June is: _____.

Table 11.1
State Efforts to Assess Postsecondary Outcomes for Students with Disabilities: Grid

State	Data Collected — Employment	Post-Sec Ed	Living	Quality of Life	Agcy. Connection	In-School Experience	School Work Experience	Transition Planning	Target Population — Graduates	All Exiters	SE Only	GE and SE	Data Collection Points — In-School Survey	6 months out	1 year out	3 years out	5 years out	Who Collects — School/District	SEA	Contractor	Who Gets Reports — School/District	SEA	Uses — Improvement Planning	Drives TA/training	Monitoring	Accountability (Sanctions)
AL	×	×	×	×	×	×	×	×	×		×		×		×			×		×	×	×	×	×		
CA	×	×	×		×	×	×		×	×	×		×		×			×	×	×	×	×	×	×	×	
DE	×	×	×	×		×				×	×			×						×	×	×	×	×	×	
FL	×	×	×	×	×		×	×	×	×		×	×	×	×			×			×	×	×		×	
IA	×	×	×	×	×	×				×	×		×	×	×			×		×	×	×	×	×	×	
ID	×	×	×		×					×	×		×		×	×	×	×	×		×	×	×	×	×	
KS	×	×	×							×				×								×			×	
MI	×	×	×	×							×	×			×	×		×	×	×	×	×	×		×	
MN	×	×	×	×	×	×	×	×		×	×		×		×	×				×	×	×	×			
NM	×	×	×	×	×	×	×	×	×		×		×		×	×				×	×	×	×	×		
NY	×	×	×	×	×	×	×	×	×			×	×		×		×	×	×	×	×	×	×		×	
TX	×	×	×	×	×	×	×	×	×		×		×		×			×		×	×	×	×	×		
VA	×	×	×	×	×	×	×	×		×	×							×		×	×	×	×	×		
WA	×	×	×	×	×	×	×	×	×				×	×				×			×	×	×	×		

NOTES AND DESCRIPTIONS

LIMITATIONS: the information contained in this grid is based on phone conversations between state special education staff or university contractors and WRRC staff during November 2002 through early January 2003.

394

DATA COLLECTED

- Employment, Postsecondary Education and Training, and Living: all states collect some form of this core set of data.
- Quality of Life: data such as overall satisfaction, transportation, drivers license, banking, friends, who provides assistance.
- Agency Connection: data about connections, links, or services provided by community organizations or agencies. Sometimes the follow-up survey inquiries result in the interviewee receiving additional information about needed services.
- In-School Experience: data about how the high school experience prepared the student for his or her postschool goals including classes taken, classes that should have been taken, whether someone in school helped the student think about and plan for the future.
- School Work Experience: data about whether the student had any volunteer or paid work experience while still in school.
- Transition Planning: data about whether the student participated in his or her own transition planning and IEP, what goals were actually written into the IEP, sometimes there is a check of the IEP document to see whether there is a correlation between what was planned and what actually happened.

METHODOLOGY

TARGET POPULATION

- Graduates: students who graduate from high school with an approved diploma.
- All Exiters: all students who graduate, drop out, or leave by other methods.
- SE Only: only special education students are surveyed or interviewed.
- GE and SE: both general and special education students are part of the sample.

DATA COLLECTION POINTS

- In School Survey: students complete some form of a survey prior to leaving school.
- 6 months Out—5 years out: points in time when survey or interview contacts are made with the population.

WHO COLLECTS

- School/District: assists with identification of students and/or assists in collecting the data.
- SEA: assists with identification of students and/or assists in collecting the data.
- Contractor: the SEA contracts with an outside agency (University or private business) to collect, analyze, and/or report the data.

USE OF DATA

WHO GETS REPORT

- School/District: information is returned to school and/or district level. Sometimes it is disaggregated at the school or district level.
- SEA: information is returned to the State Educational Agency.

USES

- Improvement Planning: some level of analysis is provided and used in various forms of improvement planning.
- Drives TA/Training: information is used to target technical assistance and or training at the school, district, regional or state level.
- Monitoring: information is used in the state monitoring of districts.
- Accountability (sanctions): the SEA uses the information to apply sanctions to schools or districts where data suggests there are compliance problems.

Note. From the University of Oregon, Western Regional Resource Center, 2003.

395

Table 11.2
New York State Post-School Indicators Data Collection

I. What Data is Collected by NYS in the Longitudinal Post-School Indicators Study?

Topic:	Demographics and Folder Search:	Senior Exit Survey:	Post-School Interviews (One year beyond school exit)	Post-School Interviews (three and five years beyond school exit)
Schedule	◆ During the senior year	◆ May or June	◆ May through August	◆ May through August
Collection Method	◆ Collected from school district electronically or on paper	◆ Paper questionnaire administered at school at the end of the senior year ◆ Accommodations provided as appropriate	◆ Personal youth interview administer over the phone or in person ◆ Accommodations provided as appropriate ◆ Alternate reporter as appropriate	◆ Personal youth interview administered over the phone or person ◆ Accommodations provided as appropriate ◆ Alternate reporter as appropriate
Employment	◆ Related Services ◆ Vocational Education Participation ◆ Tech Prep Participation ◆ Participation in Community Based Educational Experiences ◆ Use of Assistive Technology	◆ Perception of preparation by high school experiences for employment ◆ Career preparation programs & activities ◆ Career guidance activities ◆ How job skills were learned ◆ Postsecondary employment plans and status ◆ When did you decide not to attend postsecondary education and why?	◆ Perception of preparation by high school experiences for employment ◆ How jobs were found ◆ Employment status and characteristics (up to three jobs) ◆ Hours and earnings and benefit ◆ Job turnover ◆ Job satisfaction ◆ Reasonable accommodations ◆ Preparation for using technology	◆ Perception of preparation for employment ◆ How jobs were found ◆ Employment status and characteristics (up to two jobs) ◆ Hours and earnings and benefit ◆ Job turnover ◆ Job satisfaction ◆ Reasonable accommodations ◆ Preparation for using technology ◆ Assistive Technology ◆ Test Modifications
Postsecondary Education Involvement	◆ Special Education Services	◆ Perception of preparation by high school experiences for Life Long Learning	◆ Perception of preparation by high school experiences for Life Long Learning	◆ Perception of preparation for Life Long Learning

396

• Related Services • Time apart from General Education Setting • Diploma Type or other school exit reason • Testing modifications • English and Mathematics Statewide Test Scores	• Postsecondary guidance and plans • Postsecondary selection criteria • Postsecondary degree aspirations	• Postsecondary education status • Postsecondary education participation • Postsecondary credential • Major • Access to support services • Assistive technology • Testing modifications	• Postsecondary education status • Postsecondary education participation • Cumulative average • Postsecondary credential • Access to support services • Major • Access to support services • Assistive technology • Testing modifications • Perception of reasons for success or failure
Community Living • Community based educational experiences	• Perception of preparation by high school experiences for Community participation. • Household	• Perception of preparation by high school experiences for Community participation. • Household • Parents' work status • Travel within the community • Social and recreational activities • Community agency/program use • Waiting lists for service • Short and long term goals • Life satisfaction	• Perception for Community participation. • Household • Travel within the community • Social and recreational activities • Community agency/program use • Waiting lists for service • Life satisfaction
General • Ethnicity • Language Preference	• Ethnicity • Disability status • Computer access and use • Perception of their school and educational environment • Did the transition process facilitate connection to post high school activities? • Self Determination	• Ethnicity • Self Determination	• Ethnicity • Disability status • Perception of their disability • Perceived need for supports • Access to supports • Self Determination

The New York State Post School Indicators Longitudinal Study is coordinated by the Institute for Applied Research at SUNY Potsdam, Potsdam, NY 13676 (nyspsi@potsdam.edu) and is funded through the NYS Education Department Office of Vocational and Educational Services for Individuals with Disabilities (VESID).

Note Available from http://psocenter.org/Docs/state_info/NY/NY2Qoverview.doc.

2. High school experiences were helpful in preparing you to read and understand written material.

3. High school experiences were helpful in preparing you to understand and use math.

4. High school experiences were helpful in preparing you to live on your own.

5. High school experiences were helpful in preparing you to vote in elections.

6. High school experiences were helpful in preparing you to find and keep a job.

7. Your school has provided you with a good education.

8. Your school has provided you with opportunities to reach contacts for getting more education or training after high school.

9. Your school has provided you with opportunities to reach contacts for getting where you need or want to go.

10. When did you first receive information at school about careers?

11. What is the highest level of education you plan to achieve?

12. The occupation you plan to pursue immediately after high school is: _____.

Some sample questions for postschool outcomes include the following:

1. How did you leave or complete high school?

2. Since high school, have you had additional training or taken classes that lasted for 3 months or more from any of the following?

   a. Adult basic education.

   b. WIA/JTPA classroom-based (employment) training.

   c. Career-technical school.

   d. Two- or four-year college or university.

   e. Supported employment.

3. Does your school (college, university, etc.) have any special support services for students who may have difficulty with the reading, writing, math, public speaking, or study skills required in their courses?

4. Do you use any of the following assistive technology devices?

   a. Computer.

   b. Text-to-speech software.

   c. TTY/TDD.

   d. Word processing device.

   e. Augmentative communication device.

5. Do you use any testing modifications?

6. Since July 1 last year, how many months did you work in which you were paid for 35 or more hours per week (i.e., full time)?

7. How many other months since July 1 last year were you employed part time (i.e., less than 35 hours per week)?

8. Where do you live?

9. Have you used any of the following services since leaving high school?

   a. Social security benefits (i.e., SSI, SSDI).

   b. Department of Social Services.

   c. Medicaid or Medicare.

   d. New York State Job Service.

10. When you left high school, how well prepared did you feel to get along with others and to make friends?

11. What is your career or work goal for 1 year from now?

What are the results?

Data are presented for each of the variables for which information is collected. Percentages are presented for both students in general education and those in special education. One of the most interesting sets of data reported is used to determine what is called the *transition gap*. The premise for calculating the transition gap is that if the transition services provided to a student are successful, there should be a seamless gap between school-based supports and community-based supports. In other words, a successful secondary education ideally should prepare 100% of its students to participate in lifelong learning and/or postsecondary education and employment after high school (Shepard, 2003). The transition gap is the difference between 100% and the actual percentage of students who report attending postsecondary education and/or being employed either part time or full time. Results from the Class of 2001 indicated that 93.7% of general education students and 81.4% of special education students were successful. Therefore, the transition gap was 6.3% for general education students and 18.6% for special education students.

How are the data used?

Results are used to determine predictors of successful transitions. To date, New York's results indicate six variables that make a difference:

1. K–12 transition planning.

2. Career preparation, especially paid or unpaid community work experiences.

3. Safe, supportive educational environments.

4. Integrated learning environments.

5. Attaining a standards-based diploma.

6. Collaboration among students, parents, school, and community.

Results are also shared with appropriate state legislative bodies and agencies, families and stakeholder groups, and participating schools. So far, based on data collected, the following changes have been made: (a) establishing vocational rehabilitation counselor positions dedicated to serving in-school youth; (b) changing state requirements regarding content of IEPs containing transition needs assessments; and (c) creating a career and technical education enhancement to the IEP diploma.

Local-Level Transition Program Evaluation: Shelby City/Cleveland County, NC

What data are collected?

Two types of data are collected: consumer satisfaction data and student outcome (i.e., follow-along) data. Consumer satisfaction surveys are distributed to students, parents, business community members, adult service providers, and school personnel. Student outcome data are collected to determine student outcomes and satisfaction in the areas of employment, postsecondary education, living arrangements, leisure and recreation activities, and high school experiences.

How are consumer satisfaction data collected?

Consumer satisfaction data are collected annually. Questionnaires are distributed each May. The *student satisfaction questionnaire* consists of seven questions answered with a yes or no response. Student satisfaction data are gathered either in a one-to-one situation with the questions read to the student or in small groups with a teacher available to help with vocabulary. Every effort is made to ensure that the student's teachers are not involved in collecting these data. At first, student satisfaction data were gathered from as many students as possible; however, now data are collected from a random sample to ease teacher workload.

A *parent satisfaction questionnaire* consisting of 10 questions rated on a 4-point Likert scale is distributed to parents of students enrolled in the occupational course of study. Parent satisfaction surveys are sent home with students or are completed during the May IEP meeting, if the parent attends.

An *adult service provider questionnaire* consisting of six questions rated on a 4-point Likert scale is mailed to each adult service agency representative on the school-level teams. Questionnaires are returned by mail.

A *school personnel satisfaction survey* consisting of five questions rated on a 4-point Likert scale is distributed to each special education and workforce development (i.e., vocational education) teacher at each high school. Questionnaires are returned via school system mail.

Finally, an *employer survey* consisting of 15 questions rated on a 4-point Likert scale is distributed to all businesses that provide community-based training sites. Questionnaires are given directly to the appropriate person at each site and are returned by mail.

How are student outcome data collected?

Student exit and follow-along data are collected from all students who leave or graduate. Data are gathered through telephone calls made by either a transition teacher or the transition coordinator. An attempt is made to interview each student three times. The first interview is conducted 6 months after graduation, and the next two interviews are conducted at 12-month intervals. If the student is not available, interviews are conducted with a family member. Calls are made by school staff members who are known to the student and family so that they are comfortable sharing information. The questionnaire used is a revised version of the exit and follow-up assessment from the *Illinois Transition Project's Transition Planning Guide* (Bates, 1989). It consists of 39 questions designed to gather data on student demographics, employment status, enrollment in postsecondary education, residential status, social interpersonal information, leisure and recreation activities, and satisfaction with the high school experience.

What are the results?

Results indicate that students are becoming employed and/or entering postsecondary education at higher rates than the national average reported in the National Longitudinal Transition Study-1 (Aspel et al., 1998). In addition the majority of students were satisfied with their current postschool outcomes. Finally, consumer satisfaction with the current program was high for all stakeholders.

What changes have been made?

When both parents and students indicated a need for a more systematic process for linking with postsecondary education institutions, the school system responded by providing more in-depth services. Next, when parents requested smaller class sizes for curriculum and instruction classes, a new teacher was added to reduce the class load. Third, when parents indicated that they were not getting enough information about their adolescents' school- and community-based occupational training, students were required to compile a training journal to share with their families. Finally, when students indicated the need for more long-term paid placements, the school system responded by making more summer jobs and internships available.

SUMMARY

As the two case studies show, data gathered through a comprehensive transition program evaluation are invaluable in terms of helping schools and school systems provide high-quality transition programs. Therefore, collecting program evaluation data becomes the final piece of the puzzle in preparing students to make successful transitions from school to adulthood.

DID YOU KNOW?

The National Center on Secondary Education and Transition has a curriculum-based youth Web site called The Youthhood. The Youthhood is a free, interactive Web site that young adults and their teachers, parents, and mentors can use to plan for life after high school (http://www.youthhood.org).

STUDY GUIDE QUESTIONS

1. Differentiate between formative and summative evaluation. How can each be used in evaluating transition programs?
2. What are three reasons for collecting program evaluation data?
3. List and describe four types of transition program evaluation data.
4. Differentiate between follow-up and follow-along data.
5. Describe a process for collecting consumer satisfaction data from the following stakeholders:
   a. Students
   b. Parents
   c. Adult service providers
   d. School personnel
   e. Employers
6. What types of data might you collect to evaluate interagency collaboration and the IEP team process?
7. How is student self-determination reflected in the transition program evaluation process?

REFERENCES

Agran, M., Cain, H. M., & Cavin, M. D. (2002). Enhancing the involvement of rehabilitation counselors in the transition process. *Career Development for Exceptional Individuals, 25,* 141–155.

American Youth Policy Forum and Center on Education Policy. (2002). *Twenty-five years of educating children with disabilities: The good news and the work ahead.* Washington, DC: Author.

Aspel, N., Bettis, G., Test, D., & Wood, W. (1998). An evaluation of a comprehensive system of transition services. *Career Development for Exceptional Individuals, 21,* 203–222.

Austin, P. E. (2001). Post-school outcome of Alabama students with disabilities. In P. Browning, C. A. Cox, K. Rabren, & S. Tew-Washburn (Eds.), *Transition in Alabama: A profile of commitment* (pp. 230–237). Auburn University, Department of Rehabilitation and Special Education.

Baer, R. M., Flexer, R. W., Beck, S., Amstutz, N., Hoffman, L., Brothers, J., et al. (2003). A collaborative followup study on transition service utilization and post-school outcomes. *Career Development for Exceptional Individuals, 26,* 7–25.

Bates, P. (1989). *Illinois Transition Project's transition planning guide.* Carbondale: University of Southern Illinois.

Benz, M., Lindstrom, L., & Yovanoff, P. (2000). Improving graduation and employment outcomes of students with disabilities: Predictive factors and student perspectives. *Exceptional Children, 66,* 509–547.

Blackorby, J., & Wagner, M. (1996). Longitudinal postschool outcomes of youth with disabilities: Findings from the National Longitudinal Transition Study. *Exceptional Children, 62,* 399–413.

Cross, T., Darby, B., & D'Alonzo, B. (1990). School drop-out prevention: A multifaceted program for the improvement of adolescent employability, academic achievement, and personal identity. *Career Development for Exceptional Individuals, 13,* 83–94.

Darrow, M., & Clark, G. (1992). Cross-state comparisons of former special education students: Evaluation of a follow-along model. *Career Development for Exceptional Individuals, 15,* 83–99.

Fairweather, J., & Shaver, D. (1990). Making the transition to postsecondary education and training. *Exceptional Children, 57,* 264–271.

Grigal, M., Test, D. W., Beattie, J., & Wood, W. M. (1997). An evaluation of transition components of individualized education programs. *Exceptional Children, 63,* 357–372.

Halpern, A. S. (1990). A methodological review of follow-up and follow-along studies tracking school leavers from special education. *Career Development for Exceptional Individuals, 13,* 13–27.

Halpern, A. S., Benz, M. R., & Lindstrom, L. E. (1992). A systems change approach to improving secondary special education and transition programs at the community level. *Career Development for Exceptional Individuals, 15,* 109–120.

Harvey, M. W. (2002). Comparison of postsecondary transitional outcomes between students with and without disabilities by secondary vocational education participation: Findings from the National Education Longitudinal Study. *Career Development for Exceptional Individuals, 25,* 99–122.

Hoisch, S., Karen, R., & Franzini, L. (1992). Two-year follow-up of the competitive employment status of graduates with developmental disabilities. *Career Development for Exceptional Individuals, 15,* 149–154.

Indiana Department of Education & Indiana University. (2000–2001). *Review and analysis of post-school follow-up results: 2000–2001 Indiana Post-School Follow-Up Study.* Indianapolis; Indiana Department of Education: Division of Exceptional Learners.

Individuals with Disabilities Education Act Amendments of 1997, 20 U.S.C. § 1414.

Johnson, L. J., Zorn, D., Tam, B. K. Y., Lamontagne, M., & Johnson, S. A. (2003). Stakeholders' views of factors that impact successful interagency collaboration. *Exceptional Children, 69,* 195–209.

Kochhar-Bryant, C. A. (2003). Implementing interagency agreements for transition. In G. Greene & C. A. Kochhar-Bryant (Eds.), *Pathways to successful transition for youth with disabilities.* Upper Saddle River, NJ: Merrill/Prentice Hall.

Kohler, P. (1996). *A taxonomy for transition programming: Linking research and practice.* Champaign: University of Illinois, Transition Research Institute.

Kohler, P. D., & Hood, L. K. (2000). *Improving student outcomes: Promising practices and programs for 1999–2000.* Champaign: University of Illinois, Transition Research Institute.

Lawson, S., & Everson, J. (1993). *A national review of statements of transition services for students who are deaf-blind.* Great Neck, NY: Helen Keller National Center/Technical Assistance Center.

Malmgren, K., Edgar, E., & Neel, R. S. (1998). Postschool status of youths with behavioral disorders. *Behavioral Disorders, 23,* 257–263.

Rabren, K., Dunn, C., & Chambers, D. (2002). Predictors of post-high school employment among young adults with disabilities. *Career Development for Exceptional Individuals, 25,* 25–40.

Repetto, J. B., Webb, K. W., Garvan, C. W., & Washington, T. (2002). Connecting student outcomes with transition practices in Florida. *Career Development for Exceptional Individuals, 25,* 123–139.

Roessler, R., Brolin, D., & Johnson, J. (1990). Factors affecting employment success and quality of life: A one-year follow-up of students in special education. *Career Development for Exceptional Individuals, 13,* 95–107.

Sample, P. L. (1998). Postschool outcomes for students with significant emotional disturbance following best-practice transition services. *Behavioral Disorders, 23,* 231–242.

Shepard, R. (2003, April). *The New York State Post School Indicators Longitudinal Study.* Paper presented at Northwest Passages: A Western Regional Resource Center Forum on Post-School Outcomes, Portland, Oregon.

Statewide systems for collecting student post-school follow-up data. Transition Technical Assistance Center, University of North Carolina at Charlotte. Retrieved July 10, 2002, from http://www.uncc.edu/ttac/tipsheets/statewide_systems.pdf

Storms, J. (2003, April). *State efforts to assess post secondary outcomes for students with disabilities.* Paper presented at Northwest Passages: A Western Regional Resource Center Forum on Post-School Outcomes, Portland, Oregon.

Storms, J., O'Leary, E., & Williams, J. (2000). *The Individuals with Disabilities Education Act of 1997 transition requirements: A guide for states, districts, schools, universities and families.* Minneapolis: University of Minnesota, Institute on Community Integration (UAP), National Transition Network.

Wagner, M., Cameto, R., & Newman, L. (2003). *Youth with disabilities: A changing population. A report of findings from the National Longitudinal Transition Study (NLTS) and National Longitudinal Transition Study-2 (NLTS2): Executive summary.* Menlo Park, CA: SRI International. Retrieved May 20, 2003, from www.cec.sped.org/pp/nlts2.pdf. (Entire report available at www.nlts2.org).

Worthen, B. R., Sanders, J. R., & Fitzpatrick, J. L. (1997). *Program evaluation: Alternative approaches and practical guidelines* (2nd ed.). New York: Longman.

Author Index

Subject Index